Mass Hate

THE GLOBAL RISE OF
GENOCIDE AND TERROR

Neil J. Kressel

UPDATED EDITION,
WITH A NEW PREFACE BY THE AUTHOR

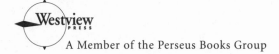

A Member of the Perseus Books Group

Westview Press books are available at special discounts for bulk purchases in the United States by corporations, institutions, and other organizations. For more information, please contact the Special Markets Department at The Perseus Books Group, 11 Cambridge Center, Cambridge MA 02142, or call (617) 252-5298.

First published in 1996 in the United States by Plenum Press, a Division of Plenum Publishing Corporation, 233 Spring Street, New York, N.Y. 10013-1578.

Visit us on the World Wide Web at www.westviewpress.com

Library of Congress Cataloging-in-Publication Data

Kressel, Neil Jeffrey.
    Mass hate: the global rise of genocide and terror / Neil J. Kressel.—Updated ed. / with a new preface by the author.
      p.   cm.
    Includes bibliographical references and index.
    ISBN 0-8133-3951-0 (pbk. : alk. paper)
      1. Genocide—Psychological aspects. 2. Terrosim—Psychological aspects. 3. Hate crimes—Psychological aspects. I. Title.

HV6322.7 K74 2002
304.6'63—dc21

                                                                        2001056773

Text design by *Brent Wilcox*

The paper used in this publication meets the requirements of the American National Standard for Permanence of Paper for Printed Library Materials Z39.48-1984

10   9   8   7   6   5   4   3   2

To
Dorit, Sam, and Hannah

CONTENTS

Mass Terror in America

"WE ARE NOT DECEIVED BY THEIR PRETENSES TO PIETY. WE HAVE SEEN THEIR KIND BEFORE. THEY ARE THE HEIRS OF ALL THE MURDEROUS IDEOLOGIES OF THE TWENTIETH CENTURY. BY SACRIFICING HUMAN LIFE TO SERVE THEIR RADICAL VISIONS, BY ABANDONING EVERY VALUE EXCEPT THE WILL TO POWER, THEY FOLLOW IN THE PATH OF FASCISM, AND NAZISM, AND TOTALITARIANISM."[1]

President George W. Bush,
September 20, 2001

Some readers of the first (1996) edition of *Mass Hate* wondered why I had chosen to discuss Muslim extremism in a book about mass atrocities and genocide. Did the terrorist threat emanating from this movement really have sufficient murderous potential to be considered in the same breath as Bosnia, Rwanda, and Nazi Germany? And why, some readers asked, had I chosen to devote so much attention to the 1993 bombing of the World Trade Center? After all, a mere six people had died—horrible, of course—but not a large casualty figure by twentieth-century standards. Even when we factored in the thousand-plus wounded and the $500 million tab, the event did not seem to qualify as a mass atrocity.

In the original edition of the book, I pointed out that

but for the terrorists' ineptitude and bad luck, the damage could have been much worse. . . . the plotters might have succeeded in toppling the north tower of the World Trade Center into the south tower, and that might have resulted in tens of thousands dead. The second Manhattan plot [discovered shortly after the 1993 bombing] also might have been very bloody had it not been foiled by law enforcement officials. One can only imagine the consequences of rush hour blasts in the Lincoln and Holland Tunnels, or the international impact of a large scale explosion at the United Nations.[2]

I further commented that "Despite the satisfaction the World Trade Center and seditious conspiracy verdicts elicited in most New Yorkers, many admitted to a haunting fear that the story was just beginning."[3] The remark was a bit of an overstatement. New Yorkers at the time had overwhelmingly returned to their normal routine and only a few continued to worry about terrorism in the city.

This was true even though, as I explained:

The [1993] terrorists showed how simple it is for a . . . group of committed fanatics to breach what had once been regarded as the impermeable Atlantic barrier. Americans no longer have to board a plane, visit Belfast, or stroll the streets of Beirut to encounter terrorists; Americans merely have to take the PATH subway train from Hoboken, New Jersey, to the downtown Manhattan business district. In the minds of many, the country runs the risk of becoming yet another battlefield in the seemingly endless war that Islamic extremists have been waging across the globe. So far, the worst consequences have not materialized. But the menace remains.[4]

Now, of course, the world has changed and America has changed. Still, even now, we do not know whether the worst consequences have yet materialized. In retrospect, the 1993 bombing of the World Trade Center, an event that once seemed so large in its own right, now appears a mere first act. And we do not know how many acts there will be. Only six died in 1993, but more than five thousand died in 2001. Many Americans now wake up with nightmares that the next wave of attacks will produce casualties in the millions as terrorists develop proficiency with biological, chemical, and nuclear weapons.

Though many aspects of American thinking have changed since the attack of September 11, 2001, one thing has not changed: the need to understand mass hatred, especially in its Muslim extremist variety, but in its other forms as well. The coordinated strikes at the Pentagon and the World Trade Center have focused the attention of Americans and other members of the civilized world on the need to fight back against terrorism. Beyond that, there appears to be little agreement.

The one question I have been asked repeatedly by reporters and others is, Why do they hate us? What motivates men, apparently competent and intelligent men, to act as the hijackers acted? They remained committed to their goal despite the certainty of their self-destruction, despite months—in some cases, years—away from their network of support. They carried out their tasks without any trace of compassion for their victims, slitting throats and drawing blood as the plan required. Why?

In an address to Congress and the American people nine days after the attack, President George W. Bush offered one answer to this question: "They hate what we see right here in this chamber, a democratically elected government. Their leaders are self-appointed. They hate our freedoms, our freedom of religion, our freedom of speech, our freedom to vote and assemble and disagree with each other."[5] This was true, in a sense. The terrorists certainly had no regard for the American institutions mentioned by the president. But congressional government and the Bill of Rights were not the aspects of America that loomed largest in the minds of the terrorists or those in the Muslim world who sympathized with them.

The question "Why do they hate the United States?" is actually several related questions. Why do Osama bin Laden and his top associates hate America? How have they been able to recruit and train so many followers—committed even to the point of embarking on suicide missions? Why do they target the United States rather than other Western nations? Why have so many Pakistanis, Egyptians, Yemenis, Indonesians, Palestinians, and others throughout the Muslim world displayed enthusiastic support for those who brought the Twin Towers down, apparently gloating over America's misfortune?

Perhaps the most significant question is not why the terrorists hate the United States, but rather why they felt empowered to attack it, despite the nation's vast military resources. To answer this query is simpler than to answer the others. First, the terrorists believed that they had God on their side. Second, and possibly more important, the behavior of al-Qaeda terrorists was shaped and reinforced by the responses of the outside world as surely as a rat's behavior is shaped in a psychologist's cage. During the decade preceding the attack of September 11, 2001, bin Laden operatives carried out a series of increasingly destructive acts against the interests of the United States. From the perspective of the terrorists, Americans answered each of their deeds with tremendous bluster—but little else. After the devastating attack on the Pentagon and the World Trade Center, former Clinton administration Secretary of State Madeleine K. Albright explained: "It [i.e., going after bin Laden's organization] was something that we focused on on a daily basis, and pursued with vigor, and I think we accomplished quite a lot. . . . I think we took it as far as was possible to go at the time."[6] Whether or not she is correct in her assessment of what could have been done, a message clearly reached the terrorists that they lay largely beyond the reach of the United States and, therefore, could act with impunity. Moreover, each successful strike conferred on bin Laden and al-Qaeda a flood of respect, adoration, and positive reinforcement from others in their circles who shared a deep-seated hostility toward the United States.

Many who start out asking why the terrorists struck at New York and Washington very quickly find themselves grappling with a different matter, why there is so much anti-Americanism in the world. This does not seem a constructive path to follow.[7] After all, hostility toward America has existed for decades without spawning similar terrorist acts. The causes of such enmity are many. There is plenty of room to disagree with U.S. policy and plenty of room to disagree with the critics of such policy, but in order to understand the origins of the September 11 attack we must retain our focus.

Writer and former CIA agent Reuel Marc Gerecht warns that the call to search for root causes inevitably implies "that we have done something wrong, and until that something has been corrected, we can expect others to be mean-spirited."[8] Similarly, some people infer from the depth and sincerity of the terrorists' commitment that their contentions must have at least some merit. This is, of course, a dangerous fallacy. Hitler and many of his followers believed every word of their nonsense about the Jews; throughout history, many fanatics have been sincere. Truth to one's own conscience—*Hamlet* notwithstanding—is no guarantor of any other type of truth.

September 11, 2001, did not mark the beginning of a new war, but rather the escalation and intensification of an old war on a new front. The innovation behind the assault did not lie in its ideology or theory, essentially the same as that which motivated the 1993 World Trade Center bombers. Where bin Laden and his men differed in 2001 was in their methods, in their ability to carry out plans that past extremists had merely salivated over. First and foremost was the leader's ability to use his financial resources and charismatic appeal to unite disparate extremist groups throughout the Muslim world. As in previous bin Laden operations, there was evidence on September 11 of meticulous long-term planning, an ability to learn from past mistakes, careful surveillance of targets, and highly effective training of operatives. The wide geographical reach of al-Qaeda also provided a tremendous asset, enabling the terrorists to move freely from country to country and to draw on a large network of support in the United States and elsewhere.

Bin Laden's ideology, however, was mainly old hat, restating many elements of the Muslim extremist world vision that has been promulgated by a wide array of demagogues and militant theologians during the past few decades. At its core stands a belief that the religious commandment of *jihad* can be fulfilled only by a violent holy war against nonbelievers, apostates, and the nations they control. Though widely accepted among militants, this view contrasts with the opinion of mainstream Muslim clerics, who claim that jihad, in modern times, refers to a struggle to advance the faith without arms. Indeed, according to the extremists, the widespread neglect of violent holy war is a principal reason why the Islamic world has not flourished in recent times. The ultimate goal of the jihad is to establish a world (or, at least, a Middle East) governed strictly by Muslim religious law, i.e., the *shari'a*. The extremists' plan, according to some observers, is for Pakistan to fall first, then Saudi Arabia, then Egypt, then Turkey.[9] The theocratic system established by the Taliban in Afghanistan offers one rough vision of their desired end result.

In February 1998 bin Laden and his lieutenant, Ayman al-Zawahiri, head of the Egyptian Islamic Jihad organization, jointly announced a *fatwa*, or religious decree, calling on all Muslims around the world to kill Americans and their allies—whether civilians or soldiers. The fatwa states: "We with God's help call on every Muslim who believes in God and wishes to be rewarded to comply with God's order to kill the Americans and plunder their money wherever and whenever they find it. We also call on Muslim ulema [clergy], leaders, youths and soldiers to launch the raid on Satan's U.S. troops and the devil's supporters allying with them, and to displace those who are behind them so that they may learn a lesson."[10] Bin Laden further maintains that those who do not participate in his jihad will be punished. In a September 2001 statement faxed from his hiding place to the Qatar-based al-Jazeera television network, he cited a religious foundation: "The Prophet, may peace be upon him, had said: He who did not fight or prepare a fighter or take responsibility for the family of the martyr fighter, God will punish before judgment day."[11]

Bin Laden also raised fairly specific political grievances against the United States. The American military and civilian presence in Saudi Arabia is, for him, an insult to Muslim honor and a desecration of the sacred soil that houses the holy cities of Mecca and Medina. That Jews and women are permitted to move more or less freely among other Americans in Saudi Arabia is particularly enraging. For bin Laden, U.S. support (or toleration) for moderate or somewhat moderate Middle Eastern states, especially those that are partly secular, is a moral anathema as well as an unwelcome barrier to the establishment of pious Muslim regimes. The sanctions imposed on Iraq are deemed unjust and cruel. The United States is thought to have stolen Arab oil from its rightful owners.

Though not a central element of his belief system, America's commitment to the survival of the state of Israel is, for bin Laden, tantamount to an alliance with the devil. Needless to say, he was also irked by America's pre–September 11 efforts to capture terrorists and disrupt their plans. More generally, he is angered by all of America's attempts to exercise power in regions he regards as Muslim territory.

All that being said, it would be a mistake to view a list of grievances provided by terrorists as their real reasons or motives for striking out against the United States. Bin Laden did not target America because of this policy or that, because of some policy that might have been avoided had only the State Department planned more carefully. America has, indeed, made policy errors, though perhaps not the ones frequently recited by its critics. After all, options in the Middle East over the past half-century have been severely constrained by local realities. No seriously democratic and tolerant leaders have managed to build a substantial following; faced with few good options and eager to preserve vital business interests in the region, the United States has often been forced to choose among distasteful alternatives.

Bin Laden and similar extremists target the United States because of its very essence. America, in their eyes, symbolizes the political, cultural, and military power of the Western world and, by contrast, the relative weakness of the Islamic countries. It stands for the irresistible thrust of modernity and for a cluster of values squarely rejected by the Muslim militants. These principles include tolerance for diversity, separation of religion and state, electoral democracy, free flow of information, and much else. America, to Muslim extremists, also means Christianity and the legacy of the Crusaders from a thousand years ago.

One aspect of Western civilization particularly irks the Taliban and, no doubt, the members of al-Qaeda: the role of women. Mohamed Atta, one of the September 11 hijackers, left behind a will in which he said he did not want women to come to his funeral or later to his grave.[12] British writer and member of Parliament Boris Johnson described Taliban Afghanistan as a place where "women are lashed for adultery; where little girls are denied education; where female teachers are sacked; and where women are kept from elementary health care. Mohammed Omar, the Taliban leader, says that mingling men and women is Western and decadent, and leads to licentiousness."[13] Similar views are held with varying intensity across the Muslim world. Johnson correctly maintains that "these prejudices are so deeply held by Islamic fundamentalists that they [or, at least, some] will die to preserve them. They look at America, and they see a world full of spookily powerful women, such as Hillary Clinton. . . . The Muslim fanatics see denatured men, and abortion, and family breakdown, and jezebels who order men around. It tempts them and appalls them and, finally, enrages them." Johnson asserts that "What Islamic terrorists are really afraid of is women"; whether or not he places too much emphasis on this issue, the extremists undoubtedly view the Western orientation toward the rights of women as threatening to their values.

American culture, in part by design, has been spreading across the globe. Muslim traditionalists see themselves as defending a way of life that is losing ground to American popular music, television, films, and consumerism. They see the Internet as one more weapon used by the West to infiltrate the Middle East and to spread un-Islamic ways. Terrorists see most traditional Muslims as doing nothing in the face of impending defeat. They see themselves as resisting a powerful onslaught against their core values using the only methods likely to succeed.

We do not know how closely the world view of bin Laden and other Muslim militants resembles that of the Taliban. However, there is—at a minimum—a great amount of overlap in the two visions. And if your image of the way things ought to be resembles that of the Taliban, it is not unreasonable to believe that you have to bring America down in order to realize it.

In this context, the Muslim terrorists' preoccupation with the World Trade Center made sense. As writer Caleb Carr explains: "Inside those buildings, the people behind this attack believe, is where the end of the societies they come from and the values that they live by was and is being planned (whether consciously or not), and *there* is where the erosion must be stopped. The terrorist obsession with the World Trade Center was, in this light, not irrational. In fact it was, viewed in the context of a war of cultures, entirely understandable."[14] American leaders have struggled hard to ensure that the war against the terrorists does not appear to be a clash of civilizations but that is precisely how it is seen by the terrorists themselves. This is why no list of policy demands preceded or followed the attack of September 11, 2001. America must cease being America in order to avoid the terrorists' wrath.

We do not yet have sufficient information to offer confident judgments about what specifically drew bin Laden, his top associates, and other individuals to the life of terror. Clearly, millions in the Muslim world agree with large portions of the al-Qaeda ideology. Yet al-Qaeda operatives probably never numbered more than ten or twenty thousand, perhaps far fewer. What motivated particular sympathizers to act on their beliefs? And what motivated certain operatives to acquiesce in, or even enthusiastically solicit, suicidal missions?

Although a tremendous amount has been written recently about Osama bin Laden, his private life remains shrouded in secrecy. Surely his intense hatred did not originate in deprivation as we generally conceive it. In his young adult years, he appears to have lived the life of a rich playboy in Beirut. The man opted out of a world of tremendous wealth and privilege. We can only speculate about why. Perhaps it was a lust for power, a warped religious commitment, guilt arising from his comfortable life, bizarre dynamics in his huge family, powerful influences from extremist teachers at university, radicalizing experiences during the Afghan war against the Soviets, or unpleasantness in his dealings with the CIA. We cannot confidently include or rule out any of these hypotheses.

The more important question concerns how bin Laden was able to generate such powerful support among his followers. The process by which ideologically affiliated Muslim extremists graduate to become terrorists is discussed in some detail in Chapter 3, and this book's more general discussion of why people participate in mass atrocities is also relevant. The process may start with the mosques or media of repressive Middle Eastern states, where potential recruits acquire a belief that Muslims are "besieged, humiliated and annihilated around the globe, whether by Serbs in Bosnia, Russians in Chechnya, Hindus in Kashmir or Israelis in Palestine."[15] Some zealots vow to defend the faith by attending proterrorist rallies, raising funds for terrorist organizations, or—in some cases—signing on for jihad-related terrorism against the West.

Many al-Qaeda members, especially older operatives, originally came from Middle Eastern states and the West to fight a jihad against the Soviet Union in Afghanistan. They felt enormously empowered by their victories against that superpower, not acknowledging the extent to which their battlefield successes depended on covert American support and Soviet internal rot. Once the war in Afghanistan ended, some of the holy warriors experienced a sense of alienation as the new battles in Afghanistan pitted Muslim against Muslim. They sought to extend their participation in a wider jihad against infidels. We may speculate that an assortment of personality traits and frustration from various personal sources also fed their militancy. Some of the individual characteristics typically associated with participation in atrocities are discussed in Chapter 7. As of this writing, we do not have much beyond speculation about the specific psychology of the al-Qaeda terrorists.

We do know that the al-Qaeda training program was very effective and included an oath of loyalty to Osama bin Laden that, if broken, was punishable by death. Once a person had joined, leaving al-Qaeda was at least as dangerous as leaving the Mafia. The training process has been called brainwashing, although—as is often the case—the term obscures more than it explains.[16] Trainees, according to Ahmed Ressam—an al-Qaeda terrorist now serving a 130-year sentence—learned "how to blow up the infrastructure of a country [including] . . . electric plants, gas plants, airports, railroads, large corporations. . . . hotels where conferences are held."[17] They were told to avoid the appearance of an observant Muslim while afield in the West. In the training camps, they frequently heard fatwas and religious decrees authorizing terrorist activity against America and Americans; one of these came from Sheikh Omar Abdel Rahman, the cleric behind the first attack on the World Trade Center, whose ideology is discussed in Chapter 3.

Islamic extremists generally recruit suicide bombers from among those in their ranks who are the most alienated, confused, and powerless. Bin Laden, Sheikh Omar Abdel Rahman, and other extremist leaders recorded many audio and videocassettes used in recruitment and training of operatives. Some reports suggest hundreds of thousands of bin Laden's recordings may have been distributed in the 1990s. Terrorist leaders typically select very young men (average age twenty-two) who see no prospects for a satisfying future. These few are then offered a pathway to instant immortality. An important part of the deal concerns their families, whom the leaders promise to provide with financial security and great communal esteem. The heart of the recruitment effort involves a guarantee of eternal bliss in the afterlife, specifically including a greeting in heaven from seventy dark-eyed virgins.[18]

At least some of the September 11 hijackers expected a similar reward. Several possessed copies of a handwritten document that promised "The time of fun and waste has gone. The time of judgment has arrived. . . . Always remember the verses that you would wish for death before you meet it if you only know what the reward after death will be. . . . You will be entering paradise. You will be entering the happiest life, everlasting life."[19] This promise, if believed, provides the prospective terrorist with a simultaneous resolution of political grievances, personal guilt whatever its source, a stressful day-to-day existence, and humanity's common existential dilemma—the search for meaning in a world where people die. The offer seems weak to those who reject its premise. But to those who believe, it can be an alluring package.

Still, the September 11 terrorists did not fit the standard suicide bomber profile in every respect. Thomas Friedman of the *New York Times* notes that "What we know of these terrorists is that they were evil, educated and suicidal. That is a combination I have never seen before in a large group of people. People who are evil and educated don't tend to be suicidal (they get other people to kill themselves). People who are evil and suicidal don't tend to be educated."[20] Though some of the hijackers may not have known that they were on a suicide mission, some surely did and they were, on average, several years older than the profile would have suggested. In addition, they were able to acquire marketable flying skills and certainly possessed options for other satisfying life paths. Though their training instructed them, as part of their cover, to avoid acting like observant Muslims, these guidelines cannot fully account for their trips to strip-tease bars and their consumption of alcohol in the United States.

More important, the September 11 terrorists had many opportunities over months or even years to change their minds. And even one person who had changed his mind could have undermined the plot. Bin Laden, himself, had a $5 million price on his head. Yet no one betrayed the network and, most likely, none of the operatives changed their minds about participating. Perhaps working in small groups created additional pressure to stay the course. Perhaps the terrorists reinforced their commitment by reviewing the training videotapes that investigators later found among their possessions. There remains much to learn about the motivation and procedures of the proficient terrorists who attacked the Pentagon and the World Trade Center.

Muslim extremist operatives would pose a monumental problem for Western policy even if they operated without much support beyond the al-Qaeda network. However, the greatest long-term threat to the United States and its allies resides in the large number of Muslims from across the globe who have voiced sympathy for the terrorists or otherwise supported them—even while their national leaders offered varying degrees of official condemnation. More than a few Palestinians, Pakistanis, Egyptians, and others from the Muslim world cheered when the Towers came down. One Egyptian teacher explained: "They are very fine young men who did this. . . . America deserves a lesson."[21] A prominent Saudi lawyer remarked that "Osama bin Laden has been called the conscience of Islam. . . . What he says and what he does represents what most Muslims or Arabs want to say and can't. What he says we like, we agree with it."[22] Another Saudi, educated in America, added: "The royal family are the only people in this country who don't like Osama bin Laden." The judgment was, no doubt, an exaggeration, but one that makes a point.[23]

Along similar lines, a popular exhibit at the prominent Al Najah University on the West Bank highlighted the enthusiasm for terrorist deeds that prevails in parts of the Middle East. The exhibit celebrated a deadly suicide bombing of a Sbarro Italian restaurant in Israel. Intermingled pizza crusts and bloodied plastic body parts were suspended from the ceiling to provide ambiance for a memorial to the "heroes" who carried out the act; at the entrance to the exhibit, visitors trampled over the flag of Israel and that of the United States.[24]

Terrorist groups, including al-Qaeda, had success in the 1990s raising money in oil-rich Arab states; they also carried out significant fund-raising among Muslims in the West. In 1998 terrorism expert Steven Emerson told the Senate Judiciary Subcommittee on Terrorism, Technology, and Government Information that groups known to have established themselves in various capacities in the United States included, in addition to the followers of bin Laden, the following: Hamas, Islamic Jihad, Hezbollah, Hizba-Tahrir, the Algerian Islamic Salvation Front and Armed Islamic Group, En-Nahda of Tunisia, the Muslim Brotherhood, Egyptian Ga'mat Islamiya, Abu Sayyaf Group, the Afghan Taliban, and Jamat Muslimeen (from Pakistan and Bangladesh). Of these, Emerson thought that Hamas had the strongest and best-organized presence on American soil.[25]

Some wealthy businessmen in the Middle East gave money because they felt it was not safe to refuse, but others gave from genuine desire. Even among the vast majority of Muslims who squarely condemned the terrorist methods of September 11, many saw some legitimacy in the terrorists' motivation and their hostility to the United States.[26] Typically, spokesmen declared that—while such acts were horrible and contrary to the spirit of Islam—they were the direct and predictable consequence of unreasonable American policies. A not-unusual headline after the attacks proclaimed "A Sense of Unfairness Erodes Support [for the U.S.] in the Gulf States."[27] Some who tied the attacks to American misbehavior did not buy into the extremist Muslim agenda, but others bought into large chunks of that worldview.

It is important to remember that virtually all perpetrators of great evil in the world—including Nazis, Serb rapists, Hutu extremist murderers, and those behind the Khmer Rouge atrocities—believed that they were victims of some longstanding prior outrage that justified their militancy. A group's self-perception of victimization should never be taken as evidence of actual victimization. And even when there has been real mistreatment in the past, we should not assume that it always, or even generally, originates with those who are targeted for retribution. Psychologists have long understood that anger is often directed toward scapegoats who are chosen because they are deemed less able to resist than the actual offenders. Especially where there is no free press—a condition that prevails in the entire Middle East (except Israel)—public sentiments may show very little correlation with reality. In states that have corrupt and dictatorial leaders, such sentiments are often the product of manipulation, where popular anger is very consciously channeled against outsiders in order to protect the regime.

As a matter of strategy—and, perhaps, conviction—President Bush has determined that America's struggle against terrorism should not be perceived as a war against Islam or Arabs. With more than a billion Muslims in the world, anything else would be utter folly. And the president is surely correct when he asserts that "There are thousands of Muslims who proudly call themselves Americans, and they know what I know—that the Muslim faith is based upon peace and love and compassion. The exact opposite of the teachings of the al Qaeda organization, which is based upon evil and hate and destruction."[28] However, to portray the extremists as a handful of politically driven madmen who have twisted unambiguously kind teachings for their misguided purposes is patently incorrect and a poor guide for policy.

As Peter Steinfels, the *New York Times* religion columnist, notes, "It takes only the slightest knowledge to recognize how incredibly diverse and complex Islam is, and if Osama bin Laden's network is only a tiny group at the end of a spectrum, at many other points on that spectrum there are Muslims closer to his world view than to the West's."[29] Similarly, Yale University professor of religion and history Lamin Sanneh explains that "By insisting that fundamentalists have misinterpreted the Koran, they [Muslims in the West] seek to downplay the widespread support for fundamentalism in the Muslim world."[30] While it certainly behooves the United States to endorse moderate readings of the Islamic religious texts, and while there certainly is a basis for such interpretation, the extremist reading of the jihad commandment also appears plausible.[31] In the final analysis, the morality of messages from all religions always depends on the way they are interpreted and implemented.

When asked by a journalist whether he considered bin Laden a religious leader or a political leader, President Bush replied: "I consider bin Laden an evil man. And I don't think there's any religious justification for what he has in mind. Islam is a religion of love, not hate. This is a man who hates. This is a man who's declared war on innocent people. This is a man who doesn't mind destroying women and children. This is man who hates freedom. This is an evil man."[32] Earlier that day, he explained: "I have told the nation more than once that ours is a war against evil, against extremists, that the teachings of Islam are the teachings of peace and good, and the al Qaeda organization is not an organization of good, an organization of peace. It's an organization based upon hate and evil."[33] However well-intentioned these remarks, they did not provide the nation with a useful understanding of the splits that exist in the Muslim world, splits among those who, in the main, reject militant interpretations of their faith and those who, to varying degrees, embrace them.

Indeed, several days earlier—while reaching out to patriotic Muslim-Americans and promoting tolerance—President Bush met with Nihad Awad, the president of the Council of American-Islamic Relations, describing him along with other Muslim-American leaders as "the good folks standing with me." Yet, according to Steve Pomeranz, former chief of Counter-Terrorism for the FBI, "CAIR, its leaders, and its activities effectively give aid to international terrorist groups."[34] The meeting also included other noteworthy apologists for Middle Eastern terrorism, such as a representative of the Muslim Public Affairs Council, which denounced America's 1998 missile strike against Osama bin Laden's training camps as illegal and immoral.

Thus, in his admirable effort to remind Americans that the overwhelming majority of the Muslim community rejects terrorism and that many Muslims bear no ill will to the United States, President Bush was blind to real dangers emanating from spokespersons who masqueraded as opponents of terrorism when they were, in reality, apologists for it. At home and abroad, the failure to perceive accurately and understand this threat of extremism weakens the ability of the West to combat it. Rather than purporting to support all Muslims except a handful of terrorists associated with al-Qaeda (and, perhaps, a few other organizations), the United States should actively seek to strengthen the hands of *genuine* moderates—of whom there are many. If such moderates know that the United States stands committed to their cause for the long term, they will feel empowered to reclaim their faith and oppose those who tarnish its image.

As columnist William Safire writes, "The suicide bombers were motivated to mass murder by the false promise of eternal joy after death, and it

is up to Muslim clergy—who know their Koran and have special credibility—to publicly and repeatedly refute that cultish brainwashing. . . .
[And] to undermine the worldwide anti-Christian "Crusader" appeal of
the radicals, [America should] . . . work with our Islamic allies to form a
Muslim legion" as "a powerful symbol of Islam's enlistment in the campaign against terror."[35] America can do much more to win the hearts and
minds of the Muslim world, but our policy must begin with a clear grasp
of what we are for and what we are against.

Genuine moderates oppose violent jihad, reject the anti-American re-
flex, tolerate non-Muslims in their midst, support the Western human-
rights agenda, and show a willingness to coexist with Jews in the region.
While short-term tactical arrangements with those who reject elements of
this agenda (but are not too distasteful) may be necessary, such opportunistic alliances should not be confused with friendship and should not
be sold to the public as such. Shortly after the terrorist massacre in September, the British foreign minister sought cooperation from Iran, a long-
time supporter of the anti-American, anti-Israel Hezbollah terrorist organization. Richard Perle, a former assistant secretary of defense, rightly
warned that "It is a grave mistake to compromise the moral high ground
by inviting terrorists to join with us."[36]

The place occupied by Israel in the Muslim extremist ideology of hate
deserves special attention. Salam al-Marayati is a prominent Muslim-
American radical who was once nominated for a position on a federal
antiterrorism commission by Representative Richard Gephardt. After a
public outcry, Gephardt withdrew his support. After the September 11 attack, al-Marayati—now director of the Muslim Public Affairs Council in
Los Angeles—said "Our country is under attack. . . . We stand shoulder to
shoulder with all Americans to bring the perpetrators of this heinous
crime to justice."[37] Then, the very same day, on Los Angeles radio, he said:
"If we're going to look at suspects, we should look to the groups that benefit the most from these kinds of incidents, and I think we should put the
State of Israel on the suspect list because I think this diverts attention
from what's happening in the Palestinian territories so that they can go on
with their aggression and occupation and apartheid policies."[38] Perhaps
mindful of his status as a Muslim leader with whom President Bush occasionally consults, he subsequently sent a clarification to Jewish leaders.
Many others around the Muslim world arrived at similar theories and

continue to believe them to this day. One absurd notion circulating throughout the Middle East is that thousands of Jews received notice of the September attacks beforehand and hence were not in the buildings, something that could be explained only if Israel had perpetrated the crime.

For many in the Muslim and Arab world, Israel has become a central element of a collective obsessional delusion. With no shortage of injustices close to home in Pakistan, Indonesia, Sudan, Libya, Saudi Arabia, and elsewhere, one wonders how so many people find so much energy to devote to social justice so far away. Even if Israel were conducting itself, as its detractors maintain, in a profoundly unjust manner, it remains to be explained why its particular moral infractions should loom so large in Muslim and Arab public consciousness.

The best answer is that the Islamic political world permits very little reality testing; there is no open debate and precious little unbiased information even in the moderate states. If political or religious leaders ever felt inclined to offer any pro-Israel sentiments, they could not do so without endangering their prominence and probably their lives. A few brave leaders have been willing to face the risk. President Sadat of Egypt (who was subsequently assassinated by Islamic extremists) and King Hussein of Jordan (whose moderate grandfather, Abdullah, also fell to an assassin's hand) come to mind. Most political, intellectual, and religious leaders, however—even otherwise reasonable ones—have understandably felt content to parrot the party line and accept the status quo. Generations of propaganda and childhood indoctrination have produced populations among which public opinion bears little connection to reality.

Former prime minister Ehud Barak's negotiating position in the summer of 2000 was judged by President Bill Clinton and nearly all mainstream American observers to be extremely fair, meeting far more Palestinian demands than most had believed possible for an Israeli leader. Yet his overture did not evoke acceptance or even a counteroffer from Yasir Arafat. Indeed, it did not even register on the radar of Muslim extremists. Even in a country like Egypt, formally at peace with Israel, the government-controlled media is generally hostile to Jews and the Jewish state. Thus, denunciation of Israel in the Arab and Muslim worlds appears to be a component of a mass delusional system. In a sense, the part played by Israel in the ideology of the Muslim extremists is not altogether different from the part played by Jews in Nazi ideology. The term anti-Semitism doesn't quite work—since Arabs are Semites—but, clearly, we are dealing with a form of anti-Jewish bigotry.

Arab and Muslim leaders may encourage anti-Israel pronouncements as a form of scapegoating designed to deflect criticism from more deserving targets. Sometimes, hostility to Israel serves a "motherhood and apple pie function," enabling those who agree on little else to find common ground. Most often for Muslim extremists, however, antagonism toward Israel is a component of the irrational impulse to holy war; Jewish occupation of the sacred land irks them in much the same way that Muslim possession of the Holy Land was, a thousand years ago, unacceptable to the Christian powers that ruled Europe. It is regarded as an affront to honor in a culture that does not take such affronts lightly.

Nothing Israel might do save mass suicide would placate those who approach the topic in this frame of mind. As columnist Thomas Friedman points out: "We know the September 11 attack was being planned a year ago—exactly when President Clinton was proposing to Yasir Arafat a Palestinian state on roughly 95 percent of the West Bank and East Jerusalem—with Israeli settlers uprooted from all but 5 percent. In other words, this terrorism was being planned *because America was trying to build Israeli-Palestinian coexistence,* not because it wasn't."[39]

Israel is, as one newspaper put it, the flashpoint, not the cause.[40] The time may yet come to negotiate a final settlement between Israel and the Palestinians, probably along lines not so different from those put on the table in the summer of 2000. But the time to negotiate is not in the middle of a war against terrorism.

Attorney Alan Dershowitz notes that although Islamic scholars have recently been asserting that Islamic law prohibits harm to noncombatants, some militant imams, "Every Friday all around the world . . . call for the death of Israeli civilians. They justify these acts of terrorism by drawing hair-splitting distinctions between 'terrorism' and 'resistance,' and they describe the suicide bombers who carry out these murderous acts as martyrs."[41] He correctly warns that "Today's justifications of anti-Jewish and anti-Israeli terrorism can easily become tomorrow's justification of anti-American terrorism."[42]

Extremist Islam as the terrorists and their supporters conceive it is not a religion in the traditional sense of the term. It is, instead, an ideology of hate—like that which drove the Bosnian Serbs, the Hutu extremists, the Nazis, and other perpetrators of great atrocities. Like all such ideologies, it comes replete with dehumanization of preferred victims (Americans, Jews, Israelis), delusional and conspiratorial theories, an approach to warfare that indiscriminately and mercilessly targets civilians, training camps for the indoctrination of a militant vanguard, and a profound sense of having been wronged throughout history.

The struggle against terrorism is not fully explained as a clash between two civilizations—Western and Muslim. American leaders have made this abundantly clear. After all, many devout Muslims stand resolutely on the side of the West, and much terrorism—past and present—arises from sources entirely unrelated to Islam. However, the struggle against Muslim extremist terrorism also should not be portrayed as an effort to uproot a single, geographically spread out, deeply entrenched but relatively small network of fanatics. If the cells of al-Qaeda are uprooted, but Muslim extremist ideology continues to flourish, others will soon organize themselves afresh to revitalize the jihad. Defense against terrorism, therefore, rests on the outcome of a struggle within Islam for the heart and soul of the faith. And the West remains neutral in that struggle at its peril—and at the peril of the entire world. This is no time for moral or cultural relativism.

Until America and its allies succeed in their efforts to control terrorism, evildoers around the world will be able to operate with greater impunity than ever before. Consider the situation in Rwanda, for example. In the late 1990s, many American leaders appeared to recognize that military intervention in the spring of 1994 might have saved thousands, perhaps hundreds of thousands, of lives. In the post–September 11 environment, however, all military and foreign policy initiatives are apt to be evaluated exclusively or at least primarily in terms of their impact on the antiterrorist campaign. And should new violence arise in Rwanda or Burundi—as is likely—I suspect the energies and attentions of the United States will be occupied elsewhere.

In addition, as the United States conducts its battle to uproot and punish terrorists across the globe, it will, if the past is any guide, become less choosy as it reviews the human rights portfolios of potential allies. The nation must strive to retain its standards and to forge alliances with those who share its core values. When the United States deals with those who do not, the nation must use whatever influence it possesses to promote re-spect for human rights. Unfortunately, it seems likely that the ability of America and the West to promote good behavior and discourage evil will diminish—at least in the short term. In a life-and-death struggle against terrorism—with massive civilian casualties on the American mainland—an alliance with a tough dictatorship capable of controlling the terrorists may be judged preferable to one with a more open society that proves less able or less willing to control its militants. Should this come to pass, the amount of suffering in the world will increase and the twenty-first century may prove bloodier and crueler than its predecessor.

N. J. K.
October 2001

ONE

The Hater's Mind

SICK PEOPLE ARE MADE BY A SICK CULTURE; HEALTHY PEOPLE ARE MADE POSSIBLE BY A HEALTHY CULTURE. BUT IT IS JUST AS TRUE THAT SICK INDIVIDUALS MAKE THEIR CULTURE MORE SICK AND THAT HEALTHY INDIVIDUALS MAKE THEIR CULTURE MORE HEALTHY.[1]

Abraham Maslow, Psychologist

The twentieth century was a century of hostility, an epoch in which the brutality of humankind erupted and flowed more expansively than ever before.

During the past nine decades, mass hatred has reached genocidal proportions in Turkey, Germany, Indonesia, Nigeria, Bangladesh, Burundi, Cambodia, Bosnia, Rwanda, and elsewhere. Blood has gushed so freely, and with such frequency, that one might consider the urge to kill one's neighbor an inborn characteristic of our species.

Moreover, the power to wreak bloody havoc on innocent civilians across the globe has fallen into the hands of terrorists whose hate knows no bounds. Barely into the new century, America has witnessed firsthand the horrific destructive power of such hateful ideologies. Terrorists like Osama bin Laden may soon use nuclear, chemical, or biological devices that will make their previous methods seem quaint.

The twentieth century took butchery to a new level. It drew great minds to evil causes, and introduced nightmarish technologies of destruction.

Worst of all, it spawned legitimizing ideologies that have provided misguided inspiration to tens of millions. Unless humanity learns to tame its
murderousness, the future promises more of the same. The only hope lies
in understanding the human impulse to hate and, more important, the
forces that transform that impulse into action.

This book will draw together the results of six decades of research on
the psychology of mass hate. It will focus on situations where large portions of nations or cultural groups have participated in mass murder, acts
of terror, or other atrocities against unarmed civilians selected primarily
because of their race, religion, ethnicity, nationality, or ideology. The goal
is to crawl into the minds of the haters, however despicable, and to share
their world, at least momentarily, to learn why they are so willing to act as
they do and under what circumstances they might be less likely to take
part in violence.

Three examples help clarify the central issues of this book, two from the
1990s and one from the Nazi era.

BOSNIA, 1992:
PSYCHOSEXUAL DESTRUCTION

An estimate of twenty thousand rapes, from data offered by independent
human rights organizations and European Community investigators, may
overstate or understate the scale of the terror. The primarily Muslim Bosnian government set the figure at fifty thousand for the early phase of the war
in Bosnia. The first figure is more plausible, though both are difficult to
confirm and, therefore, likely to provoke skepticism if cited as authoritative.
(A UN commission of experts has identified sixteen hundred specific
cases.)[2] What appears beyond question, however, is that thousands of Muslim girls and women have endured horrifying sexual degradation, sometimes repeatedly, and often as a prelude to torture or a bullet to the head.
And many experts claim that Serbian soldiers participated as part of a sanctioned "ethnic cleansing" campaign. Anna Quindlen in the *New York Times*
aptly described this campaign as "a particularly sophisticated and brutal
form of genocide . . . which relies on the psychosexual destruction of those
who would bear the next generation of Bosnian Muslims, so hated by the
warring Serbs."[3]

Victims of sexual assault seldom wish to discuss their ordeals, much less embellish and magnify them. Many women choose to suffer in silence, owing to shame, shock, societal taboos, and fear of reprisals against loved ones. Thus, we have little reason to doubt the disturbing tales recounted by Bosnian women like Rasema, a thirty-three-year-old mother who resisted a gang rape in front of her two daughters. Her Serbian attackers reportedly threatened, "We will cut out your teeth! Do you want us to slaughter your children, to watch us cutting them into pieces, piece after piece?"[4]

Another Muslim woman, Sofija, was raped every night for many months by five or six different Serbian soldiers.[5] Yet another, at the Partizan Sports Center, endured twenty-nine rapes in one night before passing out.[6] In Bosnia, during the summer of 1992 and at various other times during the war, the bodies of women and girls became just another battlefield. Even though the military conflict has ended, the scars will remain for decades, not least in the tormented lives of children born of forced impregnations.

According to feminist author Susan Brownmiller, "there is nothing unprecedented about mass rape in war when enemy soldiers advance swiftly through populous regions."[7] After all, the Japanese in World War II forced thousands of Asians to serve as "comfort women" for their troops. Advancing Soviet and Nazi soldiers also left behind a trail of rape. Pakistani soldiers did the same in Bangladesh in 1971. But the Bosnian situation may differ in degree, and to the extent that Bosnian Serbs used rape as an instrument of policy.

We are left with the question why this took place, and it is a question that burns the conscience. What does it say about human nature, that sizable chunks of modern societies, in this case thousands of Serbs, participated in the mass rape of women and children, the murder of unarmed thousands, the destruction of whole communities of human beings? And are the Serbs' crimes mitigated in the least by the atrocities perpetrated on a much smaller scale by Croatians and Bosnian Muslims?

"We were ordered to rape so that our morale would be higher," claimed Borislav Herak from a Bosnian military prison in Sarajevo. "We were told we would fight better if we raped the women."[8]

Herak, a twenty-one-year-old Serbian soldier, admitted that he had gone on a six-month rampage of sexual assault, throat-slitting, and machine-gunning in the summer and fall of 1992. In a matter-of-fact monotone, he described how he would select his victims from an ever-changing supply of Muslim girls and women kept at the Sonja Cafe near Sarajevo, an alleged "rape camp." It remains unclear precisely how many Muslims were raped or killed by Herak, although he did not contest charges at his trial that he killed thirty-five and raped sixteen. Another Serbian attacker, a policeman who raped a twenty-year-old woman from his own town, protested to his victim, "It is war, you can't resist, there is no law and order."[9]

Little from what we know of Borislav Herak's background suggests a particular propensity for him to have acted as he did; he was an undistinguished textile worker and mechanic, a low-ranking soldier, patriotic to the Serbian cause, but not especially so. When asked how he felt after killing three villagers who turned out to be Serbs, not Muslims, Herak showed little remorse. "I was not sorry because they had a color television set," he explained.[10] (Color televisions brought a good price in the black market.)

Was he, as he asks us to believe, a victim of circumstance? Did he succumb to primal urges for sex and violence that are present in all humans or, at least, all men, but deeply submerged during ordinary times? In psychiatric terms, Herak acted as a sociopath, or antisocial personality, a person who violated the rights of others without remorse, without loyalty to anyone. But where exactly does this analysis get us, when so very many others in the Serbian army acted similarly? And if Herak truly felt no remorse, why did he speak so freely about his role in the atrocities? Perhaps he enjoyed the publicity.

Are the roots of Herak's crimes to be found in his moral upbringing, his political views, his prejudices, his family life, his ambitions? What are we to make of Herak, the man? When sentenced to death, he did not object. He asked for some cigarettes.

MANHATTAN, 1993: MUSLIM HOLY WAR

The questions we ask about Herak apply to most participants in crimes of mass hatred, including terrorists.

The 1993 bombing of the World Trade Center by Muslim extremists and the barely averted attack on other New York City targets at that time demonstrated the impunity with which hate-driven terrorists could penetrate the defenses of the United States—and it foreshadowed the devastating September 11, 2001, attacks on the World Trade Center and the Pentagon.

That first strike on the World Trade Center resulted in several deaths, a thousand injuries, and tens of thousands evacuated. It should have been a wake-up call to all Americans. Had the FBI been just a little less effective, or less lucky, New Yorkers might have seen a relatively small group of conspirators succeed where large enemy armies had always failed—in bringing massive bloodshed to the American mainland. A bomb blast in the Lincoln Tunnel or the Holland Tunnel, two of the 1993 terrorists' prime targets, could have brought tile, cement, mud, steel, and water crashing down on hundreds, maybe thousands, of commuters. Likewise, the Muslim extremists' plan to blow up the United Nations possibly would have killed dozens of delegates and dealt a major setback to the international organization.

One Clinton administration official, commenting in June 1993 on the arrest of some of the terrorists, said, "What this certainly shows is that the conspiracy in New York went beyond a single terror cell."[11] As we are now all too aware, the 1993 attack in New York was merely the first strike in a conspiracy of terror fueled by terrorist cells around the globe.

Who can conceive such schemes? When we examine the list of conspirators associated with the failed 1993 plots against the UN, FBI building, and Hudson River tunnels, we see a group of devout extremist Muslims; most had ties to the expatriate Egyptian cleric, Sheikh Omar Abdel Rahman, and his mosque in Jersey City, New Jersey.[12] All the conspirators, save two, were recent immigrants: one a Palestinian from Jordan, several from Egypt, several from the Sudan. Most were in their thirties, some married, some not; none was wealthy.

One key participant in the failed 1993 plots, Siddig Ibrahim Siddig Ali, held a degree in economics from the Sudan and had worked as a security guard and a taxi driver. He trained in "self-defense" with a group of Muslim militants in Pennsylvania on weekends. He had been active in raising money for the defense of suspects in the World Trade Center bombing and for El Sayyid Nosair, who had been accused of the murder of Rabbi Meir Kahane. In secretly taped conversations with an FBI informer, Siddig Ali discussed plans to procure things necessary for an attack on the United Nations, including a vehicle, dynamite, false identity papers, and a safe house for preparing a bomb. He and the informer also considered a counterfeit scheme in order to finance the plot.[13] Later, Siddig Ali confessed to his role in the failed scheme and provided prosecutors with useful information.

Siddig Ali's coconspirators included Mohammed Saleh, a gas station operator described by friends as very religious and devoted to his three children—but also convicted of charges related to the sale of heroin.

One of the few American citizens in the 1993 group, Clement Rodney Hampton-El (known in his Flatbush apartment project as Dr. Rasheed), aged fifty-five at the time of the plot, has an especially curious background. Hampton-El, a Black Muslim whose father was also a Black Muslim, had fought for Islamic militants in Afghanistan's war against the Soviet Union. He received a leg wound of which he was particularly proud, and spoke often about returning to Afghanistan for another chance at martyrdom. Many neighbors respected Hampton-El, a sometime medical technician, and told of his opposition to drug dealers and crime. He apparently also worked with dying children and AIDS-infected patients.

But Hampton-El had ties to al-Fuqra, a violent, secretive group of Black Muslim extremists that took marching orders from the radical Sheikh Mubarak Ali Jilani Hashmi of Lahore, Pakistan. One interviewer reported at the time that Hampton-El had said he wanted to return to fight in Afghanistan because he was "afraid of what he might do here if he saw injustice and racism."[14]

What, then, motivated the 1993 terrorists? They, themselves, referred to anger over American support for Israel and Egyptian president Hosni Mubarak, whom they detested. They shared an immersion in the world of extremist Islam and, in most cases, immigrant status. All apparently believed that they were fighting injustice; and all shared a diffuse hostility toward the "Great Satan," America.

But none of these commonalities provides a very satisfying answer to the fundamental question, why? For this, we must look deeper.

GERMANY, 1933–1945: ERADICATING THE JEWISH "BACILLUS"

One would think that, by now, nobody would need to be told about the crimes of the Nazis. Hundreds of books by survivors, perpetrators, and scholars testify to the indisputability of the Holocaust; every conceivable form of evidence, written, spoken, visual, is available, and it is fair to say that our certainty about the Holocaust is no less than our confidence that a man named Hitler ever existed. Still, as several historians have amply demonstrated in recent books, a growing cadre of writers persists in denying the historical reality of Nazi genocide.[15] So it continues to be necessary to document how millions of Jews were forced from their homes; how being productive members of a "civilized society" offered no protection; how the *Einsatzgruppen* lined up defenseless villagers and mowed them down with machine guns; how women, children, and men unable to work, such as the old and disabled, were stripped, gassed, and burned to ashes in massive death camps.

Still, by now, the average educated person has heard enough of the gory details. The significant remaining question deals with motivation. Even after more than six decades of analyses by social scientists of every stripe, our understanding of how and why so many individuals joined in Hitler's plan remains inadequate. Traditional explanations based on economics and politics provide part of the answer, but the deepest understanding emerges from psychology.

Why, for example, did apparently normal engineers agree to build the crematoriums used to burn the bodies of millions of innocents who had just choked to death on Zyklon-B? Hate may in fact have contributed very little to their motivation. According to testimony given to the Soviets after the war and recently published, these engineers knew precisely what their work would accomplish.[16] One cited fear to explain his complicity: "I knew that if I refused to continue with this work, I would be liquidated by the Gestapo."

Another, who showed much initiative in his designs of the human ovens, spoke of patriotism: "I saw it as my duty to apply my specialist knowledge in this way in order to help Germany win the war, just as an aircraft construction engineer builds airplanes in wartime, which are also connected with the destruction of human beings." Yet another revered the law, obeyed superiors, and looked out for his career interests: "Whoever opposes our laws is an enemy of the state, because our laws established him as such. I did not act on personal initiative but as directed by Ludwig Topf [who owned the firm]. I was afraid of losing my position and of possible arrest." These testimonies may be disingenuous, but if we take them at their word, it seems that crimes against humanity sometimes stem from motives far removed from hatred.

Hannah Arendt, the eminent philosopher and political scholar, coined the phrase "banality of evil" in connection with her analysis of the Eichmann trial in 1961.[17] Eichmann was a high official in the Austrian Nazi party who became head of the Gestapo's Jewish section, and played a major role in the destruction of the Jews. He professed throughout his trial that he was not an "*innerer Schweinehund,* a dirty bastard in the depths of his heart"[18] and, in a sense, Arendt agreed. A half-dozen psychiatrists certified Eichmann as "normal," and she did not judge him especially driven by anti-Semitism. His prime motivations included a sense of duty, a willingness to obey authority, and a bureaucrat's drive for advancement.

Arendt's disturbing thesis about the everyday, banal origins of heinous acts has received dramatic support from several ingenious experiments conducted by social psychologists.[19] The most famous of these, the Milgram shock experiment and the Zimbardo prison study, show that, under certain conditions, average, psychologically healthy, morally typical Americans can be induced to hurt their peers and even kill them. The findings of these studies are discussed below; they may suggest that, under different circumstances, Americans rather than Germans might have staffed a network of death camps.

But not all psychologists accept the banality of evil theory or draw the same conclusions from the obedience experiments. For one thing, Nazis and other perpetrators of evil generally did not commit their crimes one afternoon, and then go home. They had to live with their deeds over many months or years, all the while committing new atrocities. Thus, they needed to forge powerful defense mechanisms, perhaps by splitting their personalities into two halves, roughly speaking the decent and the indecent, as suggested by psychiatrist Robert Jay Lifton.[20]

Also, many Germans shared the anti-Semitic values and beliefs of the regime.[21] And, while only a very small percentage manifested signs of serious psychopathology, many were drawn to their crimes by a variety of personality traits and predispositions discussed below.

The Psyche of Hate

The main objective here is to answer the question: "Why mass hate?" The goal is to uncover meaningful and valid generalizations, not for the sake of knowledge itself, but to suggest strategies to reduce crimes of hate in the future. The next four chapters each explore and seek to understand mass hatred in a different context. Chapter 2 focuses on atrocities committed by Bosnian Serbs, Chapter 3 on extremist Muslim terrorists, Chapter 4 on the slaughter of Tutsis and moderate Hutus by Hutu extremists in Rwanda, and Chapter 5 on the Nazis' efforts to destroy the Jewish people. These contexts have been selected because of their severity, their importance in world affairs today, and their relevance to American concerns.

Chapters 6 and 7 revisit, from a different angle, the question of what motivates mass hatred, presenting and interpreting the relevant research of psychologists and other social scientists. Chapter 6 looks at the power of situational pressures to overcome individual values. A central question is whether the crimes of Auschwitz, for example, were carried out by everyday, "normal" people who found themselves yielding unavoidably to the pressures of "abnormal" circumstances. Many psychological studies, like those of Milgram, Zimbardo, and others, have highlighted the fragility of human character and its susceptibility to influence. But can one really lay the blame for many of the most hideous acts in human history on a widespread tendency to obey superiors and conform to the mores of one's peers? Finally, to what extent, and by which methods, can tyrannical regimes turn unexceptional people into eager killers and cruel torturers?

Even when circumstantial pressures are similar, individuals differ sharply in their propensity to commit atrocities. Chapter 7 asks whether there is such a thing as a hater's personality, a collection of traits that predisposes a person to initiate or join in acts of mass hatred. Psychologists have suggested that several personality styles can lead to fascist beliefs and antisocial behavior. How well do these theories hold up to scrutiny, and how much do they help us to explain the perpetrators of evil? It might seem obvious that personal aggressiveness, prejudiced attitudes, ethnocentrism, and stereotyping propel a person on to hateful deeds, but recent research suggests a different perspective. Chapter 7 also evaluates the impact of education (or miseducation) on the development and perpetuation of mass hatred, assessing whether it's true that one has "got to be taught to hate and fear." Finally, Chapter 8 draws conclusions about the sources of mass hatred and considers strategies for combating it.

We, as a species, are profoundly fortunate that most of our members react to extreme instances of mass hatred with emotional disgust and moral outrage. We are perhaps somewhat less fortunate to possess two additional tendencies, namely the ability to avert our gaze from instances of great suffering and to feel tremendous satisfaction when we can assign unequivocal blame to those deemed responsible. These latter tendencies, while natural, can lead to premature and uninformed judgments. This book grows out of my belief that historical and psychological inquiry can illuminate the places where mass hatred grows, and that the public should be made aware of this knowledge.

TWO

Ethnic Cleansing in Bosnia

WHICH IDENTITIES BECOME RELEVANT FOR POLITICS IS NOT PREDETERMINED BY SOME PRIMORDIAL ANCIENTNESS. . . . WHEN T.V. TALKING HEADS AND OP-ED CONTRIBUTORS POR- TRAY "MOBS" AS "FRENZIED" AND BELIEVERS AS "FANATIC," THEY HAVE GIVEN UP THE TASK OF DISCERNING THE HUMAN INDUCEMENTS AND POLITICAL CALCULATIONS THAT MAKE POL- ITICS HAPPEN. THEY HAVE GIVEN UP MAKING MOTIVES VISIBLE AND SHOWING HOW THEY ARE TRANSFORMED. . . . THE DOC- TRINE OF ANCIENT HATREDS MAY BECOME THE POST-COLD WAR'S MOST ROBUST MYSTIFICATION, A WAY OF HAVING AN EN- EMY AND KNOWING EVIL THAT DECEIVES AS IT SATISFIES. THE HATRED IS MODERN, AND MAY BE CLOSER THAN WE THINK.[1]

Susanne Hoeber Rudolph and Lloyd I. Rudolph,
Professors of Political Science, University of Chicago

One forty-year-old Muslim woman's ordeal began when Serb sol- diers burned her home in the Bosnian town of Foca and imprisoned her along with twenty-eight other women. Day and night, at unpredictable intervals, the loudspeaker from the main mosque would blast out "Mars Na Drinu" ("March on the Drina"), a Serb nationalist fighting song that had been outlawed by the former Yugoslav leader, Marshal Tito. The music signaled that the rapes would commence. The soldiers, some local and some from a different region, would order the women to remove their clothing. Their victims ranged in age from twelve to sixty. The soldiers sometimes sought deviations from the routine—virgins or mother-daughter combinations.

On one occasion, this particular woman was raped by two soldiers, while, in full view, five other soldiers raped an eighteen-year-old girl whom they believed to be a virgin. The Serb soldiers told the older woman, "You should have already left this town; we'll make you have Serbian babies who will be Christians." To complete the humiliation, the soldiers forced her to eat pork and drink alcohol—both abominations to observant Muslims.[2]

Islamic women were not the only victims of Serb violence. Jadranka Cigelj had been a politically active Bosnian Croat lawyer from the city of Prijedor. Several days after her arrest in June 1992, she watched Serb guards beat to death another Croat woman, Silvije Saric. Saric's political involvement as head of the county committee of the Croatian Democratic Union had roused the ire of her Serb interrogators. Cigelj herself was scarred by their rifle butts and barely managed to survive the beatings. Thirty-three Muslim and Croat women, mostly professionals, had been brought to Omarska concentration camp on trumped-up charges; the arrests formed part of a general effort to destroy Muslim and Croat leadership in all areas of Bosnia conquered by Serb forces.

For Cigelj, the rapes began about four days after her arrest. First, a local reserve officer dragged her into a bathroom, hit her over the head with the handle of a revolver, cut her, beat her, and proceeded with the rape. Then, on three different nights, she was beaten and raped by Zeljko Meakic, the commander of the guards at Omarska, and by two of his underlings. According to Cigelj, during daylight hours, Omarska guards questioned and beat male detainees in the same rooms where at night they abused the women. Before the rapes would begin, the women had to scrub blood from the floors and walls. Serb guards also took pleasure in forcing these women, predominantly professionals, to do kitchen and cleaning duty.

Conclusive proof of these specific crimes may never emerge, but there is enough convincing corroboration of war crimes at Omarska to convince any fair-minded person. (The Serbs closed the camp shortly after *Newsday* reported its existence.) However, Zeljko Meakic denies Cigelj's charges: "I don't know why I would do that, because she is forty-five years old while I am twenty-six, and I don't need a woman as old as that, particularly as she is a bad and unattractive woman. The way she was, I wouldn't lean a bicycle on her, let alone rape her." Even while defending himself, he fails to conceal a dehumanizing mindset that lends credibility to the charges.[3]

For the eleven thousand Muslim and Croat men at Omarska, conditions were equally unbearable. Stories from the camp cover every conceivable torture. Throats were slit. Guards forced prisoners to eat feces, to perform oral sex on other prisoners. Men were castrated. Those who died were often thrown in the river. The Serbs would say they were feeding the fish. And Omarska was only a small sampling of the horrors. Mass murder took place in the villages, in the mountains, at camps at Manjaca, Breko, Keraterm, and Trnopolje. The tens of thousands of Muslims of Banja Luka were bombed and terrorized in every conceivable way when the town fell to Serb forces.[4] Sarajevo's suffering became legendary. "It was suddenly clear," writes Croat writer Slavenka Drakulic, "that Europe hadn't learned its lesson, that history always repeats itself and that someone is always a Jew."[5]

This frequently drawn comparison between the Holocaust and Serbian ethnic cleansing in Bosnia obscures many nontrivial distinctions. For one thing, Nazism sprang from a vastly different and more highly developed racist ideology. Nazi ideologues crafted an elaborate pseudoscientific framework covering every "racial" group on earth. Although rapes certainly did occur, Nazi doctrine actually prohibited sexual intercourse with Jewish women on the grounds that such contact defiled the purity of the Aryan race.[6] The Nazis devised a far more encompassing killing operation than the Serbs, and the Nazis' goal was more clearly extermination. As A. M. Rosenthal notes, "The Jews of Europe were hardly trying to force the Germans into a new nation under their control and the Bosnian Serbs are not hunting down and incinerating all Muslims of the world. Ethnic cleansing is vicious enough without the Holocaust analogy."[7] Furthermore, the Jews were not at war with Germany nor had they a history of conflict with the Germans, and revenge atrocities by Jews were very few. The death toll of the Nazis exceeded that of the Serbs by several orders of magnitude.

Yet these are historical points, important for analytic purposes, but essentially irrelevant to the comprehension of human suffering. The death toll at the Omarska camp, probably between one and four thousand, does not approach the figure for Auschwitz, which was about two million. There is no general agreement about the total number of Muslim casualties in Bosnia. One commonly cited figure placed the total casualties— dead, missing, and wounded—on all sides of the war in Bosnia through the end of 1994 at about two hundred thousand. In 1995, some analysts challenged that figure as too high, concluding that deaths in the conflict stood somewhere between twenty-five and sixty thousand. While no clear consensus has yet emerged, two responsible historians—Steven Burg and Paul Shoup—conclude that total deaths resulting from the war probably exceeded the November 1995 CIA estimate of 238,000 (including 81,500 combatants and 156,500 civilians). Perhaps an additional 174,000 were injured. The war also damaged 60 percent of dwellings in Bosnia. More than a million people became refugees.[8] Still, the enormity of individual suffering at Omarska, Srebrenica, and elsewhere in Bosnia is horrible by any standard, even that established by Auschwitz, Treblinka, and the *Einsatzgruppen*.

*   *   *

How are we, amid the insulated comforts of the West, to understand the war in Bosnia, where men routinely gang-raped girls barely beyond puberty, slit the throats of neighbors, and perpetrated tortures not visited on Europe since the Nazis?

Roy Gutman, the *Newsday* reporter who broke the story of Serbian ethnic cleansing, describes prewar Bosnia-Herzegovina as a "genuine melting pot" characterized by "an atmosphere of secular tolerance"; he speaks, for example, of "Sarajevo, with its skyline of minarets, church steeples and synagogues" as "testimony to centuries of civilized multiethnic coexistence."[9] Lamenting what has been lost, Gutman and other writers sometimes overstate the spirit of tolerance among Muslims, Croats, and Serbs in prewar Bosnia, at least some of which can be traced to the dictates of imperial and communist overlords.

Nonetheless, Muslims, Croats, and Serbs had lived in Bosnia-Herzegovina without violent conflict since the end of World War II. And the region, along with the rest of Yugoslavia during the 1970s and 1980s, saw its youth far more preoccupied with acquiring the trappings of Western European life—color TV, video games, rock concerts, Madonna, and MTV— than with fomenting interethnic battles.[10] There is some truth in the cynical remark of novelist Miroslav Karaulac that the Bosnian people had "acquired the fatal habit of living together, a quality which the various armies now fighting one another are, by means of a blood-bath, attempting to correct."[11]

The transformation of a previously stable nation into a nightmare was not inevitable, and required a monumental change in the feelings, values, beliefs, and concerns of hundreds of thousands, possibly millions, of individuals. How opportunistic leaders attempted to orchestrate this change and how it came about is the central theme in the tragedy of Yugoslavia.

The first news of atrocities in Bosnia came in the early summer of 1992. By the end of that summer, it became clear that the horrors of this war would exceed even what we have cynically come to think of as the "normal" excesses of armed conflict.

All parties, Serbs, Croats, and Muslims, committed some verifiable atrocities. For example, masked soldiers of the Bobovac Brigade of the Croatian nationalist army in Bosnia massacred dozens of Muslim civilians at the village of Stupni Do in October 1993. Bosnian Croats also admitted to physically abusing Muslim P.O.W.'s at camps in Dratelj and Gabela during the summer of 1993; Muslim inmates suffered random shootings and beatings, living for extended periods with little water or food. For their part, Muslim soldiers reportedly have used Croat prisoners as human shields and Muslim forces summarily executed Croat prisoners and civilians in a number of villages. A UN war crimes commission maintained that all forces had committed some rapes, and members of all communities have been indicted by the International Criminal Tribunal for Former Yugoslavia in the Hague.[12]

Independent observers generally agree, however, that Bosnian Serbs bear responsibility for the overwhelming preponderance of rapes and other war crimes. Their victims were mostly Muslims but also Croats. The United States Central Intelligence Agency (CIA) concluded, in a highly classified report that was leaked to the press, that Serbs carried out 90 percent of war crimes and that they were the only party that systematically attempted to "eliminate all traces of other ethnic groups from their territory."[13] Serbs were also the first to commit atrocities. Some officials, like Canadian Major General Lewis MacKenzie, the former top UN peacekeeper in Bosnia, threw up their hands in light of the complexity of the situation. "Dealing with Bosnia," MacKenzie testified, "is a little bit like dealing with three serial killers—one has killed 15, one has killed 10, one has killed five. Do we help the one that's only killed five?"[14] At the height of the fighting during the early stage of the war, Serbs and their allies spread much propaganda attributing equal responsibility for war crimes. After his tour of duty in Bosnia, Serbs even paid MacKenzie to make speeches.[15] However, as more evidence accumulated, Serbian efforts to establish moral equivalence appeared less and less credible. Serbian atrocities continued throughout the conflict. When, for example, Bosnian Serb forces seized the United Nations "safe haven" of Srebrenica in July 1995, they executed between five thousand and eight thousand Muslim men and boys and tossed their bodies into a mass grave.[16]

Jeri Laber, former executive director of the human rights organization Helsinki Watch, explained the atrocities committed by Muslims and Croats as mainly a reaction to the political success of Serbs: "[I]f the Bosnian Serbian army can 'cleanse' Muslims and Croats in Bosnia and be rewarded for it in Geneva, why shouldn't Croat and Muslim forces do the same? Victims of abuse often become abusers if they finally get a chance."[17] Her point is an important one. Moreover, by 1995, some Muslims and Croats believed they had the *right* to commit atrocities against the Serbs, particularly against those whom they believed responsible for torturing and murdering their families. Though it is not difficult to fathom where such feelings originate, they are politically destabilizing and morally unacceptable.

In any case, our first task should be to examine the motivation of the Bosnian Serbs who brought "ethnic cleansing" to contemporary Yugoslavia and practiced it with such terrible ferocity. Many forces contributed to their infamous campaign, and much of the violence was spontaneous rather than planned. However, the murderous program had a clear strategic component; at its core, the policy sought to force or frighten Muslims and Croats into abandoning their homes in regions of Bosnia that the Serbs wanted to acquire. As in pre-1948 Palestine, there was no practical way to partition the territory into geographic zones with homogeneous populations. Bosnian ethnic groups were intricately mixed together in regions, towns, neighborhoods, and even buildings. The Bosnian Serbs wanted reports of their brutal methods to spread among the non-Serb population in order to induce people to flee their homes. The more savage and humiliating they were, the more intimidating an impression they left. Cruelty itself was useful from the point of view of Bosnian Serbs who wanted Muslims and Croats to leave homes where their families may have lived for centuries. Consistent with this principle, the most heinous acts of violence and brutality generally occurred in those regions where Serb control was most precarious. These places were far from Serbia proper or else they had a high concentration of non-Serbs in their population.

In several reports to the United Nations, the United States government summarized credible eyewitness testimony on war crimes in the former Yugoslavia.[18] These reports read like catalogs from Hell. Twenty-four soldiers raped one woman. A witness estimates that two thousand men were killed and thrown into the Sava River. A sixty-two-year-old Muslim watched the murder of fifty-three Muslims; the report lists their names. Serb soldiers raped a Muslim woman and murdered her husband; they shot a Serb man dead for refusing to join in. A Serb woman in her twenties repeatedly and savagely beat young Muslim men on the genitals. Girls were raped while their fathers or mothers were forced to watch.

The list goes on, and after a while the destruction of individual worlds is reduced to a reader's momentary disgust.

The question of how these events could occur in the 1990s should haunt those who live in the West, not only because of the human moral tragedy, but also because Bosnia may be a harbinger of the future as nationalist movements clash not only in the Balkans but throughout the post-Communist world. Bosnia also shows the fragility of civilization, the ease and speed with which things can degenerate. This is a lesson that even those of us lucky enough to live in the West can only ignore at our peril. We must understand what it takes to transform primarily peaceful cohabitants into enemies thirsting for blood.

In Bosnia, personal bonds formed during a lifetime disintegrated in a few short years, sometimes months. Families were divided, especially where there had been intermarriages. Reluctant people on all sides, among whom national loyalty had been inconsequential or even annoying, found themselves joining the combatants. A school principal who served as commandant at one detention camp did his best to minimize abuse to inmates who included his former students; but in the end he was merely a tool in their torture, which commenced at night after he left. People with no long-standing grievances against their neighbors failed to warn them of impending attacks. Strangely, but hardly without precedent, educated members of the helping professions, a psychiatrist, a dentist, and professors, led the march against the Bosnian Muslim and Croat civilians.

How did it happen? Or perhaps, one should ask, how does it happen? First, why did such fierce, nationalistic conflict develop in the former Yugoslavia? Second, why did the Bosnian Serbs commit so many atrocities in this conflict? Third, why did so many of these atrocities take the form of rape?

THE MAKING OF NATIONALIST WARRIORS

A common Western perspective on the Bosnia conflict portrays it as the consequence of inscrutable and very ancient animosities. According to the argument, Muslims, Croats, and Serbs have detested each other since medieval times, they are combative peoples, and, under the circumstances, bloody conflict was to be expected. This position can be misleading. Taken to extremes, the perspective becomes little more than an obfuscation, born perhaps of the same spirit that moved British Prime Minister Chamberlain in 1938 to describe Hitler's attempt to take over Czechoslovakia as "a quarrel in a faraway country between people of whom we know nothing."

The "ancient animosities" explanation also recalls writer Rebecca West's description over fifty years ago of the development of an Adriatic personality type as:

> the product of Dalmatian history: the conquest of Illyria by Rome, of Rome by the barbarians; then three hundred years of conflict between Hungary and Venice; then four hundred years of oppression by Venice, with the war against Turkey running concurrently for most of that time; a few years of hope under France, frustrated by the decay of Napoleon; a hundred years of muddling misgovernment by Austria. In such shambles, a man had to shout and rage to survive.[19]

But such explanations tell little about how distant historical events become psychologically relevant and meaningful for the individual. William Pfaff, an expert on nationalism, calls the approach "mystification by history" and notes that those who wish to rationalize inaction refer to it frequently. After all, the further back one sets the roots of a conflict, the less amenable the conflict seems to outside intervention.[20]

Many Serb nationalists associated their cause in the 1990s with efforts to refight the 1389 battle of Kosovo and to restore the medieval glory of Old Serbia, but the reasons for these associations are modern. Following the "ethnic cleansing" of the town of Zvornik in northeastern Bosnia, the Serb mayor, Branko Grujic, rejoiced over the eradication of traces of the community that had converted to Islam during the hundreds of years of Turkish rule. After passing through the rubble of the town, he stopped by a cross he had built, declaring: "The Turks destroyed the Serbian church that was here when they arrived in Zvornik in 1463. Now we are rebuilding the church and reclaiming this as Serbian land forever and ever."[21] He genuinely may have viewed the recent horrors as a fulfillment of a fifteenth-century vendetta, or he may simply have seized on a convenient rationalization. However, past met present only by virtue of his efforts to bring them together, and these efforts owed far more to recent than to distant events.

Twentieth-century history leads to more credible explanations for turmoil in the 1990s. But there is even a danger in assigning too much weight to events that are decades in the past. Consider, for example, the following verdict that concludes Fred Singleton's first-rate history of the Yugoslav peoples, published in 1985:

> The wide-ranging and open debate about the future which came to the surface in the 1980s is a necessary preliminary to the working out of a consensus which will, I believe, provide a new point of departure for the creation of a more democratic but still socialist Yugoslavia. . . . My own inclinations are towards optimism and hope.[22]

Less than a decade later, there was no Yugoslavia, no socialism, no democracy, no consensus, no optimism, and precious little hope. If so many students of Yugoslav politics and society had little inkling of the events to come, how much sense can it make to view the current events as an inevitable outgrowth of historical forces?

Historians have attempted to trace the roots of the Balkan crisis to virtually every era, pointing to its sources in Turkish and Austrian overlordship, in the breakup of these empires, in World War I, in the Versailles settlement, in interwar Yugoslavian politics, in World War II, in the postwar adjustments, and in the Tito period. Still, as late as the 1980s, few experts foresaw an interethnic bloodbath. History tells part of the story, but its limitations are clear.

Several misleading theories about the origins of the conflict turn up frequently. The first sees a war born of Serbian blood lust, of a desire to visit atrocities upon mortal enemies—the Muslims and the Croats. While some Serbs, indeed, may have given vent to long-standing but submerged brutal passions, this position confuses the cause of the conflict with its consequence. Anyhow, it leaves us with the question of where that blood lust originated, unless we assume that people in the Balkans are somehow blood-thirsty by nature.

The second viewpoint assigns primary responsibility for the conflict to the United States and other Western countries, either for (1) failing to broker a peaceful dismemberment of Yugoslavia; (2) prematurely recognizing the independence of Croatia, Slovenia, and, then, Bosnia; or (3) failing to intervene militarily on behalf of the Bosnian government. These contentions may contain some truth, but they are similar to claiming that an incompetent doctor is the source of a patient's initial illness.

The third theory was often hurled by angry Serbs against their Western detractors. "Don't you see that we are fighting the West's battle against fanatical Muslim fundamentalists bent on a jihad against Europe?" they ask. "We Serbs have always been the first victims of Muslim armies, but, if the West persists in its current position, we will not be the last." The biggest problem with this theory is that it explains nothing about the Serbs' conflict with the Catholic Croats.

Moreover, explanations based on the very real threats emanating from extremist Islam are irrelevant here. Bosnian Muslims are, and have been, primarily secular and sympathetic to the ways of Europe. Most bear little sympathy for the violent acts of extremist Muslims and, perhaps of necessity, showed more commitment to peaceful coexistence than any other ethnic group in the former Yugoslavia. One writer likened them to European Jews, maintaining, "the Bosnian Muslims are urban and most are secular; their religion is less a matter of worship than a means of self-definition. The Muslims were an elite, more sophisticated and more affluent than their rural Serbian neighbors."[23] Whatever the merits of the analogy, few Bosnian Muslims were zealots at the outset of the crisis. They received assistance from the Muslim world during the years of fighting. But, even as positions hardened during the course of the war, Bosnian Muslims assumed little resemblance to extremist Muslims from other parts of the world.

Professor Fouad Ajami, a respected scholar of Islamic politics, notes that Bosnian President Alija Izetbegovic's 1980 book, *Islam Between East and West,* is hardly the work of a Muslim fundamentalist. He describes the book as:

> [T]he product of an anxious *assimilé,* a child of the Western tradition reassuring himself that all the sources of his mind add up to a coherent whole, a man of our messy world born at the crossroads of cultures. The index alone is sufficient proof of the man's eclecticism. This must be the only book on Islam with nine references to Dostoevski, seven to Albert Camus, eleven to Engels, nine to Hegel, three to Malraux, two to Rembrandt, ten to Bertrand Russell, eight to Kenneth Clark and so on.[24]

To equate the worldview of Izetbegovic or his government to that of extremists from other parts of the Muslim world is unjustifiable.

In the fourth perspective, the conflict is portrayed as ideological, a clash between democracy (the governments of Bosnia and Croatia) and the dictatorial, nationalistic remnants of the once-Communist government of Yugoslavia. Though, again, there is a kernel of truth, this interpretation misses some key points. First, Franjo Tudjman, the president of Croatia, was hardly free of dictatorial tendencies; before the war, his government initiated aggressive steps against its Serb minority and, in 1995, he masterminded a military campaign to drive Serbs out of the Krajina region of his country.[25] Second, Izetbegovic had little choice but to attempt a multiethnic government, given the population distribution in Bosnia and his own military weakness. For its part, Serbia's aggressive position owed much to President Slobodan Milosevic's grandiose and manipulative efforts to increase his power. But it also had origins in the logic of realpolitik, especially in Serbia's natural military superiority and the presence of a large number of ethnic Serbs beyond the borders of Serbia proper.

However it started, the conflict clearly turned into one between ethnic groups, all of which paid lip service to democracy and none of which proved its dedication to democratic precepts. When Bosnian Serbs held a November 1991 referendum on the question of independence from Yugoslavia, 98 percent voted to remain a part of the country. Several months later, the Bosnian government sponsored its own plebiscite; not surprisingly, Serbs boycotted this poll and 99 percent of those who did vote, mostly Muslims and Croats, said "leave Yugoslavia, and become an independent nation." It is far from clear how democracy could have produced a desirable outcome under such conditions. Members of hostile ethnic groups cast their votes solely on the basis of ethnic identification. They supported elections only as tactical ploys to advance their own group interests, and boycotted them when they anticipated unfavorable results.

For many Yugoslav peoples, nationalistic sentiments simmered quietly throughout Tito's rule and, from time to time, disturbed the domestic serenity of his nonaligned communist state. In 1966, he was forced to admit that the nationalities question had been solved "only" in principle, and that "material and political content needed to be added."[26] However, it was not until the 1980s that Serbian nationalism began to ferment into mass hatred, the result of a process of ethnic polarization that began shortly after Tito's death in 1980.

He had controlled Yugoslavia since the success of his Partisans in World War II; throughout that period, Tito showed acute awareness that the eruption of excessive ethnic loyalties could destroy Yugoslavia. To secure personal power, build strength against an ever-present Soviet threat, and break the back of ethnic nationalism, Tito established a system based on fear. Less repressive than other communist regimes, the Tito government still tolerated little dissent. He did not refrain from using the power of the state to banish his ablest successors, extinguish the voices of reform-minded critics, and prevent the emergence of liberal democratic traditions. No spirit of open and rational inquiry could develop, only outward declarations of support for the state, coupled with quiet but angry murmurs of discontent.

Tito's system acknowledged the existence of various ethnic groups but placed firm limitations on the expression of nationalistic loyalties. In view of what has happened since, one might be tempted to sympathize with this approach. However, efforts to extinguish ethnic identification seldom succeed, especially when a state is only somewhat repressive. What happened, instead, was that following World War II the various peoples of

Yugoslavia were never permitted to explore and develop freely the significance of their ethnicity. When Communism lost its ability to command popular support, expressions of national identification became a means of showing dissatisfaction with the system. Asserting one's identity as a Yugoslav, on the other hand, became tantamount to asserting one's support for the decrepit regime. Once the Communist shell cracked, people embraced their tendencies to define themselves in nationalistic and religious terms. Ethnic and religious symbols had become psychologically established as symbols of the righteous struggle. Affirmations of religious identity similarly contributed to the protest against Titoism. The fall of Communism in Yugoslavia, as in other countries, removed barriers against nationalism.

Simultaneously, there emerged dangerously high expectations for the future without any apparent means for fulfilling these expectations. Economic and political failures often lead to frustration and the search for scapegoats; this was certainly the case in post-Tito Yugoslavia.

In Serbia, intellectuals like Dobrica Cosic took the lead in stirring the cauldron of ethnic loyalty. Then, opportunistic politicians like Serbian president Slobodan Milosevic, Bosnian Serb leader Radovan Karadzic, and Krajina Serb leader Milan Babic rode the nationalist stallion to power, and kept it galloping to insure that they remained in the saddle. Of course, such strategies work only when people are willing to heed the trumpet's call.

And while people from all of Yugoslavia's ethnic groups heard the sound of nationalist trumpets blaring, it is not by accident that Serbs responded most enthusiastically. First, Serbs at 36 percent of the Yugoslavian population made up the largest ethnic group and, consequently, possessed from the outset the best chances of prevailing in a conflict. In contrast, the Bosnian Muslims, at about 8 percent, found themselves in the traditional position of minorities such as Jews who have a strong interest in stemming uncontrollable nationalism and in maintaining a multiethnic balance. Second, Serbs were the most dispersed of Yugoslavia's nations, accounting for a substantial portion of the populations outside Serbia proper in Bosnia, Croatia, Vojvodina, and Kosovo. Thus, Serb minorities always faced a real (and imagined) potential for mistreatment at the hands of other ethnic groups. As talk turned to the rights of ethnic groups, Serbs living outside Serbia proper felt especially vulnerable.

In April of 1981, ethnic Albanians in the province of Kosovo rioted against Belgrade's failure to improve their living standards, among the very lowest in Yugoslavia.[27] The Albanians lashed out against Serbs, who lived better and, seemingly, with government advantages. The backlash against these protests stirred fanatical Serbian national feelings. Local Serbs angrily denounced the Albanians and spread stories about Albanian atrocities against Serbian women. The Serb population of Kosovo was only a small fraction of the total population there, having declined significantly over the past two decades. Yet nationalist politicians played upon the nostalgic position Kosovo occupied in Serbian hearts owing to its centrality in the medieval lore of Old Serbia. The land was rightfully Serbian. The emigration of Serbs from Kosovo had been the result of Albanian terrorism and had to be stopped. During the years following the Kosovo riots, Serb intellectuals argued that the Communist system in Yugoslavia had systematically oppressed the Serbs—but not the Albanians and other troublemakers.

This rise in Serbian nationalism might have been controlled had it not been for the emergence of Slobodan Milosevic as leader of the Serbian Communist Party. Milosevic transformed himself from the representative of a discredited regime into the powerful voice of rising Serb nationalism. Milosevic, a former banker and Communist functionary, was a pure, or nearly pure, opportunist who saw Serbian nationalism as a pathway to power. Both his parents committed suicide, and some analysts have speculated that he, too, suffered from an unconscious urge to destroy himself, and Serbia in the process.[28] On the other hand, Milosevic showed many signs that he was, above all, a survivor, willing to abandon principles and allies when doing so served his self-interest. His upbringing and parents' suicides may have contributed to the development of a deficient, Machiavellian character, but without further details of his personal relationships, such speculation cannot be confirmed.

British journalist Misha Glenny, generally acknowledged as less hostile to the Serb cause than most Western journalists, described Milosevic as "a man without passion, without any real nationalist motivation (although on the surface, he appears to wallow in it), and he is a man who has never shown any affection or regard for the masses upon whom he depends for support."[29] Others, however, have seen at least some genuineness in Milosevic's concern for Serb minorities. It's difficult to tell what he feels in his heart.

In any case, Milosevic seized first on the Kosovo situation and then on a series of other nationalistic issues, using the full range of tools available to the modern dictator, including control of the mass media, deception, blackmail, corruption, and violence. Historian Christopher Bennett has correctly noted that "[t]he power of the media within Serbia cannot be over-estimated."[30] Though some opposition newspapers were tolerated, Milosevic used the official media, especially Belgrade radio and television news, to launch a massive propaganda offensive. Unlike most Communist bureaucrats who feared the populace, Milosevic turned mass demonstrations into a tool. His goal was a Yugoslavia dominated by Serbia and, hence, himself. If Croatia, Slovenia, and the other nations wanted independence, he would let them have it, but only if they handed back the portions of their territory which were home to Serbian minorities. Milosevic stoked the fires of Serb nationalism and kept stoking until the population was aflame. Student protesters denounced his methods, but he easily outmaneuvered them. By 1991 very few voices spoke publicly for interethnic tolerance.

Serbs responded to Milosevic enthusiastically partly because many believed that history had treated them unfairly and that other groups would persecute Serbs if given half a chance. Many supported the nationalist interpretation of twentieth-century history—that Serbia never got its just reward for siding with the victorious allies in two world wars. More significantly, Serbs living in the Krajina region of Croatia expected the Croatian president to impose a fascist state. They also feared Croatia's warm linkage with Germany, a bond that recalled for them the Croatia of World War II, which was a Nazi puppet. Despite certain unsavory tendencies, including some anti-Semitism, Croatian President Franjo Tudjman was no Nazi (indeed, he had fought against them in World War II), but he might have done more to dissociate himself from Croatia's past.

Serb nationalism derived considerable strength from these fears and resentments concerning the past. But it was not the events of World War II themselves that *necessarily* fueled the nationalism. Rather it was the way several key leaders handled the memories of these events. Tito, throughout his rule, attempted to repress the traumatic memories. Anthropologist Bette Denich explains: "As Communist rule entailed ideological control over the representation of the past, those horrifying events that would disrupt interethnic cooperation were not to be mentioned, except in collective categories, all 'victims of fascism' on one side, and all 'foreign occupiers and domestic traitors' on the other side."[31] The efforts of contemporary Croatian historians to minimize the scope and significance of Croatian fascism during World War II fed into Serb anger. So, too, did the Croat nationalists' revival of specific symbols associated with fascist Croatia. Had Franjo Tudjman, as the official leader of Croatia, accepted responsibility for war crimes committed in the name of the Croatian people and offered a sincere apology, he might have deprived the Serb extremists of a powerful tool. But this was hardly in his nature.

As it happened, the inflammation of Serbian national passions led almost naturally to the fanning of Croat and Slovenian nationalism. Driven by his own opportunism and nationalism, Franjo Tudjman kept step with Milosevic. His failure to address the legitimate concerns of the Serbs in Croatia made it far easier for Milosevic to carry out his plan.

Not all the events contributing to the development of conflict in Yugoslavia can be recounted here.[32] A few major events deserve some attention, however. Bosnia, sensing the potential for disaster, was very reluctant to declare its independence. After the secession of Slovenia and Croatia, and the subsequent fighting in those countries, the residents of Bosnia, Macedonia, and Montenegro faced the choice of whether to stay in what remained of Yugoslavia, knowing that it would be dominated by Serbs. The Montenegrins decided to stay, being closely related to Serbs and economically less developed. The Macedonians left, peacefully, in part because they had a very small Serb population and also because Belgrade's energy was directed elsewhere.[33]

The Bosnian government, supported by Muslims and Croats, decided to leave Yugoslavia, knowing very well that Bosnia was not militarily viable and probably hoping for Western intervention. The war in Bosnia started when Bosnian Serbs refused to accept the multiethnic, but mostly Muslim, Bosnian government. Yugoslavian National Army soldiers (Serbs and Montenegrins) stationed in Bosnia provided arms to the Bosnian Serbs and, in many cases, fought the Bosnian government—although usually after removing insignia patches identifying them as members of the army. After initially siding with the Muslims, Bosnian Croats in the spring of 1993 joined in the land grab.

Thus, the Serbs did not possess special antagonism against the Muslims that led to war. Instead, the war started as a part of the general drive to build a Greater Serbia, born of grandiose nationalism, realistic concerns for Serb minorities, and a recently revived sense that the Serbs had been persecuted throughout history. At the outset, hostility toward Muslims was not notably greater than that toward the other non-Serbs in Yugoslavia.

CHOOSING SIDES

Once they start, nationalistic wars can take on their own locomotive logic, overpowering everything in their path: individuality, professional loyalties, friendship, and moral codes. Imagine the predicament of a rational, fair-minded person unfortunate enough to find himself or herself a citizen of Yugoslavia as the conflict heated up, first verbally, then militarily. Even if an individual had not previously been a particularly nationalistic Croat, Muslim, or whatever, the pressure to choose sides grew immense.

Misha Glenny describes an interview with a Serb policeman who resided several miles outside Sarajevo. Glenny, who questioned the officer several months after the outbreak of fighting, decided that he was not an evil man:

> On the contrary, he explained how he found it very difficult to shoot at the other side of his village, because he knew everybody who lived there. But the war had somehow arrived and he had to defend his home. The man was confused and upset by the events but he now perceived the Green Berets and the Ustashas to be a real threat to his family. "We cannot let them form an Islamic state here," he said with genuine passion. "Are you sure they want to?" I asked him. "Of course they want to. I don't understand why you people outside don't realize that we are fighting for Europe against a foreign religion." There was nothing disingenuous about this simple man. His only mistake was to believe the nonsense that his local community had learned from Serbian television.[34]

On all sides, even the most discerning audiences had difficulty separating truth from propaganda—although Serb pronouncements clearly departed from reality most outrageously.

Engaged in the struggle for land, combatants seldom stopped to find out the political views of a particular Muslim, Croat, or Serb. The war

drew lines with a broad brush, and once the enemy classified you by ethnicity, it was hard to refuse the label.

Even for those far from the front, the "which side are you on?" mentality proved extremely difficult to resist. Though they may have lamented
the passing of coexistence, very few Serbs, Croats, or Muslims managed to
resist publicly the onslaught of nationalism. Those who did frequently
found themselves lost, without friends and without a homeland. In her
book, *The Balkan Express: Fragments from the Other Side of War,* Croat
writer Slavenka Drakulic captures well the power of the Serbia-Croatia
war to erase individual identity, even among reasonable people:

> Along with millions of other Croats, I was pinned to the wall of nation-
> hood—not only by outside pressure from Serbia and the Federal Army but
> by national homogenization within Croatia itself. That is what the war is
> doing to us, reducing us to one dimension: the Nation. The trouble with this
> nationhood, however, is that whereas before, I was defined by my education,
> my job, my ideas, my character—and, yes, my nationality too—now I feel
> stripped of all that.[35]

Drakulic continues with a metaphor of nationalism as an ill-fitting shirt:
"You may feel the sleeves are too short, the collar too tight. You might not
like the colour, and the cloth might itch. But there is nothing else to
wear."[36] Finally, Drakulic admits to a moral pressure toward nationalism:
"Perhaps it would be morally unjust to tear off the shirt of the suffering
nation—with tens of thousands of people being shot, slaughtered and
burned just because of their nationality."[37]

Is it true, as Drakulic writes, that a person loses all possibility of moral
choice when a war is on? One wonders what remains of morality if one
accepts Drakulic's conclusions.

FROM SOLDIERS TO WAR CRIMINALS

Not all soldiers are war criminals, and not all wars produce atrocities on
the scale of Bosnia.

One will never know the identities of those who perpetrated many of
the most violent crimes, but some of the guilty are known. Some of them
have been named, indicted, and convicted by the International Criminal

Tribunal for the Former Yugoslavia in the Hague. They fall into three categories: (1) those who actually committed the murder, rape, or torture; (2) those who encouraged, directed, and commanded the murderers, rapists, and torturers; and (3) those with political or command responsibility who failed to stop the crimes despite an obligation under international law to do so.

Slobodan Milosevic, the (Serbian) Yugoslav president during the war in Bosnia, probably falls into the second category. So, too, do Radovan Karadzic, the political head of the Bosnian Serbs during the war; Ratko Mladic, their military commander; Biljana Plavsic, the Bosnian Serb vice president; Radislav Krstic, a high-level general; and other members of the Bosnian Serb leadership. At a minimum, these leaders bear political and command responsibility for atrocities. They had clear obligations to ferret out the scum beneath them; instead, they became willing and, generally, eager accomplices. In recent years, prosecutors at the Hague have compiled evidence establishing that Bosnian Serb political and military leaders, at the highest levels, very directly planned and implemented the infamous policy of ethnic cleansing. For a while, considerable effort was expended by the international community to downplay Milosevic's responsibility for war crimes in order to encourage his cooperation in peace negotiations. When he arrived in Dayton, Ohio, for the peace talks that ultimately ended the war in autumn 1995, he was treated like a visiting dignitary. But when NATO required a bombing campaign to defeat him in Kosovo in 1999, his resurrection as a responsible statesman had clearly outlived its usefulness. When, in autumn 2000, he fell from power in Belgrade, it was only a matter of time until his former countrymen decided that it was more prudent to turn him over to the tribunal.[38]

The leaders of the militias in Bosnia also deserve clear and direct blame for inciting many war crimes. The two most murderous and brutal of these leaders, Zeljko Raznatovic and Vojislav Seselj, were honored as respected public figures in Serbia. Their roles as the butchers of Muslim women and children were well known; this not only was tolerated but seemed to enhance their mystique.

Before becoming a hero to Serbian extremists, Raznatovic, wanted by Interpol, committed murders, bank robberies, and jailbreaks across Europe; he is generally known by one of his criminal aliases, "Arkan." His criminal past served him well as the leader of a group of soldier-thugs

called the "Tigers," or Arkanovci. Some of the worst instances of mass
rape and murders were committed by these thugs; they inflicted tremendous suffering in eastern Bosnia. In his 1993 campaign, Arkan presented
himself as the most nationalistic of the nationalists. "We have a Serbian
dream," he shouted. "We are fighting for our faith, the Serbian Orthodox
Church. We are fighting for a united Serbian state. This party will believe
in God and Serbia."[39] In the shattered economy of Serbia, Arkan gave
hundred-Deutschmark bills as tips; he wore a diamond-studded Rolex
watch.[40]

Seselj, a former professor, headed units of paramilitary fighters called
Chetniks, after the Serbian anti-Nazi resistance in World War II. Asked on
a popular Serbian TV show whether his men, like their namesakes, still
killed with knives, he replied no, they had graduated to rusty shoehorns
that they intended to use on Croatian eyeballs. Later, when the comment
appeared to bring ill-repute upon his men, Seselj explained that it had all
been a joke. Though many described him as a psychopath and his units
raped, tortured, pillaged, and carried out brutal campaigns of ethnic
cleansing in Croatia and Bosnia, he remained an influential figure in Belgrade. Though he fell from favor with Milosevic in late 1993, he
reemerged as a leading candidate for the presidency of Serbia in 1997.[41]

Other war criminals who masterminded atrocities include the commanders of the concentration camps. The U.S. State Department has
named Drago Prcac, the head of Omarska, as a good candidate for a war
crimes trial. And there is Velibor Ostojic, a former minister in Karadzic's
government, whom Nazi hunter Simon Wiesenthal dubbed the Goebbels
of the Bosnian Serbs. He also bears personal responsibility for the ordering of mass rapes committed at the Partizan Sports Center.[42] Dozens of
others supervised atrocities.

It is impossible to name the thousands of underlings who participated
in war crimes, and some may be tempted to dismiss them as insignificant
players in a drama directed by someone else. Yet no atrocities would have
occurred had there not been individuals willing to carry them out. In the
Bosnia conflict, saying "no" occasionally proved dangerous when, for example, militia troops murdered Serbs who vocalized sympathy for their
Muslim neighbors. But saying "no" remained an option, albeit one that
sometimes required considerable courage. It might have been more effective to speak out against nationalist extremists earlier in the process, be-

fore they had assumed control of the situation. Every society has its prophets of evil, its power-hungry criminals, its madmen. The key question, to which we turn next, is why in Bosnia so many people were willing to act in blatant disregard of moral and social inhibitions before this behavior was accepted and became the norm.

From the standpoint of political strategy, the motivation behind ethnic cleansing is clear. Serbian soldiers committed atrocities for tactical reasons, to force the non-Serbian population from their homes and villages. The more brutal the acts of violence, the better. If the fear of mass rape was most likely to lead to an exodus, then mass rape must be the policy. Ethnic cleansing occurred most frequently and was most brutal in areas where the largest numbers of Muslims and Croats had to be intimidated into flight. Additionally, Bosnian Serbs farthest removed from Serbia proper proved among the most active perpetrators of atrocities.[43]

As one history suggests, the Serbs "evidently wished to avoid a repetition of the 'West Bank problem' faced by the Israelis—the risk of adverse international publicity that would accompany occupation of lands inhabited by a hostile population."[44] They tried to follow Machiavelli's precept, that when one must be brutal, it is more effective to be overwhelmingly cruel during a short period of time than slightly repressive over a much longer period.

For the individual soldier, the promise of plunder provided additional incentive. When they had the chance, soldiers and locals took televisions, jewelry, and whatever they could find of value. Guards at the concentration camps would torture wealthy prisoners in an attempt to learn where they had hidden their money.

Thus, the political and military leaders had a strategic goal in mind when they ordered or tolerated ethnic cleansing and the soldiers had the personal incentive of enriching themselves.

Yet it would be wrong to interpret ethnic cleansing solely as the product of self-interested rational choice. Moral and social inhibitions, under normal conditions, would keep most people from acting on these interests. A few sociopaths might partake, but not nearly so many as formed the backbone of Serbian ethnic cleansing. A process of psychological preparation for genocide had to happen first. One critical step in this process, the reinvigoration of nationalist sentiments, has already been discussed. Three more steps completed the creation of a murderous mindset: (1) the intensification of the culture of toughness; (2) the reactivation of historical fears and resentments stemming from World War II; and (3) the stimulation of a desire for revenge.

Understandably, people from the Balkans sometimes object when outsiders describe them as wild, violent, dangerous peoples. Yet many Serbs lay claim to a national character of toughness and hypermasculinity, viewing themselves as a heroic and virile race. As it often does, the coming of military conflict brought increased emphasis on toughness and a decreased sensitivity to the loss of human life. Under conditions of war, a person typically hardens, developing some tolerance for blood and gore. Sensing that one's own death may be around the corner, there is frequently a lessening of concern for moral convention—particularly concerning the lives of the enemy. Simultaneously, the assertion of toughness provides comfort, suggesting as it does that one might have what it takes to survive. Thus, at Omarska, guards reportedly made special efforts to select prisoners with muscular builds for nightly murders. Sometimes, as if to assert their own godlike powers, Serb guards would tell a prisoner that it was time for him or her to die, but then, at the last minute, allow the prisoner to live.[45]

No single factor contributed more to the Serb war criminals' willingness to ignore moral prohibitions than their reactivated anger at how their people had suffered at the hands of the Croats during World War II. At the Jasenovac concentration camp in Southern Croatia, nearly 100,000 Serbs, Jews, and Gypsies had been murdered. Many more Serbs were killed elsewhere. The scale of Croat atrocities against the Serbs even caught the attention of the Nazis, who worried that Serbs might be driven to build a more effective resistance movement. Among many Serbs, before the current conflict, the personal or inherited memories of brutal mistreatment remained vivid. Psychiatrist John Mack has commented that:

> [E]thnonational groups that have been traumatized by repeated suffering at the hands of other groups seem to have little capacity to grieve for the hurts of other peoples, or to take responsibility for the new victims created by their own warlike actions. Victims kill victims through unendingly repeated cycles that are transmitted from one generation to another, bolstered by stories and myths of atrocities committed by the other people.[46]

But Mack overstates the inevitability of the cycle. For example, Jews, after the Holocaust, remained among the political groups most concerned about the suffering of other minorities.[47] And, in Israel, military policy has not escaped internal criticism. As a consequence of anti-Semitism and the Holocaust, Jewish antennae are always up, but the consequences described by Mack have not ensued. In part, this may be because Germany has accepted full responsibility for its war crimes and made reparations to the victims. As psychoanalyst Vamik Volkan notes:

> Although one's own side may raise monuments to memorialize its suffering and thus help bring about a practical end to the mourning process, the suffering of the other side is seldom honored. But a victimized group needs to have its losses recognized by its opponents.[48]

For the Serbs under Marshal Tito, the situation was worse, for they could not memorialize their own dead. And, from a psychological standpoint, the inability to mourn may have trapped many Serbs in a mentality based on World War II.

For example, General Ratko Mladic, the military commander of the Bosnian Serbs and a man who bears much responsibility for ethnic cleansing, owed much of his worldview to World War II. His father was killed in 1945 fighting to liberate a village in Bosnia. He could not think about the 1990s without thinking about the massacres of the 1940s. He interprets the independence of Croatia as a step in the revival of belligerent German power and saw British recognition of Croatia as analogous to the surrender of Czechoslovakia to Hitler at the Munich conference in 1938.[49] Serbian propaganda successfully capitalized on such memories and managed to persuade many Serbs that another genocide was happening, this time orchestrated by a new generation of Ustashas (Croatian fascists) in league with the Muslims.

Many parties are implicated in the World War II atrocities. While the Croat Ustashas committed the earliest, and possibly the worst, of the war crimes, it is difficult to sort out all the horrors of those years—more difficult because Tito never permitted the writing of objective history. Though crimes against the Serbs were committed in the name of the Croatian people, some Croats opposed the Ustashas. Some fought alongside the Serbs with Tito's (Communist) Partisans. Support for the Ustashas proved stronger among Bosnian Croats than among Croats in Croatia. Toward the end of the war, Serb nationalist Chetniks and Partisans took their revenge on the fascist Ustashas, executing many innocents along with the thousands of guilty. Amidst this murderous situation, Tito's Communist Partisans also massacred many Chetniks.

Though this history seems to point Serb anger primarily toward Croats, propaganda has proven effective in expanding Serb wrath to include the Muslims. During World War II, Muslims sometimes collaborated with the Ustashas and sometimes were victimized by them. There was a Bosnian Muslim SS unit and, after the war, the Mufti (Muslim leader) of Zagreb was tried and sentenced on charges of inciting Muslims to murder Serbs. Most Muslim religious leaders and the Muslim population, more generally, tried to keep a low profile during the war.

Serb leaders in the 1990s played on these fears by systematically fabricating the prospect of a new anti-Serb genocide, at various times led by Croat Ustashas, Muslims, or Albanians. For example, Roy Gutman reports the words of Major Milovan Milutinovic, a principal Serb propagandist in 1992 describing anti-Serb atrocities: "Necklaces have been strung of human eyes and ears, skulls have been halved, brains have been split, bowels have been torn out."[50] Milutinovic also referred specifically to the "Islamic fundamentalists from Sarajevo" who had allegedly ordered the rape of Serbian women, aged seventeen to forty.[51] A newspaper article in the Serb daily *Borba* reported evidence of a purported atrocity of the new Ustashas—a bucket drawn from a well that contained three hundred testicles.[52] People who hear stories like these repeatedly may begin to believe them. And once they believe the stories, the situation becomes "them" or "us." The most flagrant violators of human dignity at Omarska cited "proof" that the Muslims were going to put their women in harems and breed soldiers for the jihad. For these men, the perpetration of atrocities became revenge for crimes that (with few exceptions) had never taken place. More perversely, murder, mayhem, and even rape appeared to them as protective measures, necessary to preserve their own families and communities.

As a captain in the Bosnian Serb army left Pale, the capital, for the front line in Sarajevo, he explained the necessity of war:

We are prisoners of history. All of Serbian history is a chain of war, resistance and uprisings. The reason is simply that we insist on defending our land. We can never agree to live under a Muslim regime because in our history that has always led to genocide against us. The Muslims in Sarajevo say they will treat us fairly, as equals, but history and our own experience tell us that is a lie.[53]

This soldier believed he reacted to the lessons of personal experience and the past. In reality, he reacted to the propaganda of his leaders.

THE REASONS FOR RAPE

For Susan Brownmiller, author of the feminist classic *Against Our Will: Men, Women and Rape,* the mass rapes in Bosnia were the latest manifestation of a male tendency to use sex as a weapon of domination.[54] For Brownmiller, the roots of mass rape extend into matters of *male* identity as much as they do into matters of ethnic identity. Brownmiller writes that wartime provides men with the "perfect psychologic backdrop to give vent to their contempt for women" and that rape "flourishes in warfare irrespective of nationality or geographic location."[55] She notes that, typically, the winning side does more raping than the losing side, although for reasons that obviously have nothing to do with morality. Rape is the act of a conqueror and it enables soldiers to prove their superiority and masculinity.[56] The wartime rapists are not particularly deviant, but are "ordinary Joes, made unordinary by entry into the most exclusive male-only club in the world," the armed forces.[57] Moreover, Brownmiller sees the anguish of men in the victim group as suffering related to damaged pride and lost goods. Women, during war, become booty.

Brownmiller further maintains that rape results from deep-rooted social traditions in which males have dominated all economic and political institutions that truly matter. Prostitution and pornography are only two poignant examples she cites of male domination and exploitation of females. She sees the complicity of *all* males in acts of rape. These acts, and the fear of them, in her view, reinforce male power generally. Finally, the drive for sexual gratification is seen as essentially irrelevant, taking a back seat to power motivation, specifically the desire to establish and maintain dominance over women.[58]

Nobody can dispute the prevalence of rape during wars throughout history. In ancient, medieval, and early modern times, nearly all groups sanctioned the rape and capture of enemy women. Even in the twentieth century, many wars have seen large-scale raping by invading armies. Despite their ideological prohibitions against sexual misconduct and mixing of races, the Nazis were responsible for many rapes in their conquest of parts of the Soviet Union. In 1993, the Japanese government finally owned up to horrible rapes sponsored by the Imperial army during World War II. Chinese, Filipino, Dutch, and, especially, Korean women were forced, on pain of death, to serve as prostitutes, known euphemistically as "comfort" women, for Japanese troops. These troops swept into villages, carrying women away at gunpoint. As many as 200,000 women had their lives devastated, not by one rape, but by repeatedly being robbed of their human dignity in order to meet the "needs" of soldiers.[59]

Neither these crimes nor those in Bosnia could have happened without the dehumanization of female victims; as Brownmiller points out, women were doubly dehumanized, both as women and as enemies.[60] If soldiers in Bosnia had viewed sex acts as matters of shared intimacy or shared humanity, they certainly would have felt *themselves* degraded by participating in rape. They would have been preoccupied by guilt, wondering how they could live with themselves and their present or future mates.

Many victims reported that the soldiers who raped them claimed to be acting under orders.[61] For example, Hafiza, a twenty-three-year-old woman, reports her conversation with one soldier. "You have a mother and a sister, a female in the family." The soldier said nothing, at first. Then: "I must. I must." She told him that he must not, if he did not want to. But she could not stop him.[62] Some women report soldiers taking them to houses and asking them to say they had been raped, even though they had been left unharmed. Still, those who refused to rape and those who did so reluctantly seemed to the victims far fewer than those who participated with relish. Commanders reportedly told soldiers that the rapes would boost their morale. The vast majority of Serb rapists did not appear to be sheepishly complying with distasteful commands.

Individual Serb soldiers probably responded to the rape orders differently, depending on their personalities and particular circumstances. It is not currently known to what extent it was possible for Serb soldiers to evade the orders without incurring the wrath of their superiors. But the nature of the rape act would generally permit a reluctant recruit to feign the deed. Moreover, the soldier who refused to participate faced humiliation or disgrace in the eyes of his peers, rather than death—though one cannot rule out the possibility that a few feared for their lives. The probable scenario, then, involves soldiers themselves making a choice to rape or taking advantage of orders authorizing rape, rather than slavishly adhering to orders against their wills. They regressed down the scale of civilization to a level of conduct that characterized many armies in various eras throughout history.

Research on rape suggests that at least three motives can be important: (1) the desire to hurt or humiliate the victim; (2) the desire to demonstrate power over the victim; and (3) the desire to have sex. Usually, it is difficult to determine which of the three motives predominates in a particular rape. Even in wartime Bosnia, all three played a part. But desires to hurt, humiliate, and demonstrate power seem more central than sexual motives.

According to research on rape in other settings, when sexual motives are most important, rapists usually select attractive victims and use little gratuitous physical violence.[63] In Bosnia, survivors of the rapes report that attractive girls were chosen most frequently, but many older and less attractive women were also raped. And there was much gratuitous violence and degradation. One Muslim woman, for example, reports the following ordeal:

> I was raped with a gun by one of those men, along with another woman and her daughter, while the others watched. Some of them spat on us; they did so many ugly things to us. . . . There was no passion in this, it was done only to destroy us . . . if they couldn't rape me, they would urinate on me.[64]

Even in this barbarous instance, however, one cannot rule out the possibility that perpetrators derived some perverse sexual pleasure from their crime. Several studies have shown that, under various circumstances, sexual arousal can increase aggressive tendencies and vice versa. Rapists, in particular, find violence against women sexually arousing.[65] In addition, studies show that when an angry male sees sexually explicit material, he is much more apt to behave violently toward women.[66] This might suggest that, given permission to rape, many Serb soldiers combined their anger toward the Muslims with sexual desires in a way that increased their tendencies toward sexual violence.

Most of the time, though, sexual motives were secondary, or tertiary. The Serb rapists sought to inflict humiliation and apparently reveled in their power. Their primary goal was not, as Brownmiller argues, to reinforce patriarchy, but rather to assert dominance of Serb over Croat and Muslim.

The use of rape as a tool of ethnic humiliation presupposed a willingness to treat women as objects; this was not a sufficient condition for rape to occur, but it was a necessary one. The rapists in Bosnia probably differed from rapists in times of peace in that they required less deviancy to become sexual aggressors. Still, rapists in other settings may share certain attributes with the Serb rapists, including generally aggressive personalities and histories of sexually promiscuous behavior.[67] In addition, those who committed rapes in Bosnia may have ignored traditional moral bounds in the past in their attempts to induce women to have sex with them—as is the case with American date-rapists.[68]

Males who do not commit acts of sexual aggression generally find pornographic depictions of consensual sex more arousing than violent pornography; in contrast, violence fails to inhibit the sexual arousal of the rapist. This difference in arousal patterns might have contributed to individual decisions to participate in the rapes.[69] One study in the United States examined the origins of the inclination to use pressure, coercion, and force in sexual relationships. Though this inclination is not the same as the willingness to carry out a rape, similar attitudes and experiences may be involved in both. Sexually violent men showed general hostility toward women, an accepting attitude toward sexual aggression, a considerable amount of sexual experience, and physiological arousal to depictions of rape. The desire to dominate women was an important part of their sexual motivation.[70] Similar experiences and views might have characterized the Bosnian Serb rapists. Without direct studies of these rapists, however, theories about why they committed their crimes must remain speculative.

One can conclude that the rapes of Muslim and Croat women in Bosnia reflected a combination of strategic and personal goals. Some reluctant rapists no doubt went along against their desires in order to avoid the scorn of peers and superior officers. For most, their personal involvement probably went beyond this conformity and beyond the goal of intimidating non-Serbs into leaving contested territory. Most Serbs probably committed rapes as an expression of their utter contempt for the enemy, a contempt born of real and imagined wrongs of the past and present. The central desire was to humiliate Muslims. To this end, they were equally willing to treat male bodies as objects—cutting and mutilating them for sport.

Sadism and sexual deviancy contributed to the savagery of sexual abuse in some instances. Propensities toward such deviant behavior exist in all populations at all times. But, for the Bosnian Serbs, authorization to rape enabled otherwise submerged deviant tendencies to surface. Thus, the same pathology that on one occasion led to forcing a man to eat a piece of another man's ear might lead on a different occasion to raping a girl in front of her father or mother. More generally, research suggests that rapists rarely specialize. People who are willing to violate moral injunctions against sexual coercion typically abandon other rules as well; they engage in a wide range of deviant behavior and crime. The rapists in Bosnia may have differed from nonrapists principally in their failure to have internalized moral controls. When the external rules against rape were removed, there was nothing left on the inside to inhibit horrifying antisocial behavior.

No evidence supports Brownmiller's contention that Muslim males acted out of wounded pride or anything other than genuine, humane, familial concern when they expressed outrage about the rapes of wives and daughters. Neither does any evidence support the theory that males *as a group* share a common willingness to participate in, or at least overlook, rape, because they want to preserve patriarchy.[71] Many men think of sex as "doing something to someone" rather than sharing intimacy. And gang rape is a worldwide, though uncommon, phenomenon. But, across the globe, many men view women as sex objects without possessing the requisite willingness to violate moral injunctions against rape. The distance between using a prostitute and committing a rape is not as small a step as some have argued. Additionally, a theory that implicates *all* men in the genesis of rapes fails to explain why some modern armies do not act similarly to the Bosnian Serbs or the Imperial Japanese. Rapes do occur in most wars, but not in anywhere near the same frequency nor with the tacit, or even explicit, approval of army officials.

Some aberrant males in all populations have a tendency to rape; when they can get away with it during wartime, many will. This, however, is not what happened in Bosnia. Military and political leaders used terror and humiliation as part of a clear strategy. Soldiers obeyed, but not out of dutiful compliance. Because of political propaganda that stimulated fears, resentment, and a desire for revenge against the non-Serbs of Bosnia, most participated enthusiastically. The demonstration of power and the infliction of humiliation were key motives, but for most of the rapists enforcement of a patriarchal system was not a motive. For sexual deviants and sadists in the Serb militias, official authorization to rape provided a welcome opportunity that they accepted with horrible effect.

THREE

Muslim Extremists in New York: First Strike

[MUSLIMS] MUST KILL THE ENEMIES OF ALLAH, IN EVERY WAY AND EVERYWHERE IN ORDER TO LIBERATE THEMSELVES FROM THE GRANDCHILDREN OF THE PIGS AND APES WHO ARE EDU-CATED AT THE TABLE OF [THE] ZIONISTS, THE COMMUNISTS, AND THE IMPERIALISTS.[1]

Sheikh Omar Abdel Rahman, 1992

AS AN IDEOLOGY, FUNDAMENTALIST ISLAM CAN CLAIM NONE OF THE SANCTITY THAT ISLAM THE RELIGION ENJOYS.[2]

Daniel Pipes, Editor,
Middle East Quarterly

The early winter of 1993 was a happy time for Edward Smith and his wife, Monica. The young couple from Seaford, Long Island, had learned during the autumn that they were going to have a baby, a son, and they had decided to name him Eddie. They had fixed up their house from top to bottom, listened to Eddie's heartbeat in the doctor's office, and shopped for baby furniture. Edward, Monica, and little Eddie seemed destined for a future of contentment, right up until the moment their world was shattered on 26 February.

Monica Smith and her unborn child, along with five others, perished when a bomb tore through the garage and lower levels of the World Trade Center that day. Her husband recalls:

> Nobody could have ever prepared me for the feelings I was experiencing. I had lost my wife, my best friend, my idol and my son. I would never get the chance to tell Monica how much I loved her. I would never get to tell her what an inspiration she had been. I would never get to tell her what a best friend meant to me. We would never get to hear Eddie say his first word, to say "mommy," "daddy," "love." . . . What god would want people to die in his name?[3]

The cry of the victims, in 1993, was a mere squeak, evoking sympathy for a moment, perhaps for a day, perhaps a week, then fading silently as eyes fixed on the perpetrators. In May 1994 four major defendants in the World Trade Center bombing trial received sentences of 240 years each. In October 1995 a jury found Sheikh Omar Abdel Rahman and nine others guilty of seditious conspiracy. And in January 1996 Judge Michael Mukasey sentenced them all to long prison terms, the shortest being twenty-five years. In January 1998 Ramzi Yousef, viewed by some as the mastermind of the plot, was fined $4.5 million, ordered to pay $250 million in restitution, and sentenced to 240 years in prison without visits from friends or family members. Several months later, his associate, Eyad Ismoil, also was sentenced to 240 years.[4]

The satisfaction the verdicts elicited then does little to shore up Americans' sense of security now, in the shadow of September 11, 2001. As Oliver B. Revell, a former FBI official in charge of counterterrorist investigations, observed at the time: "They are ultimately committed to waging holy war, both in the Middle East and the world at large against all of their opposition. And that means us."[5]

Now, in the post–September 11 world, the cries of victims cannot be forgotten—and America's focus on the perpetrators must be intense and unyielding. Many said, as they saw the smoke rise from the fallen towers on September 11, that the world had changed forever. The sobering fact is that the essential realities of terrorism in the world before September 11 and the world after are not that different: Osama bin Laden's operatives and others like them lived among us then, crafting schemes of mass death and destruction, and they live among us now, with the same goal in mind.[6]

Even before September 11, the substantial danger of mass violence by Islamic extremists—whether on American soil or abroad—was apparent. Militant Islamic movements have bombed American embassies and interests and threatened the survival of relatively moderate, pro-Western governments across the Middle East, Africa, and South Asia. And fatwas issued by Islamic extremist leaders around the globe have provided religious justification to terrorists. Fatwas are religious opinions that can deal with a broad range of issues, like marriage, divorce, and fasting. But, in recent years, Islamic extremist sheikhs have delivered numerous fatwas that amount to death sentences for those opposed to their extremist positions, including many in the Muslim world.[7]

During the 1990s, for example, Algerian extremists struck bloody blows against their nation's own intelligentsia.[8] The daughter of Mohammed Boukhobza, a sociology professor, was forced to watch as five fundamentalist terrorists slit her father's throat. The editor of an Algerian weekly, Tahar Djaout, was shot and killed. So was Rabah Zenati, a TV journalist, and Nabila Djahnine, a prominent feminist. After surviving three previous assassination attempts, Said Mekbel was murdered as he ate his lunch in an Algiers pizzeria in December 1994. He was the third journalist killed within a seventy-two-hour period. In May 1995, a gunman's bullet cut short reporter Malika Sabour's life at the age of twenty-two; her family was forced to watch the murder. Earlier in the same month, Mourad Hemaizi, a news anchorman on Algerian national television, was tied to a pole and shot to death by three extremist terrorists. A violent faction of Muslim fundamentalists threatened to kill every mother, sister, and daughter of Algerian government officials.

In Egypt, Farag Foda, a writer, was gunned down, partly because he defended the rights of Egypt's Coptic Christians. Egypt's Nobel Laureate in literature, Naguib Mahfouz, occupied a prominent spot on the extremists' hit list, and was ultimately stabbed by supporters of Sheikh Omar Abdel Rahman in October 1994. Salman Rushdie, the most famous literary target, has so far managed to escape, or delay, the fatwa issued against him by the Iranian government. His Norwegian publisher, William Nygaard, less fortunate, was shot and seriously wounded near his home in Oslo; his Italian translator was murdered. In Bangladesh, a price was put on the head of Taslima Nasrin, a feminist writer who called for modifying the traditional Islamic position on women's rights.

Such threats have an impact that goes well beyond the toll they exact in lives and literature. They have, in fact, brought meaningful debate on social values to a standstill in most Middle Eastern nations; from this region, no public opinion, no governmental position, no journalism, no theology can be taken at face value because all have evolved under conditions of duress.

And what of the effect on the hundreds of millions of Muslims (including most fundamentalist Muslims) who wish to pursue their faith in peace? Consider the case of Professor Nasr Abu Zeid, who published a linguistic analysis of Islam's holy book, the Koran. Despite his protestations that he was a good Muslim and intended no insult to the faith, militant Islamic lawyers sued to have him declared an apostate, a man who has abandoned his religion. But they did not stop there; they also demanded that his marriage be annulled because religious law, the law governing matrimony in Egypt, does not permit marriages between Muslims and apostates. In January 1994, a court threw the case out, not because Abu Zeid and his wife wished to remain married (which they did), but because the militant lawyers, in the opinion of the court, had no grounds for a lawsuit. In June 1995, however, an appeals court reversed the decision and annulled the marriage. The ruling forced Abu Zeid and his wife into exile in the Netherlands, where they remain. Similarly, when seventy-year-old feminist Nawal el-Saadawi allegedly remarked that the Muslim custom of making an annual pilgrimage to Mecca was a "vestige of pagan practices," she found herself in court trying to prove that she should not have to end her thirty-seven-year marriage to her husband, Sherif Hetata. This time, the court allowed the marriage to stand.[9]

Moderate Muslims throughout the world find themselves in a particularly unenviable position, threatened with physical attack by militant Muslims who disagree with their interpretations of Islam, and mistrusted by Westerners who fail to distinguish between them and the extremists. For many Westerners, it has become difficult to consider Islam apart from the images of violence and hostility it evokes. This understandable tendency is unjust, tarnishing as it does many who have been among the prime victims of the extremists.

The goal, here, is to understand the motivation and ideology behind extremist Islam. Many acts of terrorism have been committed in the name of Islam, though the majority of Muslims are revolted by terrorist acts. In the wake of the events of September 11, political and religious leaders alike have called attention to the danger of blaming Islam for the acts of criminals acting in clear contradiction to the laws of Islam. These leaders express the deeply held American belief in the respect for freedom of religious conviction. They argue that a religion that provides moral and spiritual comfort for nearly a billion people, nearly one out of five human beings, cannot justly be blamed for those who, in effect, have rejected its teachings. They urge us to condemn the crimes, punish the criminals, but respect the religious beliefs of Islam.

This position commands our support. But the analysis neglects the fact that the extremists were not merely criminals who happened to be Muslims. They were acting in what they, and many of their supporters, believed to be the deepest traditions of their faith. They, their cobelievers, and their sheikhs regard violent resistance to nonbelievers (under some circumstances) as not only condoned by Islam, but required by it. And they have declared themselves willing to fight to the death against those who disagree.

The supporters of Muslim extremism do not constitute a majority of Islamic believers, but neither are they an insignificant number. For many years, several groups of extremist Islamic leaders have been spewing words of hate against America and the West. How has one of the world's major monotheist religions become associated with justifications for murder? Why has America been drawn into this religious conflict? What are the psychological and historical roots of Muslim extremist hostility toward the United States? How has Islam been used by extremists to foment hatred against secularism, the West, Jews, and, in many instances, modernity?

It is no simple matter to untangle the ideological origins of Muslim extremist terrorists. Despite claims of unity, Islam (like Christianity, Judaism, and other major faiths) is really a group of religious belief systems, related more by a common past than by core beliefs. The fundamentalist, or revivalist, strand of Islam itself constitutes a multitude of ideologies which differ significantly in their level of militancy. Even militant Islam includes a world of movements that is forever splitting and splitting again. Ideological differences among these submovements may be negligible, but political agendas may be worlds apart. Or political objectives may be virtually identical, but divergences on ideological matters may be tremendous.

The 1993 World Trade Center bombers and Lincoln Tunnel plotters, themselves, were not a tight-knit group. Federal investigators connected representatives of various militant Islamic groups to the World Trade Center plot, including Osama bin Laden's al-Qaeda organization, the Palestinian-based Islamic Jihad, Hamas (also Palestinian-based), the Sudanese National Islamic Front, and the Pakistan-based al-Fuqra.[10] Ideologically, most of the 1993 terrorists had their immediate roots in the movement associated with Sheikh Omar Abdel Rahman, the blind sheikh who was one of the leaders of the Islamic Jihad (Munazzamat al-Jihad) group in Egypt. The Islamic Jihad, itself, represents one of the most radical offshoots of the Muslim Brotherhood movement, a revivalist group founded by Hassan al-Banna in 1928.

THE SHAPING OF A CONSPIRACY

The news in March 1993 was hard to believe. Mohammed Salameh had rented a yellow Econoline van, stuffed it with explosives, and blown a huge hole in the World Trade Center. But, amazingly, he had rented the van in his own name, reported it stolen, and then returned to the rental agency several times to reclaim a $400 deposit. Amidst the rubble, detectives found a fragment of the van with a vehicle identification number that they traced back to the rental agency and, ultimately, to Salameh. A detective's reaction at the time captured a widely shared sentiment: "I cannot believe that such devastation could be caused by someone so dumb."[11]

Over time, however, the complex network of plots hatched by Brooklyn and Jersey City Muslim extremists appeared far less the work of simpletons. Despite huge teams of detectives and prosecutors, hours of tapes from an FBI informer, defendants working with the government, and an ideological leader who had published and been in the public eye for more than a decade, there is still much we do not know about the 1993 World Trade Center bombing and the broader conspiracy that same year. The most pressing unanswered question is whether foreign governments, notably Iraq and Iran, played a part in planning and bankrolling the plots. Most analysts suspect that they did. We also lack clear knowledge of specific individuals' culpabilities. For example, we do not know whether Sheikh Omar Abdel Rahman was an operational head pulling the strings, or merely a radical theologian providing the inspiration. Much confusion still surrounds the role of Ramzi Yousef, who was not apprehended until a year after the bombing. Some see him as the originator of the conspiracy while others dismiss him as a hired gun.[12]

The charge brought against the defendants was seditious conspiracy to levy a war of urban terrorism against the United States. The plot was complex and the terrorists chose grandiose targets: the United Nations, the FBI building, the Hudson River tunnels, the Manhattan Diamond district, Egyptian President Hosni Mubarak, UN Secretary General Boutros Boutros-Ghali, New York Senator Alphonse D'Amato, and others. One plan was to kidnap former President Richard Nixon and former U.S. Secretary of State Henry Kissinger in order to arrange a prisoner swap. The terrorists had ties to the worldwide holy war network, with affiliates in Afghanistan, Egypt, the Sudan, Iraq, and Iran.

They plodded through clandestine meetings for more than three years, gathering and conspiring amidst prayer sessions in mosques, homes, luncheonettes, and bookstores in Jersey City and Brooklyn. Many of the terrorists spent their weekends attending training programs. An allied leader, Mustafa Shalabi, was murdered, probably as part of an internal power struggle and possibly involving defendants from the conspiracy case. A hate-mongering, incendiary rabbi, Meir Kahane, fell to an assassin's bullet, and the defendant was, to the chagrin of the presiding judge, at first found not guilty of the murder in a state trial. A few years later, the assassin was finally convicted of murder through federal charges and legal maneuvering that avoided the problem of double jeopardy. An informer with a mysterious past infiltrated the conspiracy, tied Kahane's murder to the broader plot, and provided the FBI with critical information on the planned assassinations and bombings. In the end, government agents were too late to stop the 1993 World Trade Center bombing, but they arrived in the nick of time to prevent the other disasters planned that year.

One of the key figures from the World Trade Center bombing, Ramzi Yousef, remained at large, hopping from country to country until one of his associates turned him in, reportedly for a $2 million reward. During this period, he set new plots in motion—to kill the Pope and blow up several American jets. But, again, the authorities were able to prevent a calamity.

While it is beyond our scope here to trace and unravel all the details of the conspiracy, we can move toward a more sophisticated understanding of why a group of nearly two dozen Muslims in the New York metropolitan area declared war on a country which had opened its doors to them.

Mahmud Abouhalima probably was not the mastermind of the bombing, but clearly he played a central role. An understanding of his life can help clarify some of the formative events that influenced many other conspirators in this plot as well as the more destructive one of September 2001. Writing in *Time* magazine, Richard Behar reflects: "So much of Abouhalima's past seems humdrum that to read his story and believe in his guilt is to be reminded of Hannah Arendt's line about Adolf Eichmann embodying the banality of evil. Look at pieces of his life, however, and one finds a growing religious fervor that could have transformed Abouhalima into a man with a motive for destruction in the name of a higher goal."[13]

Abouhalima developed his hatred for Egypt while growing up in the sixties and seventies in Kafr al-Dawar, a Nile delta town. His family was poor, though not as poor as many of their neighbors. Stories about his early years are unreliable; some say he was always devout; others claim he cared little about religion and focused his energies on soccer. By his teens, however, Mahmud became associated with the Islamic Group (al-Jama'a Islamiyya), whose members took spiritual guidance from Sheikh Omar Abdel Rahman and other fundamentalist leaders. He attended Alexandria University, and when friends in the Islamic Group were arrested, he took some steps to assist them.

President Anwar Sadat's intensification of his crackdown on Muslim fundamentalists opposed to the Egyptian secular state put Abouhalima in some danger because of his peripheral involvement with the Islamic Group's activities. When he learned that Egyptian security forces had their eye on him, he quit school and left for Germany.

Meanwhile, back in Egypt, one week after Abouhalima's arrival in Germany, Lieutenant Khalid Islambouli, an associate of Sheikh Omar Abdel Rahman, murdered President Sadat. Abouhalima sought political asylum in Germany, but his request was denied. This problem he solved promptly by marrying a German citizen, Renate Soika. According to Soika, the relationship was characterized by friendship, but not love. Abouhalima was never violent with her. Soika also claimed (after his arrest) that she suspected Abouhalima's involvement in some sort of underground movement at the time.

His life in Germany centered around the community of devout orthodox Muslims in Munich. Abouhalima openly spoke of his hostility toward Sadat, Sadat's successor Hosni Mubarak, the Germans, and the United States. His relationship with Soika soon fell apart, partly because she refused to convert to Islam. Abouhalima then found another German woman, Marianne Weber, significantly younger and willing to convert. He married her in an Islamic ceremony—but not before asking Soika to live with them as a threesome. She refused.

Soon thereafter, Abouhalima and his new wife moved to Brooklyn, entering on a tourist visa, staying illegally, and ultimately gaining permanent resident status under the 1986 amnesty program. He claimed to have been a migrant worker on a farm in South Carolina, although there is no evidence of this. Abouhalima's immersion in fundamentalist Islam increased. While working in America as a New York City cabdriver, he listened enthusiastically to sermons on cassettes. Though he frequently expressed contempt for materialistic American culture, he accepted money from his wife's parents, apparently overcharged his cab's customers, and was involved in an attempt to steal from the broker of a taxi medallion.

Amidst all this, and possibly influenced by the sermons he heard, Abouhalima often spoke of the glories of the jihad in Afghanistan. More than an idle daydreamer, in 1988 he left New York for Afghanistan. He first trained with the Mujaheddin at Peshawar, Pakistan. While there, he no doubt benefited from the billions of American dollars sent by the CIA in an effort to quash the 1979 Soviet invasion. Though we know little about the specifics of his life during this period, the war in Afghanistan appears to have been a transforming event. He intensified his commitment to an extreme fundamentalist interpretation of Islam and, apparently, became more comfortable with violence.

Fundamentalist Muslims came to Afghanistan from around the world. Veterans of the conflict exported aspects of the jihad to Algeria, Azerbaijan, Bangladesh, Bosnia, Egypt, India, Morocco, Pakistan, the Sudan, Tajikistan, Tunisia, Uzbekistan, Yemen, and elsewhere. As Noor Amin, a commander of a radical Islamic faction, announced proudly, "Yes, the whole country is a university for jihad, exactly as they say. . . . We have had Egyptians, Sudanese, Arabs and other foreigners trained here as assassins."[14] The brutal and bloody war in Afghanistan claimed the lives of well over a million Muslims; once the Soviets left in February 1989, the holy warriors began a battle for the remains of the country with the leading faction under Gulbuddin Hekmatyar committing itself to a "true Islamic republic" and a hostile, anti-Western ideology. Along with Abouhalima, several other prominent conspirators, including Ramzi Ahmed Yousef, Ahmad Ajaj, Siddig Ibrahim Siddig Ali, Clement Rodney Hampton-El, and Sheikh Omar Abdel Rahman, contributed their services to Hekmatyar's group in Afghanistan. Those who did not make the trip, like Mohammed Salameh, raised money for the cause.[15]

Upon Abouhalima's return to Brooklyn in July 1990, he served as Sheikh Rahman's part-time driver and centered his life around worship in two mosques, Abu Bakr in Brooklyn and al-Salaam in Jersey City. When El Sayyid Nosair was acquitted of murdering Rabbi Meir Kahane, Abouhalima was inspired; a well-known photograph shows him hoisting Nosair's lawyer, William Kuntsler, on his shoulders. Police considered the possibility that Abouhalima had been intended as El Sayyid Nosair's getaway driver, but they were unable to prove it. The tapes provided by Emad Salem, the FBI informer, confirm that the conspirators thought of El Sayyid Nosair as a hero. One of their objectives was to break him out of jail where he was serving time for weapons charges related to the shooting of Rabbi Kahane, or to arrange a deal to have him released. Nosair's acquittal of the more serious charge of murder can only have provided the conspirators, including Abouhalima, with encouragement.

The other defendants in the various trials connected with the 1993 conspiracy shared elements of Abouhalima's background.[16] All of those charged were men, mostly between twenty-five and forty years old. All were Muslims, generally associated with Sheikh Omar Abdel Rahman's brand of Islamic fundamentalism—though, according to defense attorneys, some had quarreled with the Sheikh. Many were family men. Abouhalima had four children; Tariq Elhassan and Mohammed Saleh each had three. Mohammed Abouhalima and Mahmud Abouhalima were brothers. El Sayyid Nosair and Ibrahim El-Gabrowny were cousins. So were Fadil Abdelghani and Amir Abdelgani (despite the slight variation in spelling the family name).

None of the defendants was a wealthy man. A few had some higher education from overseas, but nearly all worked at jobs that did not require any advanced degrees. Many were cab drivers in the New York area. For example, Siddig Ibrahim Siddig Ali, a leader of the plot to bomb the Hudson River tunnels who later pleaded guilty, had a degree in economics from a university in Sudan, but worked as a taxi driver, street peddler, and security guard.

Besides Sheikh Omar Abdel Rahman himself, only one defendant in the 1993 plot, Nidal Ayyad, had a professional career. A recent graduate of Rutgers University, Ayyad lived in the New Jersey suburb of Maplewood and worked as a chemical engineer for Allied-Signal, Inc., earning about $38,000 a year. It was Ayyad who ordered the chemicals for the World Trade Center bomb and sent a letter claiming credit for the explosion, a letter that was later retrieved from a deleted file on his computer.

One could argue that, except for Ayyad, the defendants felt personally degraded by their low economic status and that this contributed to their anger. This line of argument, however, ignores the fact that tens of thousands of New Yorkers, especially immigrants, perform work at a lower level than their skills suggest, yet few become terrorists. In fact, most of the conspirators probably had already crystallized their hostility toward America well before their arrival in the United States.

One of the 1993 plotters, Clement Rodney Hampton-El, born in the United States, followed a somewhat different path to radicalism than the others.[17] We know something about Hampton-El's background because (prior to his involvement in the bombing plot) an anthropologist, Robert Dannin, had interviewed him for a study of the relationship between America's Black Muslim movement and new Islamic immigrants to the United States.

In his mid-fifties at the time of the conspiracy, Hampton-El was the son of pioneers in the Black Muslim movement; his parents had been members of the Moorish Science Temple. Also known as Abdul Rashid Abdullah and, more colloquially, as Dr. Rasheed, he was a medical technician. Some local residents had very favorable recollections of Dr. Rasheed, noting his involvement as a Flatbush apartment complex leader, a medical advisor, and a militant opponent of drug dealers. Hampton-El, himself, often expressed fury over what he perceived to be widespread antiblack racism in the United States.

A critical event in Hampton-El's development, and one that brought him in contact with the other 1993 conspirators, was the war in Afghanistan. One of a small group of volunteers from the New York metropolitan area, he was wounded in the arm and leg. While recuperating in New York, he spoke of returning to the fight against infidels in Afghanistan and of protecting his Brooklyn neighbors against crime. A common thread was militancy and a willingness to use violence. In the bombing conspiracy, Hampton-El agreed to provide firearms and grenades for the planned Mubarak assassination. A search of his Brooklyn house turned up gun parts, ammunition, a cannon fuse, and military training videos. Hampton-El's fatalism is also psychologically relevant; as he told Dannin: "You got to die and you're not going to die until it's your time. I just chill and lay back."[18]

There were other American-born conspirators: Philadelphia resident Earl Gant, also known as Abdul Jalil and Abdul Rashid, received only a light sentence for his role in the foiled bombing plot because he convinced prosecutors that he had been duped. Although he had helped supply explosives, he claimed to believe that they were to be used to fight Serbs in Bosnia and to protect Muslims there from being raped. Victor Alvarez, a convert to Islam who was born in New York City and raised in Puerto Rico, also supplied arms for the foiled plot. A former supermarket clerk, auto mechanic, and carpenter, who was unemployed at the time of the plot, Alvarez worshipped at Sheikh Omar Abdel Rahman's mosque.

Except for Earl Gant, Victor Alvarez, and Clement Rodney Hampton-El, the conspirators were immigrants. They came from across the Arab world, including Egypt, Sudan, Iraq, Pakistan, the West Bank, and Jordan. Some of them were legally present in the United States and others were illegal immigrants. A few had recently become citizens, but most were not. The conspiracy itself can be accurately described as an imported product, not the result of stirrings in the home-grown Islamic community or in the wave of immigrants that arrived in the late 1960s.

A few general conclusions can be drawn about why they were willing to participate in a terrorist plot at great risk to themselves. Had the terrorists been wealthy, employed in high-status jobs, or members of the mainstream culture, some would undoubtedly have felt less of the alienation that contributes to a terrorist's angst. They may also have been less willing to risk things they valued. But, one should remember that Nidal Ayyad, the chemical engineer, was not deterred by his professional position. Several terrorists had family lives which they were quite willing to disrupt out of loyalty to a higher cause.

Far more important than economic status were several formative experiences: growing up in the Middle East amidst a religious upheaval; participating in the war in Afghanistan; witnessing El Sayyid Nosair's acquittal on charges of murdering Rabbi Meir Kahane; and absorbing an extremist Islamic subculture led by Sheikh Omar Abdel Rahman.

Nearly all of the immigrant conspirators brought anger toward the United States with them from overseas. While many criticized secular American society from the standpoint of fundamentalist Islam, personal experiences in the United States appear to have played a very limited role in stimulating their hostility toward America. Some of the recent immigrants brought their real or imagined grudges against Israel, secular Arab governments, and a mainstream Islam they saw as too compromising and even heretical. After his arrest, Ramzi Yousef defended the bombing of the World Trade Center in principle—without conceding his guilt. He called America a criminal state, and claimed that Palestinians had every right to fight against it for its unconscionable support of Israel.[19]

By the time most of the 1993 conspirators had arrived in the United States, their belief that America was at the root of their problems was unshakable. Thus, they proved unwilling or unable to follow in the path of prior Islamic immigrants. While many members of the domestic Islamic community have quarrels with American policies, particularly regarding the Middle East, they have generally expressed their views and observed their religion within the parameters of American law and politics.[20]

The 1993 conspirators arrived in a more recent wave of Arab immigration and some of them seem to have notably different objectives from those of earlier immigrants. The editors of the *New Republic* wrote:

[These immigrants] also were fleeing from the fires of their world. But the fires were ones that they had helped set. Unlike their [Arab] predecessors, they carried the wars in their hearts with them. Now, a few of them have brought these wars to American streets. Surely, terror brings disgust and fear to the ordinary Arab immigrant. Yet one cannot deny that there is also an Arab culture in Brooklyn and Jersey City and Detroit off which the criminals feed and which gets a grim thrill from them.[21]

Though there is some truth in this assessment, it casts its net too broadly, failing to distinguish adequately among the varieties of Islamic and Arabic subcultures, and more importantly, the degree of immigrants' involvement in these subcultures.

The literature found in the apartments of several 1993 conspirators sheds light on the values of the Islamic extremist subculture that exists in parts of Brooklyn and Jersey City. At trial, Judge Kevin T. Duffy ruled most of the literature found in the apartments inadmissible because it was likely to be prejudicial. The literature is essential, however, from the point of view of those trying to understand the terrorists' motives.

One document was described by a defense attorney as "the one that talks about the prophet allegedly saying to the Jews, 'You sons of monkeys, you sons of pigs, and you worshippers of Satan,' et cetera."[22] The prosecutor noted another reference to the Jews, in the same document: "Throughout history, kings and leaders feared this race."[23] Two of the defendants possessed a pamphlet entitled, "Facing the Enemies of God Terrorism is a Religious Duty and Force is Necessary."[24] A defense lawyer summarized an article from a magazine, *Jihad,* in which a Muslim scholar stated that "the Islamic Jihad in Afghanistan destroyed Russia. The Islamic Jihad in Kashmir will destroy India. Then the Muslims will move, God willing, to destroy the United States of America."[25] The prosecutor argued that the documents generally stated "that America is backing the Jews, America is supporting the Jews, things like that. And that's at the heart of the reason why the trade center was bombed."[26]

The themes of "America as the enemy" and "violence as the means" were echoed in a video taken from a defendant's apartment that was admitted into evidence during the trial.[27] This video was entitled, "International Islamic Resistance Presents a Course in Manufacturing Explosives." In the video, footage from a Hollywood movie, *Death Before Dishonor,* showed a terrorist bombing of an American embassy overseas. An Arabic passage stated: "There is no other alternative except to wage a holy war and to make a push against the enemies of God. In God's name, hurrah [for] the battle against our enemies, the Jews, the Christians, the Americans, and the Arab rulers and their advisers who legitimize and sanction the rule of these oppressors."[28]

At his sentencing, Mohammed Salameh announced, "Greetings to anyone who defends his usurped land or who fights to make Islam the law of the land. Peace be upon those who follow the right path."[29] Nidal Ayyad accepted his punishment with confidence: "What are you going to do to me? Are you going to put me in prison for life, or ten lives? It doesn't mean a thing. If God wants me to get out of prison, I will get out. If He wants me to stay in prison, I will stay in. The true Muslim accepts God's will."[30]

These two terrorists and most of their cohorts seemed fully absorbed in a complex religious and ideological system. To understand this system and its appeal, we need to examine the context in which it developed. This religious and ideological subculture was directly imported from Egypt by Sheikh Omar Abdel Rahman, and it is to his ideas that we now turn.

JIHAD AND EXTREMIST IDEOLOGY

Sheikh Omar Abdel Rahman's religious opinions carried, and may still carry, the power of life and death. According to tapes secretly recorded by FBI informer Emad Salem, Sheikh Abdel Rahman was asked whether the United Nations was the "house of the devil" and whether it could become a target of action. "It is not forbidden," he answered, "but it will put the Muslims in bad light. . . . People will say then that Muslims are against peace."[31] Instead, he suggested, "find a plan to inflict damage to the American army."[32] Asked about the suitability of targeting the FBI office in lower Manhattan, he replied, "By God, it needs to be studied."[33] He also urged his followers to go slowly, not to do anything in haste.[34] Abdo Mohammed Haggag, a former aide to Sheikh Rahman, testified that he asked the sheikh in April 1993 about whether he should assassinate Egyptian president Mubarak. The sheikh told him, "Depend on God, carry out this operation; it does not require a fatwa. You are ready in training. Do it. Go ahead."[35]

Sheikh Rahman has denied playing a role in any terrorist activities.[36] However, Siddig Ibrahim Siddig Ali, a defendant who pleaded guilty, confirmed Salem's account of the sheikh's guiding hand. The jury agreed. Though there is no direct evidence, it seems likely that Rahman played a similar role in precipitating several previous terrorist acts committed by his supporters. Federal investigators suspect that the sheikh passed judgment on the religious acceptability of assassinations of Rabbi Meir Kahane in 1990, rival leader Mustafa Shalabi in 1992, and Egyptian President Anwar Sadat in 1981. Less directly, his writings may have inspired the murder of Egyptian writer Farag Foda in 1992, the attack on Egypt's Nobel Laureate, Naguib Mahfouz, in 1994, and the assassination attempt on Egyptian President Hosni Mubarak in 1995; all three crimes were the work of those who looked to him for spiritual guidance. In the mid-1980s, Egyptian authorities arrested, imprisoned, then acquitted the sheikh on charges of encouraging Sadat's murder. In April 1994 an Egyptian court sentenced him to seven years in prison for inciting riots and attempting to kill two policemen. Regarding the Manhattan case, Rahman has explicitly denied authorizing the 1993 World Trade Center bombing. Nonetheless, the FBI informer's tapes and Siddig Ali's testimony are hard to refute.

More recently, Osama bin Laden has used Rahman's recorded sermons to recruit and train operatives. That an Islamic spiritual leader, one with a doctorate in Islamic jurisprudence from Egypt's prestigious Al-Azhar University, might authorize, encourage, or ignite terrorist acts would disgust many practicing Muslims, even some of those characterized as fundamentalist. But Rahman cannot be dismissed as a mad cleric. His organization in Egypt has many supporters; estimates range from ten thousand to over a hundred thousand. Clerics who interpret Islam along similar lines and who also endorse violent means command large followings throughout the Arab and Islamic nations. Tens of millions share some of Rahman's political sympathies and objectives.

Thus, Rahman's ideology and that of similarly inclined clerics must be understood in the broader context of the resurgence of Muslim fundamentalism; this resurgence, itself, should be seen against the backdrop of Islam's encounter with modernity. By the nineteenth century, it was clear to most Muslims that the West had triumphed militarily over the Islamic world.

The Muslim defeat was particularly painful because it seemed an unacceptable culmination to well over a thousand years of conflict between Christianity and Islam. At first, the armies of Islam had spread across the Middle East, North Africa, and Spain in the seventh and eighth centuries. During the eleventh, twelfth, and thirteenth centuries, Christian Crusader armies attempted and, for brief periods, succeeded in retaking parts of the Holy Land. The brutality of the Crusades left bitter memories on both sides.

The rise of the Ottoman Empire once again put Islam in a position to threaten Europe. Constantinople, present-day Istanbul, fell to the Ottoman Turks in 1453. By the early sixteenth century, Greece, Hungary, and many southern Slavic domains were in Muslim hands, and, in 1529, Ottoman armies laid siege to Vienna. The siege failed, however, and shortly thereafter the balance of power shifted in favor of Christian Europe. By the nineteenth century, Islamic power had declined to the point where Britain and France assumed control over several Islamic countries, and called the shots in several others. When Islam had witnessed an unbroken string of conquests during its first two centuries and exercised tremendous power during its golden age, these good fortunes had been interpreted as evidence of the ultimate truth of the Islamic faith. Not surprisingly, defeat brought an era of soul-searching perhaps made more wrenching by the arrogance of the imperialists.

Colonialism led to four different responses from Muslim culture.[37] The first response, direct resistance to the infidel West, had little chance of success given the disparities in military power and resources. The second strategy, an outgrowth of the first, involved reaffirmation of Islamic values and implementation of a policy of total noncooperation; in other words, refusing to have anything to do with Europeans, their schools, or their institutions. The third approach, dominant among some Arab nationalists, was to modernize, secularize, and Westernize; this seldom happened rapidly, but gradually the traditional Islamic basis of political legitimacy in Muslim societies was altered. The last response to Western dominance was Islamic modernism. Here, the goal was to bridge the gap between Islamic traditionalists and secular reformers by seeking a synthesis of Islam with the best of modern science and Western thought.

The modernists included a wide variety of religious and political figures. Jamal al-Din al-Afghani (1838–1897) urged anticolonialism, Arab unity, and Islamic solidarity. At the same time, he also argued that the Islamic world needed to appropriate the sources of the West's power, which he saw as science, technology, and democratic constitutionalism. Afghani's protégé, Muhammad Abduh (1849–1905), championed legal, educational, and social reforms, including improvement of the status of women. For example, he noted that it was extremely unlikely that anyone could meet the Koran's requirement that all one's wives be treated impartially and, thereby, rendered polygamy a practical impossibility.

In contrast to Afghani and other anticolonialists, Sir Sayyid Ahmad Khan (1817–1898) tried to modernize and revitalize the Islamic community through education, without rejecting the West; he remained a British loyalist in India throughout his life. Muhammad Iqbal (1875–1938), also in India, believed that Islam was passing through a reformation similar to the Protestant reformation in Europe; while he dismissed secularism, Marxism, and capitalism, he emphasized Islam as a religion of peace and as the potential source of indigenous Islamic versions of parliamentary democracy. Taha Husayn (1889–1973), a disciple of Muhammad Abduh, went further than other modernists and might accordingly be classified a secularist. He argued that the needs of Egyptian society would be better served by a separation of religion and politics. Even more radically, he asserted that Christianity and Islam shared the same essence and source. Collectively, the Islamic modernists suggested the compatibility between Islam, or at least its core, and the modern world; they also rekindled pride in the glorious past of Islam, pride which had been wounded by several hundred years of Western ascendancy. The Islamic fundamentalists were influenced by the modernists, but reacted passionately against their compromises.

A variety of complaints have been raised concerning the use of the term *fundamentalism* to describe the revivalist movement within Islam. John Esposito, a professor of religion and international affairs at Georgetown University, Washington, DC, objects, explaining that *all* practicing Muslims are fundamentalist in the sense that they accept the Koran as the literal word of God; he further argues that the term *fundamentalist* carries, from its association with Protestant fundamentalism, a connotation of a static, retrogressive, politically activist, and extremist movement.[38] This description, according to Esposito, applies to only a minority of the Muslims under consideration. Princeton historian Bernard Lewis similarly argues that, pertaining to Christians, the term *fundamentalist* describes those who maintain the literal divine origin and inerrancy of the Bible in contrast to liberal theologians with a more critical and historical view of the Scriptures.[39] In Islam, despite the modernist movement, no similar liberal approach has gained currency. According to Lewis, Muslim fundamentalists differ from other Muslims by virtue of their emphasis not only on the Koran, but on the entire Islamic legal tradition embodied in the shari'a and including its rules, penalties, jurisdiction, and prescribed form of government.[40] Nonetheless, he reluctantly supports the term *fundamentalist* because it is so widely used.[41]

Political scientist R. Hrair Dekmejian, of the State University of New York at Binghamton, also discusses nomenclature for the movement, noting that it has been described as revivalism, rebirth, puritanism, reassertion, awakening, reformism, resurgence, renaissance, revitalization, militancy, activism, millenarianism, messianism, the return to Islam, and the march of Islam.[42] He points out that collectively these terms help describe the complexity of this movement, but also that none is superior to *fundamentalism* as a descriptive term.[43]

Fundamentalism implies a search for the fundamentals of the faith and the Islamic polity. Many types of fundamentalism have surfaced in recent years, some Sunni and some Shi'ite. In 1985, one scholar listed ninety-one different organizations around the world.[44] All share two central beliefs: the necessity of breaking with corrupting Western influence, and the importance of substituting the laws of Allah, the divinely inspired shari'a, for the laws of men. The shari'a contains laws governing all aspects of life, including dress, diet, education, sex, marriage, justice, and politics. While Jews and Christians each have their bodies of religious law, they have, in modern times, generally accepted a limited domain for these regulations. Until recently, most Muslims around the world were willing to restrict similarly the domain of the shari'a.

Most manifestations of contemporary Islamic fundamentalism have their organizational roots in two movements: the Muslim Brotherhood established in Egypt by Hassan al-Banna (1906–1949) in 1928 and the Jamaat-i-Islami founded in India in 1941 by Mawlana Abul Ala Mawdudi (1903–1979). Sheikh Omar Abdel Rahman's extremist organization grew most directly out of the Muslim Brotherhood.

Al-Banna and Mawdudi articulated a worldview in which Islam supplied an all-purpose ideology which derived its force and content from the Koran and the *Sunnah,* the example of the Prophet Muhammad's life in the seventh century. Islamic law, the shari'a, told Muslims how to lead a righteous life. By following this body of law, the Muslim community could gain success, power, and wealth in this life. More important, faith promised eternal reward in the next life. But, during the lifetimes of al-Banna and Mawdudi, the Islamic community possessed little worldly power. They attributed this to Muslims having abandoned God's path for the infidel values of the West—capitalism and Marxism. Thus, they believed that the way to restore Muslim pride and power was through a revitalization of Islam. Science and technology could play a part, but only within the context of traditional Islam.[45]

The fundamentalist vision also includes a concept of social justice. Although Islam recognizes private property, it maintains that all property ultimately belongs to society and God. Certain methods of accumulating wealth such as loaning money for interest are prohibited. There is also a general belief that individuals and the state should fight poverty. When implemented, such views are sometimes called Islamic socialism.

The ultimate aim of Islamic fundamentalism is to establish the sovereignty of Allah over all humanity. To accomplish this goal, Muslims must strive to transform infidels into believers. Secular states in the Middle East and elsewhere must be eliminated. Non-Islamic judicial systems must be disbanded.

To expand the area over which Allah's writ may run, there is no disagreement among fundamentalists that Muslims must resort to jihad. Literally, jihad means "striving or self-exertion in the path of God."[46] God, through revelation, has imposed the duty of jihad on all Muslims. Historian Bernard Lewis writes that:

> The basis of the obligation of *jihad* is the universality of the Muslim revelation. God's word and God's message are for all mankind; it is the duty of those who have accepted them to strive (*jahada*) unceasingly to convert or at least to subjugate those who have not. This obligation is without limit of time or space. It must continue until the whole world has either accepted the Islamic faith or submitted to the power of the Islamic state.
>
> Until that happens, the world is divided into two: the House of Islam (dar al-Islam), where Muslims rule and the law of Islam prevails; and the House of War (dar al-Harb), comprising the rest of the world. Between the two there is a morally necessary, legally and religiously obligatory state of war, until the final and inevitable triumph of Islam over unbelief. According to the law books, this state of war could be interrupted, when expedient, by an armistice or truce of limited duration. It could not be terminated by a peace, but only by a final victory.[47]

One of the main points that splits mainstream Muslims and moderate fundamentalists on the one hand from extremist fundamentalists on the other is the interpretation of jihad. Can the duty be fulfilled by nonmilitant means? Must the war be waged now? Who are suitable targets for ji-had? Although Islamic history and jurisprudence clearly show that actual warfare was frequently used to fulfill the requirement of jihad, some ju-rists have held that the duty could be met "by the heart, by the tongue, by the hands and by the sword."[48] For Hassan al-Banna, violence was cer-tainly acceptable, but only if used strategically. In his words:

> As for force, it is the motto of Islam in all its rules and regulations . . . but the Brotherhood's thought is too deep and farsighted to be lured by the su-perficiality of ideas and deeds, instead of diving into the depth of things and weighing their results, meanings and purposes. The Brotherhood knows that the ultimate degree of force is the force of doctrine and belief; the force of the arm and weapons comes second.[49]

By the late 1930s, Hassan al-Banna's organization had become very powerful, attracting members from a cross-section of Egyptian society. During the next decade, the Muslim Brotherhood was widely regarded as a major threat to King Faruk's declining monarchy. Thus, Faruk ordered a period of repression, during which Hassan al-Banna was murdered by government agents.

A common enemy produced cordial early relations between the Brotherhood and the military junta that eventually overthrew King Faruk. But Gamal Abdel Nasser, soon the head of the new government, wanted a secular state, not an Islamic one. Nasser's popular pan-Arabist ideology, his charismatic leadership style, and most important, his mil-itary repression of the Brotherhood, soon devastated the fundamental-ist organization. It was Nasser's humiliating defeat by Israeli forces in the Six Day War in 1967 that led to the revitalization of fundamental-ism in Egypt and throughout the Arab world. Anwar Sadat, Nasser's successor, initially encouraged the fundamentalists, in a tactical move designed to weaken the power of Sadat's Communist opponents. As the fundamentalists grew in strength, however, Sadat too turned to repres-sive methods.

In this environment, Sheikh Omar Abdel Rahman's extremist offshoot of the Muslim Brotherhood was born; Sadat became the proverbial man who attempted to ride the tiger, but ended up inside. Although Rahman did some writing of his own, the ideology of the Jihad organization best emerges in *Al-Faridah al-Gha'ibah* ("The Neglected Duty"), a manifesto written by Muhammad Abd al-Salam Faraj.[50]

Faraj was tried, convicted, and put to death for his role in fomenting the assassination of Sadat in 1981. The *Faridah* is probably the best existing statement of extremist Islamic fundamentalism; it is certainly the best that has been translated into English. Faraj circulated the document among strict fundamentalist Muslims and did not intend it for outsiders. The *Faridah* cannot be taken as a statement of what all Muslims believe, or even of what all fundamentalists believe. It can, however, help us to peer into the mindset and ideology of bin Laden, Rahman, and similarly inclined extremists. It should also be noted that, while the Western mind would regard much of the manifesto as unpalatable, it does contain a powerful internal logic. One need not be mad to follow this logic; one need only accept the premises.

According to Faraj: "If the religious obligations of Islam cannot be carried out in their entirety without the support of an Islamic State, then the establishment of such a state is a religious obligation too. If such a state cannot be established without war, then this war is a Muslim religious obligation as well" (*Faridah*, section 16).[51] He then notes that Egypt cannot be described as a Muslim state, and that the ruler of such a non-Islamic state cannot be called a Muslim, even if his subjects are Muslims. Sadat, who was born a Muslim, therefore became an apostate the moment he started to rule. And the punishment for apostasy, according to the accumulated laws of the shari'a, is death. Mubarak, of course, is guilty of the same offense. In fact, Faraj maintains that *all* rulers of Muslims during the twentieth century are apostates and collaborators with Western Christianity. This remains true, according to the *Faridah*, even if such rulers pray, fast during Ramadan, and perform all the obligatory rites of the Islamic faith.

For Faraj, the highest form of obedience to God is jihad. He writes:

The Apostle of God [Mohammed]—God's Peace be upon Him—once described *jihad* as the best of the summit of Islam, saying: 'Someone who does not participate in any way in the raids [against the enemies of Islam], or someone whose soul does not talk to him encouraging him to wage a fight on behalf of his religion, dies as if he had never been a Muslim, or [he dies] like someone who, filled with some form of hypocrisy, only outwardly pretended to be a Muslim (*Faridah*, section 50).[52]

Faraj also dispels the notion that this struggle might be democratic. He quotes the Koran: "If thou obey the majority of those who are in the land they will lead thee astray from the Way of God" (Koran 6:116; *Faridah*, section 54).[53] And, "How many a small band has, by the permission of God, conquered a numerous band?" (Koran 2:249; *Faridah*, section 55).[54] Jihad for God's cause, according to Faraj, "in spite of its extreme importance and its great significance for the future of this religion, has been neglected by the *ulama* [leading Muslim scholars] of this age. They have feigned ignorance of it, but they know that it is the only way to the return and the establishment of the glory of Islam anew" (*Faridah*, section 3).[55] Moreover, only the militant interpretation of jihad is acceptable. According to Faraj, the real character of jihad "is clearly spelled out in the text of the Qur'an: It is fighting, which means confrontation and blood" (*Faridah*, section 84).[56] Some Muslim scholars have argued that jihad must take place in phases, the first of which is jihad against one's own soul; they conclude that, since this stage is still going on, they need not move on to fighting infidels. For Faraj, this argument reflects ignorance or cowardice, for the various types of jihad (against one's soul, against the devil, against infidels) are aspects, not stages.

Faraj also notes that Christians and Jews are permitted to live in peace, according to the Koran. The catch is that they must submit to the rule of Islam and pay a special tax. Without these conditions, all Jews and Christians are suitable targets for jihad. The war against Israel, however, occupies a less central position than we might expect. Faraj identifies the battle for the liberation of Jerusalem as a religious obligation, but claims that a victory over Israel might redound to the benefit of the non-Islamic states currently holding power. Thus, he endorses the fight against secular Arab governments as the first step.

Whoever the target, Faraj permits a wide variety of tactics. Lying to the enemy and deceiving the infidels are permissible, "but it is better to limit oneself to speaking ambiguously" (*Faridah*, section 109).[57] It should not be done without need, but killing children is acceptable, because they are "'part of their fathers,' that is, there is no objection to it because the rules applying to their fathers pertain to them as well" (*Faridah*, section 121).[58] Attacking Muslims who were forced into the army of the infidels is also permitted, since they will be united with fellow Muslims on the Day of Resurrection.

According to the *Faridah*, the neglect of jihad "is the cause of the low-ness, humiliation, division and fragmentation in which Muslims live to-day" (*Faridah*, section 100).[59] The overwhelming majority of Islamic the-ologians would reject this conclusion along with Faraj's militant interpretation of jihad. And other Islamic writers offer differing interpre-tations of the Koranic verses he cites in support of his positions. Nonethe-less, his well-argued manifesto possesses a certain internal logic which is not conducive to peaceful coexistence, not consistent with Western values, not agreeable to Arab governments, but somehow convincing to many thousands who started with more moderate Islamic perspectives. When Sheikh Omar Abdel Rahman inflamed his supporters with sermons based on the logic of the *Faridah*, the result was assassinations, bomb threats, and attacks on tourist buses. When Osama bin Laden used similar argu-ments, the result was five thousand dead in New York City. Jihad, said Sheikh Rahman, is not merely worshipping at a mosque, attending lec-tures, or praying; "Jihad is fighting the enemy, fighting the enemies for God's sake."[60]

THE SOURCES OF ISLAMIC EXTREMISM

Four steps led to anti-American terrorism: (1) the rise of the Islamic fun-damentalist movement; (2) the development of anti-Western hostility within this movement; (3) the splitting off of extremist groups; and (4) the decision of a small number of individuals to commit terrorist acts, risking or sacrificing their lives in pursuit of extremist objectives.

Western experts generally agree that Islamic fundamentalism draws much of its strength from a widespread perception among Arabs that all other strategies and approaches have failed. Fundamentalists maintain that non-Islamic social and political systems have not provided the peo-ples of the Islamic world with the solutions to their pressing problems. It is time, they say, to go back to the ways of the past, to the ideology that prevailed during the glory days of Islam's first centuries, to the shari'a. Journalist David Lamb writes that:

Young Arabs . . . have turned to religion because they have been failed by and grown weary of all the "isms"—Arabism, socialism, Palestinianism, capitalism, Baathism (a socialist Islamic philosophy practiced in Syria and

Iraq), Americanism, presidential cultism, the notion of destroying Zionism. They sought an alternative, just as young Americans did who became hippies in the 1960s and Moonies in the 1970s. And the alternative they sought was the only constant in the Arab world—Islam.[61]

Lamb's analysis is a bit fuzzy. For example, just what is Americanism, and how has the Arab world tried it? Has socialism been tried? Have those Arabs who joined the fundamentalists really grown weary of the notion of destroying Israel? And are not fundamentalists more analogous to, say, the Michigan Militia and Ku Klux Klansmen than they are to innocuous hippies and Moonies? Still, no one can dispute the conditions of poverty that prevail throughout much of the Arab world, even after huge oil windfalls. Overpopulation threatens to swallow any potential economic gains in the future, and paints a bleak Malthusian portrait. Democracies have failed to take root anywhere in the Arab world, and unscrupulous leaders have found few cruelties unsuitable for the maintenance of their own power. Nasser's promises of pan-Arab unity came to nothing. The obsession with defeating Israel devoured scarce resources, stole generations of youth, and most fatally, distracted Arab peoples from pressing economic, social, and political concerns. Under such conditions, radical and reactionary movements flourish. Muslim fundamentalist groups, many of which operate schools, hospitals, and social services, have proved very appealing alternatives to decadent, semisecular states.

The Islamic solution is a time-honored one. As nearly all analysts have noted, present-day fundamentalists can cite a long history of revivalism when things go awry. Professor Bernard Lewis writes: "There is a recurring tendency in times of crisis, in times of emergency, when the deeper loyalties take over, for Muslims to find their basic identity in the religious community; that is to say, in an entity defined by Islam rather than by ethnic origin, language, or country of habitation."[62]

The rise of fundamentalism can also be seen as a revolt against modernity and modernization. Nationalism, secular education, rights for women, minority rights, urbanization, industrialization, modern health practices, the hallmarks of modernity, have brought about, or threaten to bring about, rapid change in the Arab world as in other parts of the developing world. With these changes came rapidly rising expectations of a better, more fulfilling, life. After several decades, many Middle Easterners decided that the modernist images of the future amounted to little more than a giant mirage, and alienation set in. Fundamentalist Islam, like all traditional religions, promised a simpler world in which one knew where one belonged. Many economic challenges of modernity remained, but the psychological stresses diminished. Modernity had progressed too far to turn back on all fronts, and even the revivalist movement began to rely heavily on some modern technology, such as electronic communications and modern weaponry, to help propagate the faith. However, the battle lines were drawn incongruously, leaving on one side modern technology, and on the other, the scientific, tolerant, and meritocratic mindset which made that technology possible.

An independent-minded Moroccan scholar, Fatima Mernissi, argues that many in the Muslim world perceive modernity as nonuniversal; they see the modern world as belonging to the West. America and the European countries contributed to this perception, poignantly, for Mernissi, by planting an American national flag on the moon.[63] To buy into modernization is equated with selling out to an enemy culture.

Anti-Western, especially anti-American, sentiments have colored the politics of many nonfundamentalist Middle Eastern leaders. Nasser, after all, was the scourge of the West as well as the scourge of the fundamentalists. More recently, Saddam Hussein has played a similar role. Conversely, not all Islamic fundamentalist leaders have voiced hostility toward the West. Still, the most boisterous and ferocious anti-Western criticism in recent years has come from among the fundamentalist ranks, and they, by definition, are antagonistic to Western culture.

The simplest and most far-reaching explanation of their position is rational self-interest. In other words, the fundamentalists are not wrong in judging America as their enemy. America, in theory, at least, stands for democracy, modernity, protection of the rights of women and minorities, preservation of existing national borders, support of Israel's right to exist, respect for diverse religious traditions, and many other policies inimical to the Islamic fundamentalist belief system. Hence, Professor James Bill misses a certain point when he writes that "[t]here is nothing inherently anti-American about Islam. It is the policies of governments that have converted Muslims into critics and opponents. When these policies have been perceived to be supportive of corruption, oppression, and colonial or imperial interventionism, there has been criticism and resistance."[64]

However, to appease most fundamentalist Muslims, America would need to cease being America. Even if policy changes were enacted, such as lessening support for Israel, at most some fundamentalists would avert their gaze for a while. But they would not abandon their basic hostility, which arises out of a conflict between worldviews.

Islam, of course, encompasses much more than extremist fundamentalist Islam. As historian Bernard Lewis writes:

> The question, therefore, is not whether liberal democracy is compatible with Islamic fundamentalism—clearly it is not—but whether it is compatible with Islam itself. Liberal democracy, however far it may have traveled, however much it may have been transformed, is in its origins a product of the West—shaped by a thousand years of European history, and beyond that by Europe's double heritage: Judeo-Christian religion and ethics; Greco-Roman statecraft and law. No such system has originated in any other cultural tradition; it remains to be seen whether such a system, transplanted and adapted in another culture, can long survive.[65]

Regarding Islam's democratic potential, Fatima Mernissi of Morocco, who has been described as a psychiatrist of her culture but equally a political and theological scholar, has argued persuasively that a strong rationalist undercurrent has always existed in Islam.[66] This orientation, associated with the Mu'tazila, has been submerged and suppressed for centuries. Nonetheless, Mernissi argues that Islamic theology is capable of supporting democratic, tolerant governance along with a profound respect for scientific thinking. One reason for the weakness of the rationalist approach to Islam lies in the politics of anticolonial nationalism. To maintain unity against the colonial powers, the nationalist leaders "fought against the advances of Enlightenment philosophy and banned Western humanism as foreign and 'imported,' calling the intellectuals who studied it enemy agents and traitors to the nationalist cause."[67] In so doing, they allowed the rationalist Islamic tradition to remain buried at just the moment when it could have been unearthed and put into service. According to Mernissi, those in power tried to cement ancient fears of strangers and the West onto modern anxieties. She sees tolerance, freedom of thought, friendship with the West, and even secular humanism as entirely consistent with Islam. The problem, in her analysis, is that "the break with the medieval state, which used the sacred to legitimize and mask arbitrary rule, never took place in the Arab world."[68]

Matters of religion always boil down to questions of interpretation, and the fundamentalists' interpretation of Islam contrasts sharply with Mernissi's view. For them, the battle against the infidels, the dar al-Harb, must continue until the Christians and Jews submit. Some consultation should precede political decisions, but a democracy bearing any resemblance to Western democracy is inconsistent with the shari'a in their viewpoints.

Without question, certain concepts in the Islamic faith can push believers toward extremism; for example, the doctrine of jihad, the division of the world into the House of Islam and the House of War, the emphasis on military force in spreading the faith, the harsh punishments for apostasy, and the requirement that Jews and Christians be subjugated. But, as Fatima Mernissi shows, all of these concepts have been interpreted at various times in ways that permit, and even encourage, moderation and peaceful coexistence.[69]

Christianity, too, has been used to justify violence and brutality against nonbelievers. Charlemagne's brutal conversions by the sword, the Crusades, the Spanish Inquisition, and Luther's anti-Semitism come to mind. St. Augustine argued that Christianity exists in the real world, and must therefore play by the rules of the real world. Consequently, violence was perfectly acceptable as a tool of the Lord, and heretics had to be attacked with murderous zeal. For at least a thousand years, this harsh theology displaced Christ's focus on love as the basis for Christian behavior.

Judaism has been associated with far fewer atrocities, but, in the ancient world, the Jewish king John Hyrcanus, son of Simon Maccabee, was driven by a fundamentalist impulse to convert whole cities to Judaism by force, slaying inhabitants who refused. Moreover, the Torah instructs Jews that one group of people, the Amalekites, are so evil that they, and their descendants, must be killed on sight. More recently, Jewish extremist religious ideology played a part in motivating the assassin of Israeli Prime Minister Yitzhak Rabin and the gunman who opened fire in a Hebron mosque.

In the twentieth century, however, Judaism and Christianity, for the most part, have laid aside, reinterpreted, or rejected outright those elements of theology that fuel mass hatred most blatantly. Many Muslims have done the same with inhumane aspects of their tradition.

Why then have so many other Muslims embraced an extremist theology? The recent radicalization of the fundamentalist movement, and the growth of uncompromising groups like Rahman's organization, can be traced to the Arab defeat in the Six Day War against Israel—a tragic but ironic outcome for the Israelis. Many Muslims saw this defeat as punishment for lack of faith, and some even perceived Israel's victory as a reward for the Jews' adherence to their religion. In any case, the defeat highlighted the inability of the secular state, across the Muslim world and especially in Egypt, to deliver satisfactory results.

Radicalization also occurred in response to persecution.[70] The Egyptian government never shied away from using the state apparatus to battle its enemies. Government agents murdered fundamentalist leaders while others were tortured mercilessly. Under such conditions, it is not hard to see how fundamentalists started to lose patience with the struggle to bring about an Islamic polity by working within the confines of the system. Sadat and Mubarak's inconsistency also contributed to the radicalization of the Muslim fundamentalists in Egypt. By alternating laxity with persecution, the fundamentalists had both the incentive (revenge) and the opportunity to develop extremist offshoots.

In some ways, extremism is a natural outgrowth of all forms of fundamentalism. Barry Goldwater once noted that when you think you're right, moderation is no virtue and extremism no vice. Certainly, Islam could not have survived as a thriving culture for centuries had it not shown the ability to compromise, and, in the long history of the faith, political realism emerged far more frequently than fanaticism. But when the depth of one's earnestness and belief becomes the criterion for achieving immortal bliss in the afterlife, God's work—fighting infidels, punishing apostates, instituting the shari'a—is logically pursued with a zeal equal to the task. One does not compromise with forces perceived as satanic.

Some individuals feel the urge to fanaticism far more than others. Among the tens of thousands who support aspects of the extremist mindset, only a very small number actually undertake terrorist acts. Under ordinary circumstances, when psychologists want to know why one group of people differs from another, they administer psychological tests, questionnaires, and similar research instruments to both groups. Needless to say, such a strategy would not work in understanding the motives of fundamentalist extremists. Apart from language difficulties and the subjects' unwillingness to participate in studies, psychologists would face problems resulting from the cultural inappropriateness of many research tools and concepts. Thus, most of our insight into why individuals become fundamentalist terrorists is not based on firm research.

Two students of terrorism, C. A. Russell and B. H. Miller, developed a profile of the "typical" terrorist. He is a single male, between the ages of twenty-two and twenty-four. He comes from an affluent family, has received some university education, and is attracted to terrorism by his discontent with the current structure of society.[71] This profile fits some Middle Eastern terrorists, but not all. Only a relative few have studied at college and come from privileged backgrounds. The FBI identifies three types of terrorists: (1) a leader with a strong commitment to the group's belief system; (2) an "activist-operator" who often has a criminal background and implements the group's agenda; and (3) an idealist who finds a sense of purpose in his commitment to the group.[72]

In his definitive study, *The Age of Terrorism,* Walter Laqueur evaluates efforts to identify a personality type that typifies terrorists with a wide variety of agendas. While he accepts the search for a terrorist personality as a worthwhile endeavor, he concludes that, apart from the fact that most terrorists are young, it is difficult to find other common features.[73]

Youth, according to psychologist Erik Erikson, is the occasion for passing through an "identity versus role confusion" conflict, during which people strive to answer the question, "Who am I?" Part of the process involves developing faith in someone or something outside the self, for example, a religious movement or leader. Terrorists may have problems forming a suitable identity and, consequently, become vulnerable to "totalism," an inclination to resolve identity issues by submerging oneself in a group that promises to provide an identity.[74]

Thus, terrorists often can be viewed as people with marginal personalities. They are drawn to terrorism by their self-deficiencies and, above all, are looking for a place where they will be accepted. By virtue of their self-deficits, however, the group begins to exert tremendous influence on them. The terrorists cannot easily separate themselves from the group because their participation is what holds together their personality.[75]

Laqueur notes that most contemporary terrorists are fanatics who believe that they, and only they, know the truth and that ordinary law does not apply to them. Moreover, he comments that the less clear the political purpose, the greater its appeal to unbalanced individuals. However, according to Laqueur, terrorist personality types will, if they exist, probably be specific to causes and circumstances. In other words, the personal characteristics that predispose a person to join one terrorist organization are not necessarily the ones associated with membership in another.[76]

While no clear pathological diagnoses of the Manhattan conspirators can be made at a distance, political scientist R. Hrair Dekmejian has speculated about a personality type associated with Islamic fundamentalist fanatics (*mutaassib*), but not necessarily all Muslim fundamentalists.[77] For example, the fanatic is an "acutely alienated individual" who often follows this alienation with a self-imposed separation from society; he looks to the fundamentalist belief system not for a religion but for a new identity.[78] He is, at an early age, exceptionally rigid in his beliefs and unable to integrate new values into his way of looking at the world. His original feelings of inferiority are supplanted by feelings of aggressive superiority derived from his fanaticism. He tends to be intolerant and arrogant in dealings with unbelievers, and is preoccupied with power and the quest for domination. The fanatic is deeply distrustful of other people and government institutions, seeing evil forces at work in the world. Partly as a result of this outlook, and partly in response to state persecution, the fanatic Muslim favors secret organizations and conspiracies as a modus operandi. He manifests rigid self-discipline and austerity in social and sexual matters, displaying considerable idealism in his devotion to the cause. Finally, the Islamic extremist is obedient and conformist by nature, and pledges complete loyalty to Allah, Muhammad, and, most relevant, the charismatic leader of the movement.[79]

Dekmejian paints a plausible portrait of the mutaassib, one which draws on existing theory in psychoanalysis and social psychology. Our confidence in the portrait, however, is diminished by the lack of empirical studies that would permit greater knowledge of the terrorists' inner lives. Most seem to have committed their crimes as part of a quest for meaning. Having lost hope and possessing a very weak sense of personal identity, the terrorist offers his only commodity, his life, in pursuit of what he needs most. As David Lamb puts it, "With a gun, he is important. Without one, he is naked."[80]

The 1993 Manhattan conspirators, Mahmud Abouhalima, Siddig Ibrahim Siddig Ali, Mohammed Salameh, and the others, warded off feelings of frustration, alienation, and confusion by merging their identities with the cause of Islam. The extremism of the cause and the severity of its demands on the individual perhaps helped deflect a sense of personal emptiness. The energy created by the struggle for identity, however, propelled them down a long path that culminated in the murder of Monica Smith and the other victims of the World Trade Center bombing. They started down this path with their recognition that something had gone awry in the Arab world and with the belief that few of the traditional options were likely to provide them with satisfying lives.

They saw no viable route to individual success or meaningful political action. They felt let down by government, education, traditional Islam, socialist politics, and the military. Thus, they fell under the influence of a powerful ideology, one inspired by a long history of periodic revivalism, a doctrine of salvation through holy war, and a hatred for the infidel West. Muslim theologians must decide whether this ideology captured the essence of true Islam or is instead a corruption.

Once under the power of this movement and its charismatic leader Sheikh Abdel Rahman, the conspirators passed through a series of radicalizing experiences, including persecution by secular authorities, rabble-rousing sermons, group meetings, the Afghanistan war, and terrorist training camps. The 1993 bombing plots provided them with the opportunity to be recognized as heroic, to crystallize their sense of self, to achieve revenge for real and imagined suffering, and above all to be rewarded with eternal life. None of these things depended on the success of the plots, however. Consequently, their likelihood of success did not bear critically on their decision to participate. And, no doubt, El Sayyid Nosair's acquittal of earlier murder charges provided an added incentive to action.

The victims' plight meant very little. One wonders whether decades in jail will change the conspirators' sense that they did the right thing. And we are left with the bigger question, whether hatred traveling under the veil of extremist Islam will succeed in overpowering the more tolerant humanistic forces within the religion. Recent events leave us with few reasons for optimism.

FOUR

Rwanda—The Legacy of Inequality

IT IS SAID THAT MANY OF THE HUTU TRIBESPEOPLE WHO CROSSED THE RWANDAN BORDER INTO TANZANIA BY THE THOUSANDS IN A MASSIVE WAVE OF REFUGEES . . . HAD "A KILLER IN THE EYE." THAT WAS THE SAME MADDENED, PITILESS LOOK THEY HAD WHEN THEY RAISED THEIR MACHETES AGAINST MEN, WOMEN AND CHILDREN OF THE MINORITY TUTSI TRIBE AND EVEN AGAINST MODERATE HUTUS WHO SOUGHT TO PROTECT THEM OR WERE ASSOCIATED WITH THEM, AND SLICED OPEN THEIR ARMS AND CHESTS, STUCK BLADES INTO THEIR MOUTHS AND GENITALS AND LOPPED OFF THEIR HEADS. IT WAS THE SAME LOOK EVIDENT ON THE FACES OF THOSE WHO DID NOT COMMIT SUCH ACTS BUT NONETHELESS STOOD BY AND CHEERED THE GENOCIDE ON.[1]

Roger Rosenblatt,
New York Times Magazine, *June 5, 1994*

What will become of Pacifique Mutimura, a Tutsi boy who spent a day in 1994 hiding under a pile of dead bodies, trying to escape the very same machetes that hacked his parents to death? Will he survive? As an adult, will he be clinically depressed, psychotic, caught in the tentacles of a long-lasting posttraumatic stress syndrome? Nine years old at the time of his parents' murder, will his entire life be driven by passion for revenge, or will he, somehow, manage to elude the cycle of hate? Months after the attack, he spoke very little as he played with his friend, Mutaganzwa, also a Tutsi, in a graveyard where their parents were buried. Mutaganzwa struggled to describe what happened on 15 April 1994. "The soldiers came by helicopter and gathered all of us in a church. They were screaming. They asked us our ethnic group. Then they began to kill us. Busloads of people came with machetes. They killed my family with machetes. They thought I was dead and they left me." The Hutu attackers told Mutaganzwa that he and his family were *inyenzi*, or insects.[2]

Many thousands of children suffered similar fates, orphaned or separated from their parents during the massacres that started in April 1994 and continued for several months until the Hutu-dominated Rwandan government fell in July. At least 500,000 men, women, and children were killed, many of them in Catholic churches, where frightened families had gathered in the hope of gaining sanctuary.[3] The genocide resulted in the death of, more than half of the Tutsis in Rwanda.

Chrisostome Gatunzi, an elderly Hutu resident of Nyarubuye, bears witness to what happened in his village in April 1994. Alive since the earliest days of colonial rule, Gatunzi was too weak to intervene when militias, in groups of twenty, murdered Tutsis and tossed their bodies into mass graves. Filled with anger and despair, he recalls, "I knew some of them. I don't know why others want to kill Tutsis. We have lived together for such a long time as neighbors and friends. It's unbelievable seeing your neighbor hacked to death. These people are saying they want to create a new Rwanda. How can you do that by killing neighbors and friends? It has hurt my heart so much."[4]

In the months following the massacres, human rights organizations gathered convincing evidence of many grim crimes perpetrated by Hutu extremists—mostly against Tutsis, but also against Hutu moderates whom they viewed as accomplices of the Tutsis. Some thirty-one Tutsi orphans, segregated because of their "ethnic" group, and eleven Red Cross volunteers who tried to protect them, were killed at an orphanage in Butare. In the same region, one hundred seventy Tutsi patients at a hospital were kidnapped and, ultimately, beaten or hacked to death. Thirty Catholic priests of the Nyundo Diocese were murdered. Eighty-eight students were killed at a school in Gikongoro. At the Mabirizi Roman

Catholic Church, in Cyangugu, an extremist militia murdered two thousand Tutsis.[5] At a psychiatric hospital in Kigali, the capital, most of the six hundred and twenty patients as well as the staff and hundreds of refugees were slaughtered.[6] Thirty-seven Tutsi and moderate Hutu journalists, one-third of all journalists in Rwanda, became victims of the genocide.[7]

It will be many years before one can mention Rwanda without evoking the horror of mutilated bodies and severed limbs floating down the Kagera River.[8] Yet very few Americans, even well-informed ones, possess even the most rudimentary background needed to understand what happened there. One writer notes that ignorance of Africa is as vast as the continent and asserts that, "For many Americans, the 'real Africa' is a blurred concatenation of game parks, starving infants and genocidal warfare—or it's a Disney-fied cradle of civilization."[9] Even people who know a great deal about Africa typically know very little about Rwanda; after all, nearly five dozen countries crowd the continent, and Rwanda has had relatively little political, economic, or cultural impact beyond east-central Africa. The few Americans who knew anything at all about Rwanda prior to the massacres knew it as one of the centers of Africa's uncontrollable AIDS epidemic, or more likely as the setting for Dian Fossey's research on mountain gorillas, popularized in the movie *Gorillas in the Mist*.

Thus, Americans and most other Westerners were ill-prepared to interpret the basic political situation in Rwanda, let alone untangle the complex historical, cultural, and psychological sources of the mass hatred that culminated in genocide there. At first, a mass of confusion surrounded the events of the spring of 1994, starting with the apparent precipitating factor—the fatal downing on April 6 of a plane carrying the Hutu president of Rwanda, Juvenal Habyarimana, and his counterpart from Burundi, also a Hutu, Cyprien Ntaryamira.

In May, Robert Kajuga, the leader of the Hutu Interahamwe militia charged with many of the killings, declared that "absolutely nothing was organized. Everything was spontaneous; the people defended themselves while the rebels of the [Tutsi-dominated] Rwandan Patriotic Front attacked them."[10] He asked, "Why doesn't anyone speak of the carnage committed by the Rwandan Patriotic Front?"[11] Months after the massacres became headline news, Jean Kambanda, prime minister of the Rwandan (Hutu) government-in-exile, protested that the Tutsis had been the ones guilty of genocide against the Hutus.[12] Kajuga, Kambanda, and other

Hutu extremists denied the existence of an organized massacre; instead, they painted a picture of civil war, in which their side, the "patriotic" Hutus, engaged primarily in self-defense, though some regrettable atrocities occurred.

Many Hutus who participated in the massacres probably did believe that they were defending themselves and their families against a potential Tutsi assault. But reality squares better with the conclusions of a United Nations report issued in the late fall of 1994. According to this report, "Overwhelming evidence indicates that the extermination of Tutsi by Hutu had been planned months in advance of its actual execution. The mass exterminations of Tutsis were carried out primarily by Hutu elements in a concerted, planned, systematic and methodical way and were motivated out of ethnic hatred."[13]

At first, it seemed as if the Tutsi-dominated Rwandan Patriotic Front (RPF) rebels had downed the plane carrying Habyarimana. There is still no conclusive evidence, but now it appears more likely that the fatal missile was fired by extremist Hutus, close to President Habyarimana but dissatisfied by his recent willingness to reconcile with the Hutu opposition as well as the rebels.[14]

In any case, the Hutu government immediately erected barricades in critical areas. They limited access of United Nations officials to the site of the plane wreck. And they very rapidly distributed comprehensive lists of state enemies, which guided "reprisal" killings soon after President Habyarimana's plane went down. All of this conflicts with the "spontaneous reaction" explanation offered by Kajuga and others. And while troops associated with the RPF did participate in some atrocities against Hutus, these attacks, as the United Nations report argues, were neither planned nor systematic, nor did they approach the crimes of the Hutu extremists in either scope or scale.

Specifically, the perpetrators of the worst crimes in Rwanda included the Presidential Guard, officials in the Hutu-dominated government, soldiers in the Rwandan army, and, above all, members of two Hutu extremist militias—Interahamwe ("Those who stand together") and Impuzamugambe ("Those who have a single aim").

The genocide had two phases: First, within minutes after the crash of Habyarimana's plane, the Presidential Guard set up road-blocks in Kigali, while troops arrested and killed moderate Hutu officials (including Prime

Minister Agathe Uwilingiyamana) and Tutsi politicians. During this phase, extremist leaders distributed lists of targeted people to the death squads. Then, after about two days, the militias were given license and encouragement to kill every Tutsi they encountered—first in the capital and, then, throughout the country. Some Hutu civilians, unaffiliated with the militias, also joined the massacre. They were incited to do so by a barrage of inflammatory radio broadcasts, but the seeds of hatred had long been present.[15]

In Nyakizu, Rwanda, frightened Tutsis and Hutus went to their mayor, asking what might be done to prevent the spreading slaughter from reaching their town. He reassured them that nothing would happen, because the troublemakers were members of the Interahamwe militia and that they did not exist in the area. Several days later, two hundred Hutus approached the town. The armed mob included several policemen, a school superintendent, teachers, university students, and, at its head, the mayor himself. He told Tutsis who had gathered on parish grounds that they need not worry. They should put down their staffs. They did, and the mob attacked. Using axes, stones, spears, and guns, they murdered Tutsis wherever they could find them. The killings continued for several days. When the deputy mayor, the director of an adult education program, and several other Hutus tried to intervene, the mayor had them killed. A few days after the killings began, Rwanda's acting president, Theodore Sindikubwabo, a pediatrician, came to town; he thanked the Hutu townspeople for their accomplishments and offered to send help for the next phase.[16]

If we are to understand the origins of the genocide in Rwanda, considered by some to have been the most rapid mass murder in modern history, we must understand the mindset of these Hutu killers, a mindset forged over several centuries of Hutu-Tutsi relations but also owing much to the years and months preceding the massacre.

THE PREMISE OF INEQUALITY[17]

Rwanda is a small country, roughly the size of Maryland. Though situated near the equator, high elevation produces a relatively mild, tropical highland climate. As a result of the recent massacres, no one estimates the current population with much confidence; at the beginning of 1994, about eight million people lived there, mostly in extended family groups scattered throughout the country. A large percentage of the population, including both Hutus and Tutsis, has some affiliation with Catholicism. But Christian beliefs usually coexist alongside traditional African animist religion, and few Rwandans express concern about apparent conflicts between the two. The traditional belief system in Rwanda, like many premodern ones, has pronounced tendencies toward fatalism; thus, most Rwandans are brought up to accept fate, rather than to challenge it, believing that neither natural phenomena nor individual destiny can be humanly controlled. Fewer than one Rwandan in fifty has received a complete secondary school education.

Even in comparison to other African economies, Rwanda's economy performs poorly. This is not surprising because the country has the highest population density in Africa, an extremely high birth rate, and limited fertile land. The Rwandan economy depends almost entirely on agriculture. Coffee accounts for most of the country's exports, rendering the nation extremely vulnerable to changes in international supply and demand. Moreover, the overwhelming share of Rwanda's agricultural product is grown for domestic, local consumption; people eat most of what they grow. Aside from some traditional crafts and a dwindling mining business, Rwanda has little industry. The per capita income, a little more than $300 a year in the mid-1980s, underscores the dire state of the economy. At that time, many Rwandan leaders looked to expansion of the country's tourist industry as a likely spur to economic growth. The lure of the mountain gorillas made this a plausible solution, but, after the 1994 massacres and more recent attacks by Hutu extremist rebel factions on Western tourists, this option no longer seems promising (to say the least). The World Health Organization regards the average Rwandan's diet, largely sweet potatoes and beans, as inadequate and nutritionally unbalanced. According to a 1990 report, nearly one-third of the residents of Rwanda's capital city, Kigali, aged eighteen to forty-five, had the AIDS virus.[18]

Poverty and poor health contributed to the conditions in which Hutu-Tutsi animosity flourished. It would be a mistake, however, to say that such conditions created, or even ignited, the mass hatred in Rwanda.

Three African groups, the Hutus, the Tutsis, and the Twa, inhabit Rwanda; the Hutus are by far the most numerous, followed by the Tutsis, and then the Twa.[19] Prior to the 1994 massacre, the subsequent flight of

Hutu refugees, and the influx of Tutsi refugees, the population percentages were about 85 percent Hutu, 14 percent Tutsi, and less than 1 percent Twa. The three groups are usually described as tribes or ethnic groups, but many experts have noted that these descriptions do not capture the complexity of the situation. Alex Shoumatoff, an American writer married to a Tutsi, calls the Tutsis "not a race or a tribe . . . but a population, a stratum, a mystical, warrior-priest elite, like the Druids in Celtic society."[20] Describing historical relations among Tutsis, Hutus, and Twa, he writes that all three groups "spoke the same language and had the same gods, dances, huts, hair styles and sexual practices."[21] They also paid homage to the same leaders. Historian Alison Des Forges describes the groups as "amorphous categories based on occupation: Hutu were cultivators and Tutsi, pastoralists."[22] Cultivators survive by growing crops; pastoralists raise cattle. Anthropologist Jacques J. Maquet argues that the groups (during their precolonial phase) bore the greatest similarity to castes, based as they were on a feudal organization, hereditary occupations, and membership by birth.[23]

According to stereotype, the three groups have profoundly different physical appearances: The Tutsis are very slender, very tall, straight-nosed, and light-brown in complexion; the Hutus have Bantu features including woolly hair, broad noses, and full lips. They are generally of medium height and somewhat stockier than the Tutsis. The Twa, related to the Pygmies, are very short, with pronounced cheekbones, bulging foreheads, and flat noses. At one time, these stereotypes probably corresponded closely with reality, and it is still easy to find prominent illustrations. General Paul Kagame, the Tutsi RPF leader and Rwandan President, is 6 feet 2 inches tall and weighs a mere 128 pounds. Statistical data also confirm substantial present-day physical differences. The average Twa is 5 feet 1 inch and weighs 106 pounds; the average Hutu is 5 feet 5 inches and weighs 131 pounds; the average Tutsi is 5 feet 9 inches and weighs 126 pounds. Still, intermarriage has greatly diminished the once large physical differences among the groups.

Moreover, the social system was not entirely rigid, allowing for some people to change their birth group. On very rare occasions, an extremely successful Hutu might be granted Tutsi status. Thus, classification was often tricky, as the Belgian census takers learned when they identified Tutsis based on the number of cattle they owned, because Tutsis were generally wealthier. To clarify matters, and reinforce their own Hutu ideology, the Rwandan government used a system of classification based on the father. If your father is a Hutu, you are a Hutu. If your father is a Tutsi, you are a Tutsi. The mother's blood is irrelevant.[24] During the genocide, the government-issued identity cards became, for many, the final arbiters of life and death.

Although it has become a habit in some circles to blame most of contemporary Africa's problems on colonialism, the roots of Hutu-Tutsi animosity originate squarely in the pattern of relations between the groups that evolved well before the arrival of the Europeans in the late nineteenth century. Westerners and Rwandans alike know little about the early history of Rwanda, but it is possible to reconstruct some of the key events. The Twa, hunters and gatherers, came to the region first, followed by the agriculturalist Hutu. During the sixteenth century, the Tutsi arrived from the north, perhaps from Ethiopia, in a migration that appears to have been gradual and mostly peaceful.

Over the years, the Tutsi established a system through which they completely dominated the lives of the Hutu and the Twa. This system has been dubbed "internal colonialism," though it can be more accurately described as Rwandan feudalism.[25] The Tutsi cattle ranchers emerged as an aristocratic elite, the Hutu planters as commoners, and the Twa as potters and entertainers who were generally held in low regard by the other groups.

Much of our knowledge of the social system in precolonial Rwanda comes from an excellent study by anthropologist Jacques Maquet.[26] Power and prestige in Rwanda depended on possession of cattle. The Rwandans appreciated meat, but they would seldom slaughter an animal solely in order to eat the meat. Instead, cattle provided dairy products such as milk and butter. These products were enjoyed by the Hutu when available, but they were staples in the diet of Tutsi noblemen. Perhaps possession of cattle was most important as a symbol of status. Through their possession of cattle, the Tutsis gradually obtained ownership of nearly all the land; they also obligated Hutus to perform a wide range of services for them, in exchange for cattle. The Tutsis considered agricultural work beneath their dignity, and they evolved an ideology of themselves as a race of leaders, endowed with extraordinary intellectual abilities. They perceived the Hutu as hard workers, incapable of leadership.

The system rested on what Maquet calls "a premise of inequality."[27] It permeated life in precolonial Rwanda, to the extent that unmarried Tutsi boys would be "given" Hutu girls, temporarily, for sexual purposes. Inter-marriage occurred, but usually with successful Hutu men marrying Tutsi women. Tutsi men would take Hutu women as concubines, rather than marrying them.[28]

The feudal relationship, called *buhake,* established a link between the lord and the client that was not entirely without benefit for the client. Moreover, the complex hierarchy also placed Tutsi clients in a feudal rela-tionship with higher level Tutsi lords. And there was a process, rarely used, through which an exceptional Hutu could ascend the hierarchy and shed his "Hutu-ness." Even the average Hutu had some protection from the most brutal forms of exploitation. The norms of the *buhake* relation-ship were paternalistic; a lord had certain obligations to insure that his clients were fed and protected. In practice, Tutsis engaged in very little vi-olence against Hutus, who, for the most part, accepted Tutsi overlordship. Tutsi-Tutsi violence was more common, and was usually related to strug-gles for power and honor.[29]

The shared culture, the religion, beliefs, language, incorporated ele-ments from both Hutu and Tutsi society, so it is difficult now to trace the origins of particular aspects to one group or the other. At a political level, however, Tutsis had all the power. The Tutsi *mwami,* or king, established a fair degree of central control and the monarchy was apparently consid-ered sacred by Hutus as well as Tutsis. (The mwami's sacred power, inci-dentally, was symbolized through his possession of the *kalinga,* a drum on which were hung the genitalia of defeated enemies.)

The Tutsi mwami had established control over most of Rwanda by the end of the nineteenth century. In the extreme north, however, the Hutu population had never completely accepted the rule of the Tutsi monarchy. In the struggle for independence, and in the development of anti-Tutsi ide-ology in the 1990s, this region supplied the most avid proponents of Hutu power. For most of Rwanda, however, as Maquet notes, the system of polit-ical and economic domination and exploitation by the Tutsis "seemed to be successful and stable at the beginning of the twentieth century."[30]

From the arrival of the Europeans onward, and even before that, the history of Rwanda bears many similarities to that of its neighbor, Bu-rundi. Burundi is approximately the same size as Rwanda, with comparable percentages of Tutsi, Hutu, and Twa. Even less is known about pre-colonial Burundi than Rwanda, but it too was ruled by Tutsi kings.

The European colonialists did not expect much economic gain to come from ventures in Rwanda and Burundi. At times, they tended to romanticize about the twin kingdoms—beautiful, mountainous, flowery, far from civilization, peopled by exotic tribes, ripe for conversion to Christianity. They also were caught up in the mad scramble for colonies, in which great powers staked claims simply to prevent others from doing so first. In any event, the Germans obtained rights to the twin kingdoms, Rwanda and Burundi, before any Europeans had actually visited them.[31]

The Germans had little time to make an impact on the colony before they lost it to the Belgians in World War I. They generally worked indirectly, through the mwamis, and, in 1914, the total white population of Rwanda and Burundi was only one hundred ninety, and about one hundred thirty of these were missionaries. There were only eleven civil administrators and forty troops in a region nearly twice the size of Belgium.

The Belgians never really wanted to rule in Rwanda-Burundi; they had hoped to trade the rights they won in World War I for territory on the Atlantic adjacent to their Congo colony. Once it became clear that this was not going to happen, Belgium took up, with some degree of sincerity, the task of their League of Nations mandate, to conduct affairs for the betterment of the inhabitants.

Like the Germans, the Belgians attempted to administer the colony largely through the existing Tutsi-dominated political and social structure. Thus, the Tutsi mwami remained an influential figure. This reinforcement of the Tutsi position, clearly expedient, had a racist component. The Belgian administration declared that "the Government should endeavor to maintain and consolidate [the] traditional cadre composed of the Tutsi ruling class, because of its important qualities, its undeniable intellectual superiority and its ruling potential."[32]

Missionaries provided a pseudo-intellectual foundation for Tutsi rule with their "Hamitic hypothesis."[33] According to this theory, the Tutsis were superior because they originated in Ethiopia where they had been exposed to Coptic Christianity at an early period in their development. This indirect contact with "Western" civilization gave the Tutsis a clear edge in the eyes of the colonialists. So, too, did their more Western physical features and, above all, their possession of power.

However, Belgian policy recognized the need to address the condition of the Hutu majority, even though through much of Belgian rule, few Hutus themselves called for an amelioration of their position vis-à-vis the Tutsi. The Belgian administration asserted that "the mentality of this [Tutsi elite] class must gradually alter. A way must be sought gradually to modify its conception of authority, which must be changed from one of domination exercised solely for the benefit of its holders, to one of a more humane power to be exercised in the interests of the people."[34]

To accomplish these goals, the Belgians limited the power of the mwami and finally ended the buhake system of feudal relationships. Although the Belgians educated a much higher percentage of Tutsi than Hutu, the impact of the education of the Hutus ultimately proved decisive. Western concepts of equality, democracy, and freedom filtered down to the Hutu leadership, encouraging them, perhaps inadvertently, and against the desire of many Belgians, to challenge and eventually overthrow the Tutsi monarchy.

The Belgians set up a tier of power above that of the mwami and, in so doing, changed the avenues to and signs of prestige and status. Thus, the Tutsis retained most of their privileges and rights under the Belgians, but the perceived legitimacy of these advantages was seriously undermined. The end of feudal relationships, in 1952, destroyed solidarity between the Hutu peasants and their Tutsi lords, though without bringing the Hutu any noticeable economic or political improvements. The Belgian-sponsored system of ethnic identification cards stemmed from the earlier policy of working within the existing social structure. This system contributed to sustaining the perception of two unequal groups, even as its foundation in reality began to diminish. Through the 1950s, the Hutus, especially the Hutu leaders, grew far less tolerant of Tutsi rule. The changes that occurred under colonial rule had improved some aspects of the Hutus' predicament, but by raising expectations these very improvements made domination by the Tutsis seem more oppressive.

In Rwanda, the Belgians had imposed themselves as rulers over a previously existing system of domination. By doing so, they destabilized the prior pattern of exploitation and cast doubt on the natural superiority of the Tutsis. At the same time, the Belgians did not reorganize the structure of Rwandan society, but instead left the Tutsis to occupy most positions of privilege and power. The approach of independence infused the situation with murderous potential, for Tutsi power had always rested largely on Hutu acceptance of the Tutsis' perceived superiority. Now, however, the Tutsis occupied privileged positions with neither the power nor the ideology to sustain them. Additionally, the Belgians had exposed Rwandan society to Western notions of justice and equality. Many Hutus, for the first time, grew angry and bitter about the years of exploitation. Leo Kuper, an expert on the sociology of genocide, has noted that when two tiers of domination exist in the colonial system, decolonization is frequently charged with a genocidal potential.[35] When the colonialists pull out, they leave the dominated group angry and the dominant group without the power or authority to enforce its position. As a result, the dominated group is apt to rise up in violent rebellion against their masters. In Rwanda, blood flowed freely when the Hutus finally overthrew the mwami and brought an end to Tutsi domination.

In the summer of 1959, the colonial era was rapidly coming to an end across the globe. While Belgium considered how to transfer power peacefully to the Rwandans, the mwami, Mutara Rudigwa, died somewhat unexpectedly. His half-brother and successor, Kigeli, struck many Hutus as unequal to the tasks he faced. Most significantly, many felt Kigeli would become a tool of the local Tutsi chiefs. In their view, these chiefs had become particularly demanding and oppressive in recent years, although this perception also may have reflected a change in Hutu expectations.

By November, the rural Hutu peasantry had grown increasingly dissatisfied with the local and national situations. They rose in a violent anti-Tutsi crusade and, in a matter of days, had massacred or removed from office many Tutsi chiefs and subchiefs. In response to the uprising and the apparent breakdown of Tutsi rule, the Belgians appointed various Hutu leaders as "interim" authorities. By January 1961, the Belgians had placed Hutu leaders firmly in control of the provisional government and, in effect, abolished the Tutsi monarchy.

Independence followed in July 1962, but attacks against the Tutsis persisted throughout the first few years of Hutu rule.[36] In the struggles immediately preceding and following independence in 1962, tens of thousands of Tutsis lost their lives and hundreds of thousands more became refugees. The philosopher and social activist Bertrand Russell called the events surrounding Hutu independence "the most horrible and systematic massacre we have had occasion to witness since the extermination of the Jews by the Nazis."[37] In the mid-1960s, nearly 400,000 Rwandans, nearly all Tutsi, were listed as refugees in Uganda; from this group, nearly three decades later, sprang the core of the Rwandan Patriotic Front.

TUTSI KILLERS IN BURUNDI

Burundi followed a very different path to independence, with the Tutsis remaining on top. At first, it seemed as if Burundi might avoid a Hutu-Tutsi polarization, in part because the Burundi Tutsi, though dominant, had avoided some manifestations of superiority in their dealings with the Hutu leadership. More significantly, disunity plagued the Burundi Tutsis, who were split into the Hima and Banyaruguru factions. In addition, the institution of the mwami had survived independence from Belgium, and for a few years Mwami Mwambutsa served as an arbiter among the contending groups.[38]

The promise of a peaceful, cooperative transition to independence in Burundi, however, soon proved illusory as the Hutu-Tutsi divide widened and relations grew violent. Independence led to an intense competition for government jobs and other spoils. Most important of all, recent events in Rwanda influenced Burundi's politics; the violent overthrow of the Rwandan Tutsi sparked the hopes of Burundi's Hutu while suggesting a nightmare scenario to Burundi's Tutsi. In 1965, following Hutu victories in legislative elections, some Tutsi, not associated with the mwami's group, attempted to overthrow the government. This coup attempt led, in turn, to another aborted coup, this time organized by Hutus. In reprisal, the Tutsi-dominated army killed several thousand Hutu civilians.

The next year, the frustrated Mwami Mwambutsa gave up all efforts at balancing the demands of his warring constituencies. He abdicated in favor of his son, Charles, who became Ntare V. The new mwami's unfortunate reign lasted a mere eighty-nine days before he was deposed and exiled by his prime minister, Michel Micombero. The end of the traditional monarchy in Burundi permitted Micombero to put the country on a new, and ultimately disastrous, path that ensured continued Tutsi domination and led to a series of brutal genocidal attacks against the Hutus.

Sociologist Irving Louis Horowitz has written that, "When the ruling elites decide that their continuation in power transcends all other economic and social values, at that point does the possibility, if not the necessity, for genocide increase qualitatively."[39] The Tutsi elite did not fabricate a threat to their rule; rather, they faced a realistic possibility that the Hutu would accomplish in Burundi what they had in Rwanda. Hundreds of thousands of Rwandan Tutsi were already living in exile, many in Burundi. Thus, the policy of the Tutsi elite in Burundi did not emanate from ungrounded paranoia but rather a willingness to employ all means to maintain their power and privilege, and equally significant, to avoid a Rwanda-style overthrow.

On several occasions during the late 1960s and early 1970s, the Hutus attempted to defeat Tutsi rule. In 1969, in the face of increasing tensions, the Tutsi government arrested large numbers of Hutus to forestall a possible coup. Then, on 29 April 1972, Hutu rebels in southern Burundi, probably with some assistance from Congolese insurgents, embarked on an uprising in which hundreds of Tutsis were killed. The Tutsi government's attempts at disinformation still cloud our understanding of just what happened in this rebellion, and few trustworthy informants survive. But it appears that armed Hutu rebels swept through southern Burundi, killing Tutsis wherever they could find them. Tutsi casualties probably numbered between five hundred and three thousand.

In any case, President Micombero's Tutsi government clearly exaggerated the scale of the uprising, as well as the degree of foreign involvement, claiming that more than *fifty thousand* Tutsi had been slaughtered. The government, according to some sources, knew about the Hutu plans to rebel in advance, but intentionally did nothing to stop them. Regardless of whether this is true, following the Hutu rebellion, the Tutsi government lost no time in launching a massive, genocidal counterattack against the Hutu, under the guise of self-defense and punishment of those responsible for crimes during the uprising. The most reliable estimates of casualties hold that at least eighty thousand, and perhaps as many as three hundred thousand, Hutus were murdered in 1972. The Tutsi regime that perpetrated these massacres survived for several years afterward and, therefore, was able to prevent an accurate death count.

Noting that the genocide against the Hutu started with a massacre of Tutsi, some observers have dubbed the events in Burundi a *double-genocide* or a *mutual genocide*. These terms capture some of the dynamic behind the murderousness in Burundi, but they neglect the gross disproportion in the scale of the killings. These labels also fail to indicate that a government and an army supported the Tutsis in their murderous rampage against the Hutu. In contrast, only a band of Hutu rebels unleashed their fury against the Tutsi.

The Tutsi murderers, at some level, feared the consequences of a Hutu uprising, but most of the killings did not occur in an atmosphere of frightened frenzy. According to survivor accounts, some of the killings probably involved individuals settling personal scores. But the overwhelming majority of Hutus were murdered in a planned, cold, and calculating way. The government did not, as Micombero claimed, seek out only the guilty; the government's reprisal was comprehensive and systematic, and probably planned well before the Hutu uprising of 29 April 1972.

Many Hutu were taken from their homes at night; others reported to police stations in response to misleading requests. The government-supported killers frequently used machetes and did not rely heavily on bullets, a foreshadowing of the machete massacres by Hutus against Tutsis that would take place twenty-two years later in Rwanda, in 1994.

The 1972 genocide included many Hutu peasants among its victims, but the primary target was the modern class of Hutus—priests, teachers, managers, clerks. The Tutsi ruling class struck against a contending elite. The preferred victims fell into four categories: (1) Hutus with government jobs; (2) Hutu soldiers; (3) Hutus who were wealthy (those with bank accounts, those whose homes had iron roofs); and (4) Hutus with some secondary or college education. The Tutsi government intended to eliminate all Hutu competition for leadership of Burundi for at least the next decade.[40]

For the most part, the Tutsis succeeded in this objective. Although tensions between Hutus and Tutsis did not go away, and the Micombero government fell in 1976 to a coup led by another Tutsi, Lieutenant Colonel Jean-Baptiste Bagaza, the decimated Hutu population lost its ability to mount a serious threat to Tutsi rule for about fifteen years.

By 1987, Hutus had begun to reemerge in all walks of life, but discrimination still limited Hutu participation in secondary schools and universities, and the Hutu occupied only a small number of token, minor posts in government and the military.

In 1988, another wave of ethnic violence brought massive bloodshed to Burundi. It appears that Hutus living in some northern provinces became convinced that another large-scale massacre was imminent. They launched a preemptive attack against the Tutsi that claimed several thousand lives. Once again, the Tutsi government called for punishment of the guilty. This time, however, President Buyoya, who had replaced Bagaza in 1987, ordered action against only armed rebels and was perhaps sincere in his hopes for moderation. Nonetheless, what followed was another slaughter of the Hutus by the Tutsi-dominated Burundi army, with casualties exceeding twenty-five thousand.[41]

After the massacre, President Buyoya, partly in an effort to outflank competing Tutsi factions, showed signs of reaching out to the Hutus by launching a serious investigation into the excesses of the army. In June 1993, Buyoya's government sponsored the first free elections in Burundi's history. These elections led to his own defeat and the election of Melchior Ndadaye, the first Hutu president of Burundi. But shortly after taking office and setting up a unity government of Hutus and Tutsis, President Ndadaye ran afoul of the military, still dominated by Tutsis. A coup attempt in October 1993 left Ndadaye dead and Tutsi control of the army unshaken.

At first, Hutus killed Tutsis in response to the assassination of President Ndadaye. Then the Tutsi army started to kill Hutus. Once again, no one is certain about the number of casualties, but the death toll in this round of murder, according to Washington-based Human Rights Watch/Africa, numbered between thirty and fifty thousand—mostly Tutsis, but many Hutus as well.[42] Hundreds of thousands fled their homes, and many Hutu ended up as refugees in Rwanda, where they participated in the massacre of Tutsis in 1994.[43] A state of civil war has persisted in Burundi since the assassination of Ndadaye in 1993. Interethnic relations remain grim and, despite a recent power-sharing agreement that was negotiated by Nelson Mandela, new genocidal massacres would surprise nobody who has been following the situation there.[44]

During much of the sixties, the people of Burundi looked over their shoulders at Rwanda and wondered whether their country would follow the same blood-soaked path. The Rwandan Hutus, in the seventies, eighties, and nineties, watched events unfold in Burundi and feared what the Tutsis might do should *they* ever return to power in Rwanda. Hutu refugees from Burundi were always available to remind them of the potentially deadly outcome of Tutsi rule. In both Rwanda and Burundi, however, the fears of the masses, both Hutu and Tutsi, could be, and frequently were, manipulated to serve the self-interests of individual leaders from each group.

Potential killers on all sides paid careful attention to the world's restrained reaction to the genocides in Burundi. In 1972, nearly all African governments ignored the massacre or pledged their support to the government in Bujumbura; only Rwanda protested strenuously, and it was unable to have any impact on events in Burundi. (Rwanda, at the same time, had to contend with Uganda's General Idi Amin, who threatened to destroy Kigali, the capital city, because of Rwanda's good relations with Israel.) The newly independent African countries wanted a free hand to deal with their own "internal" problems in whatever manner they saw fit; they did not want to set any troublesome precedents by castigating Micombero.

Burundi was one of the most heavily Catholic countries in Africa, but Catholic clergy there and around the world had little to say about the killings. Western governments noted the events with concern, but perceived their interests in Burundi as marginal and their protests as futile. Moreover, they reasoned that the problem was an African one, and they had no business making a stink when African countries themselves were silent. Only Belgium reacted sharply, denouncing the massacres and threatening to cut its sizable foreign aid. It never followed through on the threat. The Burundi massacres of 1988 and 1993 were similarly treated as back-burner issues around the globe. One wonders whether the world would have made its voice heard if the white government in South Africa tried to put down an insurrection by black South Africans with such brutality.[45]

THE GENOCIDAL IMPULSE IN RWANDA

Although Rwanda faced poverty, AIDS, and other problems in the late 1980s, it seemed considerably more stable than most of its neighbors.[46] President Habyarimana had been a fixture since 1973, when he toppled Grégoire Kayibanda in a bloodless coup. Habyarimana was a ruthless despot, to be sure, but he brought an austere stability to the country through the iron rule of the *akazu*—relatives and cronies he installed in key governmental and military posts. In its early years, the Habyarimana government attracted foreign aid and even seemed to make some eco-

nomic progress. Hutu-Tutsi antagonism persisted, but it did not fester
into severe, open conflict during the seventies and eighties. Tutsi refugees
had launched several poorly organized efforts to retake Rwanda, in the
sixties, and these had been followed by harsh reprisals against Tutsi civilians. But mass killings had not been seen since well before Habyarimana's
takeover. The Hutu government rigidly adhered to an "affirmative action"
quota system in which Hutu were allotted 85 percent of civil service jobs
and places in the schools, while the Tutsi received 15 percent.[47] The system, based roughly on the population distribution, left out some qualified
Tutsi, but given the country's history and the conditions in neighboring
Burundi, intergroup relations could have been much worse. The central
question is how Rwanda so rapidly degenerated from this state into the
site of one of the worst massacres of the twentieth century.

More specifically, what led thousands of Hutu politicians, militiamen,
and peasants to participate in the murder and dismemberment of hundreds of thousands of Tutsi? What rendered them willing to turn their
homicidal wrath even on fellow Hutu with whom they disagreed? The
deep roots of this behavior, as we have already seen, lay in the historic
domination of Rwandan Hutu by Tutsi masters. But this domination
could, after all, have been dismissed as ancient history by a people who,
themselves, had dominated Rwanda's affairs for three decades. The more
immediate answer lies in the rise of Hutuism, an extremist ideology holding genocide against Tutsis and their supporters as the only solution to
the long-standing Hutu-Tutsi problem.[48]

Serious abuses of human rights usually occur in the context of war. And
though most of the killings in 1994 were not direct casualties of the fighting and often took place many miles from the front, Hutuist ideology
would not have taken root without the military threat posed by the Rwandan Patriotic Front. A generation of Rwandan Tutsi had grown to adulthood without ever stepping foot inside their ancestral homeland. Some
resettled permanently outside Rwanda, but many languished in temporary residences in border countries, mistreated by their hosts and committed to returning home. In 1979, a group of these refugees organized
themselves, originally as the Rwandese Alliance for National Unity. They
maintained a very low profile until the late 1980s, but gained important
experience serving in Yoweri Museveni's Ugandan rebel army. When Museveni succeeded in Uganda, Tutsi from Rwanda occupied high posts in

his government and army. Museveni, despite his denials, provided the RPF with strong military support and enabled the group to invade Rwanda in 1990.[49]

The RPF rebels called themselves *Inkotanyi*, or the Indefatigable Ones, a reference to their estimation that the road ahead would be a long one.[50] From the beginning, the RPF offered a multiethnic, democratic ideology.[51] Girard Gahima, a spokesman for the group, downplayed the Hutu-Tutsi dimension of the conflict. In 1992, he stated:

> This is not a tribal war or a secession war, but a war of unification. We want to do away with the invidious ethnic distinctions that have caused so much suffering. We are fighting not just for the Tutsis, but for the good of all Banyarwanda. We do not want power; we want real democratic changes, not just cosmetic ones, the half-hearted reforms of an old dictator trying to cling to power.[52]

The RPF demanded a right for refugees to return and a share of political power.

In the years following the 1990 invasion, the Hutu-dominated Rwandan government accused the RPF of many atrocities. Less interested parties also suggested that the RPF's methods were brutal, but it is difficult to gauge the true extent of its human rights violations. Most outside observers judge the tactics of the postgenocidal government to be less brutal than those of most African governments and rebel movements around the world. Nonetheless, these standards generally fall short of present-day Western military codes.

Although the 1990 invasion did not succeed, the RPF rebels enjoyed sufficient success on the ground to push Habyarimana to accept a negotiated solution. The Arusha (Tanzania) accords of August 1993 provided a formula for ending the conflict, based on a restructuring of the Rwandan armed forces to include a substantial RPF representation. In addition, a transitional government including the RPF and other opposition groups was to be formed, pending the outcome of general elections in the future. When Habyarimana signed the Arusha accords, he signed his own death warrant, and when he began to implement them, the sentence was carried out. He had alienated his base of support, the akazu. The downing of his plane in April 1994, and the government's murderous reaction against the

Tutsis, led immediately to renewed fighting with the Tutsi rebels. During this fighting, the RPF forces, now numbering about fourteen thousand and including many Hutu, achieved remarkable battlefield success against government forces armed by the French, Egyptians, and South Africans. Military experts attribute the RPF's ultimate victory to excellent leadership, tight discipline, and a committed fighting force.[53]

Throughout the years of fighting with the rebels, the akazu and other extremist Hutu groups attempted to incite and manipulate public opinion against the Tutsi. Even without their propaganda, Rwanda would have been fertile ground for mass hatred. Although Hutu and Tutsi lived side by side, stereotypical thinking prevailed among the majorities of both groups and there was a deep undercurrent of distrust and disdain. Rwandan Hutus did not have to be told that an RPF victory would bring home many thousands of refugees who might wish to reclaim land taken from them or their families decades earlier. They knew what had happened in Burundi and shared a fear of Tutsi rule. From personal experience or parents' tales, Hutus recalled what life had been like under the Tutsis, and their recollections often exaggerated brutal aspects of the earlier period. What the propaganda of the Hutu extremist leaders did was to reinforce (rather than create) the historic fears of the Hutu public, to distort facts about the present, to inspire a cadre of anti-Tutsi fanatics ready to join militias, and to fire animosities to a genocidal level in the spring of 1994.

The exclusion of Tutsis from power and the prevention of an RPF victory were in the obvious self-interest of Hutu power holders, but their hatred of the Tutsi sprung from something deeper than mere opportunism. Extremist Hutu politicians made no secret of their deep hatred for the Tutsi, even after the massacres. François Karera, the former mayor of Kigali, defended the attacks on the Tutsi: "If the reasons are just, the massacres are justified."[54] Bigotry and resentment about the past fuel his views on the Tutsi. "They are murderers. The Tutsi have given the white people their daughters. Physically they are weak—look at their arms and their legs. No Tutsi can build; they are too weak. They just command. The others work."[55]

In an infamous speech to a party conference nearly a year and a half before the massacres, Dr. Léon Mugesera, a Hutu politician associated with President Habyarimana, called on Hutus to kill Tutsis and dump their bodies in the rivers. He told the Tutsis that Ethiopia was their home and that they would be returned via the shortcut of the Nyaborongo River.[56]

The extremist Hutu elite, in control of the government and media, never allowed Rwandans to forget their group differences, and worked hard to imbue these differences with invidious meaning. In 1990, Hasan Ngeze, a northerner from Gisenyi, started a publication, *Kangura,* that proved particularly significant in building hatred. It published the highly influential "Hutu Ten Commandments," number eight of which was "The Hutu must not have mercy on the Tutsi."[57] The paper did all it could to sabotage the Arusha accords, seeking instead a fight to the end. One issue warned:

> You Hutus who re-possessed your property in 1959 when the cockroaches (Tutsis) fled, you'd better beware . . . the peace accord is allowing the cockroaches to come back to seize their property. Hutus, you will be injected with syringes full of AIDS viruses because the peace accord gave the ministry of health to the cockroaches . . . sleeping Hutus, be prepared to be killed in your beds by cockroaches. Hutu soldiers be ready to surrender your weapons and become peasants.[58]

In August 1993, Ferdinand Nahimana, a former director of state media fired by President Habyarimana for his extremist ideas, took a decisive step to fan the flames beneath the cauldron of mass hatred in Rwanda.[59] He set up Radio Television Libre des Milles Collines, a booming voice for Hutuism, dubbed by one journalist, "Rwanda's Killer Radio."[60] For months before the outbreak of violence in April, folk songs, slogans, speeches, and inaccurate news reports demonized the Tutsis and warned against Tutsi plans to retake the land, kill the Hutu, and reclaim their preindependence role of dominance. Broadcasts depicted Tutsis as snakes, animals, and most often, cockroaches. Government leaders would urge the killers on with slightly more cautious euphemisms, telling them to "clear the bush," "get to work," or "clean around their houses." Peasants understood well these encouragements to slaughter their neighbors.[61] Radio Milles Collines tied all Tutsi to the RPF and branded certain Hutu as traitors who deserved to die. The United Nations report on Rwanda confirms that individuals targeted in the broadcasts of Radio Milles Collines were among the first killed in April 1994.[62]

After Habyarimana's death, Radio Milles Collines became a mobile genocidal headquarters, traveling in an armored vehicle. It told the Hutus, "The enemy is out there—go get him" and reminded them that, "The graves are only half full."[63] Once the killings began, the state-operated Radio Rwanda joined in, spreading false rumors about RPF atrocities and telling the Hutu that, unless they joined the battle, the RPF would eventually kill them. On June 1, Radio Milles Collines announced that the Tutsi rebels were "gathering people in a village and killing them with bullets, gathering people in a mosque and killing them with machete, throwing people tied up into the Akagera River, killing a pregnant woman and taking out the fetus, which is ground and given to the family to eat before they are killed."[64] The station claimed to have international confirmation of these abuses, though no outside confirmation ever existed. Most significantly, Radio Rwanda and Radio Milles Collines succeeded in blurring the distinction between RPF soldiers and Tutsi civilians. For example, Radio Rwanda warned its listeners that RPF rebels "change their clothing appearance most of the time, trying to be confused with ordinary people who till the soil and go to the market."[65]

However deadly the impact of the mass media in Rwanda, most Hutus did not receive their news directly from radio broadcasts and newspapers. In accordance with what communication theorists call the multistep flow model, rumor mills filtered, amplified, and modified the information imparted by the mass media.[66] Indeed, political leaders intentionally fed the rumor networks, which historically have played an important part in Rwanda and Burundi. Observers have noted that people in these countries are especially apt to believe rumors because news has traditionally come to them via oral channels.[67] Moreover, a large percentage of the population is illiterate. In any case, many Hutus in the militias and the general public believed that Tutsis were killing Hutus indiscriminately, that they would continue to do so if they were victorious, and that the only safe route for Hutus was to kill Tutsis first.

Those responsible for most of the killings, members of the two extremist militias, received special training and indoctrination. Habyarimana's party, the National Republican Movement for Democracy, sponsored the Interahamwe; the even more extreme Hutu party, the Coalition for the Defense of the Republic, sponsored the Impuzamugambi. Both groups recruited most successfully among young, unemployed Hutu from the northern part of the country. Ali Yusuf Mugenzi, a Rwandan journalist, claims they were "bought by politicians for small sums of money and large quantities of beer."[68] At a training camp in Mutara, in groups of three hundred, Interahamwe initiates participated in three-week indoctrination programs. Extremist politicians taught them that the only way to move Rwanda forward was to kill Tutsis. They must, they learned, kill women and children as well—because only then could they prevent future descendants from rejoining the battle. The young militiamen responded particularly well to promises that they would receive their victims' land; but this promise, too, highlighted the need for total extermination lest a family member return to reclaim the family land. The Impuzamugambi trainees received similar instruction, from the Presidential Guard and elements of the Rwandan Government Army.

No studies have addressed the question of why individual Hutus, from the militias and the general public, joined in the slaughter. The explanations given by perpetrators captured by the RPF provide one source of insight. However, in RPF captivity, it was hardly in the prisoners' interests to admit that they killed out of hatred. Some, like Samuel Karemera, blame their participation on fear. While in RPF captivity in June 1994, Karemera, a forty-one-year-old farmer from Kibongo and a member of the Interahamwe, admitted to killing three of his neighbors, a man and two women, with a big club.[69] He claims that on April 13 the Mayor of Murambi, Jean Baptiste-Gatate, ordered them to start killing nonextremist Hutu as well as all the Tutsi. "So we had to do it or be killed ourselves as traitors or sympathizers with Tutsi."[70] Karemera said he regretted the killings and hoped for a pardon. Others who killed Tutsi also claimed that they did so to prove their loyalty to the Hutu during a frightening period. Even if these explanations are partially true—and they no doubt are— they do not explain why nearly all property of value was taken from victims' homes, or why many of the Hutu prisoners had joined the Interahamwe in the first place.[71]

Many of the killings did not seem like mechanical acts of obedience. A witness tells of a Hutu woman, a mother, married to a Tutsi. She begged for her life, as Interahamwe killers made two piles of bodies—the dead and the nearly dead. The militia men jabbed at her with their machetes and laughed. Finally, they tossed her atop the nearly dead pile and hacked everyone on the pile to death.[72] If these members of the Interahamwe acted out of fear, it must have been a fear transmuted into bravado and cruelty by a psychological defense mechanism.

Other prisoners, like Alfred Kiruhura, a twenty-nine-year-old illiterate peasant farmer, claim they were misled by their leaders and the mass media. Kiruhura, also a member of the Interahamwe, explains, "I did not believe the Tutsis were coming to kill us, but when the government radio continued to broadcast that they were coming to take our land, were coming to kill the Hutus—when this was repeated over and over—I began to feel some kind of fear."[73] According to Kiruhura, the radio stations "were always telling people that if the [RPF] comes, it will return Rwanda to feudalism, that it would bring oppression. We didn't know the RPF. We believed what the government told us."[74] Many witnesses from all over Rwanda heard rumors that the Tutsis had started a genocide and were bent on murdering the Hutu. The credibility of these rumors owed much to historical precedent, namely, the Tutsi massacres of Hutu in Burundi and the Hutu massacres of Tutsi in Rwanda. In addition, two hundred thousand Hutus from Burundi had fled to Rwanda during the violence following the October 1993 assassination of Burundi's first Hutu president, Melchior Ndadaye; these refugees brought with them the message, "Never trust the Tutsi."[75]

Genocide by the Tutsis seemed plausible, even likely. Major Frank Rusagara, a public affairs officer in the (post-genocide) Rwandan army, reports that "The former government created a climate of fear by saying that the Tutsis could come and invade the country at any time to kill the Hutus' families, to change the fabric of Rwandan society. The scare was deliberate, a part of government policy. It was common to tell children when they were bad that the RPF would come to take them away to use them as slaves. People were conditioned to fear and hate the Tutsis from birth."[76] Had the media portrayed the RPF differently, Rwandan Hutus may not have been so ready to believe the Tutsis capable of mass murder; perhaps the Hutus would even have subjected their own behavior to more serious inquiry. The media's dehumanization of the Tutsis was even more significant, and helped to create the deadly notion that all Tutsi civilians were in league with the RPF.

WHY IT HAPPENED

Officials from the genocidal Rwandan government claimed that the Hutu masses rose up spontaneously against the Tutsi after the downing of President Habyarimana's plane on 6 April 1994. Then, during the next few months, Hutu citizens simply defended themselves against murderous RPF attacks. From his exile in Zaire, the former information minister of the Hutu government, Eliezer Niyitegeka, protested discussion of the genocide. "Why do you want to talk about these dead Tutsis?" he complains to a reporter. "What about my human rights? I can't even go home."[77] The deposed Hutu leaders attempted to recast the slaughter as an unfortunate event, in which neither side conducted itself in saintly manner, and both sides perpetrated some massacres. This effort to establish moral equivalence is a fabrication. Its purpose is to diminish sympathy for the new government of Rwanda and to reduce awareness of the extent to which the genocide was systematic and planned.

As in the case of Bosnia, many outsiders interpret the bloodshed as a consequence of "ancient" animosities between ethnic groups. As we have seen, the Hutu and the Tutsi are not simply ethnic groups and, at least before the late 1950s, the groups seldom fought. Moreover, many moderate Hutus were numbered among the victims of the extremists. Historian René Lemarchand correctly attributes the violence to "the extent to which collective identities have been reactivated, mythologized and manipulated for political advantage."[78] But ruthless politicians did not manufacture these identities and historical "myths" *ex nihilo*. The historical reality of Hutu-Tutsi relations in Rwanda and Burundi made the manipulations possible.

The precolonial Tutsi domination of Hutus in Rwanda had certain benevolent aspects, but it was clearly an exploitative system. When the system fell apart and the exploited realized what had happened, their anger intensified. The persistence of denigrating stereotypes added to their fury. ("They think they were born to rule; we will show them.") Moreover, many Hutu remained psychologically fearful of returning to their former predicament. When the realistic threat from the RPF appeared, it was a relatively simple matter to activate a nightmare scenario. The genocide, by this logic, had its deepest roots in a precolonial social system based on a "premise of inequality."

The Belgian colonial rulers sometimes receive blame for making the massacres possible. In its most plausible form, this argument holds the Belgians responsible for destroying the legitimacy of the Tutsi monarchy, shaking the system, vesting power in the Tutsi elite, then quickly switching sides during the last few years of their rule. The end result was very angry Hutu masses confronting a weakened Tutsi elite. In a fantasy Africa without European intervention, the exploitative Tutsi monarchy might have persisted, and, in this manner, genocide would have been avoided. Alternatively, the Belgians might have moved more vigorously to reorganize Rwandan society along more egalitarian lines. This would have required considerable force, less respect for indigenous institutions, and a longer period of colonial rule. The progressive world would hardly have approved of these tactics.

A cycle of genocide fed the massacres in Rwanda. Just as abused children may grow up to abuse their own offspring, so the victims of genocide can perpetuate a murderous hatred of their own. As in the case of abused children, the cycle can be broken. But, more often, fear of a repeat occurrence and a desire for revenge create fertile soil in which demagogues can propagate hatred.

Such demagogues were not lacking in Rwanda in the 1990s. Politicians, army commanders, and other leaders had a vested interest in blocking the implementation of the Arusha accords, under which they would probably lose much of their power. To preserve their status and position, these Hutu leaders aroused the fears, suspicions, memories, and resentments of the masses, successfully employing a classic array of propagandistic methods. However, hostility toward the Tutsis was not purely instrumental, as many of the militant Hutu leaders seemed driven by genuine feelings of hatred as well as political self-interest. These leaders imparted their murderous anger to special extremist militias, which became indispensable tools of genocide.

Once fired up and misled by inflammatory media broadcasts, a frenzied mob psychology also propelled many Hutus in the general population over the brink to mass murder. Had these people been asked to act alone, they might never have become killers. Even hate-poisoned, angry, and misled people would possibly have felt moral inhibitions against picking up machetes and using them against unarmed women and children. But as French social psychologist Gustave Le Bon noted, a crowd acquires "new characteristics very different from those of the individuals composing it."[79] When mobs operate, they display a profoundly inferior mentality, an increased intensity of emotion, and a diminished capacity for moral judgment. The crowd setting of many murders in Rwanda, their brutality and the apparent abandon with which they were carried out, suggest that some of the murderers, at least, acted with lessened self-awareness and diminished individual judgment, both products of mob psychology.

We are left with the critical question of why some Hutus joined in the massacres, while others did not. Unfortunately, no psychological studies have been conducted on this matter, and very little direct evidence exists.[80] Seven attributes might be expected to have rendered a Rwandan Hutu more likely to participate in the genocide: (1) greater personal aggressiveness; (2) greater hatred of Tutsis; (3) greater fear of a Tutsi takeover of the government; (4) greater fear of Hutu reprisals for refusing to participate; (5) greater susceptibility to manipulation by the media; (6) greater susceptibility to mob influence; and (7) greater proximity to areas where the slaughters were taking place.

According to *New York Times* correspondent Raymond Bonner, "It was not just a few young toughs and uneducated peasants who killed. The guilty cut across the social and economic strata."[81] We might expect that better educated Hutu, not affiliated with the government, would have been more resistant to the propaganda. Also, Hutu who were relatively prosperous would have been less likely to join the Interahamwe militia. Hutus who had positive experiences with Tutsis may have been more resistant to the genocidal hysteria as well. All of this, of course, remains speculative and imprecise, as do questions about the impact of relative modernity and Catholic religious beliefs. If the situation in Rwanda stabilizes, it may become possible to conduct research into these questions.

The mass killings in Rwanda took place about one year after the worst atrocities occurred in the former Yugoslavia. Although the two societies differed tremendously in terms of history, politics, economics, culture, and social conventions, there were some similarities that deserve mention. Both massacres arose in countries which lacked a concept of legitimate political competition and a tradition of respecting the loyal opposition. In both, the leaders who engineered the slaughter had shaky claims to power, which they attempted to bolster by fomenting conflict between

groups. But one cannot, in either case, readily determine the relative contributions of opportunism and fanaticism to the leaders' motivations.

Extremists in Serbia and Rwanda used the mass media very effectively
to ignite and fan the animosities which had historical origins but which
had not flamed up recently. In both instances, the target of the hate propaganda was a group that had, itself, been associated with mass slaughter
in the past. Thus, Serb leaders were able to obscure the critical distinction
between Croats and Muslims in the 1990s, on the one hand, and Ustashas
from the World War II era on the other. Extremist Hutus drew on the
knowledge that Tutsis *in Burundi* had murdered tremendous numbers of
Hutu in 1972, 1988, and most recently in 1993; they also revived fears that
returning Tutsis would reappropriate Hutu land and restore the Hutu to
their historically subordinate position in Rwandan society. Thus, Serb
and Hutu militants created a public atmosphere of fear, where a strategy
of mass murder became widely perceived as the only effective defense
against attack. In both cases, a willingness to murder dissidents from their
own group strengthened the hand of the extremist leaders and shielded
them from internal criticism. Finally, trained and well-indoctrinated militias committed the bulk of the atrocities in both Rwanda and Bosnia.
While these common elements do not negate the importance of differences between the situations, they do highlight the ease with which powerful leaders can rapidly create a genocidal mood in countries where the
political culture is deficient and memories of slaughter prevail.

FIVE

Why People
Followed Hitler

WE MUST LEARN TO ACCEPT THE DIFFICULT TRUTH THAT HITLER'S REGIME WAS THE MOST POPULAR GOVERNMENT IN GERMAN HISTORY; YET WE KNOW AS WELL THAT FEW GERMANS AFTER THE WAR WOULD CONFESS HAVING GIVEN ANY LOYALTY TO THE NAZI MOVEMENT. THIS WAS NOT A LIE IN THE SOUL OF THE GERMAN NATION; IT WAS A PART OF A COLLECTIVE DELUSION THAT ALL THE FASCIST MOVEMENTS BROUGHT UPON THEIR FOLLOWINGS. IT WAS AS IF THE MOVEMENTS THEMSELVES, AS THINGS INDEPENDENT OF THE MEN THAT EMBODIED THEM, WERE RESPONSIBLE FOR THE THINGS THAT HAPPENED.[1]

Gilbert Allardyce, Historian, 1971

WELL-PUBLICIZED AMONG GERMANS, ALREADY BEFORE HITLER CAME TO POWER AND DURING A PERIOD WHEN HE STILL DEPENDED ON THEIR CONSENT RATHER THAN COERCION, WERE THE MANY ACTUAL DEEDS OF BUTCHERY. . . . SOME DAY THE SAME GERMANS, NOW CHEERING HITLER'S STRUT INTO PARIS, WILL SAY TO THEIR AMERICAN FRIENDS AND TO THEIR BRAVE GERMAN ANTI-NAZI FRIENDS: "WE DID NOT KNOW WHAT WENT ON, WE DID NOT KNOW"; AND WHEN THAT DAY OF KNOW-NOTHING COMES, THERE WILL BE LAUGHTER IN HELL.[2]

Peter Viereck, German-American Scholar, 1940

Reinhard Heydrich ordered the immediate annihilation of Jews and Communist officials in the conquered Soviet territories; he headed the Gestapo, directed the concentration of Polish Jews into ghettos, and convened the notorious Wannsee conference to announce the Final Solution. He had his hand in every significant anti-Jewish action in Nazi Europe until his assassination by Czech resistance fighters in June 1942. Had he survived that attack, he would in all likelihood have continued to pilot the Nazi destruction of European Jewry to the bitter end.

His first biographer, Charles Wighton, portrays him as a man with some political and organizational talent, but driven by a depraved character to become Hitler's most satanic henchman. This view has fallen from favor and in its place have emerged two portraits of Heydrich as more the product of his culture and era. The first, advanced by the Israeli historian Shlomo Aronson, sees him in terms not altogether different from the way his widow, Lina, would like us to see him, as an ambitious but apolitical man who entered the SS only by chance and whose position at the pinnacle of the Nazi campaign to exterminate the Jews owed little to his personality or political beliefs. In contrast, Edouard Calic, a German historian and former political prisoner of the Third Reich, views Heydrich as a committed Nazi, a man who had already absorbed anti-Semitism, extremist nationalism, and a penchant for harsh methods years before he signed on with Hitler in 1931. According to this perspective, the roots of Heydrich's evil lie in his anti-Semitic family and schooling, his reaction to Germany's defeat in World War I, and his association with ultranationalist groups in the immediate postwar period.[3]

Historians have disagreed about the motivation of many top Nazis, and their views often parallel positions staked out in the Heydrich debate. The leaders of the Third Reich are sometimes portrayed as psychotic, sometimes as satanic, sometimes as amoral careerists ascending the bureaucracy, and sometimes as enthusiasts of Nazi ideology. Unlike Heydrich, some architects and perpetrators of the Holocaust lived long enough to face an angry, perplexed world which demanded some explanation for their behavior. Though self-serving, their answers deserve examination for the flicker of understanding they may offer about how human beings become genocidal.

As chief of the German High Command from 1938 until the end of the war, Field Marshal Wilhelm Keitel issued orders that unleashed the SS in conquered Soviet territories. Acting on Hitler's orders, he called for the retaliatory murder of hostages and directed that all Soviet Commissars be shot immediately upon capture. The record confirms that he, personally, felt little enthusiasm for these measures, but nonetheless acquiesced in them. Primarily a military man, Keitel did not dream up plans to murder European Jews, and his role in implementing the scheme was peripheral. However, he was second only to Hitler in directing the war effort and his actions (or perhaps inactions) resulted in monumental suffering. When the Nuremberg Tribunal condemned him to hang, Keitel did not plead for clemency. As his lawyer put it, he wanted to save not his neck, but his face. Keitel said

> I hope that those members of the Allied Control Council who have been soldiers will have some understanding for my guilt, which was born of a virtue recognised in every army of the world as an honourable and necessary basis for being a good soldier. Even if I failed to recognise the proper limits that ought to have been set upon this soldierly virtue, at least I do not feel I have therefore forfeited my right to atone for this error by the mode of execution [firing squad] that is the right of the soldier.[4]

For Keitel, his "error" originated in the creed of the Prussian soldier class, in his faith in the inviolability of the leader's will. The Tribunal turned down his final request, and he was hanged.[5]

Albert Speer, the German minister of armaments from 1942 to 1945, succeeded in raising arms production only by squeezing the life out of millions of forced laborers and concentration camp prisoners. At the Nuremberg Tribunal, he accepted responsibility for the crimes of Nazism, even those of which he was purportedly unaware, like the extermination camps. After serving twenty years in prison, he published his memoirs, in which he portrayed himself as an apolitical technocrat, not driven by hatred but nevertheless guilty, most of all, for his *acquiescence* in the destruction of European Jewry. Speer may not have known so very little. Still, his best-selling memoir offers a plausible explanation of how he originally joined Hitler in 1931. A well-educated architect, he came from a wealthy family and was, therefore, a bit atypical for a Nazi recruit in those days. He recalls hearing a Hitler speech and growing entranced by the Führer's hypnotic style.

> Quite often even the most important step in a man's life, his choice of voca-
> tion, is taken quite frivolously. He does not bother to find out enough about
> the basis and the various aspects of that vocation. Once he has chosen it, he
> is inclined to switch off his critical awareness and to fit himself wholly into
> the predetermined career. My decision to enter Hitler's party was no less
> frivolous.[6]

He further claims that, "Had Hitler announced, before 1933, that a few years later he would burn down Jewish synagogues, involve Germany in a war, and kill Jews and his political opponents, he would at one blow have lost me and probably most of the adherents he won after 1930."[7] Of course, Hitler had announced these things in *Mein Kampf,* several years earlier; why hadn't Speer paid attention? He answers: "This failure was rooted in my inadequate political schooling. As a result, I remained un-critical, unable to deal with the arguments of my student friends, who were predominantly indoctrinated with the National Socialist ideology."[8]

Even the death camp commandants, men who directed the daily mur-der of thousands of Jews and sanctioned some of the most abusive "med-ical" experiments ever, have attempted to sanitize their places in history by arguing that their motives did not differ so very much from our own. Rudolf Hoess, in an autobiography written while awaiting execution in a Polish prison, spoke of his loving relations with his family and of his deep, lifelong affection for animals. From his memoirs, one might conclude that here was a shrewd administrator who had the bad fortune to end up at Auschwitz: But for an unfortunate incident during adolescence, when a Catholic priest betrayed his sacred trust, Hoess might even have become a man of the cloth. In confession, Hoess had told the priest how, in a scuf-fle, he had accidentally pushed a classmate down a stairway and how the boy had broken his ankle. That night, the priest, a close friend of Hoess' father, dined at their house and, the next morning, his father punished him for the pushing incident. According to Hoess, the betrayal shattered his faith forever.

Hoess maintains that throughout his life he strongly valued obedience and authority, but he was no sadist. He had a human heart. He was not evil. He even shot a guard, once, for abusing a prisoner against his orders. Hoess assures us he had nothing in particular against the Jews. He was no less, and no more, than a patriot—rendering a necessary service to his country.[9] "Don't you see," he told Dr. Gustave Gilbert, the prison psychologist at Nuremberg, "we SS men were not supposed to think about these things; it never even occurred to us. And besides, it was something already taken for granted that the Jews were to blame for everything."[10]

Franz Stangl, the commandant at Treblinka, and, before that, at Sobibor, discussed his profound lack of enthusiasm for his task with journalist Gitta Sereny. He had tried, on several occasions, to get out of these distasteful assignments, but his superiors wouldn't hear of it. He too had no strong dislike of Jews and he felt little responsibility for what had happened at Sobibor and Treblinka. His actions, after all, were not his own. He merely lacked the courage to resist. The gore of the camps disgusted him and, consequently, he tried to observe as little of the brutality as possible, focusing instead on more honorable administrative matters.[11]

Following his capture, no less a figure than Reichsmarschall Hermann Goering, the number two man in Nazi Germany, denied having anything to do with the SS, the racial laws, or the death camps. He was determined to be remembered in German history as a "great man." "In fifty or sixty years," he predicted, "there will be statues of Hermann Goering all over Germany."[12] He dismissed questions about the extermination camps, saying that Hitler never discussed such matters with him. They were Himmler's department. Told about an alleged plan to kill Hitler and deliver Himmler to the Allies, Goering was outraged: "[D]o you think I would have handed Himmler over to the enemy, guilty as he was? Dammit, I would have liquidated the bastard myself!"[13] But such machismo was not evident with regard to Hitler. Asked by Dr. Gustave Gilbert why he and the others had been such abject "yes men," Goering replied: "Please show me a 'no man' in Germany who is not six feet under the ground today."[14] This was a somewhat surprising response from the highly decorated, intrepid, "Iron Man," the last commander of the legendary Richthofen Squadron in World War I. "I was never cruel," he told Gilbert.[15] His motives had been political but honorably so; he wanted to restore Germany to a position of honor and power, to undo the wrongs of the Versailles Treaty.[16]

From their statements after the war, one might conclude that few Nazi leaders agreed with Nazi ideology, fewer still knew about anything outside of their direct organizational responsibilities, and that virtually none disliked the Jews. One might be led further to the conclusion that even those who committed the most heinous war crimes did so out of soldierly obedience and with a deep sense of guilt, often because they perceived no way out of difficult situations. To the extent that they acted out of personal motives, these were (1) to be good soldiers; (2) to move up the career ladder; and (3) to save their own skins.

What are we to make of this vision? Some facts seem glaringly inconsistent. Hoess, after all, had already served time for murder, several years before he assumed command at Auschwitz. Other officers trained in the Prussian military tradition could not bring themselves to serve, in Keitel's place, as Hitler's "yes" men, and some, finally, plotted to kill the Führer. Keitel's obedience clearly exceeded passive compliance. As he explained in a preliminary interrogation in August 1945: "At the bottom of my heart, I was a loyal shield-bearer for Adolf Hitler; my political conviction would have been National Socialist."[17] Speer apparently altered documents that demonstrated his more active role in war crimes. Stangl's involvement in "mercy killings" of the chronically ill at Sobibor and finally Treblinka makes him seem more like an active climber up the career ladder of the murder business than a reluctant, disgusted participant. And Goering, in July 1941, ordered Heydrich to carry out all preparations regarding the "total solution of the Jewish question in the German sphere of influence in Europe," an order that many historians believe set the Final Solution in motion and hardly qualifies as noninvolvement.[18] More to the point, his massive collection of plundered artwork and his self-indulgent life-style suggest a man more motivated by greed than patriotism—at least in the final years of the Third Reich.

Nonetheless, some truth may remain in the explanations offered by Nazi leaders. They square rather well with the findings of some social science studies (discussed in the next chapter). And if obedience, career ambition, and fear constituted the primary motivation of these top dogs, shouldn't we conclude that they played an even greater role for midlevel bureaucrats and low-level grunts?

The eminent Holocaust historian Raul Hilberg notes that no one agency of the German government was established to deal with Jewish affairs and no fund was set aside to finance the destruction process. "All components of German organized life were drawn into this undertaking.

Every agency was a contributor; every specialization was utilized; and every stratum of society was represented in the envelopment of the victims."[19] For example, the Interior Ministry handled dismissals from the civil service, prohibition of mixed marriages, and the definition of the term *Jew*. The Transport Ministry managed transports to the ghettos and camps, as well as the acquisition of Jewish personal property. Private firms utilized forced labor and provided ample stocks of poison gas for the death chambers. The Education Ministry agreed to remove Jewish students, professors, and researchers. The churches provided believers with proof of non-Jewish descent. The direct perpetrators of many of the worst crimes usually came from the SS, whose selection and training predisposed them to such tasks. But Nazi genocide was also carried out by tens perhaps hundreds of thousands of bureaucrats, professionals, businessmen, policemen, workers, and soldiers—people from every walk of life.

The destruction of European Jewry was not as it sometimes appears in popular consciousness, one massive crime, the crime of the death camps, committed by Nazis acting in unison from common motives and with similar objectives. While millions of Jews met their deaths in the gas chambers at Auschwitz and elsewhere, millions died by other means—in bludgeonings by angry guards, from starvation and disease in the Polish ghettos, in officially sanctioned old-style pogroms, in mass machine-gunnings in the Ukrainian and Byelorussian countryside, in mobile gas vans, and in a variety of unique tortures devised by their tormentors. While all the perpetrators shared a willingness to murder Jews, or assist in their murder, their motives differed substantially. Many who did not personally pull the trigger, or release the Zyklon-B gas, did not see themselves as perpetrators. The bureaucratic division of labor permitted them to see themselves as "doing their job" and to see others as "the killers." And one cannot conclude, for example, that a low-ranking soldier who obeyed an order to fire at Jewish civilian hostages in Serbia acted from the same motives as the foreign office bureaucrat who championed deportation of the Jews to Madagascar, or the anti-Semitic former stormtrooper who joined the party in the 1920s and derived pleasure from beating inmates at Treblinka.

After reviewing thousands of studies on the Holocaust, historian Michael Marrus concluded that the greatest challenge for historians was to explain why people followed Hitler even to the extent of eliminating a cultural inhibition against mass murder.[20] Economists, political scientists, and sociologists have all applied the tools of their trades to this problem, and have contributed important explanations. Our focus here is on psychological motivation, not the whole story but a key part of it. To understand what motivated the Nazis and those who marched with them, three questions must be addressed. First, how do we explain the motivation of the Germans who helped bring Hitler to power by screaming their support at rallies, battling opponents in street fights, and casting their ballots in Weimar elections? Second, why did so many Germans who opposed Hitler prior to his assumption of power in 1933 experience so dramatic and complete a conversion that by the end of the 1930s his hold on Germany seemed absolute? Finally, why were so many people willing to violate, even abandon, the moral precepts of European civilization as they participated in crimes associated with the Final Solution to the "Jewish Question"?

STORMTROOPERS, ZEALOTS, AND VOTERS BEFORE 1933

Writing several years after Hitler's consolidation of power but well before the Holocaust, the German-American scholar Peter Viereck argued that

> The German enigma is not Hitler. Nor is it the behavior of either frauds or police-sadists (these are latent in all countries in about the same proportion, though hardly in the same high posts). The real enigma is the honest, unsadistic German majority that unleashes them rather than throwing them in jail. Hitler's shoddy day-dreams are not interesting. What is interesting is that an outstanding educated nation crusades for them.[21]

Despite Viereck's comments, Hitler's "shoddy day-dreams" have commanded the attention of nearly everyone who has sought to understand World War II and the Holocaust. As one biographer notes, more has been written about Hitler than about anyone else in history, except Jesus Christ.[22] And, after this intensive scrutiny, most students still come away befuddled by the disparity between the smallness of the man and the enormity of the events he set in motion.

Far from being the inevitable outgrowth of long-term historical, economic, and social forces, German military and anti-Jewish policy during

World War II conformed largely to contours defined by Hitler's personality—his conflicts, desires, frustrations, and obsessions. Had Hitler never
lived, some other leader may well have resurrected German militarism, but
with an altogether different style and agenda, perhaps without its central
anti-Semitic component.[23] Some historians now question whether Hitler
ever gave a clear, specific, or written order to commence the Final Solution;
it may have begun as the brainchild of eager-to-please underlings anticipat-
ing his desires and striving to resolve the "refugee" problems created by his
earlier anti-Jewish policies. More likely, the order did come directly from
Hitler in 1941, as a fulfillment of his January 30, 1939, pledge that a new war
would bring "the annihilation of the Jewish race in Europe."[24] In either case,
Hitler's personal preoccupation with the Jewish "cancer" endowed German
anti-Semitism with its essential murderousness; without this obsession,
Jews would have escaped mass slaughter, even if persecution persisted.[25]

Anti-Semitism, for Hitler, was no mere tool, no popularity building de-
vice, no Machiavellian trick (though he occasionally downplayed his hostility when it served the interest of the party). Hitler's hatred of Jews and
his racial imperialism were not tactics in his drive to power; they were *the
reason why* he sought power in the first place. If there was any one thing in
which Hitler truly believed, it was anti-Semitism. When he said, "The
Jew's skull will be smashed by Germanic will," twenty-one years before the
construction of the death camps, he gave voice to his most sincere wish.[26]
According to historian Lucy Dawidowicz:

> The Jews inhabited Hitler's mind. He believed that they were the source of
> all evil, misfortune, and tragedy, the single factor that, like some inexorable
> law of nature, explained the workings of the universe. The irregularities of
> war and famine, financial distress and sudden death, defeat and sinfulness—
> all could be explained by the presence of that single factor in the universe, a
> miscreation that disturbed the world's steady ascent toward well-being, af-
> fluence, success, victory.[27]

Even when it threatened his war effort, Hitler insisted on proceeding
with the anti-Semitic program. General Stroop wanted to give Hitler a
present that would please him; what came to mind was the razing of the
Jewish ghetto in Warsaw. And when Germany lay in ruins, Hitler consoled
himself that, at least against the Jews, the war had been won.

Where did such destructive, and ultimately self-destructive, passions originate? In *Mein Kampf*, Hitler traces his "conversion" to anti-Semitism to his early adulthood in Vienna, where he read anti-Semitic pamphlets that abounded in that city during the first decade of the twentieth century. He also mentions two successful anti-Semitic politicians of the day—Schoenerer and Lueger—though he strives to paint his own Jew-hatred as original, something he discovered, rather than copied.[28] If we are to believe his pal, August Kubizek, however, Hitler's father Alois also held anti-Semitic beliefs and Hitler studied under several Jew-baiting schoolteachers. Indeed, one might be tempted to attribute Hitler's anti-Semitism to his upbringing.

But this would be like attributing U.S. businessman Donald Trump's drive for money to the American consumer culture; it's not exactly irrelevant, but by its failure to distinguish him from most others in his society, it muddies far more than it clarifies. Though the environment of his youth and early adulthood no doubt helped channel Hitler's wrath against Jews, it does not explain the fiery intensity and all-encompassing centrality of his hostility.[29]

Pinpointing the sources of Hitler's destructive mindset may require a type of thinking uncommon among traditional historians. Psychoanalysts, who professionally probe the depths of the unconscious in order to unravel the mysteries of bizarre behavior, have always judged Hitler and, especially, his fanatical anti-Semitism as suitable grist for their interpretive mills. Most experts agree that Hitler was childish, humorless, rigid, and forever disturbed by feelings of unworthiness; indeed, so consumed was he by feelings of guilt that he decried conscience itself as an essentially Jewish invention. While few question his physical bravery, a fact attested to by his performance in World War I, psychological fears and obsessions dominated Hitler's universe. He spoke frequently of the imminence of his own death and showed lurid interest in the death of others. He displayed inordinate concern about dirt, cleanliness, and impurity. One need not be a trained psychologist to notice the strangeness of his mannerisms.

One of the most psychoanalytically oriented biographers of Hitler, Robert Waite, writes: "Since his fears were so many, so great, and so unbearable, he felt a great need to consolidate them all into one single fear that he could recognize, one that would explain all others, and one upon which he could release all his pent-up anger and hatred. He found it . . . in the Jewish people."[30] Psychoanalysts have pored over the record of Hitler's early years, searching for themes and details that might suggest where history's most destructive scapegoating began.

Several analysts take us back to the Oedipus complex, a key they use to open many, perhaps too many, locks. Hitler, the argument goes, felt a powerful ambivalence toward his father; publicly he spoke of him with respect, but privately he hated him and saw him as a competitor for his mother's love. These feelings normally arise in boys around age six, but for Hitler they persisted into adulthood, reflecting a failure to achieve a successful resolution of his oedipal crisis. Under ordinary conditions, a boy passes through the oedipal stage; for Hitler, the unresolved oedipal issues colored his entire life.[31]

In one version of the story, after Hitler's father died, a Jewish physician, Eduard Bloch, emerged as a father-substitute in Hitler's mind. Hitler developed a conscious appreciation for Dr. Bloch's services, while at the same time harboring a strong, unconscious resentment toward him. He had witnessed the doctor filling what appeared to be several of his father's roles: entering his beloved mother's bedroom, undressing her, and seeing her unclothed. In his mind, Hitler perceived Bloch as a competitor for his mother's affections and also as a lecherous attacker—the same way, according to the oedipal theory, that he perceived his father. When Hitler's mother died, he consciously expressed gratitude to Dr. Bloch for the doctor's attempts to aid her, but unconsciously he saw this Jew as the brutal killer, violator, and mutilator of his mother. The unconscious horror became more powerful because of Hitler's belief, also unconscious, that Dr. Bloch had caused his mother's death when he gave her a painful drug, iodoform. When Hitler, himself, received treatment for poison gas exposure during World War I, he underwent another trauma which reactivated the earlier trauma surrounding his mother's death; he then had a vision in which he saw himself announcing his duty to resurrect Germany and save it from its Jewish enemies.

Some of Hitler's word choices in his speeches support this theory of the oedipal roots of Hitler's pathology, especially if one accepts the psychoanalytic notion that such choices are seldom chance occurrences. Hitler often spoke of the Jews as a "cancer," "seducer," or "corrupter" of Germany; he showed particular preoccupation with themes of the Jew as sexual defiler of the race and, especially, of German women. For Hitler, Germany became a mother-substitute (which he often referred to as the "Motherland," in contrast to the more common "Fatherland") and the Jews became a father-substitute.[32] Killing the Jews became a psychological means of murdering his father.

Another psychoanalytic perspective derives from Hitler's well-known suspicion that he, himself, might have had partly "Jewish" blood coursing through his veins. In an anti-Semitic environment, this proved a terrifying threat to his identity, one which only intensified as he became more and more anti-Semitic. By seeking to wipe out the Jews, he struck in effect at his deepest insecurity and attempted to eradicate it. (Similarly, Heydrich's fears of Jewish blood may have fired up *his* anti-Semitic passions; superiors investigated these rumors and found them false, but nonetheless used them to keep him in line.[33])

Still other psychoanalytic explanations of Hitler's personality focus on: (1) his hunger for an ideology, a hunger that often occurs in those undergoing the identity crisis of late adolescence, and that remained important because Hitler never fully mastered this crisis; (2) powerful insecurities stemming from a reputed absence of a testicle; (3) lifelong guilt because of his unconscious incestuous desire for his mother; and (4) guilt concerning his reputed sexual perversions.

This last matter formed the core of psychiatrist Walter Langer's secret wartime report for the OSS. Hitler purportedly projected onto the Jews a deep sense of guilt and self-hatred arising out of his own perverted sadomasochistic sexual practices. According to his former ally, Otto Strasser, by most counts an unreliable source, Hitler's niece, Geli Raubal, after some prodding, revealed that he had engaged her in a variety of unusual sexual practices. Among other things, Hitler purportedly demanded that she urinate on him.

A bit more convincing, this niece, and six of the seven women who may have had some intimate sexual involvement with Hitler, attempted or committed suicide. But some did so for apparently political reasons and, therefore, those psychoanalysts who accept this theory mainly rely on Hitler's general patterns of behavior outside the bedroom (from which they infer the likelihood of perverse sexuality) and on the frequent sexual imagery in Hitler's speeches, private conversations, and writing.[34]

The efforts of psychoanalysts to understand Hitler's psyche take us into deep, uncharted territory. Often, they rely on "facts" that have not been conclusively established. Hitler may not have been a sexual pervert; he may have had two normal testicles. Nobody is exactly certain when he became a rabid anti-Semite, so it is difficult to agree on which events were triggers. His father may have been a brutal tyrant, causing the unresolved oedipal sentiments, or he may, as Erich Fromm insists, have been a kindly man who loved life but believed in a sense of duty and responsibility. In addition to so much uncertainty about the building blocks of psychoanalytic explanation, there is little consensus about the theories both among the wider community of psychologists and psychiatrists, but also among psychoanalysts. Some, or all, of their insights about Hitler may be accurate, but it seems prudent to regard them as speculative.[35] What does seem plausible is that Hitler's hatred of the Jews and his drive for world domination owed some of their intensity to the externalization of his own internal struggles.

Most psychologists and psychiatrists agree that, in some sense, Hitler was nuts. But in what sense? Some have found evidence suggestive of organic disorders, like Parkinsonism. He did have excessive flatulence (which caused him much embarrassment), stomach disorders, and uncontrollable sweating. Dr. Douglas Kelley, the psychiatrist at the Nuremberg tribunals, did not, of course, have direct access to Hitler; on the basis of information provided in interviews with other top Nazis, however, he diagnosed Hitler as "a psychoneurotic" who was obsessed, paranoid, and prone to hysterical symptoms. Others have classified him as a psychopath, a person completely lacking in conscience, having what psychologists now call an antisocial personality disorder.[36]

A few years ago, psychiatrist Norbert Bromberg attempted to make a definitive diagnosis of Hitler and arrived at this conclusion: "narcissistic personality with paranoid features, functioning on a borderline personality level."[37] This diagnosis implies a number of personal traits. A narcissist openly reveals his megalomania, but craves admiration, praise, and flattery. He has little sense of humor, he cannot form significant relationships, and blows to his self-esteem can elicit violent anger. He has a paranoid distrust of others. He can appear self-confident and secure, but deep down feels shame, insecurity, and inferiority. He has little interest in a

normal sex life, but is preoccupied with perverse fantasies. The borderline
personality falls short of a true psychosis, retaining a fairly good ability to
appraise the real world—most of the time. He tends to view other people
as "all good" or "all bad," and people move easily from one category to the
other. He may, at one moment, appear a charming, benign benefactor,
and the next moment turn into a raging, aggressive attacker. He lacks impulse control and is very likely to act on his aggressive feelings. He has a
distorted conscience. Depression is common. Bromberg and Small cite
many instances where Hitler's behavior conformed to what we would expect from this diagnosis, though they are a bit too eager to stretch interpretations in order to squeeze everything into place. They are also needlessly wedded to psychoanalytic definitions of the diagnostic categories.

Any diagnosis is merely a label, a heuristic category, that cannot by itself
explain the enormity of Hitler's character. Hitler, himself, accepted and
propounded many grandiose myths about his ideology and personality.
At the very least, a clinical diagnosis cuts him down to size.

Had he lived, however, he would not have met the prevailing standards
for an insanity defense; he knew that his actions constituted crimes that
transgressed social norms and values. He possessed the ability to restrain
himself, but chose not to do so. Had Hitler been psychotic, say, a paranoid
schizophrenic, he might have fallen under the provisions of the insanity
defense. More important, he would never have risen to power. Hitler
maintained sufficient control over his fantasies and adequate contact with
reality in order to function from day to day. After an exhaustive review of
medical records, psychiatrist Fritz Redlich recently concluded that, despite abundant physical and psychological pathology, Hitler knew what he
was doing and chose to do it with pride and enthusiasm. His crimes and
errors were not caused by illness. Hitler's symptoms were enough to fill a
psychiatry textbook, but they, in themselves, cannot explain—far less, excuse—the man or his deeds.[38]

Serious psychiatric disorders, under other circumstances, might have
rendered a successful political career improbable, but in Hitler's case his
narcissistic-borderline personality may have contributed a major ingredient to the glue that bound him to the German people. Hitler deemed this
connection provident. In 1936, he said to the nation, "That is the miracle
of our times: that you found me—that you found me among so many
millions! And that I found you is Germany's fortune!"[39] What made this

"miracle" possible? Why, to return to Viereck's question, didn't the German masses throw him in jail, send him for psychiatric help, or at least ignore him as he ranted and raved in Munich's beer halls? The answer begins with the early history of the Nazi party.

Hitler joined in September 1919, as Party Comrade number fifty-five and the seventh member of the executive committee. From the outset, his oratorical skills proved an asset to the group, though progress was far from meteoric. In the two years following his assumption of party leadership in the summer of 1921, Hitler perfected his oratory and sharply honed his ability to rouse a crowd. But at the time of his first attempt to seize power in the Munich beer hall putsch in November 1923, party membership barely exceeded fifty-five thousand out of a population of about sixty million; fewer than one German in a thousand had become a Nazi. The putsch landed Hitler in jail and ended the legality of the Nazi party for a brief period. By 1929, the party had once again become a legal organization, and included about one hundred thousand members. But prior to the 1930 elections, the vast majority of educated Germans still considered Hitler and his followers an insignificant group of loud-mouth extremists, superpatriotic and virulently anti-Semitic, with no chance of attaining power.

Widespread economic misery and unprecedented unemployment were the most immediate cause of the change in party fortunes. Two days before Chancellor Bruening, one of the last pre-Nazi leaders, was dismissed in 1932, he noted: "When the standard of living drops to a certain low point all inclination to listen to lectures, arguments of state, or the voice of reason will disappear with psychological necessity."[40] Nazism became a national phenomenon in depression-era Germany, still derided by many, but obviously growing. By the end of 1931, membership exceeded eight hundred thousand. The party never stopped growing until Hitler's final defeat, nearing two-and-a-half million by 1935, five million by the beginning of the war, and surpassing eight million just before the Allied occupation in 1945.

Hitler's decision to pursue power via the ballot box, following the failed 1923 beer hall putsch, had proved momentous. With stormtroopers and street battles, Weimar elections can hardly be judged an example of democracy at work. But the National Socialists won many supporters through old-fashioned, "grass roots" campaigning. They entered party politics, at first stumbling, then marching forward with a horrible thunder. Their best efforts in the parliamentary Reichstag elections of 1928 left them a mere fringe party. But, by the elections of September 1930, Nazi support had grown to eight times the level of 1928, from 2.6 to 18.3 percent, paralleling the growth in party membership during the same period. In the elections of July 1932, the Nazis reached a plurality of 37.3 percent, setting the stage for Hitler's deal with the "old gang" of conservatives and business interests he had been criticizing mercilessly in months just past.

The story of party politics, wheeler-dealing, and above all monumental underestimation that culminated in Hitler's appointment to the Chancellorship has been told many times.[41] The military and big business attempted to tighten their grip on political power by harnessing the popular appeal of the strange, former corporal, a pawn whom they never doubted could be removed at will. The leftist parties quarreled among themselves, also certain that their internecine difficulties would not prevent them from defeating the terrible, but ridiculous, Nazis. These political machinations and miscalculations had historic impact, but only because Hitler commanded a huge wellspring of popular adoration.

Though hugely consequential, Germany's economic depression and unemployment alone cannot account for Hitler's enormous and enthusiastic following. The economic crisis need not have spawned a social and political crisis; and this disaster, in turn, need not have festered into a dismemberment of the democratic system. The United States and England, after all, underwent serious economic jolts, and though both experienced some fascist activity neither came close to succumbing to any Hitler-figure.[42]

In the decade following Hitler's ascension to Germany's helm, some writers located the Nazis' appeal in the general trends of European history and culture. Marxists, such as R. Palme Dutt, saw the arrival of the fascists as part of the expected demise of the capitalist system. He noted the alliance between fascists and business interests, but had more difficulty explaining the mass appeal of this reactionary movement. Why hadn't the workers flocked to the communists in the face of capitalism's crisis, as they had been expected to do? For Dutt, the answer lay in the treachery of socialists who preached reform, rather than true Marxist revolution.[43]

Erich Fromm, in 1941, also saw Hitler as a reaction to the failures of monopoly capitalism, but drawing on his particular blend of Marxism and Freudian psychology, focused on the stress and malaise of contemporary life. For Fromm, freedom had not brought modern people a positive sense of their potentialities, but rather had increased their anxiety and sense of powerlessness. These pressures, according to Fromm, had especially overwhelmed lower middle-class Germans who "were as eager to surrender their freedom as their fathers were to fight for it; . . . instead of wanting freedom, they sought for ways of escape from it."[44] Even those Germans who did not seek an escape from freedom had judged it unworthy of a spirited defense. The turn to Nazism was a psychological mechanism designed to reduce the stress felt by lower middle-class elements in an advanced, modern, industrialized society. The ultimate problem was an inability to handle an untamable freedom.

Across the political spectrum, conservative economist Peter Drucker, in 1939, attributed the rise of the Nazis to the breakdown of the old world economic and political order, and more importantly, to the absence of a new order to replace it. Following the abysmally destructive First World War and the devastating Great Depression, one could no longer place much faith in either the socialist or the capitalist creed. According to Drucker, the concept of human beings as free and equal members of society, people whose fates depended on their merits and efforts, had proved illusory. No rational escape from this problem seemed to exist in the 1930s. The masses in Germany, therefore, sought escape through the essentially absurd, "magical," and "miraculous" Nazi system because they saw themselves stuck between a past they could not regain and an apparently unscalable wall of future despair.[45]

All these explanations deemphasized the specifics of German history, Nazi ideology, and Hitler's personality—factors which many later historians and psychologists have judged paramount. Germans, after all, created the Holocaust, and one might reasonably examine the specific ways in which Germans differed historically from other Europeans in culture, social values, and intellectual life.

Very often, it has been noted that Germans were more authoritarian than other Europeans, displaying a greater respect for leaders, a stronger sense of duty, and a heightened willingness to obey orders.[46] This pattern of psychological authoritarianism may have resulted from the structure of German family life and its rigid, obedience-oriented, child-rearing practices. The tradition of authoritarianism fed into, and was fed by, the related tradition of Prussian militarism. Prussia, by far the largest of the German states prior to unification in 1870, had a worldwide reputation for its military excellence and for the inculcation of values necessary to maintain this excellence. Soldiers earned the greatest respect in Prussian society, and many attributed the unification of the German states to militarist virtues. Hitler would have had a more difficult task fomenting a war of aggression in a nation that lacked the Prussian militarist tradition.

According to another explanation, a strong thread of irrationalism ran through German intellectual life in the nineteenth century. Nietzsche was the prime example, with his attack on the Enlightenment and his elevation of the will to power. (Nietzsche, despite his concept of the "superman," was not an anti-Semite and probably would have detested the Nazis; his responsibility for what followed, if any, was indirect.) The irrationalist mindset, to the extent that it existed, may have heightened receptivity to Nazism especially among the educated class.[47]

Much more concretely, one can point to the long tradition of anti-Semitism among some German intellectuals as something which tilled the ground for Hitler's poisonous seed. In 1542, Martin Luther, the spiritual father of many Germans' faith, had urged the emperor and princes of his day to expel the Jews without delay and warned that if they did not, the clergy and the people would. He described the Jews as a "plague, pestilence, pure misfortune in our country."[48] Composer Richard Wagner's legendary anti-Semitism warmed the heart of his devoted fan, Adolf Hitler. Throughout the nineteenth century, hatred of Jews flourished among many German nationalists. It became a major political force in the latter decades of the nineteenth century with hateful anti-Semites such as Adolf Stoecker, Georg Ritter von Schoenerer, and Karl Lueger gaining large followings.[49]

Long-term trends in cultural and intellectual life, such as anti-Semitism, irrationalism, authoritarianism, and militarism made the Nazis' task easier, but they cannot have been decisive causes of Hitler's rise to power. Nobody, looking at Germany before World War I, would have foreseen the rise of a figure like Adolf Hitler, and very few, even in their dreams or nightmares, would have imagined the possibility of a Holocaust brought about by Germany. (This, I believe, is a powerful argument against Daniel Goldhagen's central thesis.) However militaristic, anti-Semitic, irrational, and authoritarian Germany might have been, most Europeans continued to view it as a center of world civilization and progress.

In the late nineteenth century, anti-Semitic parties achieved some success in Germany, but they were at least as strong in democratic France where Edouard Drumont's best-seller, *La France Juive*, delineated Jewish responsibility for just about everything that went wrong in French history. Drumont's newspaper, *La Libre Parole*, waged daily battle against Jews in the republic, as did the Catholic newspaper, *La Croix*, sponsored by the Assumptionist Fathers. The tradition of hating Jews lay far deeper in Russia and Poland where pogroms were a national sport.

When Britain and France went to war in 1914, their citizens marched with an enthusiasm equal to that of their "militaristic" German counterparts. The appeal of irrationalism hardly stopped at Germany's borders. What's more, Germany was home not only to irrationalism and militarism but to a liberal, humanist tradition as well. Finally, not all militarists were Nazis in the making. Bismarck, for example, was a militarist par excellence, but it is hard to imagine him goose-stepping with the Nazis.

Thus, Hitler's rise to power is best understood as a consequence of events arising in the aftermath of World War I. German soldiers had entered the war, full of confidence, expecting a quick victory, and naively unaware of the horrors that awaited them in the trenches. They rapidly became disabused of their nineteenth-century notions, and grew accustomed to the grim realities. Right up until the very end, however, most Germans remained convinced that they would win the war, or at the very least, not lose it. The defeat that came in 1918 had an unreal quality, especially because Germany escaped destruction and occupation. Though the war had been lost on the battlefield, and an armistice requested by the military leadership, many Germans did not accept the defeat psychologically. Returning soldiers found it difficult to endure the revolution at home, the departure of the Kaiser, and the humiliation of defeat. They had suffered as long and as hard as the victors, but they were not greeted by parades, only political and economic instability in a strange new world.

Against this backdrop, the Nazis were only one group among several that promoted the "Stab in the Back" legend, the belief that Germany had not lost the war on the battlefield but had been defeated by Jews and Communists on the home front who sold them out. Similarly, they promoted the myth of [President Woodrow] "Wilson's trickery," that the Germans had been promised self-determination and a benevolent peace;

what they had received was dismemberment of German territory and the harsh reparations terms of the Versailles treaty.

Historian Michael Kater has carefully analyzed Nazi party records to determine precisely who it was that Hitler attracted through his denunciations of Versailles, the Communists, and the Jews. Using a sophisticated quantitative approach, he determined that Nazism held the least appeal for the working class, who apparently did not buy into the quasi-socialist aspects of the National Socialist agenda; still, many workers did join the movement, particularly in the later years. Kater's research confirms the impression of many earlier writers that Hitler drew his greatest support from the lower middle-class—craftsmen, lower and intermediate white-collar employees, self-employed merchants, lower and intermediate civil servants, etc. Surprisingly, in light of Hitler's desire to replace the traditional powers that be, Nazism also fared reasonably well among the elite—managers, higher level civil servants, academically trained professionals, the university-educated, students, and wealthy entrepreneurs. Kater offers three plausible reasons for the elite's disproportionate support of Hitler: (1) they had lost faith in the old order to which they nominally belonged; (2) they jumped on the Nazi bandwagon to avoid losing their positions; and (3) they joined the party in an effort to moderate the movement and, thereby, to protect their class and themselves from extinction.[50]

The bigger question concerns the response of the lower middle class, which provided Hitler with the overwhelming mass of his support. Years later, Hjalmar Schacht, former president of the Reichsbank and Nazi economics minister, remarked about Hitler: "He could play like a virtuoso on the well-tempered piano of lower middle-class hearts."[51] But why? The vast majority of lower middle-class Germans lacked anchorage in any political movement during the postwar years. They held strongly nationalist views and detested the "Marxist" republic, but could hardly envisage a return to the class-ridden, privileged life of the prewar world. They sought a renewal of the nation and were ready for a chauvinist, antisocialist, populist movement on the right.[52]

The Nazis captured the hearts and minds of this group, but for the most part the affair, though fiery, was short-lived. Few Germans came through World War II, the postwar years, and the denazification programs with their support for Hitler intact. Some true believers retained their

Nazi ideas, and a few argued convincingly that they never bought any of the Nazi nonsense in the first place. Overwhelmingly, however, Germans speak with mystification of Hitler's "hypnotic" appeal. The word shows up again and again; Hitler is said to have mesmerized the nation, captured them in a trance from which they could not break loose until the shock of defeat and the death of the Führer in 1945. Then, all of a sudden, as if arising disoriented from a nightmare, they realized what they had wrought.

When Germans call on the concept of "hypnotic appeal" to explain their attraction to Hitler, they cannot mean actual hypnosis in the sense that psychologists use the term. What they mean is that they were drawn to Hitler himself in a way they cannot understand, explain, or justify. They recall themselves screaming furiously at rallies and they do not recall why they behaved in a manner that now seems ridiculous, even to them.

Hitler's appeal actually depended on several things: (1) his significant oratorical skill and a well-implemented strategy designed to manipulate the masses; (2) a program and ideology that appealed to many, and was acceptable to many more; and (3) a personality that fit well with the psychological needs of a fairly large segment of the German population in the 1920s and 1930s.

In *Mein Kampf*, Hitler revealed a shrewd understanding of propaganda, and his skills as a speaker were legendary; his disciple, Dr. Joseph Goebbels, also proved a master of public manipulation. They had a code of principles. When you lie, tell big lies. Never hesitate, never qualify, never concede an inch. Be passionate, vehement, fanatical. To say Hitler had tremendous talent as a speaker is certainly not to say he had powerful debating skills or a fine command of the German language; he excelled in his ability to read an audience and to build it to an unprecedented and feverish level of excitement. When an audience was likely to ask tough questions, Hitler sometimes canceled the speech rather than face the music. But more than any other speaker of his day, Hitler conveyed a ruthless desire to dominate others and a fanatical sense of commitment.[53]

Hitler and Goebbels also tended carefully to the cultivation of a "Hitler Myth," and throughout the Nazi years, this myth proved immensely useful in binding together disparate constituencies, first within the party, and after the assumption of power, within Germany as a whole.[54] Hitler was nearly always the reason people joined the party in the early years; it is hard to find someone who recalls liking the party but not Hitler. In later years, Hitler's popularity among Germans always exceeded that of the Nazi party. The fully drawn image of the Führer did not appear until the war. This image painted Hitler as (1) personally sincere and moderate in contrast to more radical Nazis; (2) the most virtuous of Germans, selfless, the personification of the nation; (3) the architect of German prosperity; (4) the upholder of public morality; (5) a brilliant statesman; (6) an incomparable military leader; and (7) a bulwark against Bolshevism and the Jews. Much of this was clearly in sharp contrast with reality, but Hitler and Goebbels used all the tools of propaganda to hammer these themes home again and again. Even in the earliest years of the party, in the twenties, Hitler managed to craft an image of himself as a paragon of virtue and even as a latter-day Christ-figure. The "leader principle" of unquestioning obedience to a Godlike Führer undoubtedly stood firm because it rested on a preexisting belief, especially among the right, that such a leader would appear and rescue Germany.[55]

Ian Kershaw, the historian who has done the most to shed light on the construction and function of the Hitler myth, argues that Hitler's popularity owed far more to the myth of his persona than to the content of his ideology.[56] But one should not be so quick to dismiss the appeal of the Nazi platform. No party offered a louder and less qualified denunciation of the Bolsheviks, at a time when fear of revolution had reached a crescendo and in fact was quite realistic. None gave a more thunderous voice to German resentment of the "harsh" provisions of the Versailles treaty. None articulated better the widespread disgust with the Weimar system and the dislike of democracy among the authoritarians. Hitler's economic message always lacked clarity and really amounted to little more than an unthinking mishmash of socialism, capitalism, and national self-sufficiency. But this enabled him to be all things to all people, sometimes the ally of labor, sometimes of business. For the lower middle-class German, frightened by the political and economic uncertainties of the modern world, devastated by the unexpected defeat in World War I, and unexcited about the return of prewar privileges to the aristocracy, Hitler's message of assertive national revival won many supporters. Hitler's hypnotic appeal may have stemmed largely from the good fit between what he was saying and what his supporters wanted to hear at the time (but came to see as satanic in the postwar years).

To Hitler himself, the anti-Semitic doctrine shined as the gem in the crown of Nazi ideology. Corrupting elements of Darwinian theory, he viewed life as a struggle among races in which the strong, that is to say, the Aryan, would come to dominate the weak. This cognitive map ultimately incorporated thousands of ridiculous and horrifying details, including attempts by "scientists" to catalogue all the traits of the world's races and a morbid drive to preserve Jewish artifacts for the benefit of museumgoers and scientists after the success of the "Final Solution." But in the early years, Hitler's anti-Semitism lacked its pseudoscientific backing and seemed merely the most virulent strain of common, garden variety, racist Jew-baiting.

Hitler's supporters showed no moral qualms about joining a group permeated by extreme bigotry, no doubt as a consequence of the country's deep anti-Jewish traditions.[57] But, most likely, only a small percentage of followers sought out the Nazis *primarily because* of their anti-Semitism. Hitler even learned to moderate his hostility to the Jews during the late 1920s and early 1930s in order to avoid stimulating the consciences of potential supporters. Not even those who became leaders—Goebbels, Himmler, Goering, Frank, Hoess, Eichmann, or the Strasser brothers— had been initially drawn to the party for its anti-Semitic plank.[58] The stormtroopers, Hitler's street fighters, did include many rabid anti-Semites, but most of his supporters, especially the later ones, had other things on their minds. They were certainly anti-Semites, and they had neither second thoughts nor feelings of guilt when they heard cries of "Death to the Jews," but most joined the party for other reasons.

In sum, one group of Hitler's early supporters had been manipulated by his propaganda and another agreed with his message. This, for many historians, ends the story of why people joined the Nazi movement in the years preceding the takeover of power. Yet some historians, particularly those of a psychoanalytic bent, have crawled deeper into the psyche of the German people and attempted to stake out the contours of what might be described as a collective national pathology. More specifically, they argue that Hitler may have captured the soul of Germany because his bizarre personality led him to fulfill instinctively the psychic needs of many Germans at the time. He may have benefited from a coordination between his own private fury and the traumatized yearnings of the German public, the least fortuitous coming together of minds in modern history.

The German scholar Ernst Nolte, like other biographers, notes Hitler's infantile personality and monomaniacal obsessions, but suggests that his ability to launch Germany into twelve years of darkness originated in a trait Nolte calls "mediumism." Hitler, according to Nolte, was "the medium who communicated to the masses their own deeply buried spirit."[59] He told rallies what they unconsciously wanted to hear, even if consciously they expressed very different views. Hitler did not focus on specific policies, but on great, universal hopes—of unity, a functioning economy, love of Germany, a strong army, and the like. Nolte suggests that his delivery had a mystical quality:

> When Hitler chatted, his manner of talking was often unbearably flat; when he described something, it was dull; when he theorized, it was stilted; when he started up a hymn of hate, repulsive. But time and again his speeches contained passages of irresistible force. . . . These are always the places where his "faith" finds expression, and it was obviously this faith which induced that emotion among the masses to which even the most hostile observer testified.[60]

According to Nolte, Hitler's monomaniacal obsessive nature drove him onward with incredible energy while his infantile wishful thinking carried him "beyond the workaday world with its problems and conflicts."[61] These traits combined with his ability to function as the ultimate medium and delivered Germany into his grasp. His bizarre mannerisms were genuine and contributed to his appeal. No one could have fabricated such an outrageous persona.

The German psychiatrist and family therapist Helm Stierlin draws on a very different psychological premise, the idea that children often act out the fantasies of their parents, but arrives at an explanation not so far from Nolte's. He presents Hitler as a "delegate" acting out his mother's repressed fantasies of power and revenge for a life of mistreatment by her husband and sadness engendered by the death of three of her children. The Jews, in Stierlin's view, became a substitute for Hitler's father, and thus, a suitable target for the son's, and indirectly the mother's, displaced wrath. Moreover, by substituting service to Germany for service to his dead mother, Hitler was able to fulfill the requirements of delegacy while, at the same time, achieving his own desire for independence. Hitler also became a "delegate" of the German people, expressing their darkest fantasies and repressed desires. By doing so, he filled very powerful needs and earned their intense loyalty. Hitler satisfied the collective craving for dependency on an absolute leader and the national need for unity among diverse constituencies. He provided the Jews as a scapegoat whom Germans could blame for the "wrongs" of the Versailles treaty.[62]

Brandeis professor Rudolph Binion, author of a controversial biography of Hitler, offers yet another depiction of the bond between Hitler and Germany. He notes the need of one who has undergone a trauma to relive the experience in order "to control, to master it after having been overcome by it the first time, and to inure oneself to it so that it will 'pass' after all."[63] Germany's unexpected, shattering, and traumatic defeat in World War I paralleled Hitler's own traumatic loss of his mother. World War I triggered for many Germans a host of unconscious conflicts and out of these conflicts arose a need to relive, and relieve, the trauma. For example, while Hitler's militant pursuit of *lebensraum,* or additional territory for living space, met his own psychic purposes, it also satisfied the German collective need to avenge their defeat in 1918. Hitler knew just what to say to Germans at rallies because "his breakdown coincided with Germany's in time, and his traumatic project complemented Germany's."[64] Again, Hitler emerges as the embodiment of the unconscious desires of the German people.

Still, a strong conscience might have erected an insuperable barrier between the leader and the led; desires, especially unconscious desires, often remain unfulfilled, and conscience might have deterred Germans, however needy, from joining the Nazi ranks. Those Germans who followed Hitler did not seem to feel the restraints of morality, and those who followed him most enthusiastically apparently were least likely to feel pangs of guilt. Historian Peter Loewenberg attempted to understand the origins of weakened conscience in the young followers who formed the core of Hitler's support. He notes that these youths had been children during World War I and experienced massive health, material, and nutritional deprivation—even a decline in breast-feeding, as many mothers took jobs as part of the war effort. Many of their fathers died in the war. Those fathers who survived had spent crucial years away, and when they returned they were never able to rebuild their role in the family or to make up for lost time. Freud and the psychoanalysts argue that a child learns moral precepts by identifying with parents, primarily of the opposite sex, and that parental absence can result in a weakened conscience (superego). This, according to Loewenberg, is precisely what happened, and a generation of Germans ended up with weakened character structures. They burned with intense inner rage and possessed an unusual inclination to aggressive behavior. They were also particularly likely to employ psychological defense mechanisms, such as idealization of their absent parents. They craved submission to an absolute leader and father figure. When the Great Depression imposed new strains and stresses on this unfortunate generation, it became an ideal audience for Adolf Hitler.[65]

These attempts to understand the collective unconscious of Nazi Germany, like the efforts to mine Hitler's individual unconscious, leave many people unconvinced. The theories that Hitler functioned as a "medium" or a "delegate" seem plausible as metaphors, but they require us to accept the existence of powerful unconscious needs throughout the German public. It is difficult, if not impossible, to establish these needs in individuals; how much harder is it to convincingly establish their presence, and dominance, in the psyche of an entire people? Do nations possess a need to relive traumas in the same manner as some individual trauma victims probably do? Parental absence and loss and deprivation due to the war were very great in World War I Germany, but they also characterized the victor nations. And while it is undoubtedly more difficult for single parents to raise families, it may stretch credulity to assert that their children suffer weakened consciences to the extent postulated by Loewenberg. Still, the concept of Hitler appealing to the unconscious (and sometimes conscious) needs of many young Germans for revenge, restored national pride, unity, leadership, and a scapegoat for their problems remains credible.

A unique source of insight into the early appeal of Nazism survives because of the prescience of a Columbia University sociologist in 1934. Theodore Abel sponsored an essay contest for "the best personal life history of an adherent of the Hitler movement" who had joined before January 1, 1933. Six-hundred-eighty-three Nazis sent their life stories, ranging in length from one to eighty pages. Some hoped to show their movement in favorable light and others hoped to convince the Nazi hierarchy of their deep loyalty—so the accounts cannot be viewed as necessarily accurate. Still, these "life stories" provide a snapshot of sentiments at a critical moment before all subsequent statements by Nazis became self-justifying efforts to evade personal responsibility for Auschwitz and an enormously destructive and aggressive war.[66]

The autobiographical statements reveal many different paths to National Socialism in the early years. Nearly all the early Nazis shared a hatred of Marxists, the Weimar government, and the civilians who, in their view, failed to remain committed to Kaiser and country during the war. No simple economic motive for joining the party emerges, although many cite a variety of economic reasons associated with their own occupational group. Perhaps this reflects the lack of clarity in Nazi economic policy. The experiences of World War I, fighting, traumatic defeat, the culture shock of returning home, the "revolution," and the counterrevolutionary postwar violence proved very significant for the generation of Nazis who reached adulthood prior to the end of the war. This group had been raised in militaristic and authoritarian homes; their families had been ethnocentric, traditionally anti-Semitic, and law-and-order-minded. As Nazis, they became superpatriotic and preoccupied with avenging the defeat. World War I had rendered them unfit for any company other than that of fighting men and it had taught them that problems could only be solved in a military, authoritarian manner.

For the generation that came of age in the postwar years, the war had a much less direct and less noticeable impact. This group came mainly from virulently anti-Semitic homes dominated by a more explicit and all-encompassing racist ideology than the older group. As Nazis, they formed a Hitler cult, waxed romantic about the Nordic-German race, and displayed tremendous excitement about the struggle itself.

The postwar generation provided Nazism with a crucial second wave of supporters that enabled it to grow until the takeover of power. They also supplied the cadre of street fighters and stormtroopers that gave Hitler an essential edge in his competition for supporters. The autobiographies indicate that one critical ingredient in Hitler's formula was the "marcher-fighters." They were men of action, unencumbered by ideas or empathy. Often they grew up without fathers, and had been battered children. Their violence knew no ideology, but was instead random and volatile. These men eagerly sought opportunities for physical and verbal violence, and were grateful to the party that provided them with public rationalizations, comrades, and charismatic leaders. Often, they would wear their uniforms to work, or seek other means for stirring up trouble.

Unlike the marcher-fighters, young extremists were obsessed with the Jews and Nazi ideology, but less likely to engage in violent behavior; some youths apparently joined for the ideas while others craved the opportunity to bang heads. Without their "more thoughtful" and ideological associates, the marcher-fighters could never have propagated a successful movement, but together they gave the movement teeth.

Many early Nazis, including marcher-fighters, joined the brownshirts or stormtroopers. Until Hitler killed the leader of this group (the SA) and replaced it with Himmler's SS in 1934, the brownshirts performed all of the party's dirty work and assisted Hitler on innumerable occasions. The Abel autobiographies show that this organization attracted members largely because of the appeal of group life and the opportunity to belong to the camaraderie of a fighting community. As youths, many brownshirts had been associated with other antirevolutionary groups. Some had been drawn by the program and the ideology; many were deeply anti-Semitic. But personal motives, such as the young adult's need to rebel, to march with a purpose, and to join a dynamic group, frequently mixed with political motives.

Peter Merkl concludes his study of Abel's Nazi autobiographies with a sensible reminder:

> Human motivation is far too complex to be reduced to one factor alone, such as the impact of mass unemployment, the absence of fathers, the violent legacy of war and revolution, or the mobilization of organized youth cultures. Taken together, on the other hand, all these factors and some others can add up to a plausible combination that explains the setting in which the political act of will was conceived that we seek to explain. Reconstructing the world of meaning as the stormtroopers and party men saw it goes a long way toward explaining their decision to march and fight and proselytize, as long as we remember that it was still their free decision to join and work for the movement.[67]

EXPANDING POPULARITY AND
THE END OF DISSENT

When Hitler became Chancellor of the Reich in January 1933, he commanded the sympathies of far fewer than half of the German people. The left regarded him as the loathsome lackey of the capitalists; organized labor detested him. The large Catholic minority viewed him as brutal, warmongering, and worse, hostile to the interests of the Church. Many on the right remained uncertain and condescending. His party, after all, was National *Socialist* and some worried (needlessly, as it turned out) about its quasi-socialist plank. Hitler had been an unemployed painter and a lowly corporal, hardly fulfilling the expectations of the traditional conservative elite and military establishment. The Nazis, despite intimidation and propaganda, garnered fewer than half the votes cast—43.9 percent in the March 1933 Reichstag elections.

But when 95.7 percent of Germany's voters went to the polls seventeen months later, nearly 90 percent said *Jawohl* to Hitler and his assumption of dictatorial powers. The turnout figure is more significant than the actual vote tally, because voting against Hitler at that stage seemed futile and entailed some risk. By the end of the 1930s, however, the German people gave few reasons to doubt their overwhelming and enthusiastic support for Hitler and his program. Public opinion piped with the devil during these critical years.

For Hitler's support to have grown so rapidly, new forces must have been at work, different from those that operated in the period preceding the takeover of power. Terror was the most obvious of these compelling influences. The Nazis did not have to terrify each and every potential dissenter; they merely selected ringleaders and a few random followers. Many thousands of sensible, courageous, and ethical Germans paid the ultimate price for their refusal to still their tongues in the face of Nazi evil. Dachau drove the message home with icy clarity. Heed the teachings, obey the rules, or suffer the consequences.

Still, terror alone might have produced only mass compliance, not the enthusiastic support that is so evident in the historical record. A second explanation of the growth in Nazi popularity relies on the popular half-myth that Hitler had united Germany by eliminating class conflict and instituting a strong, united state for the first time since the days of Kaiser Wilhelm. Most Germans were better off materially and felt better psychologically after several years of Nazi rule. As historian David Schoenbaum writes, "If no social group did well in the Third Reich, no social group did badly—or so badly that its discontent was not compensated by the contentment of another group. Labor's defeat was business' triumph, agriculture's frustrations labor's relief . . . the consumer's aggravation agriculture's compensation."[68] Although the Nazis brought no new, effective solutions to Germany's long-standing social and economic problems, they did bring a seemingly new social structure. Ever-increasing numbers of Germans bought the ubiquitous message of Nazi propaganda that Hitler was Germany's messiah, a savior sent to restore the nation's rightful place in the world and to institute a powerful, secure, and proud state.

With very few exceptions, the German churches failed miserably to establish among Germans any sense of the immorality of the Hitler regime. German Catholics felt additional pressure to prove their often-questioned loyalty to Germany. When the Vatican signed a pact with Hitler in 1933 and asked God to bless the Reich, Catholics across Germany correctly interpreted support for Hitler as acceptable to the Pope. Most German Protestants, under the influence of their anti-Semitic Lutheran heritage, not only refrained from opposing the Nazi regime, but gave it their total support. The swastika flew atop many churches. Sometimes the clergy, themselves, knew better, but felt their first duty to the interests of their religious institutions. Sometimes, they did not perceive any conflict between Hitlerism and their own beliefs. The honor of Christianity was preserved by the very few who actively protested the regime, even when they had to suffer dire consequences. But all told it was a dark era for German Christianity, which proved itself at worst uninterested in the struggle against the Nazis and at best unequal to the task.[69] Catholic and Protestant clergy could have declared Nazism an affront to God; instead, they sent the message to their flocks to the very end that Hitler's deeds were acceptable.

These developments explain part of Hitler's new appeal to his former adversaries, but they do not explain how so many millions quickly abandoned the moral and political principles they had known since childhood and practiced into adulthood until 1933.[70] Two well-established principles from contemporary social psychology, the "attitude-follows-behavior" phenomenon and the "foot-in-the-door" phenomenon, help to clarify how this dramatic transformation of attitudes and values transpired.[71]

According to the attitude-follows-behavior principle, a person may engage in behaviors for reasons completely unrelated to his or her attitudes or beliefs. Then, as a consequence of having engaged in the behaviors, he or she may develop consistent attitudes. Two major theories can explain this phenomenon. According to cognitive dissonance theory, an unpleasant tension frequently results from possession of attitudes that conflict with one's deeds. To reduce this tension, called cognitive dissonance, people feel pressure to change either their attitudes or their behaviors. Often, it is easier to modify internal attitudes than to alter public behaviors.

Self-perception theory, the second explanation of the attitude-follows-behavior phenomenon, states: "In identifying his own internal states, an individual partially relies on the same external cues that others use when they infer his internal states."[72] In other words, to learn how one thinks or feels about something, one observes how one acts toward that thing and then attempts to draw plausible conclusions. Thus, a person who sees himself behaving in a way that a person who holds opinion X might behave comes to assume that he holds opinion X. When someone reads a particular newspaper regularly, for example, he or she may develop a preference for that newspaper, even when the initial motivation for reading it was convenience or affordability. Both cognitive dissonance theory and self-perception theory note that the cause of behavior may be entirely unrelated to the individual's attitudes or opinions. While social psychologists generally accept the existence of the "attitude-follows-behavior" phenomenon, some prefer the cognitive dissonance explanation and others prefer the self-perception explanation.

The attitude-follows-behavior phenomenon can help explain the internalization of anti-Semitism and other Nazi attitudes. From the standpoint of self-perception theory, by obeying Nazi laws, reading Nazi newspapers, attending Nazi rallies, voting for Nazis in plebiscites, and taking oaths to Adolf Hitler, many Germans came to believe that they held Nazi attitudes. Viewed from the cognitive dissonance standpoint, by performing Nazi behaviors that were dissonant to non-Nazi attitudes, Germans increased their cognitive dissonance; to reduce this dissonance, they developed consistent Nazi attitudes. Finally, by performing Nazi behaviors *publicly,* they became committed to the behaviors and subsequently needed to develop justifying attitudes. Watching others model the behaviors contributed to the pressure to conform. If people whom you respected were behaving like Nazis, then perhaps such behaviors were not immoral after all. As Professor Kurt Lewin, a refugee from Nazi Germany and a founder of modern social psychology, wrote in 1943:

> While it is correct that change of values will finally lead to a change of social conduct, it is equally correct that changes of action patterns and of actual group life will change cultural values. This indirect change of cultural values probably reaches deeper and is more permanent than direct changes of values by propaganda. There is no need to point out how thoroughly Hitler has understood this fact.[73]

We are left with the question of why Germans initially engaged in Nazi behaviors. The issue of original motives is essential, because not all causes of Nazi behavior would be expected to have the same impact on the ultimate attitude change. The impact will be minimal if a person perceives a clear, external source of his or her action. Only when the original source of the Nazi behavior is subtle or obscure will the above psychological mechanisms operate.

The person who obeyed Nazi laws at the point of a gun would be least likely to internalize Nazi opinions. Thus, if terror alone motivated people to engage in Nazi behavior, the attitude-follows-behavior phenomenon would not be especially helpful in explaining Hitler's rapid rise in popularity. But the assumption of power gave the Nazis many more subtle means of influence. In a totalitarian state, everyday life involves acknowledging the regime to some degree. The Nazis controlled access to the best jobs. They determined school curricula and the content of the news media. If a person wanted to read a newspaper, he or she had to read one that supported the Nazis; there was no alternative. If parents wanted to send their children to school, they sent them to Nazi-regulated schools. If their children returned home with pro-Nazi ideas, they could either speak out against these ideas, and create trouble for their children, or remain silent.

The necessities of everyday life enmeshed Germans in Nazi culture, and, as a result of the attitude-follows-behavior phenomenon, led in many cases to the formation of pro-Nazi attitudes.

The change did not occur overnight. According to the "foot-in-the-door" effect, it is easier to gain compliance with a large request if one first gets someone to go along with a much smaller request. For example, if you want someone to contribute $500 to a cause, have them first agree to a request for $25. Psychologist Ervin Staub speaks of Nazi steps along a "continuum of destruction" against the Jews.[74] Hitler moved against the Jews gradually, first obtaining the German people's assent to relatively "minor" anti-Semitic acts, then more significant ones, and ultimately genocide. The first decrees against the Jews allowed exceptions, such as for Jewish veterans of World War I. Soon all Jews were dismissed from certain jobs. Then came the Aryanization of Jewish businesses. Next followed the Nuremberg laws prohibiting marriage and sexual relations with Jews, and so on. Staub notes:

> Even passivity changes bystanders. But Germans had a semi-active role as they participated in societal actions against Jews. Devaluating Jews even more, regarding them as blame-worthy, would make it easier to watch and passively accept their persecution and suffering and one's own involvement. This, together with a changing self-concept, a view of themselves as capable and willing to harm others for "justified" reasons, prepared some people for increasingly active roles as perpetrators. As people participate in harming others, it becomes increasingly difficult to stop and break the continuity.[75]

Hitler understood this principle of human nature well. He took small steps, pressing onward a bit at a time. From the vantage point of those Germans who did not support his anti-Semitism, the early sanctions proved insufficiently outrageous to mobilize even passive opposition. But, soon, they felt themselves part of the process and soothed their consciences by adjusting psychologically their perceptions of Jewish guilt. According to trial testimony, memoirs, and historical accounts, many of those who participated in the worst anti-Jewish crimes had not been bitter anti-Semites in 1933.

Psychiatrist Henry V. Dicks elaborates on a likely psychological process:

At *first* a person with an averagely humane conscience would condemn himself for [a] lack of moral courage and self-betrayal. This became too intolerable—so the second stage was a denial: surely there had to be *some* truth in what Nazi beliefs he had to assent to in his group. "He was not a hypocrite," he did want to accept what was good. By the time such a person saw, for example, a respected Jew or anti-Nazi "disappear" from his office he had already to say to himself: "Surely I am not supporting criminals—these methods cannot be crimes—they arise from tragic necessities of fate—I am witnessing a great happening in history," etc. . . . [In] the *fourth* phase of spiraling down the scale of de-individualization . . . the painful memory of the injury done to a hitherto respected human being is replaced by dehumanized stereotyped anti-Semitic and prejudiced opinions and utterances.[76]

THE ORIGINS OF MURDEROUSNESS
IN THE HOLOCAUST

The bulk of Germans who supported Hitler before and after his takeover of power do not readily fit any diagnosis of psychological abnormality. Most acted from motives that, while hardly indicative of superior psychological functioning, resemble those of "normal" populations. Though these Germans might have failed a test of democratic responsibility, neighborliness, or moral development, their motives cannot be described accurately as sociopathic, satanic, or evil to the core. During the past three decades, many historians and psychologists have arrived at precisely the same conclusion about the tens of thousands of Nazis who actually planned and carried out the mass murders.

The case of Hans Biebow illustrates this perspective. Biebow had initially hoped to succeed his father in the insurance business. This plan fell apart when the business failed, but Biebow was undeterred. He founded a coffee import company which, by 1939, employed over two hundred people. It was not until 1937, well after Hitler's takeover, that he joined the Nazi party—and one might infer that he did so as a pragmatic move. Soon after the invasion of Poland, he became head of the Office of Food Supply and Economics in the Lodz ghetto—in effect, ghetto manager of a prison for 160,000 Jews. At the urging of Chaim Rumkowski, the controversial head of the Lodz Jewish Council, Biebow successfully advocated transforming the ghetto into a self-supporting work camp—a move that temporarily prevented mass deaths among the Jewish inhabitants. Soon, however, he grew enthused with the prospect of increasing ghetto productivity as a goal in itself; on several occasions, he resisted bringing tens of thousands of additional Jews into the ghetto on grounds that it would diminish the economic efficiency of the operation. And when Biebow discerned the higher-ups' firm commitment to gassing the Jews in death camps, he gave himself over to this project with tremendous energy. He even visited the death camps to ensure the return to Lodz of valuables belonging to "his" Jews and showed considerable interest in the salvage of "human material." By the summer of 1944, Biebow had sent all of Lodz's Jews to the death camps. Though he had not been motivated by anti-Semitism, he never stopped to ask whether there really was a Jewish problem in need of a solution. He never initiated a policy, or even an act, of mass murder. He had never been told specifically of the extermination plans. But he assimilated the policy and, after a few minor objections, made it his own. Never obsessed with hatred and hardly a madman, ambition was the grievous fault of this midlevel bureaucrat.[77] Biebow was not a psychopath, and he did not suffer from any antisocial personality disorder. He simply accepted the prevailing, and legal, moral standards set by his countrymen.

The Holocaust included so many crimes and so many criminals that the entire range of human motives must have come into play at one time or another. Thus, a wide range of theories have been advanced to explain the mindset and behavior of the perpetrators, and many have some truth.

Some Nazis may have been terrified slaves coerced by Hitler's notorious henchmen into doing his dirty work, but they were very, very few. The regime sent outspoken critics to concentration camps; it did not, however, typically imprison or kill those who requested reassignment away from the killing operations. Such a request certainly did not help one's career. On occasion, it may have landed a person in a dangerous military setting, such as the Eastern front. But the historical record contains no references to Germans killed for their refusal to participate directly in the extermination. Though the "work" itself was widely viewed with distaste, the right to perform this duty to the Fatherland was considered a high honor by the members of the SS.[78]

The view of Nazi mass murderers as disturbed people, driven by their pathology to kill, gained popularity immediately after reports and photographs of the death camps began to circulate. At the time, the tendency was to view the Nazis as overwhelmingly similar to each other and different from the rest of us.[79] To investigate this notion, psychologist Gustave Gilbert and psychiatrist Douglas Kelley interviewed the major Nazi war criminals at Nuremberg; the group included Hermann Goering, Baldur von Schirach (head of the Hitler Youth), Ernst Kaltenbrunner (head of the Gestapo, Einsatzgruppen, and death camps), and the other surviving top Nazis in custody. Kelley and Gilbert also assessed their IQs and responses to Rorschach Inkblot Tests.

Perhaps not surprisingly, every one of the top Nazis at Nuremberg scored above the mean (100) in IQ: Schacht (143), Seyss-Inquart (141), Goering (138), Doenitz (138), Papen (134), Raeder (134), Frank (130), Fritsche (130), Schirach (130), Ribbentrop (129), Keitel (129), Speer (128), Jodl (127), Rosenberg (127), Neurath (125), Funk (124), Frick (124), Hoess (120), Sauckel (118), Kaltenbrunner (113), and Streicher (106).[80] Whatever else they were, the Nazi leaders were not stupid, and several, including the boorish Goering, qualified as intellectually gifted.

In the Rorschach procedure, subjects purportedly project their inner lives into responses to a series of ambiguous inkblots. Using a variety of scoring methods, skilled interpreters can then make judgments about the presence and type of psychological abnormality. The Rorschach is a controversial procedure, primarily because the agreement among different interpreters is not as high as one might like.[81] Still, data from the Nuremberg Rorschachs provide one source of insight into the minds of high-level Nazi bureaucrats implicated in the Holocaust.

Kelley and Gilbert asked ten leading experts to interpret the Nuremberg Rorschach results; after receiving the Rorschachs, none of the experts agreed to publicize their findings, perhaps because they anticipated a cool response to their conclusions in the late 1940s. Careful analyses of the Rorschachs appeared several decades later. The study employing the most sophisticated methods started by proving that a panel of judges could, in fact, detect mental disturbances from Rorschach results. But these same judges then concluded that six of eight Nazi war criminals in the study displayed no serious mental disturbance, and that two of these were exceptionally well adjusted. Two of the Nazis, Ribbentrop and Speer, were judged to have "impoverished personalities," but they may have been reacting to the stress of the upcoming trial and the possibility of hanging for their crimes.[82] The researcher did not tell the judges that they were examining Nazi Rorschachs; rather, she asked them whether the subjects were likely to be from any of the following groups: war criminals, middle-class Americans, clergy, political assassins, psychologists, or superior adults in spotlight positions. Most of the judges did not detect commonalities within the Nazi group, but one thought they were middle-class Americans, another well-known superior adults, another military men, and yet another members of the clergy.

After reviewing three major studies of the Nuremberg Rorschachs with great care, Gerald Borofsky and Don Brand of Harvard Medical School concluded in 1980 that "the results to date are such that no major differences between the psychological functioning of the [Nazi war criminals] and the psychological functioning of other comparison groups have yet been demonstrated."[83]

British psychiatrist Henry Dicks conducted in-depth interviews of a sample of lower-level mass murderers and, similarly, rejected the notion that SS killers were "'insane' or uncontrollable people, in any generally understood clinical sense."[84] He further concluded that the men were not driven to their crimes by a particularly intense anti-Semitism. Historian Christopher Browning's sensitive case studies of midlevel bureaucrats and low-level police-killers led him to similar conclusions.[85]

Were the Nazis sadists and brutes? When one recalls the testimony of death camp survivors, it becomes difficult to conclude otherwise. In a book prepared for German high school students, Hannah Vogt summarizes survivor portraits of inmate life:

> Blows, beatings and kickings were part of the daily routine, so much so that one of the accused camp-torturers declared during his trial that such measures did not constitute mistreatment! Prisoners had to do "gymnastics" until they fainted with exhaustion, or, for hours on end, had to give the Saxon salute, i.e. remain in a deep knee-bend with arms laced behind their heads. These were merely the harmless "jokes" indulged in by the camp guards. Prisoners were whipped for the slightest offense—or for none at all. . . .
>
> Prisoners disliked by the guards were arbitrarily selected for injections . . . which means they were murdered through injections of Phenol or Evipan, only one of a number of methods of killing. Prisoners were often trampled to death with nailed boots, or drowned in cesspools, or driven into the elec-

trically charged barbed-wire fences of the camps, or, in an especially bestial manner, hosed to death with high-pressure water hoses.[86]

Far from requiring these tortures, the Nazi hierarchy sometimes frowned upon them, though little was done to prevent gratuitous cruelty. The camp guards were fulfilling a sacred duty to rid Europe of the enemies of the Reich, and were, at least in theory, expected to do so with the dignity and professionalism of a soldier.

In one sense, simply participating in such acts qualifies a person as a sadist. Yet some evidence contradicts the notion that the majority of guards had sadistic tendencies that pervaded their lives. Most of the guards exhibited total willingness to act brutally to fulfill their orders, but only a minority appeared to thrive on cruelty. Few sought out assignments in the camps. Ella Lingens, a physician imprisoned at Auschwitz, testified that "there were few sadists. Not more than 5 or 10 percent were pathological criminals in the clinical sense. The others were all perfectly normal men who knew the difference between right and wrong."[87] Of course, it is impossible to calculate reliably the percentage of sadists in the death camps, and some former prisoners offer substantially higher estimates. Yet, another physician imprisoned at Auschwitz, the noted psychiatrist Viktor Frankl, even recalls some guards who were capable of acting with genuine kindness toward inmates.[88] The overwhelming majority of the guards, including the ones who acted brutally, were not sadists outside the context of the camps, and, after the war, did not engage in criminal behavior. Many behaved with great kindness toward their families, children, friends, and subordinates. A few experienced trying bouts of guilt. The leaders of the Einsatzgruppen, the mobile killing squads that operated behind Hitler's armies in the Soviet Union, also showed few signs of sadism before or after their brief careers as mass murderers.[89] Few of the "ordinary men" of Reserve Police Battalion 101, who, by their own hands, killed tens of thousands of Jews, enjoyed participation in acts of cruelty.[90]

For a small number of murderers, however, the Holocaust may have been the nirvana for which they had been waiting. They may have possessed a lust for murder which, in normal times, had remained submerged but which, under the Nazi regime, found opportunity for expression. In some cases, virulent anti-Semites, particularly Nazified Germans living beyond the borders of the Reich and some non-Germans from

Lithuania and elsewhere in Eastern Europe, jumped eagerly at the opportunity to join the genocide; they were not generically sadistic, but rather were driven by their hostility against a particular segment of humanity.

Freud wrote widely about the aggressive instinct and mankind's ambivalent effort to rein it in; for him, the veneer of civilization was thin, and innate, brutal urges pushed hard to break through.[91] The Holocaust does not confirm this view for humanity in general, but the death camps and Einsatzgruppen did give license to a deep urge for cruelty in at least a small percentage of the perpetrators. As psychoanalyst Erich Fromm put it, "people with a sadistic character wait for the opportunity to behave sadistically, just as people with a loving character wait for the opportunity to express their love."[92]

Members of the SS committed most of the war crimes, and this gives rise to another explanation of Nazi murderousness.[93] Originally a bodyguard unit for Hitler, the SS, under the leadership of Heinrich Himmler, became, in 1934, the most reliable enforcer of Hitler's schemes. Its first major task was to attack and destroy the power of its rival, the SA. From the outset, the SS membership displayed a willingness to strike against fellow Germans. Throughout the years of the regime, the scope of its activities and power continued to increase. The Nazis presented the SS as the elite of Germany, and, in 1936, Hitler set the organization above conventional law and established independent "courts of honor" to regulate it. Members often came from privileged backgrounds, and to ensure the organization's racial purity, were required to document Aryan blood back to 1750.

Recruits received rigorous training in the norms and values of the SS, central among which were obedience and loyalty to Adolf Hitler. Every aspect of a member's life belonged to, and was overseen by, the organization. Even marriages had to be approved to ensure the continued purity of the blood. Such a life-style appealed greatly to many of its members. Some had been attracted by an intense sympathy with Nazi values, and some by the opportunity to fill a military or pseudomilitary role during peacetime. Most realized that membership in the SS conferred considerable material advantages. The SS member would do Hitler's dirty work without question, with total loyalty, and with great efficiency; and the Party would confer great rewards upon him—the higher the rank, the more the payment. For most SS members, however, the appeal of the organization went far beyond materialism. According to sociologist and death camp survivor John Steiner, who conducted interviews with former SS members, membership in the SS provided, for many, a "kind of therapy for damaged identity" and "a transition . . . from a state of existential angst to a therapeutic sense of esprit de corps."[94] When these men were called upon to fulfill the Final Solution, they did not think to rebel. The SS presented the task as distasteful work that had to be done. They accepted it as such. Years earlier, they had surrendered a large part of their individuality to the organization.

But not only the SS committed murders, and the success of the organization's socialization processes is, at best, an incomplete explanation. The SS put tremendous effort into shaping its members, but many people seemed willing to participate in the Final Solution on the basis of much less intense socialization.

The prevailing sense of good and evil became inverted in the wartime Nazi state. Hannah Arendt, the philosopher, political scientist, and formulator of the "banality of evil" thesis notes:

> [J]ust as the law in civilized countries assumes that the voice of conscience tells everybody "Thou shalt not kill," even though man's natural desires and inclinations may at times be murderous, so the law of Hitler's land demanded that the voice of conscience tell everybody: "Thou shalt kill," although the organizers of the massacres knew full well that murder is against the normal desires and inclinations of most people. Evil in the Third Reich had lost the quality by which most people recognize it—the quality of temptation.:[95]

To the extent that this moral upheaval transpired, one did not need extraordinary qualities to become a mass killer. Ordinary ones were sufficient.

Eichmann probably was not the best example of the "banal" killer. He possessed extraordinary cunning, unusual drive, a deeper-than-typical attachment to Hitler, and a total commitment to the goal of ridding Europe of its Jews.[96] Still, many Germans, for example, Hans Biebow, did not require seething hatred to become involved in crimes against the Jews.

Many rolled slowly down a slippery slope that began with an acquiescence in minor acts against the designated victims and culminated in active implementation of a policy of mass murder. They slid easily because their society had been preparing them gradually through anti-Semitic traditions, an emphasis on obedience, and weak moral training. Arch-careerism may have been a significant motivator as well; with the Nazis in control of the state's ability to confer status, wealth, and power, Germans often gave themselves over to the mass murder project as a means of protecting or advancing their careers.

At his trial, Eichmann maintained that his participation as a principal architect of the destruction of Europe's Jewry was, in essence, an accident; almost anyone could have taken his place.[97] This does not square well with the obsessive dedication he applied to his task. But he, and many of the other Nazi war criminals, justified their deeds in terms of a devotion to duty that they could not bring themselves to question. The Nazis had taken this virtue of the Prussian soldier and elevated it to the highest of all moral principles. Not all Germans accepted the apotheosis of obedience to authority, but many did, especially in the SS.

Even so, Germans who participated in the mass killings experienced severe stress. This was the result of an inability to reconcile their deeds with what remained of their Christian values. For those who shared the regime's passionate animosity toward the Jews, the dissonance was more manageable; they accepted the goals of the extermination policy and only had to come to terms with the gory methods. Blood and guts disturb even the most devoted ideologue, witness Heinrich Himmler's nausea on visiting one of the death camps. Germans who did not detest Jews faced an even more wrenching psychological problem. Thus, among the Einsatzgruppen killers and, to a lesser extent among the concentration camp guards, alcoholism and burnout abounded.

Yet many persisted in committing brutal crimes in the context of lives that otherwise seemed fairly normal. Perhaps this was possible because they adopted a number of psychological mechanisms of defense. These mechanisms, suggested by the psychoanalysts, blunt human feelings and protect people from the psychologically harmful consequences of their actions. Some killers probably used "dissociation," whereby they compartmentalized their mental existence and allowed their evil deeds to be carried out by a portion of their personality that they regarded as separate. In dissociation's most extreme form, "doubling," a person psychologically creates a second self, related to the first, but functioning more or less autonomously. Thus, a person could behave with great gentleness toward family, friends, children, or neighbors in the morning and then exterminate a hundred Jews in the afternoon without sensing any inconsistency.[98] Psychiatrist Robert Jay Lifton speaks of Nazi doctors creating an "Auschwitz self" to perform inhumane experiments and to divest themselves of any sense of responsibility for their destructive behavior.[99] Another mechanism of defense actually increased the brutality of concentration camp guards. Participation in the killing left many SS men feeling anxious and unsettled; this they attributed to the Jews, who obviously had little power to defend themselves. To balance the situation, they struck aggressively against the perceived source of their discontent.[100]

The Nazi killers also used other tactics to deny responsibility for actions they carried out on a daily basis, sometimes at the urging and instruction of the SS leadership. They made copious use of euphemisms; for example, describing their Einsatzgruppen murders in the Soviet Union as "a cleaning-up operation" or "securing the army's rear." They projected moral responsibility upward to Himmler or the Führer. They focused only on their small piece of the killing operation (i.e., "I only arranged the transports"). They "convicted" the victims of imaginary or immaterial offenses; for example, trying to steal food, trying to escape, plotting terrorism, and the like. Psychologically, the killers distanced themselves from the responsibility for murder to the point that they could see themselves as the true victims. This strategy of self-pity was perhaps the most pathetic. Said one Gestapo leader: "I protested when it was suggested that our men became sexually excited . . . at these executions. . . . It is regrettable that over and above this unsavoury work . . . we also have mud slung at us when we are merely doing our duty."[101]

In sum, Nazis killed for many reasons. Only a few murdered because they were terrified slaves and even fewer had serious mental disorders in the clinical sense. Some were evil-to-the-core sadists who regarded their assignments as fortunate and enjoyed the opportunity to brutalize their victims; among these, many discovered their penchant for brutality only after their assignment to a killing post. Brutality, in itself, may have been on some occasions an attempt to strike psychologically at the perceived cause of the killers' anxiety. Almost nobody became a killer overnight; most responded to years of socialization, first in anti-Semitic pre-Nazi Germany, then under Hitler's authoritarian system, and often as members of the SS. Gradually, killers came to classify Jews as enemies or, at least, as expendable; they also came to accept murder as a suitable means for resolving this "Jewish problem." However, few of the killers can be distinguished from other Germans on the basis of their commitment to anti-Semitism. Some, like Goebbels, Eichmann, and Himmler, stood apart by virtue of their commitment to Hitler. Most often, ordinary motives led human beings to become mass murderers in Nazi Germany. Ambition and uncontrollable devotion were the principal culprits. Any personal impediments to participation in the genocide were defanged finally by an unquestioning willingness to follow the orders of those higher up.[102]

Social scientists often downplay the role of choice. The Holocaust, however, was the culmination of many choices by millions of Germans. Tens of millions made a Faustian bargain when they gave their votes to Hitler; he made no secret of his hostility to the Jews or his willingness to launch a new war. Whether their support derived from misguided patriotism, political anger, or economic self-interest, they cast their ballots willingly. Hitler's ascension to power forced millions more to decide where they stood, and most chose a position at Hitler's side. Opposition had become costly, but most Germans even failed to maintain neutrality. Some viewed Hitler's programs as successful, and some started marching with the Nazis to retain their economic and social status. They could have chosen differently. Their failure to foresee the consequences of their choices does not free them from responsibility; the writing was on the wall. And, as to the tens of thousands who participated directly in the murders, they did so as a consequence of their choices. Eichmann was correct that millions could have replaced him. They would, no doubt, have chosen the devotion to career, duty, and authority over the moral injunction against murdering innocents, especially innocent Jews.

The Power of
the Situation

*OUR APPRECIATION OF HOW HARD IT IS TO DO RIGHT WHEN
FATE AND CIRCUMSTANCES CONSPIRE TO TRICK US CANNOT OB-
SCURE THE FACT THAT THE MEASURE OF HUMAN NATURE IS OUR
CAPACITY TO DO WHAT IS RIGHT AND RESIST WHAT IS WRONG.*[1]*

John Sabini and Maury Silver,
Social Psychologists

"If a system of death camps were set up in the United States of the
sort we had seen in Nazi Germany, one would be able to find sufficient
personnel for those camps in any medium-sized American town."[2] So
suggested Professor Stanley Milgram, not on the basis of armchair cynicism or hostility toward American culture, but as the considered verdict
of one of the best designed and most influential research programs in the
history of American psychology. Milgram's obedience studies dramatically reshaped the way many social scientists thought about Nazism,
genocide, and the human capacity to commit mass atrocities.[3] His book,
Obedience to Authority, has been translated into German, French, Japanese, Dutch, Danish, Italian, Spanish, Swedish, Portuguese, Indonesian,
and Serbo-Croatian. His experiments were the subject of a 1976 television
drama, *The Tenth Level*, starring William Shatner. There is even a home
page on the World Wide Web, www.stanleymilgram.com.

After Milgram's research in the early 1960s, few psychologists would confidently assert that monstrous acts required monstrous actors. Many found themselves agreeing with Adolf Eichmann when he protested, "I am not the monster I am made out to be. I am the victim of a fallacy."[4] More generally, Milgram dealt a severe blow to the notion that humans behave in ways consistent with their character and personal morality. So powerful were his conclusions that a South African court accepted "obedience to authority" as one extenuating factor in a trial where thirteen defendants were accused of committing murder as part of a mob; nine were saved from the death penalty.[5]

There was nothing startling about Milgram's finding that typical Connecticut residents were ready to obey without question the orders of an authority which they perceived as legitimate. What was unexpected was the *potency* of this impulse to obey, leading people to override moral restraints, personal feelings, and any sense of justice to inflict potentially lethal shocks on a totally innocent, unobjectionable person.

Milgram's obedience studies and related research by other social psychologists have formed the core of an influential psychological approach to the origin of mass atrocities. In his book, Milgram cites C. P. Snow's comment that "When you think of the long and gloomy history of man, you will find more hideous crimes have been committed in the name of obedience than have ever been committed in the name of rebellion."[6] Milgram clearly had the Holocaust in mind. Although he acknowledged some differences between his experimental design and the Nazi environment, he believed that the situations were alike in their essential features. He wrote that "[t]he Nazi extermination of European Jews is the most extreme instance of abhorrent immoral acts carried out by thousands of people in the name of obedience."[7] In the years since Milgram's research, "obedience to authority" has been invoked frequently as an explanation of why people have participated in mass atrocities in Argentina, Rwanda, Bosnia, Cambodia, and My Lai.[8]

This approach makes several claims. First, obedience rather than personal aggression lies at the heart of most organized human destructiveness. Second, without obedience, the hateful ideas of individuals could never be transformed into large-scale policies. Third, although personality, social class, and individual background may influence slightly the likelihood of obedience, the impulse to obey is extremely widespread, cutting across era, sex, culture, nationality, educational level, religious affiliation, and personality type. Fourth, people obey because they enter an "agentic state" in which they relinquish personal responsibility to an authority whom they perceive as legitimate; thus, the likelihood of obedience depends far more on the relationship to the authority figure than on the nature of the command. Fifth, people who obey evil commands do so mainly because they are overwhelmed by the situations in which they find themselves, and not because they lack character or appropriate morality.

Back in 1913, the behaviorist psychologist John B. Watson aroused much controversy with his famous contention:

> Give me a dozen healthy infants, well-formed, and my own specified world to bring them up in and I'll guarantee to take any one at random and train him to become any type of specialist I might select—doctor, lawyer, artist, merchant-chief, and, yes, even beggar-man and thief, regardless of his talents, penchants, tendencies, abilities, vocations, and race of his ancestors.[9]

The "obedience" model of human destructiveness seems to suggest an even more malleable humanity, never more than a few steps from the most sinister of deeds. It would not take America's leading psychologists years to shape a thief, or a murderer. The typical person, even the typical psychologist, might already be a potential murderer, ready to spring into action if the wrong circumstances happened along.

The moral consequences of this position are troubling. If Serbian rapists, Hutu machete-wielders, and Nazi death camp commandants differ from average citizens in Western democracies principally by virtue of having been in the wrong place at the wrong time, by what right can the rest of us condemn them? And if by carrying out orders dutifully, they merely acted on a fundamental human tendency, can anything but amoral pragmatism justify their punishment?

This "situationist" or "killer-by-accident" approach initially flies in the face of intuition. Though this explanation is uniquely popular with perpetrators of atrocities, most people cannot imagine that the murder of hundreds of thousands in Rwanda did not require large numbers of hateful, immoral killers. The idea that the killers simply obeyed orders out of a mindless sense of duty seems implausible. Similarly, most people find it difficult to believe that the Bosnian Serbs who raped Muslim women were "just following orders."

Proponents of the "situationist" approach argue, however, that the counterintuitive nature of the theory is explainable. Dozens of studies conducted during the past three decades suggest that people generally underestimate the importance of circumstances, and overestimate the significance of personal dispositions, in attempting to explain why people do things. This bias, "the fundamental attribution error," leads people to infer automatically that a person does good things because he or she has desirable traits and bad things because he or she has undesirable ones, even if circumstances exert a powerful pressure to act one way or another.[10] Thus, the preference for attributing participation in atrocities to an evil, hateful, or even obedient *nature* is entirely consistent with the way human beings typically explain events. As a result, people may be predisposed by their cognitive makeup to endorse such personality-based explanations even when there is little evidence to support them.

The "obedience to authority" interpretation of mass atrocities squares well with the "banality of evil" argument crafted by Hannah Arendt in her book on the Eichmann trial. In fact, her portrayal of Eichmann as a relatively-free-from-hatred, order-obeying, everyday Hans fits so neatly with the Milgram perspective that many psychologists have been a bit too eager to accept Arendt's credentials as the definitive historian of Nazi motivation.[11] They have also relied too much on the case of Adolf Eichmann, who is cited as proof of historical relevance whenever the obedience studies are mentioned. The Milgram studies can be, and have been, used to explain every situation where orders to kill were issued and obeyed. During the Spring of 1992 and at various times throughout the war in Bosnia, some Bosnian Serb commanders issued orders to terrorize and rape civilians. Captured perpetrators have explained that they were "just following orders," a position accepted by many commentators. Similarly, imprisoned Hutu from the Interahamwe and Impuzamugambe militias in Rwanda have pleaded that they had little choice but to obey the orders of their superiors to kill Tutsi and moderate Hutu. The murderers in Cambodia, Argentina, and East Timor all acted in a manner consistent with orders given by authorities whom they could reasonably judge legitimate. Lieutenant Calley used the "obedience to authority" defense during the trials concerning the My Lai massacre, and a large portion of the American public judged his defense appropriate.[12]

Still, it is by no means obvious that the Milgram approach applies to these situations. One may, after all, follow orders for a variety of reasons, including fear of retribution, agreement with the orders, hatred of the victims, and desire for career advancement. Milgram's study did not focus on any of these forces. Social scientists also may have been too gullible about what was, in fact, the only defense available to captured perpetrators of mass evil. More than three decades have passed since Milgram's initial studies; his main findings have been replicated by others around the world at least forty times, and his approach remains extremely influential. During these three decades, however, historians have expanded, enriched, refined, and modified our understanding of Nazi motivation. It is time to reassess the "obedience," and related "situationist," orientations, focusing especially on their relevance to Nazism and more recent mass atrocities in Rwanda, Bosnia, and elsewhere.

LESSONS FROM THE LABORATORY

What really matters is not who you are, but where you are. Study after study in the social psychological laboratory has seemed to hammer home this unsettling message. In one of the earliest demonstrations, the classic Asch study in the 1950s, people believed that they were about to participate in a study of visual perception. In a series of trials, they were shown three lines and asked to identify the one that best matched another line in length. The task was a very easy one and solo participants had little difficulty with it. The outcome changed dramatically, however, when subjects judged the lines *as part of a small group.* Without telling the subjects, the experimenter employed stooges, who were instructed to give obviously incorrect answers in some instances. After the first stooge gave the wrong answer, the subject typically giggled nervously or otherwise expressed disbelief at the blatant error. But after all the other participants, a total of six to eight people, echoed the incorrect response, the subject faced a dilemma—conform to the unanimous majority, or stand alone.

Fifty to eighty percent of the participants, depending on particular conditions, yielded at least once to the erring crowd. Only a minority of the subjects maintained their independence throughout the trials, never bending to group pressure. The study, repeated many times in dozens of variations around the world, shows the power a group can exert on individuals. Even a very small group can elicit conformity to a unanimous verdict. When issues are more ambiguous than the line judgments in the Asch study, higher rates of conformity are observed.

Though many people conform to views inconsistent with their private perceptions, the message is *not* that people are "sheep." For one thing, the urge to conform is partly rational much of the time because a unanimous majority may possess additional information or a better understanding of the situation; under such conditions, a deferral to group pressure may result in a more accurate judgment. More important, people will defend a minority view against an overwhelming majority under some circumstances. As long as one other person sides with the dissenter, conformity rates drop off very sharply and dissenters become much more common. The studies on conformity suggest that many people do have the courage of their convictions, but on an occasional basis rather than a consistent one. Differences in personality have something to do with who conforms and who doesn't. But, much of the time, it is the situation, rather than an underlying personality or disposition, that determines who will stick to their guns.[13]

Another laboratory demonstration of the power of the situation concerns how people decide whether or not an emergency exists. In a simple but poignant study, an experimenter left Columbia University students in a room to fill out a questionnaire; soon afterward, a stream of smoke poured into the room through a wall vent eventually filling the entire room. When the subjects had been alone in the room, 75 percent left to report the smoke. When two other subjects also had been in the room, 38 percent reported the smoke. But when the two other participants were stooges told to remain passive and continue working, only 10 percent of the subjects left to report the smoke. Thus, students who watched other subjects resume work on the questionnaires after noticing the smoke were apt to conclude that everything was okay. They displayed what psychologists call "pluralistic ignorance," a phenomenon where bystanders assume that nothing is wrong because nobody else appears panic-stricken. Subjects were most likely to decide that an emergency existed and to act on this decision when they were left alone in the room. Yet the students who participated in the group settings showed little awareness that the presence of others had influenced their own behavior.

In another experiment, subjects heard someone whom they believed to be a fellow participant having an epileptic seizure while talking to them over an intercom. Eighty-five percent of subjects intervened when the experimental setup led them to believe that nobody else was listening. When subjects thought one other person could hear the seizure, the intervention rate dropped to 62 percent. And when they believed a total of five people could hear the person in need, only 31 percent intervened. Circumstances again overpowered character, this time in determining who would offer help to a person in need.

In another study on bystander intervention, seminary students were asked to speak to a group of high school students. On a random basis, some seminarians were told that they had plenty of time to get across campus to the event while others were put on a tight schedule. Along the way, the seminarians observed a young man collapse in front of them; some helped, and some did not. But the matter cannot be reduced to how well they had learned morality lessons in the seminary. Those with a tight schedule found intervention too costly, in the sense that helping would make them late for the speaking engagement. Those with ample time judged assisting the stranger in need a deed eminently worthy of seminarians. In a telling touch, the experimenters had asked some of the future religious leaders to address the high school students on why they had chosen to enter the seminary, while others were asked to lecture on the parable of the Good Samaritan—the New Testament hero who assisted a fellow traveler who had been beaten and robbed. This seemingly relevant variable, what was on the subject's mind, didn't make a bit of difference.

In all three experiments on altruism, circumstances—the situation in which one found oneself—proved more powerful than personality, values, or character. As in the case of the conformity studies, the most likely conclusion is not that the subjects, or people in general, lack an impulse to help strangers. In the first two studies, the presence of others led to a diffusion of responsibility that did not occur for solo participants. In the seminary study, the costliness in time of the intervention proved prohibitive.[14]

Milgram's research on obedience grew out of his desire to know whether the conformity observed in Solomon Asch's line judgment study would occur in matters of more apparent human significance. As part of his doctoral dissertation at Harvard, he had reenacted the Asch study, except that subjects were asked to determine which of two acoustic tones was the longer and they were told that results would be applied to the design of aircraft safety signals. Thus, he linked participants' performance in the study to a life-and-death issue. This did not mitigate the impact of group pressure. Milgram's results confirmed Asch's findings, and, because he did the research in Norway and France, accumulated some evidence for their cross-cultural generalizability.[15]

As a consequence of this study, Milgram grew even more curious about the limits of group influence. He recalls conceiving the famous obedience experiment while working for Asch at Princeton University:

> Could a group, I asked myself, induce a person to act with severity against another person? . . . I envisioned a situation very much like Asch's experiment in which there would be a number of confederates and one naive subject, and instead of confronting the lines on a card, each one of them would have a shock generator. In other words, I transformed Asch's experiment into one in which the group would administer increasingly higher levels of shock to a person, and the question would be to what degree an individual would follow along with the group.[16]

But to assess the power of group pressure, Milgram needed to know, for comparative purposes, how far a person would go *without* group influence. To obtain this information, the experimenter would have to tell the subject to give progressively higher shocks, in order to determine the level at which the subject would refuse to comply. Milgram ultimately did explore the impact of group influence, but he immediately recognized the phenomenon of individual obedience to the experimenter-authority figure as important in its own right. A review of Milgram's experiment will serve to highlight some salient details.

Participants responded to direct mail solicitations as well as an ad placed in local papers seeking persons for a study of memory and learning. The initial studies called for subjects between the ages of twenty and fifty, and did not use high school students, college students, or women, although subsequent studies did. Significantly, Milgram used participants from many different socioeconomic backgrounds, including postal clerks, high school teachers, salesmen, laborers, and professionals. As soon as they arrived at the Interaction Laboratory at Yale University, each received four dollars plus fifty cents carfare—an amount equivalent to considerably more in contemporary dollars.

Milgram hired two confederates to assist with the experiment, a thirty-one-year-old high school biology teacher who played the part of the experimenter, and a forty-seven-year-old, mild-mannered accountant who played the learner-victim. Both were white males. Most observers judged the experimenter as stern looking, but considered the learner-victim quite likable.

After discussing some theoretical matters briefly to increase the plausibility of the ruse, the experimenter told the subject (and the confederate) that the purpose of the study was to "find out just what effect different people have on each other as teachers and learners, and also what effect *punishment* will have on learning in this situation."[17] The experimenter then conducted a drawing to determine who would be the teacher and who the learner; it was, of course, rigged so the subject always would end up as the teacher and the confederate as the learner. The experimenter then took the teacher and the learner to an adjacent room where the learner was strapped into an "electric chair" apparatus.

Milgram built into the procedure many touches designed to insure that the subject would believe the ruse, especially that the shocks were real. For example, the experimenter explained that the straps on the chair would prevent the learner from moving excessively while he was being shocked. The electrode paste would avoid blisters and burns. In response to a question by the learner, the experimenter noted that, "Although the shocks can be extremely painful, they cause no permanent tissue damage."[18] In addition, each *subject* received a *genuine,* "sample" shock of forty-five volts prior to beginning his role as teacher. The shock generator itself had a scary appearance; its instrument panel consisted of thirty switches in a horizontal line, indicating voltages from fifteen to four hundred fifty at fifteen volt increments. Beneath the voltage designations, the panel read "Slight Shock," followed by "Moderate Shock," "Strong Shock," "Very Strong Shock," "Intense Shock," "Extreme Intensity Shock," "Danger: Severe Shock," and ominously, "XXX." Lights, buzzing, and appropriate clicks were activated whenever the subject depressed a switch.

In the basic version of the experiment, the teacher and learner are in separate but adjacent rooms. When the learner-confederate failed at his task, which he did in a prearranged pattern, the experimenter told the teacher-subject to administer a shock. Moreover, he instructed the teacher to "move one level higher on the shock generator each time the learner gives a wrong answer."[19] Thus, Milgram could see how far teacher-subjects would go in delivering shocks to the learner-victims in response to the experimenter's demands.

The teacher had good reason to believe that the learner actually received the shocks. At seventy-five, ninety, and one hundred five volts, the learner emitted small grunts. At one hundred twenty, he shouted that the shocks were becoming painful. At one hundred fifty, he demanded that the experimenter let him out. By two hundred seventy, his aggravated grunts had become "agonized screams." Three hundred volts sparked a revolt with the learner refusing to participate, but the experimenter told the teacher to treat "no answer" as an incorrect answer. The learner no longer provided answers, but screamed after the shocks. At three hundred forty five, the screams too disappeared. From this point on, until the four hundred fifty volt level, nothing was heard from the victim.[20]

The experimental design also called for the experimenter to use a series of prods, should the teacher-subject request guidance or refuse to continue. First, he would say, "Please continue." Next, "The experiment requires that you continue." Then, "It is absolutely essential that you continue." Finally, "You have no other choice, you *must* go on."[21]

How far would people go? Asked to predict their own behavior in a similar experimental situation, none of a typical group of middle-class adults believed they would continue to administer shocks beyond the three hundred volt, "Intense Shock" level; the average predicted break-off point was about one hundred fifty volts, the level labeled "Strong Shock." When groups of college students and psychiatrists at a leading medical school were asked to estimate their own behavior in the described set-up, they offered similar guesses. The psychiatrists also predicted that most people would not go beyond the one hundred fifty volt level, at which the learner-victim would first ask to be excused from the remainder of the study. The psychiatrists further maintained that only one person in a thousand would go all the way to the highest level—450 volts, labeled "XXX".

They were very wrong. More than six people in ten (62.5%) delivered the highest level of voltage, ignoring the printed warnings of danger as

well as the screams and protestations of the victim. Out of forty participants in this version of the experiment, not a single one stopped before
the "Strong Shock" level. The average maximum shock exceeded three
hundred sixty volts, just below the "Danger: Severe Shock" level. Remember, the subjects didn't hate the victims; they didn't even dislike them. In
fact, most of those who persisted in delivering the shocks to the very end
did so with great reluctance. They asked for permission to discontinue the
shocks and they called the experimenter's attention to the victim's suffering. They obeyed, but not because of aggression.

Milgram notes:

> Many people, not knowing much about the experiment, claim that subjects
> who go to the end of the board are sadistic. Nothing could be more foolish
> than an overall characterization of these persons. It is like saying that a per-
> son thrown into a swift-flowing stream is necessarily a fast swimmer, or that
> he has great stamina because he moves so rapidly relative to the bank. The
> context of action must always be considered. The individual, upon entering
> the laboratory, becomes integrated into a situation that carries its own mo-
> mentum. The subject's problem then is how to become disengaged from a
> situation which is moving in an altogether ugly direction.[22]

Milgram proceeded to explore the impact of different situations on levels of obedience, using a new group of similar subjects for every condition. The following are among his many findings. When the victim remains in the same room as the subject, obedience diminishes, but 40
percent of subjects still deliver the highest voltage. Even when the teacher-
subject must force the victim's hand onto a metal plate in order to shock
him, 30 percent go on to the bitter end. In one variation, a soft, nonag-
gressive person replaced the stern biology teacher as experimenter and a
tough guy was substituted for the victim; the impact on obedience was
very slight—50 percent still delivered the highest shock. When women
participants delivered the shocks, their performance paralleled that of the
men. When the victim mentioned a heart condition and then protested
that his heart was beginning to bother him, there was absolutely no impact on the level of obedience.

Some observers commented that, whatever one might think about Yale
University, it was implausible that such an austere institution would per-

mit the murder of experimental subjects. Sensitive to such criticism, Milgram moved the experiment to an ordinary office building and conducted the study under the auspices of "Research Associates of Bridgeport." Obedience dropped off a little, but nearly half of the participants still delivered the highest level of voltage. When a confederate of the experimenter pulled the switch and the subject merely had to assist in a subsidiary task, only three subjects out of forty refused involvement as an accomplice to the evil act.

Still, some situations led to a considerable reduction in the level of shocks delivered. When, for example, the experimenter instructed the teacher to give whatever shock he or she thought appropriate, the majority chose very low voltage levels, and almost none continued beyond the first protest by the victim. This variation indicates that subjects in the other conditions were not using the shock machine to release personal, pent-up aggression. In another variation, the experimenter told the subject to stop after the *victim* screamed in pain, but the victim then demanded to be shocked in order to reassert his manliness; here, the subjects generally refused to administer shocks. In yet another version, when the experimenter left the laboratory and continued to give his orders by phone, obedience dropped substantially, with only about 20 percent going to the end. And when two experimenter-authority figures disagreed about whether to continue shocking the victim, none of the subjects took advantage of the opportunity to deliver the shocks—all stopped almost immediately after the disagreement. Finally, when subjects participated as part of a group responsible for delivering the shocks, very few would agree to continue after their peers (confederates of the experimenter) had rebelled.

Milgram concluded from this research that "[t]he force exerted by the moral sense of the individual is less effective than social myth would have us believe."[23] It's not that people lack empathy or moral feelings. On the contrary, Milgram notes that most of the participants felt terrible about inflicting pain on an innocent victim. But people could not muster the resources necessary to disobey. Though they wanted to do the right thing, enormous anxiety prevented them from standing up to the experimenter. There was no fear of punishment. But they had absorbed a firm rule from their social surroundings: thou shalt not violate the orders of a legitimate authority figure. According to Milgram, "Men who are in everyday life responsible and decent were seduced by the trappings of authority, by the control of their perceptions, and by the uncritical acceptance of the experimenter's definition of the situation, into performing harsh acts."[24] By bringing the victim closer and making his suffering more apparent, some people could be induced to disobey. And by rendering the authority figure less credible or less legitimate, one could increase the incidence of disobedience. But once a subject entered an "agentic state" in which he or she relinquished authority to another, the subject would most likely do as told. Equally important, the subject would continue to deliver higher and higher shocks, in order to evade responsibility for shocks already given. Breaking off would require the subject to acknowledge, in effect, that everything done until the stopping point was bad. But continuing with the procedure can permit the subject to avoid any uncomfortable realizations about the morality of his or her past performance.[25]

Oddly enough, *etiquette* plays a crucial role in sustaining obedience: it would be rude to challenge the authority figure. One does not do such things. In one of his classes, Milgram proposed to students in New York City that they ask strangers on the subway to give up their seats—without using any initial justification, like "I'm feeling nauseous," "I'm dizzy," or "I'm doing a psychology experiment." All students but one were unable to carry out the assignment; the one who did claimed it was among the most difficult things he had done in his life. Milgram himself initially felt overwhelmed by "paralyzing inhibition."[26] When finally he managed to make the request, the seated man got right up. But the learned professor immediately dropped his head between his knees and turned pale. In effect, his ill behavior restored the etiquette of the situation. A healthy male does not ask for someone else's seat, but a sick one might.

This episode demonstrates the enormous power of unspoken social rules that govern our lives. For Milgram, these rules provide a key to why people pulled the switches in the obedience experiment. He explains, "Embarrassment and the fear of violating apparently trivial norms often lock us into intolerable predicaments."[27]

All commands are not equally effective in inducing obedience. A person must judge an order consistent with the role of the authority figure. Thus, the experimenter must concoct a pretext that is, at a minimum, superficially credible to the subject. In the obedience study, the experimenter orders harm to others in the name of noble science. No one has tested the idea, but subjects probably would not have obeyed an order to steal five bucks from a victim's wallet or to urinate on the floor—unless offered a suitable pretext. On the other hand, as Milgram notes, Masters and Johnson routinely were obeyed when they requested women to masturbate in the context of studies on sexual response.[28] The key issue appears to be whether the nature of the order undermines a person's perception of the legitimacy of the experimenter. In the obedience experiment, people apparently show a willingness to accept the idea that a legitimate scientist might order the infliction of pain on innocents in the pursuit of scientific truth.

Not everyone agrees with Milgram's explanation of why people pulled the lever.[29] Some, like psychologists Martin Orne and Charles Holland, believe various subtle cues give away the deception and tip off that the *teacher* is the real subject of the experiment. The weirdly passive and imperturbable behavior of the experimenter, for example, might suggest that nobody is really being hurt. They ask:

[H]ow different this experiment is from the stage magician's trick where a volunteer from the audience is strapped into the guillotine and another volunteer is required to trip the release lever. The magician is careful to do a professional job of deception. He demonstrates that the guillotine will split a head of cabbage and allows the volunteer to satisfy himself about the genuineness of the guillotine. Though releasing the lever will lead to the apparently inevitable decapitation of the victim, he has little difficulty in obtaining "obedience" because the [subject] knows full well that everything is going to be all right. This does not, of course, prevent the [subject] from being somewhat uncomfortable, perhaps showing nervous laughter, when he is actually required to trip the lever, if only because such behavior is appropriate in this context.[30]

Orne and another colleague asked subjects to throw "fuming nitric acid" into a person's face, telling them that their task was to behave "as if" they were hypnotized. Under some circumstances they obtained high levels of compliance—for a different reason, they conclude, than that suggested by Milgram. When an experimenter asks someone to carry out a dangerous and destructive task, he or she may simultaneously communicate that it would really be safe to do so.[31]

Milgram objected strenuously to this line of argument. "Orne's suggestion that the subjects only *feigned* sweating, trembling, and stuttering to please the experimenter is pathetically detached from reality, equivalent to the statement that hemophiliacs bleed to keep their physicians busy."[32] To support his objection, he presents some evidence. In experiments conducted by other researchers, he notes, subjects have willingly obeyed commands to harm *themselves,* for example, by eating very bitter crackers soaked in quinine or accepting near traumatizing shocks. Since these subjects *themselves* were the victims, they could hardly have denied the reality of those situations. More to the point, the comments uttered by Milgram's subjects during and after the experience strongly indicate that they believed the shocks were real. Responding to a follow-up questionnaire, more than 75 percent of obedient subjects admitted, after zapping the victim, that they probably or fully believed in their reality. Most expressed tremendous relief upon learning that the victim had not been harmed; coupled with their intense anxiety during the study, one would have to stretch the imagination to accept Orne's argument that they merely played the role of "good subjects" to please the experimenter.[33]

Some psychologists have taken a middle road on this issue, asserting that people in Milgram's study thought they were shocking innocent strangers and inflicting pain, but did not believe that they were causing any enduring harm.[34] Still others have called attention to the type of authority figure in the Milgram study. Erich Fromm, for example, notes:

> The psychologist was not only an authority to whom one owes obedience, but a representative of *Science* and of one of the most prestigious institutions of higher education in the United States. Considering that science is widely regarded as the highest value in contemporary industrial society, it is very difficult for the average person to believe that what science commands could be wrong or immoral.[35]

Similarly, philosopher S. C. Patten suggests that an experimenter possesses authority by virtue of his presumed expertise, in this case, concerning shock machines and learning. Knowing how people respond to this type of authority really tells us little about how people might respond to other types of authority figures—say, political leaders.[36]

There is yet another way to explain why so few people disobeyed the experimenter. Social psychologists Lee Ross and Richard Nisbett ask us to reexamine the predicament of the subjects:

> The events that unfolded did not "make sense" or "add up."... The subject's task was that of administering severe electric shocks to a learner who was no longer attempting to learn anything, at the insistence of an experimenter who seemed totally oblivious to the learner's cries of anguish, warnings about a heart condition, refusal to continue responding, and ultimately, ominous silence. What's more, the experimenter evinced no concern about this turn of events, made no attempt to explain or justify that lack of concern or, alternatively, to explain why it was so necessary for the experiment to continue. He even refused to "humor" the subject by checking on the condition of the learner.[37]

If subjects were very clever, or if incongruities exceeded a certain point, they might have seen through the deception and, presumably, told the experimenter where to go. Even if they did not grasp the true nature of the ruse, however, they probably perceived enough inconsistencies to prevent them from arriving at a stable "definition of the situation." Under this scenario, people would typically lack the decisiveness and confidence to rebel against the experimenter. Thus, confusion, rather than slavish obedience, led people to inflict apparent pain on their fellow human beings.[38] This analysis is a slim straw for optimists to grab, but a plausible one.

*   *   *

So much for Milgram's subjects. What about perpetrators of mass atrocities in the real world? How well does their behavior match that of the Connecticut participants? How closely do their circumstances approximate those of the New Haven and Bridgeport laboratories?

Many social scientists have focused on similarities between the Milgram subject and the Nazi bureaucrat. Professor Gordon Allport of Harvard, one of the century's most prominent psychologists and author of the monumental volume, *The Nature of Prejudice*,[39] called the obedience study "the Eichmann experiment." Milgram judged the appellation apt and explained:

> In the laboratory, through a set of simple manipulations, ordinary people no longer perceived themselves as a responsible part of the causal chain

leading to action against a person. The way in which responsibility is cast off, and individuals become thoughtless agents of action, is of general import. One can find evidence of its occurrence time and again as one reads over the transcripts of the war criminals at Nuremberg, the American killers at My Lai, and the commander of Andersonville. What we find in common among soldier, party functionary, and obedient subject is the same limitless capacity to yield to authority and the use of identical mental mechanisms to reduce the strain of acting against a helpless victim.[40]

Despite his judgment of their essential relatedness, Milgram did note some clear differences between his subjects and Nazi bureaucrats. For one thing, he conceded that his study obtained obedience in the name of an ostensibly positive human value—the increase of knowledge. And the authority figure told his subjects that their acts would not result in any permanent damage to the victim, something no Nazi ever suggested. Face-to-face surveillance played a critical role in influencing the subjects in Milgram's experiment. In Nazi Germany, obedience depended much more on internalized values and beliefs, often taking place when no authority figure was physically present—a condition that significantly *lowered* obedience in the experimental scenario. Still, for Milgram, the most important psychological process underlying Nazi atrocities was slavish obedience, of the sort observed in his research.

The differences noted by Milgram seem substantial enough to raise questions about the extent to which the research design zeros in on the core psychology of the Nazi perpetrator. Moreover, the circumstances surrounding Nazi atrocities differ in many additional ways from the situation of the obedience experiment. The entire Milgram study lasted about an hour; most Nazis committed their crimes time and time again over a period of months or years. In a brief experiment, a subject can behave, more or less, mindlessly, never pausing to contemplate the implications of his or her deeds. People can also persist in mindless behavior over the course of months or years, but it is harder; generally, a person would need to invoke a more effective and subtle system of defense mechanisms. Indeed, even in the short time span of the experiment, some of Milgram's subjects showed signs of denigrating and devaluing the learner in an effort to reduce the strains associated with delivery of the shocks. Afterward, others focused on their own purity of heart to facilitate denial of their complicity. Case studies of Nazi criminals show that those who did not share party ideology and extreme antipathy toward Jews frequently employed dissociation, doubling, and other protective tactics to hide from their deeds.[41]

If the Milgram subjects had time to ponder their day's activities over dinner with their spouses, one wonders how many would have returned for a previously arranged second day of zapping new victims. Additionally, one might ask how many subjects would have continued if Milgram had wheeled out a real corpse after the victim had been shocked and then instructed the subject to continue with the procedure on a new, healthier pupil. This situation would more closely resemble the circumstances surrounding many instances of mass murder in the real world.

Unlike the Milgram subjects, many Nazis sought out their destructive roles, entering the party, attending rallies, and joining the SS. They did not usually show signs of serious mental illness, but they may well have shared an inclination to violent, obedient, or discriminatory behavior. The Nazi institutional support system then pushed them down a corridor of hatred and violence. They may, in the end, have responded to situational pressures, but to a large extent they did choose and help create their own situations.

When Milgram's subjects delivered dangerous shocks to victims who, for the most part, resembled themselves, they did so with great reluctance. Some Nazis, as historian Raul Hilberg has noted, were "bearers of burdens," consumed by guilt, but, in stark contrast, many others are better described as "zealots" and "vulgarians."[42] Whereas conscience plagued Milgram's subjects, it seemed painfully absent from the mindset of many Nazis, at least with regard to anti-Jewish acts. And while few of the teacher-subjects in the obedience study acted with any cruelty at all, death camp survivors recount that many guards, even those who showed no signs of sadism in other contexts, committed acts of great brutality in the death camps.

Though the Nazis attempted to shroud the Holocaust in a euphemistic cloak, only a very small percentage of perpetrators can plausibly claim ignorance about the likely consequences of their deeds. In the 1930s, many Germans did not have a clear sense of where Hitler's policy was headed. But by the time of the Holocaust, few of the *killers* could have had doubts that Jews were being slaughtered. For the members of the Einsatzgruppen and the staffs of the concentration camps, there could be no doubt at all. Yet, as we have seen, Milgram's subjects may well have succumbed to the pressures of the situation *precisely because of its ambiguity.* The confusion that prevailed in their minds could not have existed in those of most Nazis instrumental in the murder of the Jews, except perhaps for a few bureaucrats inhabiting offices far from the gas chambers and killing fields of the Einsatzgruppen.

One of Milgram's key conclusions is that obedience diminishes sharply if even a single role model disobeys. The German resistance did not attract huge numbers, but some Germans did disobey the regime and many more opted out of murderous duty.

Nazi leaders hardly resembled Milgram's experimenter in credibility, demeanor, or objective. Yet these ungodly souls were often perceived as legitimate. One can imagine a person obeying the experimenter because of respect for experimentation or because some unwritten social rule advises against questioning a knowledgeable scientist. But would a normal person plucked out of an everyday Connecticut environment feel the same way toward Rudolf Hoess, the commandant at Auschwitz, or Heinrich Himmler, the SS chief? German citizens did treat the Nazi leadership as legitimate in spite of an agenda that violated traditional Western norms. They accepted their argument that atrocities served the higher moral purpose of advancing the interests of the German race. For Milgram, this parallels the behavior of subjects who hurt others in the name of science. But one might reasonably ask whether the acceptance of Nazi ideology, as opposed to the endorsement of science, requires an entirely different set of social and political preconditions. And, more important, one can justly question whether the key to Hitler's effectiveness lay to a greater extent in his ability to arrange these preconditions and orchestrate monumental change in Germany, rather than in a ubiquitous human tendency to obey.

The Nazi Holocaust reached such a huge dimension because it relied on bureaucracy rather than spontaneous hatred. Obedience propelled this bureaucracy forward, but so did individual initiative and a shared set of beliefs, values, and goals. The motives of those who follow an authority figure symbolizing knowledge and those who obey a leader who stands for racial superiority cannot be equivalent. Unquestioning trust in either can lead to disaster, but surely the Milgram subjects had probability on their side. One can participate in thousands of psychological studies without ever seriously hurting another person; one cannot say the same about following the orders of Nazi leaders.

For some perpetrators, Nazi murders were as bloodless as the shock experiments, but many others had to stomach butchery and gore of unprecedented proportions. Though sometimes described as a bloodless genocide, there was plenty of blood, and more than a little cruelty. Would Milgram's subjects have tolerated this as well?

Among the many paths followed by Nazi mass murderers, some may have fit the Milgram model. Though most people in Nazi Germany were anti-Semites to one degree or another, a few may have entered the scene without much anti-Semitism and encountered authorities who seemed legitimate and whom they trusted completely. They then subordinated their own better judgment to these figures, following a social norm that one always obeys legitimate governmental authorities. This, in turn, led them to participate in murders of Jews, despite tremendous personal misgivings and overwhelmingly guilty consciences. Even for subjects who fit this model, however, the obedience studies tell us little about what happened next, more specifically, how they managed to return day after day to persist at their murderous tasks.

Many more Nazis sought to build their careers on the blood of their victims, though they too were not motivated in the main by anti-Semitism and hatred. The members of the SS obeyed, but largely because their deeds did not violate any deep personal values and because they had merged psychologically and socially with the organization. Large numbers, too, identified with the goals of the Nazi party and, more important, the person of Adolf Hitler. All probably felt some inclination to obey authorities whom they wrongly accepted as legitimate. In itself, however, the impulse to obey legitimate authorities was a necessary and sufficient condition for only a few.[43] Nonetheless, Milgram's work correctly focuses our attention on the social and situational pressures that can lead people to commit acts of which they would not dream, or perhaps of which they would only dream, under different circumstances.

The mass rapes in Bosnia have also been described as instances of destructive obedience. Some imprisoned militia members in Bosnia have asserted that they had no option but to kill civilians and rape Muslim women. Some claim that the alternative was death, that they were told, "Rape, or be killed." The Bosnian Serb leadership authorized the rapes and encouraged them as a matter of policy because they contributed to empty-ing lands that they wanted to annex. Lower-level officers communicated the acceptability of murder and rape; no doubt, they also exerted social pressures on their subordinates to participate—a reluctant soldier might easily have felt isolated. In any case, victim accounts indicate that most of the rapists participated with relish. They seemed consumed by hatred. Many also capitalized on an opportunity to indulge animalistic urges that civilized people generally lack or, at least, suppress; in an atmosphere where the social contract was nowhere to be found, and where life and dig-nity collapsed easily, they committed rape with disgusting eagerness. These rapists, in a sense, responded to situational pressures, but stretching Mil-gram's model to account for their behavior strains credulity.

Reports abound of cruelty at the Omarska concentration camp, created by the Bosnian Serbs in the spring of 1992. The genocide perpetrated by Bosnian Serbs lacked any hint of sanitized, bureaucratic detachment. Drawing on the residue of past conflicts, and more significantly, fired up by several years of hate propaganda, most soldiers in the Bosnian Serb cause detested their Muslim opponents. And most of those who carried out, and to some extent initiated, the worst atrocities and ethnic cleansing brought even angrier and more virulent animosities to the task. It is likely that, five or six years earlier, many of these men disliked their Muslim neighbors, but few would have mistreated them. And even fewer, perhaps none, would have physically attacked them. But by the spring of 1992, "slavishly but reluctantly obedient" is hardly an apt description of their frame of mind. In this bloody conflict, everyone on all sides grew more militant as the casualties mounted; many sought revenge for the death of comrades or family in the recent past. As a result of memories and propa-ganda, many more felt anger concerning real or imagined crimes against the Serbs in the more distant past. For some, the matter boiled down to "Kill them now or they'll kill you later." The Serbs had been transformed into killers who felt much affinity for the orders they obeyed, and even a need to inflict humiliation on their victims.

Reasonable people on all sides of the Balkan conflict report feeling tremendous pressure to conform and choose sides, even when this ran against their inclinations. Most succumbed. But they were far less likely to join Arkan's bloodthirsty militia or other groups responsible for the atrocities and rapes.

Though the circumstances surrounding ethnic cleansing do not approximate very closely the predicament of subjects in the Milgram experiment, one cannot discount the power of the military norm to obey. The norm to obey is far stronger in the wartime military than in civilian life. Though plenty of precedents establish a soldier's right to disobey unlawful orders, massive pressures limit the practicality of exercising this right. Recruits, in Bosnia, may have bought their leaders' propaganda line, bowed to group pressure, or been pushed into the military by the "Which side are you on?" logic of conflict. Then, without having thought much about the matter, they might have received an order to kill the Muslim residents of a village, perhaps under some guise deemed plausible. By this time, they may already have killed Muslim soldiers in battle. With sympathy for the victims, or at least with some trace of moral reluctance, they may have carried out the murders. Here, again, the Milgram obedience experiment illuminates the path that some may have followed. It remains impossible to determine how many arrived at their genocidal bent via this indirect route, though the prevalence of hatred and cruelty seems to suggest that this was not the most common path.

In Rwanda, the situation was somewhat similar. A cycle of genocide instilled in many Hutu a fear of what the Tutsi might do if they gained power. There was also a widespread desire for revenge. The crimes of the past to which they reacted were in some cases real, but in any event always salient in their minds because of the waves of hate propaganda emanating from the radio and elsewhere. Without this conscious effort to stir up animosities, the warring groups might have coexisted in peace.

The members of the Interahamwe and Impuzamugambe militias did not reflect a random cross-section of Hutu society; instead, they may well have been selected and trained in part because of their propensities to hate Tutsis and to follow orders. Still, the order to murder Tutsis and moderate Hutus came without much notice, and many found themselves faced with an immediate dilemma: to follow orders or to rebel. The radio broadcasts led them to believe that the Tutsi would not hesitate in killing them; at a minimum, this must have reduced reluctance to obey. The fact that moderate Hutu numbered among the extremists' victims also stimulated fears. In some areas, Hutu civilians who chose not to kill were told that each must slaughter at least one Tutsi or else he or she could, later on, identify the murderers. As one interpretation of the subjects' predicament in the obedience study suggests, militia men and civilians may have acted out of confusion resulting from difficulty arriving at a stable definition of the situation; perhaps they were unsure of whether they were engaging in self-defense or the murder of innocents. Without a clear sense of what was going on, they lacked the fortitude to disobey. Again, however, the genocidal situation differs from the laboratory situation in significant ways. The killers knew, for certain, that the victim's death would result from their actions. Some acted with incredible cruelty. They possessed a hatred for the victims born of years of conflict and fed by virulent and effective propaganda.

There are few meaningful parallels between the obedience experiment and the situation presented by the Muslim extremists. Simply put, Muslim extremists across the globe do not resemble the Connecticut subjects in their essential psychology. The militants seek out their terrorist tasks and regard them as morally justifiable in terms of their religious beliefs. Nonetheless, these extremists do view the radical sheikhs as legitimate authorities and, for the most part, surrender moral and religious-legal responsibility to them. Thus, they do not ask whether destroying the World Trade Center is an ethical act; they inquire whether Sheikh Omar Abdel Rahman, Osama bin Laden, or some other leader approves.

A somewhat better case can be made for the relevance of the obedience experiment to the behavior of some American troops in Vietnam. Milgram himself cites the My Lai massacre as an excellent illustration of destructive obedience at work, and many other political and social analysts agree.[44] The events of 16 March 1968, in the Vietnamese village of Son My, bear some important similarities to the obedience experiment. The time frame was short, only a few hours one morning. The purpose of the act was ostensibly noble: to advance the American effort to free Vietnam from the scourge of a vicious totalitarian regime, and to advance the interests of the Free World in the struggle against an ever-expanding Communist threat. No officially sanctioned hate campaign stimulated fear and anger toward the Vietnamese people. The American killers had not chosen to join extremist organizations, and most seemed to resemble the Connecticut subjects. The mechanical, "doing-my-job" mentality approached the surreal, as the men of Company C who had just completed a horrifying massacre of old men, women, and babies paused for lunch. Two young girls who had escaped the slaughter wandered back from a hiding place, were observed by the soldiers, and invited to share lunch. Having finished the job, the normal human values of the soldiers had reasserted themselves.

But the parallels with the Milgram study are not perfect. The day before, the soldiers had attended the emotional funeral of a sergeant who had been killed by a Viet Cong booby trap. Many thirsted for revenge, and were ready to find Viet Cong anywhere. The soldiers could have suspected that a few VC numbered among the many they had murdered. Some of the killers at My Lai also raped their victims, something which certainly had not been included in the orders of Lieutenant Calley or anyone else. And while the American government had not preached hatred against the Vietnamese, many American soldiers certainly had absorbed a considerable amount of prejudice against them, as evidenced by the widespread use of disparaging names like "Gooks."

Insofar as Milgram's experimental situation differs in so many essential aspects from circumstances surrounding mass atrocities in the real world, the study *proves* little about how such crimes could occur. However, the obedience research does help to explain several elements of mass murder in Nazi Germany, Bosnia, and Rwanda. First, if people lacked a powerful tendency to obey the orders of authorities, the architects of mass murder would not be able to coordinate effective policies; pogroms and other manifestations of mass hatred would occur, but they would not reach the levels observed in Rwanda, Bosnia, Nazi Germany, or elsewhere. Second, perpetrators nearly always find it easier to commit atrocities when they can surrender moral and legal responsibility to an authority whom they perceive as legitimate. Third, some percentage of murderers in every genocide act without any hatred toward their victims, or at least without much hatred, and some experience considerable guilt; these obedient killers are one type among several, not the majority, but they do kill for much the same reason that Milgram's subjects pull the lever. They simply lack the presence of mind or moral courage to challenge an authority figure. Fourth, group pressure apparently drives many people to suppress any inclinations they might have to question or disobey authority.

By focusing on a short-term laboratory situation where the consequences of the teacher-subject's act were by no means certain and where the authority figure represented a generally benevolent institution, Milgram probably exaggerated the probability that everyday Americans would *in their current psychological states* commit mass atrocities. Milgram's results derived at least partly from subjects' confusion about what was really transpiring.

In addition, the "obedience" model of mass atrocities misses, or deemphasizes, some critical points about the psychology of genocide. While mass atrocities are not generally the direct consequence of certain individuals expressing deep hatred, a personal lust for blood, or psychopathology, such individuals are disproportionately likely to join organizations that perpetrate atrocities. Moreover, their most vile tendencies emerge and dictate their behavior as they follow orders and embroider on them; thus, some soldiers ordered to kill may end up raping or torturing their victims.

The "obedience" model also pulls attention away from the overarching importance of an ideology of hatred—the Nazi racial doctrines, the vision of a Greater Serbia, Hutuism, Islamic extremism, and the like. Over the course of years, opportunistic or genuinely hateful leaders use control of the state, the media, and other institutions to flood people's minds with messages teaching them to devalue their victims. People must perceive those who give genocidal orders as legitimate authorities, and they must be willing to accept that genocidal orders *do not diminish a figure's legitimacy.* The ideological campaign of hate sets the stage so potentially obedient killers will not challenge claims to legitimacy; to some extent, at least, the followers now share the vision of their leaders. Many atrocities are crimes of obedience, but many more are crimes of agreement and even initiative.

The people who commit atrocities may have, years earlier, resembled the "nice" people of Connecticut, but by the time they commit their acts of aggression, they have been substantially transformed. As much as he would like us to believe otherwise, Eichmann was not a nice person.

Additionally, most atrocities occur in the context of war. Nearly always, war cheapens life, as soldiers kill other soldiers, or see friends die at the hands of the enemy. Often, these experiences engender fear and a desire for revenge, even when completely misdirected, as in the case of Nazi Germany.

And in the military, obedience takes on an altogether different character. Milgram himself notes its essentially logical character when he writes that "the maintenance of discipline becomes an element of survival, and the soldier is left with little choice but to obey."[45] True, there should be limits to obedience, but those who suggest that we train soldiers to disobey are being overly simplistic. No military organization, not even one engaged in reasonable defense, could function without a powerful norm against disobeying orders. Soldiers would be placed at unnecessary risk, and most likely the end result in the armies of Western nations would be an *increase* in atrocities. Individuals at war are placed under tremendous strain; soldiers would, no doubt, be apt to loot or even kill or rape without the restraints imposed by the norm to obey legitimate authorities.

From time to time, some of us notice an individual donning a button, popular a few years back, that says: "Question Authority!" Within limits, this makes sense. But the adolescent urge to disobey should not be mistaken for a social philosophy. Even in civilian life, obedience helps to hold society together. Would America function better if people stopped obeying the law and started making their own decisions in every instance? Do we want everyone asking, "Is it really wrong for me to take this apple when I'm so hungry and he has so many?" The proper response when the teacher says, "Write a fifteen-page paper," is not to ask, "Why?" Obedience in itself is not the enemy. In any case, the tendency to obey probably is deeply entrenched in most societies, good and bad, and, consequently, an ill-advised place to intervene in order to discourage mass murder.

Milgram offers some advice. "First, we need to be aware of the problem of indiscriminate submission to authority. . . . Second, since we know men will comply, even with the most malevolent authorities, we have a special obligation to place in positions of authority those most likely to be humane and wise."[46] This is reasonable advice, but easier said than done.

SOCIETAL PRECONDITIONS FOR SLAUGHTER

Psychologist Herbert Kelman of Harvard University believes strongly in the power of the situation, but takes a broader view, focusing on how a *society* becomes genocidal. He concludes that:

> [T]he occurrence of sanctioned massacres cannot be adequately explained by the existence of psychological forces—whether these be characterological dispositions to engage in murderous violence or profound hostility against the target—so powerful that they must find expression in violent acts un-

hampered by moral restraints. Instead, the major instigators for this class of violence derive from the policy process. The question that really calls for psychological analysis is why so many people are willing to formulate, participate in, and condone policies that call for the mass killings of defenseless civilians. Thus it is more instructive to look not at the motives for violence but at the conditions under which the usual moral inhibitions against violence become weakened.[47]

Kelman calls attention to three ways this happens, through "authorization," "routinization," and "dehumanization."[48] These social processes, or pathways, often work together, establishing the preconditions and laying the groundwork for mass atrocities.

A massacre is authorized when an authority figure explicitly orders, implicitly encourages, tacitly approves, or, at least, permits the atrocities. Under this condition, the impulse to obey propels the killers onward. Though not everyone will succumb, people, in general, become much less likely to invoke their code of morals or to think for themselves. Instead, many feel that the only "ethical" course is to follow orders dutifully. Somehow, personal responsibility falls out of the equation.

The process of authorization seems essential to large-scale massacres, and may also play a role in some crimes that require initiative. For example, the extremist Muslims in the 1993 attack on the World Trade Center wanted to strike against the United States, but first they required the approval of Sheikh Omar Abdel Rahman. Had he withheld his approval, the plot would not have proceeded. Once his authorization had been given, none of the conspirators bothered to delve any further into the moral implications of the deed.

Once people commit their first evil act, often without much thought, a new logic pushes them on toward more heinous atrocities. Before their first evil act, the fear that such behavior was criminal would impede their participation. Now, to justify the first act and avoid facing its implications, they become even more deeply involved in subsequent malevolent pursuits. Still, the possibility exists that moral scruples will reemerge. To lessen the chances of this, the organizers of the genocide try to render the acts of mass murder as routine, making them as mechanical, repetitive, and programmed as possible. By reducing the need for thinking and making decisions, the routinization of the massacre diminishes the chance that participants will recognize the moral dimension of their acts.

While routinization characterizes some mass atrocities, it is not relevant to all. It was certainly evident in the Nazi death camps. But there was not much mechanization or programmed procedure in the ethnic cleansing perpetrated by the Bosnian Serbs, and none in the massacre of the Tutsis and Hutu moderates in Rwanda. And even when routinization *is* present, the murder of another human being is still a powerful act with a moral significance difficult to obscure.

The process of dehumanization makes it even easier to disregard the moral implications of murder. Dehumanization transforms the victims into creatures for whom the usual morality no longer applies. No mass atrocities in the contemporary world have occurred without some form of dehumanization. The Nazis labeled Jews "a cancer," "a rat infestation," "subhuman." The extremist Muslims classify nonbelievers who do not submit to their rule as "infidels." The Hutu extremists call the Tutsi "inyenzi," or insects. And once the perpetrators begin to attack the victims, they notice and take comfort in the consequences of the degradation. The "animals" start to act like animals and smell like animals. As one social psychologist explains, "We are ordinarily unaware of the degree to which our being treated as civilized, decent, autonomous, moral agents depends on our ability to look and act like such agents. To the degree that we make it impossible for other people to look and act that way, we make it easy to treat them as less than human."[49]

CREATING BRUTALITY

Dictators nearly always assume power while enjoying the support of some of their subjects, but usually they do not command the hearts and minds of the majority. Consequently, they frequently capitalize on the vast array of tools delivered into their hands along with the reins of government. These tools, some blunt, some subtle, enable them to chip away, chop, and crush the resistance of those who initially opposed the regime. The success of many modern dictatorships comes from an ability to mix threats, manipulation, persuasion, and bribes to change a person politically and psychologically, without that person ever grasping why he or she has changed. Direct control or indirect influence over the media, schools, police, military, and other institutions, over time, can result in the wearying and transformation of many formerly decent souls. Very often, dictators also develop tightly controlled organizations which transform ideological supporters into mindless pawns who can be indoctrinated, manipulated, and empowered to do the regime's dirty work, not reluctantly but with relish. Those psychologists who emphasize the power of the situation have something to say about how these disastrous mental, emotional, and behavioral changes can occur.

Nazi Germany and the former Soviet Union provide classic examples of regimes using state power to dominate the lives of individuals. Those individuals who ran afoul of the state had little chance to pursue their careers or lives in peace. The state conferred governmental appointments, honors, awards, and influence across the spectrum of human endeavor. The regime became coterminous with the state and the nation, thus benefiting from vast repositories of nationalism, patriotism, and ethnic pride. Despite some noble efforts to the contrary, it proved immensely difficult to love Germany and hate the Nazis in the 1930s; by the 1940s, it was virtually impossible. There, the state also controlled the legal institutions, so that one's respect for the law led to one's respect for the regime as well. Just living one's life meant engaging in a broad range of behaviors tainted by the corrupt regime. Inevitably, those who initially disagreed felt a tension between their overt behaviors and their ostensible beliefs. The tension could be lessened by allowing one's internal beliefs to conform to the dictates and official beliefs of the regime.[50]

Perhaps most important of all, the regimes controlled or influenced the mass media and, therefore, possessed a potent implement with which to craft people's definition of reality and truth. In Rwanda, Radio des Milles Collines not only preached hatred, but also established a variety of critical lies as facts in the minds of listeners. First Milosevic and later the Bosnian Serb leaders used the media to great effect. Throughout the Muslim world, free media are scarce; where Muslim fundamentalists have influence, opinions contrary to their worldview cannot be openly expressed. Even where such expression is permitted, dissenting journalists often risk physical attack in the streets. Control of the mass media also leads to control of another important mode of influence: the selection and publicizing of role models to emulate and, in contrast, of victims to ridicule.

The dictator's powerful tools can turn opponents into the uncommitted, and the uncommitted into supporters. But special organizations must be created if the leader wants totally reliable foot soldiers for the cause who are unlikely to be troubled by independent thinking, ethics, familial pressures, or fear of the disdain of others. Many dictators, and all who have launched mass atrocities, build such organizations. Hitler had many, starting with the SA, or Stormtrooper, organization. When these thugs threatened to endanger his consolidation of power by virtue of their unbridled, and potentially disobedient, enthusiasm for the cause, Hitler transferred his affections to the SS and associated organizations like the Gestapo. Stalin had the KGB. In Bosnia and Rwanda, no one individual controlled the extremist organizations, but they played similar roles. In Bosnia, the Serb leaders Zeljko Raznatovic ("Arkan") and Vojislav Seselj organized militias that carried out the most vicious ethnic cleansing. In Rwanda, the Interahamwe militia carried out the worst of the Hutuist agenda. In Argentina, during the years when the military made "leftist" and "Communist" sympathizers disappear, a special group of soldiers was trained to do the dirty work. These organizations nearly always selected people predisposed to their tasks. But special training programs and psychological strategies helped to transform them into killers capable of the very worst crimes ever committed by human beings.

Two studies, the first a laboratory simulation and the second an analysis of interviews with former torturers, shed some light on how brutality can be created and reinforced. Philip Zimbardo is a psychology professor at Stanford University who by coincidence attended James Monroe High School in the Bronx with Stanley Milgram in the late 1940s. He and his colleagues created a mock prison in a basement corridor of the psychology building at Stanford.[51]

One day, real officers from the local police department unexpectedly "arrested" on suspicion of burglary or armed robbery ten normal, healthy male college students at their homes in California. Though they were advised of their rights, handcuffed, and searched, the students were not criminals. They had agreed to serve as research subjects in a simulated prison without knowing whether they would be chosen as prisoners or guards. A contract promised fifteen dollars per day, a minimally adequate diet, clothing, housing, and medical care in exchange for their "intention" to participate for the duration of the study. The contract noted that some of the prisoners' basic civil rights would be suspended as part of the study, but that there would be no physical abuse.

Zimbardo and his colleagues chose the ten prisoners, along with eleven guards, from an initial pool of seventy-five volunteers. After interviews and completion of a variety of questionnaires, these twenty-one subjects had been judged the most stable mentally and physically, the most mature, and the least likely to commit antisocial acts. Then, they were randomly assigned to be guards or prisoners.

For obvious practical and ethical reasons, the psychologists could not literally replicate a prison; they could, however, create the functional equivalents of prison life, producing "feelings of power and powerlessness, of control and oppression, of satisfaction and frustration, of arbitrary rule and resistance to authority, of status and anonymity, of machismo and emasculation."[52] Many of these feelings also characterized life in the Nazi concentration camps, Omarska, and other scenes of mass atrocities.

To simulate the degradation of the prison experience, "prisoner" subjects were stripped, deloused, and given loose-fitting gowns without underwear. Each prisoner had a number that appeared on the front and back of the gown. Guards, too, wore uniforms designed to reinforce their roles. Their uniforms consisted of plain khaki shirts and trousers, a whistle, a police night stick, and reflecting sunglasses to prevent eye contact. For the prisoners, the experience continued twenty-four hours a day, but the guards could return to their normal lives when their eight-hour shifts ended.

The experimenter, as warden, established some basic rules. In an effort to depersonalize the prisoners, guards were to refer to them only by number. Prisoners were to be served three bland meals and permitted three supervised visits to the toilet each day. Two hours per day, prisoners could read or write letters. Zimbardo and his colleagues then set the guards loose on the prisoners, permitting any mode of positive or negative interaction except physical punishment.

These mock prisoners and guards very quickly started to act like their counterparts in the real world. The guards soon started to treat the prisoners unpleasantly, and in no time at all began to fit stereotypes of abusiveness. The experimenters note:

Many of the guards showed in their behavior and revealed in post-experi-
mental statements that [the] sense of power was exhilarating.

    The use of power was self-aggrandizing and self-perpetuating. . . .

After the first day of the study, practically all prisoner rights (even such
things as the time and conditions of sleeping and eating) came to be rede-
fined by the guards as "privileges" which were to be earned by obedient behavior. Constructive activities such as watching movies or reading (previously planned and suggested by the experimenters) were arbitrarily canceled
until further notice by the guards—and were subsequently never allowed.
"Reward" then became granting approval for prisoners to eat, sleep, go to
the toilet, talk, smoke a cigarette, wear eyeglasses, or the temporary diminu-
tion of harassment.[53]

The guards, on occasion, withheld permission for a prisoner to go to the
bathroom, forcing them to use buckets in their cells. They put some troublesome prisoners in solitary confinement, and made others perform a
variety of degrading tasks: some had to clean toilets with their bare hands,
some had to do push-ups. A guard shot a fire extinguisher at a prisoner.

    The prisoners, for their part, engaged in a variety of traditional pris-
oner activities. They staged a rebellion. When it failed they grew demoral-
ized, and suffered a lessening of self-esteem. Some passively demanded attention and help by "developing" emotional disturbances. Others put all
their energy into acting the role of the good, obedient prisoner. When one
prisoner started a hunger strike as a protest, others treated him as someone who deserved to be punished for disobedience. In fact, the demoral-
ization of the prisoners became so intense, and things got so out of hand,
that the experiment had to be canceled after six days instead of the
planned two weeks.

    Over the course of six days, some American college students, screened
for maturity and emotional health, had started down a path toward brutality. They never actually struck a fellow student, nor did they believe
they were causing any lasting harm. Despite their knowledge that they
might just as easily have been the prisoners, they engaged in behaviors
that must be described as cruel. How had it happened? Why did the level
of discipline slide from reasonable force to brutality?

First, it is important to note, not all of the guards grew tyrannical; Zimbardo sets the fraction at about one-third. Another third acted as "tough but fair" correctional officers and the final third, the good guards, did small favors for prisoners and interacted in a friendly manner. However, the good guards and the dutiful guards never made the slightest effort to interfere with the commands of the bad guards. Zimbardo reports:

> [T]hey never told the others to ease off because it was only an experiment, and they never even came to me as prison superintendent or experimenter in charge to complain. In part, they were good because the others were bad; they needed the others to help establish their own egos in a positive light.[54]

Similarly, the behavior of the bad guards was influenced by the behavior of the good guards. By treating prisoners with open cruelty, the aggressive guards, in effect, announced that their deeds fell within the realm of acceptable behavior. The good guards could have objected, but when they did not, they communicated the false message that they condoned what they saw.

One explanation for the behavior of the good guards might have to do with etiquette; people in our society generally feel quite reluctant about telling others, particularly strangers, that their behavior is morally wrong. The actions of the bad guards, too, may be related to the power of societal norms to influence behavior. Under ordinary circumstances, normal human beings encounter plenty of provocations but refrain from aggressive, hostile retaliations. Most people even refrain from reacting with harsh language. For a variety of reasons, however, these inhibitions did not come into play in the Stanford University mock prison. The prison environment discouraged people from approaching the situation as individuals with previously established personalities, values, and perspectives. Guards and prisoners did not lose their identities, but in a sense they shut them off. In psychological terms, they became deindividuated.[55] They easily slid into their new reality, and drew on notions of how guards and prisoners typically act. They readily filled their roles, as people often do in real world settings. And in the strange new world of prison life, the power of usual societal norms to regulate behavior diminished, as an entirely different set of norms took over.

Zimbardo designed the prison to reflect the degradation of prisoners that he believed occurred regularly as a feature of the American correctional system. As we have seen, such degradation and dehumanization occur to a much greater degree whenever mass atrocities are committed.

Unlike the Milgram study, in which subjects obeyed mechanically and felt remorse, the Zimbardo experiment contributes to our understanding of the *cruelty* and *brutality* of those who participate in mass atrocities. As a laboratory simulation, however, it only approximates very roughly the conditions of concentration camps and other sites of collective aggression. Janice Gibson and Mika Haritos-Fatouros provide us with a glimpse of the brutalization process as it operates in real-world torturers.[56]

On 21 April 1967, following a period of political instability, a coup led by Colonel George Papadopoulos brought an end to democracy in Greece. During the next seven years, the harsh military junta relied heavily on torture to control and destroy political opponents. To carry out grotesque physical abuse, the regime used soldiers of the ESA—the Army Police Corps. Repeatedly, these men committed acts of aggression that most people would judge inhumane in the extreme. Researchers Gibson and Haritos-Fatouros examined in detail the testimony of twenty-one former torturers, given at their 1975 trials in Athens; they also conducted in-depth interviews with sixteen of the ESA veterans after the trials. Many had been convicted and served prison sentences by the time of the interviews.

Gibson and Haritos-Fatouros concluded that a penchant for torturing others was, in fact, a skill that could be taught. Unlike members of the SS, the Interahamwe, and the Bosnian Serb militias that committed the worst crimes in the Balkans, members of the ESA were drafted, first into the regular military, and then into specialized units responsible for torture. Though none had prior records of delinquency or disturbance, they had been screened for physical strength, "appropriate" anticommunist views, an aggressive nature, and an ability to keep their mouths shut. Officers also selected men whom they believed would trust the regime and follow its orders blindly.

Training included several steps. Recruits underwent physically brutal initiation rites. They were cursed, punched, kicked, and flogged; they had to promise on their knees to obey the military leader. At the same time, and somewhat paradoxically, the officers told them how fortunate they were to belong to such an elite organization. They were told that their actions would never be questioned and that "You can even flog a major." A daily program of "national ethical education" provided them with the requisite ideological indoctrination. Their prisoners, they learned, were "worms" whom they must crush.

A carrot-and-stick strategy proved highly effective. The torturers, after training, received many special benefits, including the right to wear civilian clothes, free restaurant meals, job placement after military service, and leaves of absence after obtaining confessions. But constant threats and punishment for disobedience also played their part. One torturer reports that, "An officer used to tell us that if a warder helps a prisoner, he will take the prisoner's place and the whole platoon will flog him."[57] Under this threat, few members of the ESA could think sensibly about what they were doing.

Gibson and Haritos-Fatouros maintain that prospective torturers grew less sensitive to the horrors of inflicting pain on another person by watching others commit violent acts and then receive rewards. Moreover, as psychologists all know, gradual exposure to any emotionally rousing event leads to progressive desensitization; psychologists frequently use this principle in therapy to overcome phobias. Without the combination of techniques designed to increase a sense of connectedness to the ESA and to reduce the strain associated with obedience and the infliction of pain on others, Gibson and Haritos-Fatouros conclude that the torturers would not have been able to carry out their tasks.

Psychiatrist Henry Dicks arrived at a similar conclusion in his study of SS killers; with perhaps one or two exceptions, he thought none of the men he interviewed likely to become "common murderers" under normal conditions. They had to undergo a gradual and comprehensive process of brutalization.[58] Muslim and secular Arab terrorists, too, receive an education in violence; at training camps throughout the Middle East, the carrot-and-stick strategy is carefully supplemented by ideological programming to produce enthusiastic killers. The biographies of extremist Muslim terrorists also reflect how many became progressively more brutal through experiences in Afghanistan and exposure to regular rhetoric denouncing the "infidels" and "Zionists." Some may also have been desensitized by mistreatment of themselves and friends during crackdowns by the Egyptian police.

In sum, social psychologists have produced a number of studies that support the power of circumstances to shape a mass killer. When a dictator bent on destroying a large group of people possesses the power to structure situations, he and his cohorts can transform many law-abiding people into the perpetrators of horrible atrocities. Using many social and psychological processes, these leaders not only produce obedience, but also agreement with their programs and unlimited brutality in the furtherance of their goals. Still, not all succumb. The next task is to understand why some individuals succumb to the pressures they face, while others do not.

SEVEN

The Personality of the Perpetrator

*PERHAPS THE MOST PERPLEXING PROBLEM IN THE ENTIRE
FIELD OF HUMAN RELATIONS IS THIS: WHY DO SO RELATIVELY
FEW OF OUR CONTACTS WITH OTHER PEOPLE FIT IN WITH, AND
SATISFY, OUR PREDOMINATING AFFILIATIVE NEEDS, AND WHY
DO SO MANY FIND THEIR WAY INTO SENTIMENTS OF HATRED
AND HOSTILITY? WHY ARE LOYALTIES AND LOVES SO FEW AND
RESTRICTED, WHEN AT BOTTOM HUMAN BEINGS FEEL THAT
THEY CAN NEVER LOVE OR BE LOVED ENOUGH?[1]*

Gordon W. Allport, Psychologist,
The Nature of Prejudice

A mild-mannered, neatly dressed, thirty-two-year-old industrial engineer pushes his chair away from Stanley Milgram's shock generator. "The man, he seems to be getting hurt," he protests. The experimenter insists that he proceed, offering the usual justifications: "The experiment requires that you go on," "There is no permanent tissue damage," and, "You have no other choice." This last remark riles the young engineer, a member of the Dutch Reformed Church and an immigrant who left Holland after World War II. "I *do* have a choice," he responds indignantly. "Why don't I have a choice? I came here of my own free will. I thought I could help in a research project. But if I have to hurt somebody to do that, or if I was in his place, too, I wouldn't stay there. I can't continue. I'm very sorry. I think I've gone too far already, probably."[2] At this point, the engineer, like one out of every three of Milgram's subjects, terminates his participation in the study.

What in this man's personality, beliefs, and background led him to disobey where so many others continued? Perhaps his religious beliefs, his intellect, or his formal education played a part. Or perhaps it was his experiences as a teenager in Nazi-occupied Europe. Was he responding to the victim's apparent suffering, or to the experimenter's attempts to infringe on his freedom of choice? More generally, the Milgram study leaves us wondering what separates the obedient from the disobedient. Milgram himself commented, "I am certain that there is a complex personality basis to obedience and disobedience. But I know we have not found it."[3]

Consider Bosnian Serb soldiers just prior to their unit's first participation in a campaign of ethnic cleansing. Their leader transmits orders from some higher up commander. Though worded euphemistically, the orders leave little doubt that the soldiers are to terrorize Muslim civilians in a nearby village. The situational influences are all there—peer pressure, a directive from an authority perceived as legitimate, the military ethos of obedience, and a wartime environment. Moreover, the members of the militia almost universally share hatred, fear, and anger toward the Muslims, though in varying degrees. One can assume, however, that these Serbian fighters differ in their personalities, and, therefore, in their predisposition to engage in anti-Muslim aggression. Some may ache to kill; others may be tenderhearted, or at least may wish to avoid participation in bloody scenes as much as possible. Some, perhaps more than a few, may crave the opportunity to indulge violent appetites for sexual domination and humiliation. Differences such as these seem likely to bear upon who takes the lead in the impending massacre, who follows, and who shoots into the air or refuses to participate.

Or consider the congregation of the mosque in Jersey City, New Jersey, in the early 1990s, where Sheikh Omar Abdel Rahman delivered sermons seething with hatred for anyone or anything remotely connected to the United States or Israel. Most Muslim-Americans, including most recent Muslim immigrants, choose more moderate environments in which to worship. What predisposed these particular Muslims to attend a radical mosque? And, though some situational pressures—for example, the impulses to conform to the congregation's views and to obey a learned religious leader—militated in favor of adopting the sheikh's extremist norms once a person joined his flock, these pressures were not impossible to evade. Only a handful of Rahman's faithful took his activist message to heart and signed on with the plot to bomb targets in New York City. The strength, depth, and variety of religious commitment may have separated terrorists from passive listeners. Alternatively, other personality traits or attitudes may have distinguished between them.

When it comes to mass atrocities, it is seldom easy to separate the impact of external pressures from the role played by personality and individual differences. In climates where decency prevails, haters often suppress their hatred; similarly, in hateful climates, relatively decent people sometimes participate in brutal and destructive acts of mass hatred. One cannot reliably estimate the importance of a personal predisposition to hatred, violence, or obedience by interviewing perpetrators. In many cases, situational pressures reinforce personal traits, feelings, and beliefs. And, after the fact, it always serves the self-interest of the perpetrator to claim that he or she acted in response to the circumstantial pressures, and decidedly not as a consequence of some inner nature or corrupt value system.[4]

Still, two conclusions seem reasonable. First, the greater the pressure of the situation, the less likely that individual differences in personality and beliefs will influence how a person acts. The strongest consciences will cave in to some powerful pressures, while even weak ones may make a stand if they can do so easily. Second, when circumstances permit some freedom of maneuver, and they almost always do, those predisposed by their nature to hate and kill will take the lead, eagerly indulging their lust for destructiveness at the first and every subsequent opportunity. Those with a moderate predisposition will follow, while those lacking the tendency, or predisposed in a contrary direction, will attempt to avoid or escape the situation. When they cannot, they will make efforts to infuse a thread of humanity into their deeds.

Even these conclusions may be a bit simplistic, however. One's personality does not exist, or develop, independent of the social pressures of one's surroundings. Circumstances can remold personalities. As a noted student of personality and politics has commented: "A stable conscience breaks down if it loses all its external reinforcements, or an individual may adopt a mechanism of defense if this mechanism is widely used by members of a social group to which he belongs."[5] Or, to put it differently, one may not be the same person anymore after one has spent a few weeks in the Hutu Interahamwe or Arkan's militia. In addition, the types of pressures that a society puts on its members may themselves result from the sorts of personalities and beliefs that predominate in that society. Thus, a country populated primarily by aggressive and bigoted people might create a social and governmental system that pressures people to behave in bigoted or aggressive ways. Or a country of egalitarian-minded people might develop institutions and policies pressuring individuals to abandon agendas based on the domination of others.

What's more, there may not be one type of predisposition that inclines a person to participate in acts of evil against others. Insofar as obedience, conformity, and other situational pressures can propel a person toward the commission of mass atrocities, one might focus on the influence-prone, conformist, or obedient personality. But the willingness to obey is only part of the answer: holding prejudiced beliefs, which clearly relates to the tendency to dehumanize victims, might increase the likelihood that a person would participate in crimes of obedience against others. Bigoted beliefs also provide the initiative required to launch terrorist acts, or enhance campaigns of violence against out-groups. If certain people are drawn dispositionally to prejudice, as many psychologists believe they are, this personality type may be important to understand. Additionally, aggression-prone personalities may lead people to seek out or respond more readily to opportunities for hurting others and for behaving cruelly. Finally, people probably differ in their willingness to buy into simple-minded, bizarre, or cock-eyed ideologies; thus, one might search for an ideology-prone personality type.

During the late 1940s and early 1950s, with the ashes of Auschwitz still fresh, social scientists devoted a great deal of study to questions such as these. One monumental work captured the imagination of the educated world, holding that all of the tendencies just noted, toward obedience, prejudice, aggression, and simple-minded thinking, came together in one type of person: the authoritarian. At the time, many social scientists believed they had solved or were close to solving the problem not only of who becomes a fascist, but also of who carries out fascism's most atrocious acts. Now, more than five decades later, they are not so sure.

THE FASCISM-PRONE PERSONALITY

Years before the publication of *The Authoritarian Personality*[6] in 1950, European thinkers had begun to speculate about the unconscious foundations of support for fascism. The day after Hitler came to power in Germany, Max Horkheimer, the director of the Institute of Social Research in Frankfurt, moved his home from the suburbs to an apartment near the train station. Several days later, he and other scholars from the Institute boarded trains for Switzerland. It had not required their unquestionably powerful minds to figure out that Germany in 1933 was no place for a group of radical Jewish sociologist-philosophers, devoted to reconciling the gospels of Freud and Marx.

However, they felt particular confidence in their pessimistic prognosis because of earlier studies they had conducted on political beliefs in Germany. In these studies, they had learned that while most German workers identified themselves as Social Democrats in public opinion polls, they showed an entirely different set of underlying values and attitudes when attempts were made to tap their hidden, unconscious feelings. Here, the Social Democratic workers showed themselves to possess personalities and beliefs consistent with support for fascism. As a result, Horkheimer and his associates concluded that German labor would not mount an effective opposition to Hitler.[7]

Oddly enough, one of the first psychologists to sketch the contours of the profascist personality was a Nazi—E. R. Jaensch. In 1938, he defined two character types. One type exhibited strong, clear, unambiguous perceptions and unwavering rigidity. Jaensch contrasted this eminently profascist person with the confused, effete, vacillating, uncertain type, who was, of course, predisposed to support democracies.[8]

But most of the research came from the antifascist side, perhaps because, as *The Authoritarian Personality* maintains, fascists don't like to think in psychological terms. Several noted psychoanalysts and psychologists—Erich Fromm, Erik Erikson, Wilhelm Reich, Abraham Maslow, and Ross Stagner—had all explored the fascism-prone character before the authors of *The Authoritarian Personality,* suggesting that the roots of fascist support lay in various unmet personal needs, usually unconscious in origin. Thus, *The Authoritarian Personality* built on several prior works; the book's main contribution lay in its clear portrayal of what the authors called a "new anthropological type," and in their valiant efforts to support speculation about this type with reliable scientific investigations.

The four authors of the study came from very different backgrounds. In 1943, Nevitt Sanford, a Berkeley professor, and Daniel Levinson, a graduate student, began to develop a scale to measure anti-Semitic beliefs; both men were American-trained psychologists, sympathetic to Freud's psychoanalysis but well versed in scientific methodology. Else Frenkel-Brunswik, an immigrant with a doctorate from the University of Vienna, soon joined them. Max Horkheimer, who had also recently arrived in the United States, had received a large grant from the American Jewish Committee to direct a series of studies on anti-Semitism; he learned of the research at Berkeley, California, noted some similarities with work that had been conducted by his group at the Institute for Social Research in Frankfurt, and at once suggested a collaboration. He himself did not join the project, though he ultimately wrote a preface to the volume. But, on his suggestion, another immigrant scholar, Theodor Adorno, signed on as the representative of Horkheimer's Institute for Social Research. Adorno was a left-wing German philosopher, sociologist, and musicologist, who, despite his contribution to the field, never really felt at home in social psychology or the United States. In the 1950s, he returned to Germany.

The Authoritarian Personality reflected the personal insights of those who had escaped fascism as well as the intellectual perspectives of psychoanalysis and, to a lesser extent, Marxism. To all of this was added some sophistication in the research methodology that was characteristic of American social science. The 990-page volume presented many theories and several different research studies. The authors used every relevant research technique, case studies, clinical interviews, psychoanalytic techniques, attitude scales, and opinion questionnaires; there was a constant interplay among sociological theory, neo-Freudian insight, in-depth interviews, and statistical analysis.

Using these methods to study a sample of white California residents in the late 1940s, the researchers identified a type of person whose traits rendered him especially susceptible to antidemocratic propaganda.[9] Authoritarians, they suggested, want to dominate subordinates, those weaker or lower in status, and they make efforts to do so. At the same time, they defer meekly to superiors, those above them in organizations or society. This obedience to higher-ups goes well beyond the normal, balanced, and realistic respect for valid authority that most healthy people have; it reflects an exaggerated, emotional need to submit. Theodor Adorno describes the authoritarian personality metaphorically as resembling a cyclist: "Above they bow, below they kick."[10]

Often, authoritarians align themselves with those in power, because this enables them to fulfill simultaneously their needs for strength and submission. Not surprisingly, in light of these needs to dominate and be dominated, authoritarians also pay careful attention to power relationships; they want to know who's strong and who's weak, who's the boss and who's the follower, who's tough and who's not. Perhaps this preoccupation with toughness is what leads them to their extreme cynicism about human nature. They see the world as a jungle where "wild and dangerous things go on." It is, they believe, human nature to make war on one's neighbors.

When it comes to thinking, authoritarians abhor the unconventional, preferring instead to adhere rigidly to whatever values prevail in their surroundings. Thus, they often find themselves idealizing the moral authorities of the ethnic, religious, or political groups to which they belong. Authoritarians, for example, would find it extremely difficult to accept that their religious leader could lie. Complexity and ambiguity are anathema to authoritarians, who frequently divide the world into strict, sharply delineated categories. Everything must be black or white. You're with them or against them, smart or stupid, strong or weak, pro-American or anti-American.

Authoritarians are very likely to rely excessively on stereotypes and be superstitious about many things. They also dislike imaginative approaches to problems and particularly detest psychological insights into human behavior. They would, for example, tend to agree with a questionnaire item that "Nowadays more and more people are prying into matters that should remain personal and private."[11]

As a consequence of their inflexible need to defend conventional values, authoritarians are always on the lookout for violators of these values, whom they seek to condemn, reject, and punish harshly. Thus, they would accept that "an insult to our honor should always be punished" and that "sex crimes, such as rape and attacks on children, deserve more than mere imprisonment; such criminals ought to be publicly whipped or worse." This trait, often called authoritarian aggression or punitiveness, reflects more than normal disgust or anger at injustice; it involves a hearty enthusiasm for severe and damaging punishments.

Finally, authoritarians possess two tendencies that emanate from deep within the unconscious. They exhibit a puritanical preoccupation with sex reflected in a potent concern about other people's sexual business. Thus, authoritarians (in the 1940s) believed that "The wild sex life of the old Greeks and Romans was tame compared to some of the goings-on in this country, even where people might least expect it." They also agreed that "Homosexuals are hardly better than criminals and ought to be severely punished."

The Berkeley researchers also suggested that authoritarians tend to project their own, unacceptable inner impulses onto other people. In part, their belief in a dangerous world reflects an outward projection of their own deep-seated aggressive feelings. They are particularly likely to see plots and conspiracies everywhere; they may also fear germs. In these cases, they are, according to the theory, reacting symbolically to subterranean dangers that they sense within themselves. Their extreme concern with sexuality betrays profound unconscious desires to violate conventional mores in this area. They must, because of their heightened conventionality, deny all of what the Freudians call id drives—the powerful tidal waves of sex and aggression.

Psychoanalytic theory provides the glue that holds together the diverse elements of the complex authoritarian personality syndrome. According to this approach, the authoritarian is a product of his upbringing. All children experience stress as they learn to control their basic, inescapable, and biologically rooted impulses. But this stressful period proves especially trying for children whose parents are harsh authoritarians. Such parents show little sensitivity to their children's needs and establish severe, even brutal, disciplinary rules. Their basic household principle is a simple one: "Do what I say because . . ." Authoritarian parents are demanding, controlling, and unreasoning. As a result, the children cannot learn to manage their sexual and aggressive energy effectively. Instead, they construct powerful but unconscious psychological defenses designed to head off any confrontations with their sexual and aggressive passions, which they fear to be uncontrollable. While such children may appear well adjusted to the untrained observer, psychoanalysts argue that they have merely internalized and submerged deeply troubling conflicts.

The many interviews with authoritarians and nonauthoritarians conducted by the authors of *The Authoritarian Personality* confirmed that although the authoritarians outwardly presented idealized pictures of their parents, they also recalled their childhood years as threatening, traumatic, and overwhelming. The authors had little difficulty explaining the apparent contradiction: "Forced into a surface submission to parental authority, the child develops hostility and aggression which are poorly channelized. The displacement of a repressed antagonism toward authority may be one of the sources, and perhaps the principal source, of his antagonism toward outgroups [i.e., groups to which he does not belong]."[12] The hostile parent is remembered as benign; and, as a consequence of this, the authoritarian must redirect anger and resentment against some more acceptable target, or targets. Else Frenkel-Brunswik further explains: "Since the moral requirements in such a home must appear to the child as overwhelming and at the same time unintelligible, and the rewards meager, submission to them must be reinforced by fear of and pressure from external agencies. Due to the lack of a genuine identification with the parents, the fearfully conforming child does not make the important developmental step from mere social anxiety to real conscience."[13]

So authoritarian parents produce authoritarian children who mature into authoritarian adults. The parents themselves became authoritarians in the first place because of their own parents. But why? Here, the authors of *The Authoritarian Personality* show how they were influenced by Marxist sociology. They explain that "people are continuously molded from above because they must be molded if the overall economic pattern is to be maintained."[14] Parents, in effect, transmit to children the personalities they need to function effectively as pawns of the capitalist system.

In sum, the authoritarian is Archie Bunker, but without the occasional lapses into human warmth. He is the adult manifestation of mechanisms of psychological defense that were first developed in childhood. The authors of the study, themselves, did not expect to find many "pure" authoritarians displaying all the attributes; they merely introduced the type as a heuristic simplification. However, their research did document that many individuals with signs of bigotry and ethnocentrism also revealed a sizable cluster of authoritarian traits.

To measure authoritarianism, the Berkeley group developed an instrument called the F-scale, named for its presumed ability to predict fascist potential. They claimed that the instrument enabled them to predict a person's level of prejudice, hostility to democracy, and potential for supporting dictators, and that it did all of this without ever mentioning a minority group or giving away its aims. In fact, mentioning particular minority groups was unnecessary. People who hated one group tended to hate many, not by coincidence, but because bigotry addressed and, to some extent, resolved their deepest needs. From a psychological vantage point, the authoritarian's selection of particular hate targets is a bit of an afterthought, guided by convenience and social convention.

During the five decades since the publication of *The Authoritarian Personality,* the work has had a strange history of ups and downs in popularity. During the 1950s, research on the authoritarian personality dominated the field of social psychology, and hundreds of studies based on the F-scale appeared in scientific journals. Much of this work sought to identify the correlates of authoritarianism. In other words, what else do we know about a person when we know his or her score on the F-scale?

Over the years, researchers learned that high-F's repeatedly manifested the most prejudice toward a wide range of groups including Jews, blacks, ethnic minorities, and more recently, AIDS patients. In addition, studies indicated that authoritarians were more likely to: (1) favor faculty loyalty oaths during the McCarthy era; (2) support the Vietnam war; (3) oppose socialized medicine; (4) favor the prosecution in criminal trials; (5) prefer directive leadership and a high degree of structure in organizations; and (6) prefer conservative political candidates. More relevant to their likelihood to participate in mass atrocities, the studies revealed that high-F's tend to conform to group pressure in experimental settings and to obey the experimenter in the Milgram scenario. They also resist the efforts of educators to reduce their prejudice. But when a high status person tries to persuade them to become *more* bigoted, they are especially susceptible.[15]

From the very beginning, however, many social scientists criticized the theory, methods, and findings presented in *The Authoritarian Personality.* In retrospect, many critics have assailed the study for its lack of methodological sophistication. By present-day standards, this may be correct, but in fairness it should be noted that the study's methods received such intense scrutiny precisely because of its bold contentions and provocative findings. The methodological flaws are too many and too detailed to discuss here. For the most part, critics make a strong case that the theory presented in the 1950 volume was not "objectively and impartially sub-jected to the rigorous demands of scientific method."[16] Still, this does not imply that the theory is false. Some flaws were corrected by later re-searchers, and many social scientists still maintain that "the positive sta-tistical interrelationships among anti-Semitism, ethnocentrism, and au-thoritarian attitudes seem to appear consistently."[17] In any event, Adorno later wrote: "We never regarded the theory simply as a set of hypotheses but as in some sense standing on its own feet, and therefore did not in-tend to prove or disprove the theory through our findings but only to de-rive from it concrete questions for investigation."[18]

Two particularly damning criticisms of *The Authoritarian Personality* were never resolved adequately, and have led to other approaches. First, even if the authoritarian syndrome of personality traits and attitudes does exist, little evidence has been adduced to support the contention that it originates in childhood stresses, unconscious needs, and a web of defense mechanisms. The syndrome may be simply learned and absorbed from one's social environment. Second, early critics noted that while the au-thors may have succeeded in identifying a right-wing type ready to follow fascists, they missed an important counterpart—authoritarianism on the left. Historically, tendencies toward obedience, aggression, and hostility have sustained left-wing dictatorships as well as those on the right. Yet the authors of *The Authoritarian Personality*, with their Marxist roots, had been blind to this possibility, even in an era when Stalin's Communists had murdered millions. Thus, conservatives and Republicans in the United States scored high on the F-scale, while liberals and leftists did not. This finding suited the politics of some social scientists just fine, but oth-ers attacked the approach for what seemed a manifest political bias.

By the mid-1960s, social psychologists had achieved little consensus about *The Authoritarian Personality*, but they turned their attention to other matters. Most social scientists apparently believed that the topic had been milked for all it was worth. It seemed as if authoritarianism, like General MacArthur, the hero of many 1950s authoritarians, had not died, but would slowly fade away. Yet the 1980s and 1990s witnessed new inter-est in the theory, in modified, updated forms.[19]

The intense, and convincing, criticism of the original study's methods led many researchers to abandon use of the F-scale as a measure of au-thoritarianism. While some psychologists merely attempted to fix blatant technical errors, others focused on new dimensions of personality, some related to authoritarianism, but conceptually distinct. Milton Rokeach, for example, argued that authoritarianism is actually a way of thinking about the world, representing a close-minded cognitive style.[20] As a result, he introduced, and measured, two new personality traits: dogmatism and opinionation. Rokeach claimed that his dogmatism scale indicated the degree to which a person's system of beliefs was open or closed; unlike the F-scale, which measures only right-wing authoritarianism, Rokeach's dogmatism scale picks up both right- and left-wing authoritarians— along with those whose close-mindedness relates primarily to nonpoliti- cal matters. Research confirms that those scoring high on the dogmatism scale are much less likely to tolerate their "least-liked group," whomever it might be.[21] Rokeach's opinionation scale measures the degree to which we accept or reject others based on whether they agree with us.[22]

Another researcher, John Ray, an Australian psychologist, has focused on an aspect of authoritarianism that he calls "directiveness," or leadership de- sire. His measure includes such questions as "Do you tend to boss people around?" and "Are you the sort of person who likes to get his own way?"[23] This scale may measure, rather overtly, an authoritarian's tendency to dominate others, but it probably fails to pick up the urge to submit.

In a well-integrated and frequently cited series of studies, Canadian psychologist Bob Altemeyer has attempted to revive authoritarianism as a popular explanation of fascist destructiveness. He discusses his interest in the topic:

> The central concern of my research program has been the apprehension that there may be a vast potential for the acceptance of right-wing totalitarian rule in countries such as Canada and the United States. . . . The mood of a populace can create a climate of opinion that promotes totalitarian move- ments. It can intimidate politicians, journalists, and religious leaders who might otherwise oppose repression. It can encourage a bold, illegal grab for power, as it did in Italy in 1922. It can elect a Hitler to office, as it did in Ger- many in 1933. It can encourage military leaders to overthrow duly elected governments, as it has so many times since.[24]

Altemeyer drops many aspects of the traditional authoritarian person- ality that Adorno and his colleagues considered essential; he also leaves out the psychoanalytic underpinning of the theory, preferring to view the character-type as something a person learns from his or her environment. What remains are three key tendencies: (1) to submit to authorities who are perceived as established and legitimate; (2) to direct aggression against people who are perceived as conventionally sanctioned targets; and (3) to adhere to values and beliefs perceived to be endorsed by established authorities. He calls these tendencies "attitudinal clusters," by which he means orientations to respond in the same general way toward certain classes of people, groups, and values.[25]

On the basis of these three tendencies, Altemeyer has been able to measure his notion of authoritarianism on a scale called the RWA, for Right-Wing Authoritarianism. Someone who scores high on Altemeyer's RWA is also likely to approve of illegal wiretaps, illegal searches, and efforts to stop peaceful protests, provided that they are carried out by government officials. Such a person finds "regular" criminals more repulsive and disgusting than do those who score low on the scale; the high-RWAs want to impose long prison sentences, and they admit to pleasure at the thought of doing so. In experiments where they believed they had the opportunity to shock peers, those with high scores tended to select higher voltage punishments than did those with low scores. White South Africans with high scores showed more anti-black prejudice than did low-RWAs. Similarly, high-RWA white Canadians showed a greater tendency toward ethnocentrism and prejudice than did those with low scores.[26]

Altemeyer attempted to duck the charge of political bias by *defining* his scale as a measure of *right-wing* authoritarianism. But as one reviewer puts it, "[he] makes no secret about whose side he is on. . . . [H]is self-righteousness and superiority over those who demonstrate right-wing authoritarian tendencies color the entire book."[27] Altemeyer clearly prefers not only low-RWAs, but more generally, liberals, both politically and culturally. Thus, a person might obtain a high RWA score partly by agreeing with the following statements: (1) "The way things are going in this country, it's going to take a lot of 'strong medicine' to straighten out the troublemakers, criminals, and perverts"; (2) "In the final analysis the established authorities, like parents and our national leaders, generally turn out to be right about things, and all the protesters don't know what they're talking about"; and (3) "Young people sometimes get rebellious ideas, but as they grow up they ought to get over them and settle down."[28]

It is hard to see how such beliefs carry a person very far down the road to Nazism.

One researcher criticized Altemeyer's scale as "just another conservatism scale," noting that, statistically speaking, the same people scored high on both.[29] Although this is overly harsh criticism, it correctly points out that the RWA scale does not adequately distinguish between a psychological tendency to support fascist-type governments and behaviors on the one hand, and conservative beliefs on the other.[30] As Altemeyer suggests, conservatives probably *are* more likely than liberals to fall prey to destructive political schemes of the far right. But so too are liberals more likely than conservatives to support destructive agendas emanating from the far left. Altemeyer, and social scientists generally, have shown more concern and awareness of the former problem than the latter.

Recently, a team of psychologists from Stanford University launched a research project designed to explore a newly identified personality dimension related to authoritarianism. Felicia Pratto, Jim Sidanius, and their associates call this trait "social dominance orientation."[31] They start with a controversial theory that "societies minimize group conflict by creating consensus on ideologies that promote the superiority of one group over others."[32] The powers-that-be use these self-serving ideologies to teach that some people are not as good as others and, hence, deserve fewer things of value, such as jobs, gold, blankets, government appointments, and protection from disease.

The authors label these ideologies "hierarchy-legitimizing myths."[33] When they are widely accepted, they contribute to stabilizing oppression against target groups. Pratto, Sidanius, and their associates cite anti-black ideology as a hierarchy-legitimizing myth that flourishes in the United States. Support for a meritocratic system also strikes them as contributing to an oppressive society. In contrast, they cite beliefs such as "all humans are God's children" as reducing the tendency to divide people into categories and groups, thus increasing social equality. Needless to say, many of their views reveal a left-of-center political orientation; for example, they suggest that "conservatism generally can be viewed as a legitimizing myth" and that racism is a pillar of the contemporary American system.[34]

On the basis of their theory, the researchers suggest that individuals differ in the degree to which they want their own group to be superior to other groups and to dominate them. These individual differences in "social dominance orientation" have important implications. Pratto, Sidanius, and their colleagues see desire for social dominance as "the central individual-difference variable that predicts a person's acceptance or rejection of numerous ideologies and policies relevant to group relations."[35] Once we know how much a person wants their own group to dominate others, the researchers believe we know a great deal about their views on many social and political matters. They also believe the social dominance dimension tells us about a person's likelihood of taking on occupations and roles in life that contribute to maintenance of inequality.

Pratto, Sidanius, and their colleagues begin their study with a reference to conflicts around the world, including Bosnia and the Middle East. Unfortunately, however, they test their theories on about two thousand students from California. Thus, when they talk about nationalism, they mean nationalism in the United States (California to be more precise), which, as they acknowledge, may have an altogether different relationship to oppression than nationalism, say, in Serbia or Rwanda.

Moreover, their definition of terms draws too heavily on their political views. Thus, their five-item "Anti-Arab Racism" scale includes such items as: "Iraqis have little appreciation for democratic values" and "People of the Muslim religion *tend* to be fanatical" (my emphasis). These are debatable points, not indicators of bigotry. Similarly, they measure support for "Wars of Dominance" partly by the extent to which one would go along with a war "for U.S. national security purposes" or "to keep an enemy from acquiring chemical or nuclear weapons." Their fourteen-item "Social Dominance Orientation Scale" includes items like: "It is important that we treat other countries as equals."[36] It is hard to believe that, as they seem to suggest, the world would have *less* inequality if all the countries in the United Nations, including the many despotic regimes, had a voice in world affairs equal to that of the United States.

In a study that might have set a record for statistics per page, the Stanford researchers concluded that knowing a person's level of social dominance orientation tells us a great deal about their other views and tendencies as well. People high in social dominance orientation showed more anti-black racism, more belief in the existence of equal opportunities, more patriotism, more political economic conservatism, less support for social programs, less support for women's rights, less tolerance for diversity, and less altruism. Some of these relationships were moderate, and some were weak.

As noted earlier, the biggest problem lies in the way the Stanford team defines their terms. They define social dominance orientation in a way that seems to measure, in part, how much one disagrees with liberal ideology. Racism and many of the other beliefs they are trying to understand are also defined in ways that are confounded by where one stands on the liberalism-conservatism continuum. Thus, in effect, part of what these psychologists have discovered is that conservative Americans tend to be conservative Americans. No doubt, the study goes beyond this, also telling us something about people who believe that their group, whether religious, ethnic, national, or political, must dominate others. Conceptually, this dimension seems important and it should be studied without the political biases of the Stanford group. Even more critical, to learn how a person's orientation toward social dominance influences his or her susceptibility to destructive ideologies, research must be conducted in countries where nationalism has run amok, not in the United States where its influence in recent years has been, more or less, benign.

The social dominance theorists, like many who have conducted research on prejudice, appear to possess some not too hidden assumptions: first, that the American system leads to pervasive bigotry at home and suffering abroad, and second, that conservative Republicans represent the embodiment of evil in the United States. Starting with these convictions, they fail to push ahead as far as they might in their efforts to isolate the true psychological attributes underlying mass hatred on all sides of the political spectrum. Does any historically aware person really believe that one has arrived at the heart of the matter when he or she declares that people on the left will resist pressures toward mass hatred, when they arise, while people on the right will not?

The original model of the authoritarian personality had an impressive conceptual and intellectual coherence; the parts fit together logically and the model captured many aspects of personality that, intuitively, seemed to incline a person to support destructive dictators. But, as we have seen, follow-up studies soon demonstrated a swarm of methodological difficulties and it is now obvious that the authors of the original study came nowhere near to proving the theory. More than five decades later, one remains uncertain about which aspects of the authoritarian personality, if any, actually predispose a person to authoritarian behavior. Punitive tendencies, dogmatic habits of thought, submissiveness, a tendency to project one's inner conflicts outward, conventionalism, and cynicism may *jointly*, or *individually*, bear on participation in mass atrocities under different circumstances.

Unfortunately, researchers have devoted very little attention to understanding the role played by authoritarianism in crimes of obedience or other types of human destructiveness. Most studies have focused on the attitudes of adults, and, even more often, students, in Western countries where few mass atrocities have occurred in recent years. Additionally, authoritarianism may differ substantially from one era to another. As one of the authors of *The Authoritarian Personality* remarked nearly a quarter century after its publication, "The trouble with research on authoritarianism is that it has been research on *The Authoritarian Personality*."[37] He urged people to consider the possibility that "personality dispositions which in the 1940s belonged to the F syndrome today belong to something else, or may indeed be different in meaning or in underlying source."[38] Studies have also told us very little about how the tendency toward authoritarianism plays out in different cultures. An exception, one study in the Soviet Union in 1991, showed that authoritarianism, even on Altemeyer's scale, strongly predicted support for pro-Communist, antidemocratic, reactionary leaders and for military actions. Russian authoritarians also opposed non-Russian leaders. In a poignant demonstration that authoritarianism can exist on the left, highly authoritarian Russians also *opposed* laissez-faire individualism and voiced strong *support* for socialist equalitarianism.[39]

But, social scientists know very little about authoritarianism in atrocity-prone situations and cultures. We have no measures of how prevalent the fascism-prone personality-type is in the parts of the Islamic world where extremism has flourished, or whether Muslim extremists show more authoritarianism than other Muslims. We don't know how common it is in Rwanda or Burundi, or even whether the concept makes sense in those cultures.[40]

We know a bit more about Yugoslavia.[41] One study of high school youths conducted in two Serbian cities in the early 1970s found a very high level of authoritarianism, as measured by the F-scale. The Yugoslavian authors, N. Rot and N. Havelka concluded, about a decade-and-a-half before the rise of Milosevic, that "it is difficult to accept that these results signify . . . subjects' extraordinary readiness to accept an antidemocratic and even fascist ideology."[42] Needless to say, recent events have rendered it easier to accept this sort of interpretation. Rot and Havelka suggested that high levels of authoritarianism did not reflect a permanent character formed by bad relations in the family; instead, they argued that the students had absorbed authoritarian views from their culture. In 1991, Ivan Siber, a political scientist from the University of Zagreb, reviewed the Rot and Havelka study, along with several others conducted in various parts of the former Yugoslavia. He confirmed their view that a high level of authoritarianism prevailed in Yugoslavia. He also noted a connection between authoritarianism and ethnocentrism and argued that authoritarianism was "linked to the absence of a critical attitude towards different ideological orientations." According to Siber, this implies that "every contention is accepted regardless of its real meaning, provided its source is perceived as . . . legitimate and reliable."[43] Finally, Siber concluded that Yugoslavia represented an ideal breeding ground for conflict and for wholesale manipulation of the public. While it would be useful to know how much authoritarianism existed among various ethnic, social, and economic groups in the former Yugoslavia, the studies that were conducted do not provide this sort of information.

Several scholars have noted similarities between authoritarians and the mass killers, or potential killers, they have studied. During World War II, psychiatrist Henry Dicks examined the differences in fanaticism among freshly captured German soldiers, sailors, and airmen. He focused on the extreme fanatics, whom he termed "High Fs," coincidentally using the same label that Adorno and his colleagues employed for those who scored high on the fascism (F) scale. The label wasn't all they had in common.

Without knowing about the work being done at Berkeley on the authoritarian character, Dicks painted an almost identical portrait of fanatic Nazis. The Nazi fanatics (1) behaved deferentially to superiors, but dominated and punished inferiors; (2) despised tenderness; (3) followed a "cult of manliness"; (4) expressed satisfaction with the violence they had inflicted during the war; and (5) tended to "project and see hostile intent outside the self."[44] That Dicks arrived at this portrait independently suggests some confirmation, though he and the Adorno group started with similar assumptions rooted, as they were, in psychoanalysis. Years later, Dicks studied in detail a small number of SS murderers. He found that they too showed some of the central attributes of the authoritarian, but with one major exception. The killers differed from run-of-the-mill authoritarians because they had "particularly destructive mother-images." As children, all had been dominated to an abnormal extent by their mothers.[45]

Similarly, sociologist and former concentration camp inmate John Steiner, several decades after the war, administered a modified F-scale to a sample of two hundred former members of the SS and the German Armed Forces. The SS men, those who carried out the Reich's worst atrocities, scored significantly higher than the members of the regular armed forces. However, both groups showed a preference for monarchical or dictatorial forms of government. They also revealed satisfaction with their past military or paramilitary activities. Finally, the former SS and the former soldiers both valued loyalty and honor over justice.[46]

Discussing the personality of the *mutaassib*, or Muslim fundamentalist fanatic, political scientist R. Hrair Dekmejian draws a portrait that reflects many aspects of the authoritarian personality.[47] Rigid beliefs, intolerance toward unbelievers, preoccupation with power, vision of an evil world, austerity in sexual matters, and above all, obedience, characterize the mutaassib. However, his idealism and unconventional beliefs do not fit the authoritarian personality; in fact, the mutaassib seems closer to Rokeach's notion of a close-minded, rigid-thinking dogmatist. Dekmejian's portrait would be more credible if it were supported by studies of actual fanatics, particularly those who engage in terrorist acts. Needless to say, such groups do not readily cooperate with inquisitive social scientists.

THE UNIVERSALITY OF ETHNOCENTRISM

Back in 1906, the sociologist William Graham Sumner coined the term *ethnocentrism* as "the view of things in which one's own group is the center of everything. . . . Each group nourishes its own pride and vanity, boasts itself superior . . . and looks with contempt on outsiders."[48] To the extent that a group differs from one's own, it is viewed with disapproval and even scorn. Since Sumner's day, ethnocentric tendencies have been located in virtually every society on earth. The current view among psychologists is not only that ethnocentrism is normal, but that it is probably here to stay. According to Roger Brown, a noted Harvard scholar, "It is not just the seeming universality of ethnocentrism that makes us think it ineradicable but rather that it has been traced to its source in individual psychology . . . and the source is the individual effort to achieve and maintain positive self-esteem. That is an urge so deeply human that we can hardly imagine its absence."[49] Regardless of how groups are formed, "people's perception and memory of outgroups is that 'they are all alike, different from us, and bad besides.'"[50]

The point is, authoritarians may well be ethnocentric, but so is just about everyone else. Similarly, nearly everyone thinks with stereotypes some of the time, even those who are predominantly unprejudiced. The human mind possesses a great store of oversimplified images of various groups—occupational, national, religious, ethnic, and racial. People do not always rely on their stereotypes, but their presence is normal, widespread, and difficult if not impossible to eliminate. People use stereotypes because they are easy to use, and though they sometimes lead to erroneous judgments, they often do not. Their principal advantage is that they save time and energy.

The profiles of other groups that people paint in their minds are frequently negative, owing to the impact of ethnocentrism. It is important to emphasize that, most of the time, this process is neither abnormal, nor the result of hateful and insidious motives. More often, erroneous stereotypes stem from unintentional processes related to attention, memory, attribution, and logical reasoning.[51] While all people sometimes use enthnocentric and stereotypical thinking, they do not all rely on these processes to the same extent. Thus, a strongly prejudiced person may engage in stereotyping in a deeper, more thorough manner than others. Such a person would have harsher and nastier stereotypes, ones which are far more resistant to disconfirmation and less open to the possibility of exceptions.[52]

Researchers have started to explore why some people engage in more stereotyping than others. According to psychologist Mark Schaller and his colleagues, people differ substantially in their personal need for structure, the need to simplify and order their environments.[53] This dimension is somewhat related to Rokeach's concept of dogmatism as well as to the intolerance for ambiguity that has been noted in authoritarians. People who have a high personal need for structure tend, in experimental situations, to use more thinking based on stereotypes.

Social psychologists have drawn another, far more dramatic conclusion about prejudiced attitudes. Many studies, conducted over several decades, suggest that people who hold prejudiced *attitudes* are not that much more likely than people who are unprejudiced to engage in discriminatory *behaviors*. If all one knows is how prejudiced someone is against a particular group, one actually knows very little about how that person will *behave* in a particular situation toward members of that group. R. T. LaPiere conducted the first study of this type in the early 1930s. He accompanied a young Chinese couple in travels around the United States. Together, they visited two hundred fifty-one restaurants, hotels, and other establishments; only once were they refused service. Then, a few months later, LaPiere wrote to the establishments, asking whether they would accommodate members of the Chinese race in their establishment. One hundred twenty-eight businesses responded, and *ninety percent of these answered "no."*[54] Needless to say, this early study did not prove that prejudiced attitudes have no bearing on discriminatory behavior. For one thing, the letter did not necessarily present the proprietor's personal attitude, but rather his policy on how to respond to written requests for such information. Moreover, many attitudes, not just those involving prejudice, may have influenced the proprietors' behavior. For example, their feelings about losing customers or money may have overpowered their feelings about Chinese people.

The study did show that situational pressures can bear heavily on how a person behaves toward people of another race. Prejudiced beliefs apparently play a surprisingly small role in determining how a person will act toward members of a minority group in a specific, short-lived situation. These beliefs become highly relevant only when we observe how people behave toward minorities in many different situations over a long period of time.[55] Even then, hateful beliefs can very often be overpowered by other beliefs, such as the beliefs that murder is wrong, that crimes tend to be punished, that rudeness is unacceptable, or that one must not follow illegal orders.

Stereotyping and ethnocentrism occur too frequently in the general population to distinguish usefully between individuals who would accept destructive ideologies and those who would not. What's more, the presence or even the prominence of hateful beliefs cannot be viewed as reliable indicators of who will follow the propagators of hateful ideologies and who will not. On the other hand, personal tendencies toward obedience and conformity may prove significant as predictors of who follows destructive regimes once they take control.

THE OBEDIENT PERSONALITY

François Xavier Nkurunziza, a Rwandan lawyer whose father was a Hutu and whose mother and wife were Tutsi, offered his thoughts on why so many Hutus allowed themselves to become killers: "Conformity is very deep, very developed here. In Rwandan history, everyone obeys authority. People revere power, and there isn't enough education. You take a poor, ignorant population, and give them arms, and say, 'It's yours. Kill.' They'll obey. . . . And, in Rwanda, an order can be given very quietly."[56]

Obedience does not lie at the root of all participation in mass atrocities, but it certainly plays a part much of the time. As we have noted, researchers have used a variety of strategies to understand why some people obey illegitimate orders and others do not. One approach, in 1971, was to ask people the following question:

> What do you think *most* people would do if they were soldiers in Vietnam and were ordered by their superior officers to shoot all inhabitants of a village suspected of aiding the enemy, including old men, women and children? . . . What do *you* think you would do in this situation—follow orders and shoot them, or refuse to shoot them?[57]

The researchers then analyzed the attributes of those who said "shoot." How one answers in this hypothetical situation, however, may reveal little about how one would have behaved in the jungles of southeast Asia. Additionally, answers may reflect a person's degree of trust in the integrity of the American military; in other words, if the army says they're Vietcong, do you believe them? But responses do tell us something about people's attitudes toward obedience. Those who had more education, more income, and more prestigious jobs were most likely to *say* that they would defy illegitimate demands. In 1990, a public opinion poll presented the same question to a random sample of Moscow area residents,

substituting "Afghanistan" for "Vietnam." Again, educated people declared more willingness to disobey.[58] Consistent with this finding, other
researchers have found that people who are relatively high in education,
income, wealth, and social standing are less willing to conform to the
wishes of authorities. One way to interpret this finding is to consider the
jobs of the upper and upper middle classes; they typically require a
somewhat more independent attitude. Sometimes they have some authority themselves.

Another way to study the obedient personality is to focus on who
obeyed and who did not in the Milgram obedience experiments. Milgram
summarizes his own early efforts to analyze the differences between the
two groups:

> The findings, although generally weak, pointed in the following directions.
> Republicans and Democrats were not significantly different in obedience
> levels; Catholics were more obedient than Jews or Protestants. The better
> educated were more defiant than the less well educated. Those in the moral
> professions of law, medicine, and teaching showed greater defiance than
> those in the more technical professions, such as engineering and physical
> science. The longer one's military service, the more obedience—except that
> former officers were less obedient than those who served only as enlisted
> men, regardless of length of service.[59]

Only the relationship between low education and obedience showed up
consistently in many studies of obedience.

Later researchers tried to identify specific elements in a person's character that led him or her to obey in the Milgram experiment. Gender didn't
make a difference. Authoritarian personalities, those who scored high on
the F-scale, tended to obey more than nonauthoritarians, although the
difference between the two groups was not so great as one might have expected. Moreover, authoritarians were also less well educated, so it is hard
to tell which factor is more important here.

Another personality trait, the "locus of control," may have something to
do with whether a person obeys. Some people, called "internals," believe
that they have the ability to control whether good or bad things happen to
them. Other people, labeled "externals," believe the opposite, that luck,
chance, and powerful people determine whether their fortunes will be fa-

vorable or not. People with an internal locus of control may resist efforts by others to influence them, and they may react more strongly when they think someone has taken away their freedom of choice.[60] Recall the Dutch-American engineer, discussed earlier, who grew angry when the experimenter told him that he had no choice.

Other studies have sought to identify the roots of the *conformist* personality. Again, a few broad contours emerge but no precise image. The conformist may, on average, have lower self-esteem and, not surprisingly, a strong need for approval from others.[61] Conformists also tend to have authoritarian attitudes. They probably differ from nonconformists on a dimension called self-monitoring, the extent to which they pay attention to the impressions they make on others. Low self-monitors, those who pay less attention, are also less likely to conform to peer pressure. Unfortunately, efforts to understand the conformist personality haven't proceeded very far, and no personality trait very consistently distinguishes between conformists and nonconformists.

THE UNEDUCATED KILLER

In Cambodia, between 1975 and 1979, the Khmer Rouge regime massacred about two million people. Pol Pot, the head of the murderous government, directed the bloody campaign against "potential enemies," defined to include officers of the old regime's defeated army, government officials, intellectuals, educated people, and professionals. In some instances, the Khmer Rouge killers deemed the mere knowledge of a foreign language or even the wearing of eyeglasses offenses worthy of death. On Pol Pot's orders, the army emptied cities and appropriated every last morsel of many not-too-well-off people's property. Where did he and his associates devise such plans? At the Sorbonne in Paris. They apparently took the first decisive steps down the road to genocide on the Left Bank of the Seine. This coterie of intellectuals developed the Khmer Rouge ideology while debating Marxist politics and writing theses on the Cambodian peasantry. Pol Pot and his associates represented the cream of their nation's intelligentsia.[62]

The Bosnian Serb leader Radovan Karadzic bears as much responsibility as anyone for atrocities directed against the Bosnian Muslims. He is a trained psychiatrist. His sixty-five-year-old deputy, Biljana Plavsic, "the empress," was famous for her enthusiasm for the cause, as evidenced by a much-publicized kiss she planted on the cheek of Arkan. Plavsic, now on trial for war crimes at the Hague, was a former biology professor who spent time in New York on a Fulbright fellowship. Milan Babic, the Serbian ruler of the occupied Krajina region in Croatia, has plenty of blood on his hands, but not much of it came from his work as a dentist. In Rwanda, many of the Hutu leaders had received fine educations. One of the first to call for the mass murder of the Tutsis was Leon Mugesera, a doctor. Sheikh Omar Abdel Rahman, the militant Muslim leader, holds a doctorate in Islamic jurisprudence from Al-Azhar University; Ayatollah Khomeini wrote scholarly works on Islam. And one might also recall *Dr.* Goebbels, the impressive IQ scores of the Nuremberg war criminals, and the grotesque involvement of many physicians in the Auschwitz killing process.

Something doesn't seem quite right about explanations that place the preponderance of responsibility for crimes of destruction at the feet of the uneducated. Yet many different types of evidence suggest that education, in general, renders a person more tolerant, more supportive of democracy, less obedient, less dogmatic, less authoritarian, less racist, and less anti-Semitic. All of these attributes would seem to render the educated person more resistant to destructive ideologies and less likely to follow the commands of illegitimate, destructive leaders. By contrast, the uneducated seem the perfect foot soldiers of evil.

In the 1950s and 1960s, a number of sociologists and psychologists in the United States began to question whether the cluster of authoritarian traits really originated in unconscious needs and certain child-rearing patterns. The authoritarian style showed up more frequently in certain cultures (including Germany, Lebanon, and South Africa) and especially among the less educated and the working class. Couldn't the authoritarian personality be more simply explained as a product of learning? Perhaps a person absorbed parental values and the values present in his or her surrounding environment. Or perhaps a formal education made the biggest difference.

This latter position received strong support from a major American study of anti-Semitic attitudes, and the findings have held up over the years.[63] Using a sophisticated survey and statistical methods, the sociologists who conducted the study concluded that the cluster of authoritarian traits and beliefs could be best explained by looking at a person's level of formal education. Education influenced people's anti-Semitic beliefs and other authoritarian attributes in several ways. First, bigoted and antidemocratic attitudes can be viewed as a form of intellectual unenlightenment, a deficiency in reasoning, logic, and information. Formal education immerses people in a new culture and it gives them a new worldview. Education also teaches new styles of thinking, imparts new information, and, above all, transmits the principles of democracy, equality, civil liberties, and civil rights. But an education is also a social experience, where students, in general, are placed in a more liberal and tolerant environment where they are exposed to people from different backgrounds. Additionally, education provides a ticket to the middle class, a setting where authoritarian attitudes are generally somewhat less acceptable.

One can, perhaps, become prejudiced, dogmatic, and authoritarian by three different, but sometimes overlapping, routes. A person who lives in a culture or class where such views prevail may simply absorb them from the environment. Or a person subjected to harsh child-rearing practices and a repressive family setting may develop some of the authoritarian traits in order to meet their deep personal needs. Finally, those with little or no formal education may adopt the authoritarian's perspective because it fits their intellectual, cognitive, and social world, while those who are educated may reject authoritarianism for similar reasons.

The amount of formal education one has received also makes a big difference in determining how much one participates in the political process. At least in the United States, the rule has been the more education, the more participation. The uneducated lag far behind the educated in support for democratic values, principles, and procedures. Thus, one 1988 survey indicated that only 25 percent of those with only a grade school education would permit a homosexual to teach at a college or university; 85 percent of those with a college education would do so. On nearly all similar questions, the educated come across as more tolerant.[64]

How can the evidence from survey studies be reconciled with the obviously prominent role of the educated in many destructive regimes? Some of the discrepancy may reflect the ability of the better educated to detect and deliver the socially desirable answers to interviewer's questions. Thus, one survey found that a high percentage of educated people would *not* allow a *racist* to teach at colleges or universities. They have learned that it is socially *chic* to condemn racists, but not homosexuals, though the underlying principle, condemning an out-group, is the same.[65]

Another explanation for the discrepancy may be that the educated classes are learning different things in the United States, where most of the surveys were conducted, than they are in the parts of the world where most of the atrocities have occurred. Most important, though both educated and uneducated people show a willingness to succumb to orders, pressures to conform, and other types of influence, it is the educated who are more likely to take the lead in devising schemes of destruction for others to follow.

THE AGGRESSIVE KILLER

Indescribable poverty and the world's worst AIDS epidemic prevailed in Rwanda in the years preceding the 1993 genocide. Civil war and a floundering economy threatened to deliver a future of continuing instability and repression. Hutus and Tutsis sometimes lived worse than the nation's renowned mountain gorillas, who were themselves frequent victims of poaching by desperate men.

The Muslim world, even before the resurgence of Islamic revivalism, experienced sharp internal rifts, class against class, country against country, sect against sect, faction against faction. Despite tremendous stores of petroleum, the vast majority of Muslims remained impoverished. Unhealthful conditions abounded, except in some parts of the richest nations. Repeated failures to defeat Israel on the battlefield were also a source of frustration.

Yugoslavia, before the break-up, had witnessed a series of economic failures and was politically adrift, seemingly beyond reach of terra firma. Turkey, prior to the World War I massacre of the Armenians, had been the "sick man of Europe," a once powerful empire at its last gasp. Cambodia, before Pol Pot, had been a poor nation, devastated by the war in Indochina, and ruled by a despot. And Germany, at the time of Hitler's rise to power, had faced overwhelming unemployment, warring political factions, and an obviously ineffective political system. Many Germans still smarted over the loss of World War I and the resulting impositions of the Versailles treaty which required Germany to pay large reparations to the victors.

Difficult conditions predispose nations in the direction of aggressive regimes and mass violence. In such times, individuals feel blocked in their efforts to reach personal goals. They also feel diminished indirectly by their nation's inability to realize shared objectives. On the other hand, poverty, internal divisions, insufficient health care, and unrealized international ambitions exist across much of the globe. And whereas places under such conditions are indeed vulnerable to mass hatred, most do not approach destructiveness on the scale of Bosnia or Rwanda.

Psychologists' theories of aggression can help explain why some nations slip into an abyss of intergroup hatred and murder, while others manage to deal with their hardships less destructively. These theories can also provide clues about individual differences in aggressiveness. Such differences become important in every genocidal situation, for they suggest how people will act when the opportunity arises to inflict harm on others. As we have noted, more aggressive people will seek out, create, and enhance opportunities to behave destructively and hatefully. Sometimes they will become terrorists. They may also reap some satisfaction from their deeds.

In the 1930s, a team of psychologists at Yale University presented a substantial body of research supporting two propositions: that aggressive behavior *always* presupposes the existence of frustration, and that frustration *always* leads to some form of aggression. Frequently, aggression cannot be directed against the source of the frustration. In these cases, the aggression is displaced and redirected onto more available targets.[66] More than half a century later, the "frustration-aggression" theory remains influential, but with some important refinements and modifications.[67]

Frustration, it is now thought, will lead to aggression only if it is preceded by feelings of anger. If these feelings do not occur, there will be no inclination to act aggressively, even if a person has been blocked in his or her efforts to achieve important goals. Thus, for example, an apology may smooth ruffled feathers and head off a confrontation, even when an individual has been seriously injured.

Several psychological events may lead a person from simple frustration to anger. The perception that one's frustration stems from unjust treatment can be a powerful source of anger and aggression, especially when one feels impotent to address the injustice by other, more legitimate means. Many Hutus felt that the Tutsis had historically mistreated them and that the RPF was waging an unjust war. Many Germans, after their defeat in World War I, felt mistreated by the victor nations and the Versailles treaty. Many also felt betrayed by socialists, democrats, and other domestic elements in Germany. Muslims throughout the Middle East lamented their treatment at the hands of the Western powers. They had a vision of their faith as a glorious conqueror, yet they found themselves subordinated to the infidel West. Many also resented exploitation brought about by leaders of their own countries.

Of course, the *perception* of injustice is not the same as *actual* injustice. Moreover, deprivation is not the same as frustration. The world is full of people who feel mistreated, even though they are not. Equally common, perhaps, are people who have been tremendously deprived, yet feel and behave as if they have not. The economically deprived do not always grow angry or aggressive; neither do the sexually frustrated. Psychologists and sociologists have focused on the importance of *relative* deprivation. People are especially likely to feel frustrated if they have (or get) less than they have been led to expect or less than people similar to themselves have. When conditions start to get better, people's expectations often rise even quicker than the improving circumstances. This is one of the problems facing Eastern Europe and the states of the former Soviet Union. With Communism dead, inhabitants of these regions rapidly developed a taste and expectation for Western comforts. Yet even a successful economic program cannot meet these expectations. Thus, frustration and aggression often come into play, threatening the very processes that promise long-term gains. Similarly, American blacks rioted in the 1960s after circumstances began to change for the better. In Yugoslavia, Tito's death and the end of the Communist regime brought rapidly rising expectations that no government could easily satisfy. And, in the Arab world, the immense wealth that resulted from rising oil prices in the 1970s also produced rapidly growing expectations that, for most Arabs, remain unmet.

Psychologists have suggested other sources of aggressive behavior, some of which are self-evident. For example, people tend to become aggressive when they are provoked. This simple fact goes a long way toward explaining hostility in genocidal situations like Bosnia or Rwanda, where people on all sides have committed atrocities.

Also, some studies have suggested that the presence of aggression-related items, like guns and other weapons, increases tendencies to behave violently. Hot temperatures, overcrowding, humidity, air pollution, and offensive odors have also been linked to the expression of aggressive urges. Other studies indicate that people who drink alcohol excessively are more likely to commit acts of aggression because the drug removes their inhibitions. Sometimes, this lowering of inhibitions is intentional. They drink to hide from their deeds and to enable them to act without dealing with the mental and emotional consequences. The leaders of the Einsatz-gruppen, the Nazi murder squads in Eastern Europe, expressed great concern about their drunken troops. Victims of other atrocities have reported that their tormentors seemed intoxicated, as well.

Why do individuals in the same societies differ in aggressiveness? One answer is that more aggressive people have experienced greater hardships. More likely, however, these individuals process information about frustrating events differently and in ways that create deep anger. Aggressive people may, as the psychoanalysts insist, be reacting to misguided child-rearing, and, as adults, are working out their internal conflicts through hostile behavior. Alternatively, aggressive people may have learned their ways from their parents and others who rewarded them for behaving aggressively, or who failed to provide role models for the effective management of frustration. Yet another possibility is that more aggressive people differ biochemically from less aggressive people.

Regardless of how they became that way, aggressive people, as one would assume, show up often among the perpetrators of mass atrocities. They are especially apt to commit terrorist crimes and to initiate their own atrocities within sanctioned massacres. But they are not the ideal bureaucratic killers, for they lack the ability to turn their aggressive tendencies on and off.

WHO BECOMES A MASS MURDERER?

The authors of *The Authoritarian Personality* thought that obedience, conformity to conventional values, ethnocentrism, stereotyping, prejudice, dogmatism, intolerance for ambiguity, and a few other characteristics combined into a coherent, if misguided, personality; this type of person, they believed, would fuel evil regimes and obey evil orders. More recent research suggests that destructive regimes do not depend on any single type of person. Although a case can be made that uneducated people share many of the predisposing traits, the highly educated do, in fact, take the lead in planning and implementing some hateful acts, particularly those requiring initiative, rather than obedience.

Most psychologists now see ethnocentrism and stereotyping as part of the way people normally process information about their environments. The human mind groups people, as well as objects, into categories. This process of categorization helps us to simplify the present and predict the future more effectively. It is, however, a small step from categorization to stereotyping and favoritism for one's own group.[68] Most people take this step without becoming haters of those in other groups. Nonetheless, taken to extremes, and rigidly applied, habits of mind based on ethnocentrism and stereotyping can foster prejudice. And deeply prejudiced people respond with greater enthusiasm to bigoted ideologies.

In general, close-minded people, even those who are *not* deeply prejudiced, seem susceptible to a variety of rigid, and potentially destructive, ideologies. When these ideologies rest on right-wing notions, they appeal particularly to authoritarians on the right. When mass hatred is couched in leftist ideology, as in Cambodia, or religious ideology, as in the world of extremist Islam, supporters have a different political profile. Nationalist hatred is particularly potent and can cut across the spectrum of political opinions.

Subject to extremely powerful situational pressures, many otherwise decent people succumb. When these pressures are weaker, only certain types of people are likely to participate. Less educated people and those with lower social status generally show greater obedience to murderous authorities. So too do those with low self-esteem, those highly attentive to the opinions of others, and those who feel that they do not control their own destiny.

Another relevant dimension has not yet been the subject of much study by psychologists; this trait can be called moral consistency. Recall the Nazi bureaucrats who so easily abandoned their values to aid their careers. And, in Bosnia, people on all sides regularly subjugated their morality to self-interest. All people abandon their values at times, but certainly not to the same degree. How firmly one stands by one's values is, of course, a different matter from what those values are, or how loudly one professes them. In contemporary America, this personality trait might be related, for example, to a person's willingness to write advertisements for a cause or product which he or she opposes, providing the price is right. In harsher times, low levels of moral consistency might produce ambitious, hard-working Nazi bureaucrats who, later on, may honestly declare that they did not act from hatred. They acted from greed and a lust for status and advancement.

Finally, aggressive people may respond to ideologies based themselves on aggression; when their personality is, then, supported by a murderous ideology, they may seek out and create opportunities to harm others. Many Muslim extremist terrorists fall into this category; they are especially frustrated by the hardships of their lives, and they interpret these hardships as arising from ubiquitous injustice. Thus, their personalities are well suited to the extremist ideology of their radical Muslim theologians. Each reinforces the other, and the end result is a person seething with anger and longing to strike out against the West. Aggressive people are particularly likely to thrive on cruelty, as demonstrated by the Bosnian Serb rapists who sought to humiliate their victims, and the Nazi death camp guards who tortured the inmates. In situations where authority figures sanction evil behavior, they come into their own.

EIGHT

Can Anything
Be Done?

CONFLICT BETWEEN GROUPS IS LIKE A STURDY THREE-LEGGED STOOL. IT IS STURDY BECAUSE TWO LEGS ARE UNIVERSAL INERADICABLE PSYCHOLOGICAL PROCESSES, ETHNOCENTRISM AND STEREOTYPING, AND THE THIRD LEG IS A STATE OF SOCIETY, UNFAIR DISTRIBUTION OF RESOURCES, WHICH HAS ALWAYS EXISTED EVERYWHERE.[1]

Roger Brown,
Social Psychologist, Harvard University

Some of the raw materials of mass hate can be found in almost every society on earth, often in plentiful supply. People everywhere tend to think in terms of "us" and "them," and to prefer their own group. Across the globe, even the most tolerant people sometimes rely on simplistic stereotypes. No society has yet been able to free itself of sociopaths, extreme bigots, and aggressive personalities. And frustrating life conditions of one sort or another exist in every nation.

Fanatics always seem to be sprouting evil schemes, though their ideologies vary from place to place. Not infrequently, a fanatic emerges with charismatic appeal. More threatening, still, a large percentage of every population seems ready to obey authorities, conform to peers, and subordinate moral principles to personal self-interest or the wave of the moment.

Despite these ingredients for destructiveness, mass hatred has reached murderous proportions in a relatively small number of societies. For someone seeking to understand large-scale atrocities, therefore, the most important question is not where prejudice or any other raw material of mass hate originates. The key issue is how these ingredients combine in an explosive mixture.

THE DESTRUCTIVE SOCIETY

No simple formula can account for the many routes by which societies have arrived at mass hatred. Each travels down a path marked by the idiosyncrasies of its history, politics, traditions, and leadership. Still, the fires of hate and destructiveness are more likely to ignite in some societies than in others.

Widespread and intense public anger usually accompanies mass hatred, and this anger typically bears some relationship to the amount of frustration a population experiences. Economic deprivation, persecution, epidemics, military defeat, and other problems may breed frustration on a societal scale. But harsh circumstances alone do not lead directly, or necessarily, to seething frustration and anger. People in many lands endure such conditions with equanimity, and, conversely, the absence of apparent deprivation hardly guarantees that people will *not* experience frustration. People become most disheartened when the rewards they get out of life fall far short of those they expected. Thus, rising, or unrealistically high, expectations sometimes contribute as much to mass frustration as does actual deprivation.

Similarly, a frustrated society need not, automatically, become an angry one. Only when people view their situations as unacceptable *and* as the result of injustice will anger prevail. When many people in a society decide that they are suffering unbearably because of oppression or mistreatment, the risk of mass hatred increases substantially. Experiences of real injustice lie at the heart of some destructive impulses, but a sense of inequity need not arise out of any actual persecution, nor from the deeds of the eventual targets.

Many Germans felt deeply frustrated by real economic problems during the Weimar period. But this frustration intensified manifold because of their memories of prewar prosperity and their conviction that Germany should lead the world in economic power and living standards. German frustration turned into bitter anger when they accepted the false assertion that Jews, Western democracies, and socialists had landed the nation in its difficult situation.

In those parts of the Muslim world where extremism flourishes— Egypt, Algeria, Afghanistan, Iran, and the Gaza Strip/West Bank area— economic, political, military, and cultural gains have failed to keep pace with rising expectations. First independence from colonial rule, then the battle against Israel, and finally immense oil wealth raised hopes of a new golden age. But advances stalled on all fronts. Many Muslims now fill themselves with rage over the perception that their society's stagnation has been a consequence of mistreatment by secular leaders, the infidel West, and the Zionists.

Psychologists have shown that people naturally have a self-serving bias that they use when they explain life's ups and downs. While people usually take credit for accomplishments, they frequently assign blame for failure to others.[2] In every spot where hatred has flourished, a popular ideology has capitalized on this psychological tendency by exaggerating real injustice and by teaching that all, or most, of a group's suffering arises because of some evil "other."

Extremist Muslim ideology teaches that the infidel and the apostate are the sources of evil, and that they stand between the believer and a satisfying life. In Rwanda, extremist Hutuism stoked and sometimes created the "memory" of oppressive Tutsi overlords. Advocates of a Greater Serbia built support by feeding memories of oppression during World War II and throughout history. According to the Serb extremist ideology, many different groups had oppressed the nation at various times, including Germans, Croats, Soviets, and others. But by equating Bosnian Muslims with the medieval Turkish Muslim conquerors, Serb extremists activated an especially powerful symbol of resentment.

Ideologies of hate do more than identify the evil enemy, they excite a lust for revenge. Nearly always, destructive doctrines couch the call to arms in a vocabulary of self-defense: "We must attack them now in order to prevent them from attacking us later." Often, no real threat exists. Jews in Germany valued their German nationality, and possessed very little power to harm the fatherland. But Nazi teachings portrayed them as demonic and dangerous foes who had hurt Germany in the past and were bent on destroying her in the future. Anti-Semitic policy came to fulfill a manufactured desire for revenge as well as an unrealistic perception that a preemptive strike was needed.

At times, an ideology of hate exaggerates a real present risk or treats past persecution as though it were contemporary. Serb nationalists called for a war against Croatia, describing Croats as present-day fascist Ustashas who wanted to pick up where they had left off in the 1940s. The cycle of genocide in Rwanda and Burundi made many Hutus receptive to the extremist canard that the Rwandan Tutsis were planning to murder Rwandan Hutus, just as Burundian Tutsis had slaughtered Hutus in that country in 1972, 1988, and 1993. No such intentions existed, and the purported defensive strategy amounted to a cloaked genocidal program organized by extremist Hutus.

The risk of murderousness increases greatly when ideologies of hate take steps to dehumanize victims. The use of animal imagery is particularly foreboding, as in Nazi depictions of the Jews as rats and Hutu references to Tutsis as insects. Such allusions to the subhumanity of enemies can be an early sign of the potential for mass bloodshed.

To carry out the destructive agenda set forth in an ideology of hate, leaders often create special organizations to hone supporters and recruits into sharp implements of mass murder. These units undergo harsh training, designed to eliminate the sensitivities of civilian life. The toughness of the discipline also serves to build commitment. At the same time, members of the units may be treated as an elite and granted special privileges. A spirit of camaraderie grows and the potential killers soon define themselves largely in terms of their membership in the group. Leaders devote considerable care to the ideological indoctrination of these special units, seeking to forestall the emergence of any remnants of conscience or critical thinking.

The Nazi SS is the classic example of a killing organization, but special groups designed for murder figure prominently in most mass atrocities. In Rwanda, the elite Presidential Guard, the Interahamwe, and the Impuzamugambe bear responsibility for many of the murders. In Bosnia, several militias, including those headed by Arkan and Seselj, committed the most horrible crimes. And extremist Muslims in many parts of the world have formed their own cadres of believers who study under a cleric, train in paramilitary procedures, and plan acts of destruction.

Societies which yield to mass hatred may possess norms and values consistent with violent behavior. For years before the Nazi assumption of power, Imperial Germany gloried in its militarism, and treated the ability to make war as a preeminent virtue. Many parts of the Arab world, for centuries, have been violent places where people frequently resorted to bloodshed over matters of personal insult.[3] And, by the 1990s, Rwanda and Burundi had seen so much violence that, as horrified as they were, people in both countries showed few signs of surprise when the machetes started swinging again.

Above all, however, one frequently overlooked characteristic separates societies where mass hate flourishes from those where it does not: an established democratic political culture. R. J. Rummel, a political scientist from the University of Hawaii, has argued:

> The more power a government has, the more it can act arbitrarily according to the whims and desires of the elite, the more it will make war on others and murder its foreign and domestic subjects. The more constrained the power of governments, the more it is diffused, checked and balanced, the less it will aggress on others and commit democide [mass murder]. At the extremes of Power, totalitarian governments have slaughtered their people by the tens of *millions*, while many democracies can barely bring themselves to execute even serial murderers.[4]

No democracy has ever made war on another democracy. Even nondemocratic states fight less frequently if their leaders are subject to some restraints on their power.

The Roman orator Cicero first said that "Laws are inoperative in war." In democracies as well as dictatorships, the greatest abuses of legality and human rights occur during wartime. Thus, Roosevelt authorized internment of Japanese-American citizens during World War II and Lincoln suspended various constitutional protections during the Civil War. But,

compared to other forms of government, democracies have shown considerably greater reluctance to kill civilians and otherwise violate human
rights, even in wartime.

Genocidal policies in nearly every instance have been launched by dictators in the midst of military conflict. Sometimes, the dictators launch
aggressive policies or take advantage of wartime emergencies as a smoke
screen for their plans to murder target groups. Alternatively, nondemocratic leaders have used mass killings to divert attention from unsuccess-
ful military ventures and to discourage the growth of internal opposition.

If one examines death tolls associated with governmental power, it becomes clear that nondemocracies are much more prone to murder civilians. As Rummel puts it (in a variant of Lord Acton's famous maxim):
"Power kills, absolute Power kills absolutely."[5] He has assembled statistics
on government-sponsored killings, excluding war dead, for those governments with the most blood on their hands. Such figures are always in-
exact and difficult to confirm, but one does not require precision to get
the point. The leaders in government-sponsored killings are: USSR
(1917–1987), 61,911,000; Communist China (1949–1987), 35,236,000;
Germany (1934–1945), 20,946,000; Nationalist China (1928–1949),
10,075,000; Japan (1936–1945), 5,890,000; Cambodia (1975–1978),
2,035,000; Vietnam (1945–1987), 1,659,000; Poland (1945–1947),
1,583,000; Pakistan (1971), 1,500,000; Yugoslavia (1944–1987),
1,067,000; Turkey (1915–1918), 1,000,000. None of these countries was a
democracy at the time of the deaths.[6] Smaller-scale atrocities also occur
much more frequently under dictatorships and Communist regimes
than in democracies.

Still, democratic governments have themselves been responsible for
some mass killings in cold blood, mostly through indiscriminate bombing of populated areas during wartime, but also from a range of atrocities
in Vietnam and various colonial wars. There is room to argue with Rummel's classification system here, especially his inclusion of the bombings
of Hiroshima and Nagasaki as unjustifiable atrocities. But, even if we accept his figures, the government-sponsored deaths associated with
democracies amount to less than one percent of all government-sponsored deaths. And many of the worst crimes of democratic governments
take place far from the public eye; when such crimes become widely
known, democratic publics and their representatives typically condemn

them. No form of government has proved incapable of murder, but democracies have shown the greatest resistance to mass hatred and its destructive consequences.

In a democracy, the power to control policy does not belong to any single person or group. Even the most charismatic leaders are severely restrained in their ability to mobilize followers down a path of fanaticism. Government bureaucracies, political parties, lobbyists, corporations, unions, churches, and other institutions compete with each other for influence, fighting to protect their interests. Just think how hard it is to get one bill passed. For the government to embark on a policy as drastic as domestic or foreign mass murder, a driving consensus would have to emerge among all, or most, of the groups that share political influence.

Many powerful and independent groups would have to be convinced, coopted, or stripped of power. In democracies, particularly in the United States, members of the elite feel themselves subject to the impact of cross-pressures from the various ethnic, professional, religious, regional, and political groups to which they belong. These multiple loyalties render them unlikely to march behind a banner of fanaticism based on group membership. Equally important, the democratic free media possess the power to expose, debunk, and derail any incipient plans for mass hatred. Television enhances this function dramatically by bringing the consequences of government action into voters' living rooms every night.

Citizens in democracies do, of course, experience economic deprivation, political disappointments, and many other sources of frustration. Moreover, difficult life conditions can be tougher to bear in a democracy where expectations for prosperity are usually high. However, democratic cultures provide an outlet for frustrations in legitimized protest and electoral contests. An ethos of debate further limits the buildup of frustrations and anger.

Radical philosophers have sometimes lamented these release valves as counterrevolutionary, and they do reduce discontent with "the system." But the release is more than a mere emotional catharsis. People are less likely to buy into extremist agendas of the left or right because they believe that today's poverty might be followed by tomorrow's prosperity, and today's electoral defeat by tomorrow's assumption of power. The emphasis on fair democratic procedures further reduces the likelihood that individuals will attribute their misfortunes to the evil behavior of another group. Blacks may blame whites for their troubles, and whites may blame affirmative action, but both groups know that they can take their complaints to the polling booths and the courts.

Of course, the relative resistance of democracies to mass hatred does not suggest that hate-mongers will find such societies altogether infertile for their creeds. Some homegrown extremists in democratic countries preach angry doctrines of hate that play second fiddle to none. In the United States, during the 1960s, violence often came from groups on the left, such as the Weathermen and the Black Panthers. The bombing of the Federal Building in Oklahoma City focused Americans' attention in the 1990s on the danger emanating from self-styled "patriot groups," armed militias, and associations of paranoid fanatics.[7]

Despite the damage done by Timothy McVeigh and other antigovernment extremists in the United States, the paranoid fringe has yet to make much headway among the bulk of the American people. Out of a population of two hundred seventy million, there are about three thousand five hundred skinheads. And fewer than one American in every thousand belongs to an extremist militia; of these, very few have shown an inclination to move beyond macho talk to acts of violence.[8] Even when hate groups limit themselves to extremist talk, they are condemned squarely by nearly all political leaders, whether liberals or conservatives, Democrats or Republicans. This is a very different state of affairs from that which existed in Weimar Germany, or any other setting in which mass hate has prevailed.

Abraham Foxman, the national director of B'nai B'rith's Anti-Defamation League, warns that "Cruel history has taught us that we dare not ignore the first sounds of jackboots."[9] His advice is sensible, but right-wing extremists in present-day America do not stand much chance of reaching even 5 percent of public support, much less of gaining control of the apparatus of government. The dozens of paranoid, hate-mongering groups quarrel among themselves; at present, they show few signs of uniting into an effective, centralized movement.

Homegrown extremists, driven by delusions of impending victory, will certainly continue to pose a deadly *terrorist* threat to the United States. The images of Oklahoma City that frightened, saddened, and angered most Americans probably inspired some fanatics, although most of the organized groups dissociated themselves from the bombing. And the democratic system with its extensive constitutional guarantees will have trouble combating this threat. But militancy of the sort manifested in the Oklahoma City bombing gives every indication of remaining the province of the lunatic fringe.

Compared to most democracies, the United States benefits from two particular protections against the eruption of murderous bigotry. First, according to several studies, those individuals who show the greatest propensity toward authoritarianism, aggressiveness, and prejudice are also the ones least likely to pay attention to, or participate in, politics.[10] Second, the American public, because of its extreme diversity, cannot seem to agree on whom to hate. One survey in 1987 showed the least liked group in the country as the Ku Klux Klan (32%) followed by the Communists (24%). Many people dislike one ethnic group or another, but the public as a whole is so far from a consensus that no program of repression has been able to get off the ground.[11] Unlike France, Britain, Israel, and most other democracies, few people in the United States feel confident of their own membership in any in-group. This insecurity restrains the popularity of movements committed to official persecution.

Despite the relative resistance of Western democracies to policies based on mass hatred, many scholars have accused democratic countries of complicity in genocidal, quasi-genocidal, or terrorist behavior. For example, America has been blamed for its refusal to take in refugees fleeing Hitler and for its failure to bomb the Nazi death camps. More recently, the United States has been accused of callous neglect for its failure to intervene strategically at an early stage in the dissolution of Yugoslavia and for its lack of concern about Rwanda and other parts of Africa. Critics additionally have attacked the United States for its conduct of relations with abusive regimes on the right (e.g., Zaire, Indonesia, Saudi Arabia, and South Africa) and, less frequently, on the left. These analyses raise important concerns about the moral limits of realpolitik and one nation's degree of responsibility for atrocities in another. They also suggest questions about where and when outside intervention might be helpful in averting mass atrocities. Critics of Western policy should not, however, obscure the fact that democracies have been far more resistant to hatred than any other form of government.

The crucial distinction between greater and lesser evils is sometimes lost. Israel Charny, the Executive Director of the Institute on the Holocaust and Genocide in Jerusalem, notes a disturbing trend in some German academic circles. The Holocaust is portrayed as "no different from what has always happened throughout history, is still happening, and will always happen."[12] Then, drawing upon their cynical relativism, these scholars reason that no one should be particularly outraged about the Holocaust or any other genocide. Ignoring all those societies that do not turn genocidal, they excuse German behavior before and during World War II on the grounds that this is the way "human beings always have been and will be in the future."[13] Similarly, those who wish to deny the significance of genocidal events compare them to other instances of suffering and death, such as the AIDS crisis, the bombing of Hiroshima, urban poverty, famines, war, and earthquakes.[14] By transforming the Holocaust (and, less often, other instances of genocide) into meaningless metaphors for all varieties of human suffering and misfortune, these "moral relativists" allow genocide to evade the extreme moral outrage and condemnation it deserves.

Another variety of relativism holds that the United States, by virtue of its treatment of blacks and Native Americans, is ethically no different from genocidal nations. The greatest moral failure in American history was the enslavement of blacks, but the question is not whether slavery was morally equivalent to genocide; the issue is whether slavery was the product of American democracy. The human suffering brought about by slavery cannot be over-stated. But the system of black slavery in the United States developed during an earlier era, before democracy, when the anti-slavery ethos had not yet developed. Slavery, at the time, was common in many parts of the world. Indeed, the same enlightenment forces that gave birth to democratic principles and the establishment of the United States as a nation were ultimately responsible for propagating the notion that slavery was wrong.

The United States permitted slavery to continue during the early years of the Republic, but the nation during those years had not reached its democratic potential; voting rights were restricted to a small percentage of the white, adult male population. Even so, sufficient pressures existed to force an end to slavery, albeit after a long, hard fight. Since the emancipation of the slaves, the American creed has become an increasingly powerful weapon for those opposed to racial injustice.

Twentieth-century America began to realize the ideals of democracy, gradually extending equal treatment to all groups. Still, as late as the mid-twentieth century, significant impediments remained to full equality for blacks and others. Whether one believes that major roadblocks remain, or that they were removed by legislation in the 1960s and beyond, it cannot be convincingly argued that contemporary mistreatment of blacks or any other group in the United States approaches the level of injustice found in nondemocracies, and it certainly cannot be argued that American inequities today are fundamentally similar to those in genocidal regimes. Whenever one blurs this distinction between the great evils of genocide that have occurred around the world and the lesser evils that have taken place within democracies, one runs the risk of inadvertently adding to the perceived legitimacy of the former.

WHY INDIVIDUALS PARTICIPATE

Several common explanations of why people take part in mass atrocities are inadequate. Contrary to popular opinion, few perpetrators evince signs of mental illness or severe psychological disturbance. Hitler probably fit the requirements for a diagnosis of borderline personality disorder, but this explains little about why he designed his genocidal program. About one person in every fifty has a borderline personality, and not many of these have Hitlerian obsessions. Few of Hitler's followers met formal criteria for any diagnosis of psychopathology. Most cannot be distinguished from others in a normal population on the basis of their mental health. Though psychopaths and sadists in Nazi Germany and elsewhere frequently made the most of opportunities afforded by genocidal programs, the preponderance of crimes of mass hatred can be traced to those whom psychologists would regard as "normal."

In addition, most participants in genocide become involved for reasons that do not derive directly from absorption in ideology or bigotry. While these killers are seldom free of hateful doctrine, they may commit their crimes for other reasons, such as the desire to advance their careers. And many of those who plan and carry out mass destruction show no signs of hateful attitudes or aggressiveness on a personal level. Indeed, a truly aggressive person may lack the ability to rein in impulses and toe the line, probably making him or her less desirable as a tool of systematic and controlled mass murder.

On the other hand, one should reject the theory that mass murderers are everyday, nice people who carry out their orders dutifully, and with the greatest of guilt and regret. Few participants in crimes of mass hatred comply out of the mechanical, slavish obedience found in the Milgram experiments. And very few kill because they fear death if they do not obey. Situational pressures push many to join a genocidal program, but these pressures are more subtle and drawn out than those in Milgram's experiment. Most perpetrators of atrocities understand exactly what they are doing, yet they persist. Few feel much troubled by conscience.

Still, there are exceptions to each of the above generalizations. To understand why a particular individual participates in mass murder, one must consider a long list of possibilities. Individuals may participate because (1) they fear punishment by superiors if they do not; (2) they are deeply committed to an ideology of hate; (3) they lack awareness of the consequences of their actions; (4) they possess very weakly developed consciences; (5) they seethe with hatred for the target group; (6) they see murder as a means of obtaining material reward; (7) they want revenge for real or imagined offenses; (8) they fear retaliation or punishment for crimes already committed by their group; (9) they encounter situations where they cannot control their aggressive or sexual drives; (10) they cannot muster personal resources to disagree with their peers; (11) they perceive no justification for disobeying orders from a legitimate authority; or (12) their sense of identity depends on continued association with the killing group.

Individuals may take part in genocidal or terrorist acts for any of these reasons. But it is possible to classify crimes of mass hatred into two broad categories: crimes of submission and crimes of initiative. These categories reflect the psychological activity or passivity of the killer.

In crimes of submission, individuals may have absorbed some aspects of an ideology of hate, but they lack a deep belief in, or personal commitment to, the ideology. They are not driven by a strong hatred for the target group. Whenever they reflect on their participation, they feel genuine regret and they derive no clear personal or psychic gain from their involvement. They may feel obliged to follow orders, even if they disagree with them. Alternatively, they may fear for their own or their families' well-being. Or they may go along simply because they cannot bear the thought of standing up to their peers and disagreeing.

Sometimes, perpetrators seem to act out the *role* of murderer, making decisions independent of their own values and beliefs. Milgram's subjects fall into this category, so do Zimbardo's guards, and so also do some Nazi bureaucrats. Most of the time, terrorists do not commit crimes of submission, because situational pressures seldom push one toward involvement in a terrorist act. When a person is allowed to desist from participation in a crime of submission, he or she is often relieved. And when situational pressures change or are removed, the perpetrator shows no further signs of murderous behavior.

The perpetrator of a crime of initiative, on the other hand, seldom feels much guilt, and may even be disappointed when the killing must cease. As in crimes of submission, many different motives may apply. But one factor is present in every crime of initiative: the perpetrator wants to participate and actively takes steps to increase his or her involvement in the planning or implementation of atrocities. Individuals may be driven by identification with the regime, its leader, or its ideology of hate. They may be fanatics, whose sense of meaning, purpose in life, and identity are tied up with service to the cause.

Paradoxically, many of these killers think of themselves as idealists. They may indulge in what one psychologist has called "superego-tripping." The superego is, of course, Freud's name for the individual's conscience and values. Superego-trippers choose to act in ways that soothe their superego. Alan Elms explains:

> [S]uperego-tripping is *acting on the assumption that whatever behavior best satisfies the demands of one's superego will be most effective in attaining one's realistic goals. . . .* [I]f you judge the effectiveness of your overt acts in terms of whether they make you feel good morally, rather than whether they have changed external reality in the ways you had planned, you're superego-tripping.[15]

Elms uses the concept to explain the ineffectual behavior of some American leftists in the 1960s—for example, antiwar protesters who were more concerned about demonstrating their moral purity than building a popular support base. However, the "superego-tripping" concept also applies well to those terrorists and murderous extremists who feel driven by their *warped* consciences or plans for a new world. These are the only compasses they use to guide their behavior. The real-world consequences of their deeds are irrelevant, and they show little awareness or concern that they may be hurting their own objectives. Some Muslim extremists fall into this category. So, too, may some Hitler-devotees and ideological purists of the SS who in their enthusiasm for world domination ignored clear signs that they were driving the Reich into the dust.

In contrast, some who commit crimes of initiative have little commitment to the cause at all. They are in it for what they can get out of it. Hermann Goering comes to mind, pilfering the great art collections of Europe. Some Serb killers who robbed the belongings of their victims also may fit in this category. Lastly, crimes of initiative include those acts perpetrated by individuals who have failed to control their aggressive or sexual urges. Such individuals reap satisfaction when they murder or rape. They may be sadists who regard their killing orders as good fortune. Those who commit crimes of initiative seek out opportunities to kill or otherwise participate. Some meet the criteria for psychopathology, but most do not.

FIGHTING MASS HATE

In the decades since Neil Armstrong's "giant step for mankind" from the Apollo landing craft to the surface of the moon, no giant step has been taken in curbing human destructiveness. During this period, Communist China, Pakistan, Burundi, Indonesia, Cambodia, Argentina, Serbia, and Rwanda all have launched campaigns of mass hatred and murder, some of which reached genocidal proportions. In addition, terrorists proffering every political ideology except moderation have brought fear and havoc to nations around the globe.

Civilized people cannot observe the horrible suffering that results from mass hatred without asking whether somehow the Western nations might have done something to mitigate or prevent the disasters. Larry Martz, editor of *World Press Review*, published an early symposium addressing Western policy toward the genocide in Rwanda. He identified some problems that not only concerned Rwanda's situation, but are inherent in any Western response to mass hatred. Martz writes:

The impulse to help is generously human, but we have never come to terms with the questions of how, at what cost, and under what circumstances. Intervention may effectively halt atrocities and ease suffering—or our help could prove to be self-serving, misguided, or just counterproductive. Nations are sovereign: When are outsiders justified in imposing their own standards? Where does involvement end? Are we prepared to follow police action with warfare, conquest with colonial administration? Are we sure what is the lesser evil? And who precisely are "we"?[16]

Though the most extreme option of colonial administration is impractical in most contemporary situations, each of Martz's questions must be examined case by case.

Concerning Rwanda, the United States did not consider the situation in that country a high priority, even after the genocide began. The RPF leaders and many writers have objected that President Clinton did far too little to stigmatize and isolate the perpetrators of the massacres.[17] In 1998 Clinton—himself—visited Kigali to apologize to the Rwandan people for not doing more to limit the genocide. Earlier and more vigorous protests by the United States might have been desirable from the standpoint of moral consistency and future relations with Rwanda. But, most likely, they would have had little impact on the death toll, given the low level of American financial and military involvement in the region.

Early pressure from the French might have been somewhat more effective, because France, during the years preceding the tragedy, had propped up the regime of Hutu President Habyarimana with military assistance.[18] In retrospect, this French support amounted to an underwriting of genocide, though at the time Habyarimana may not have seemed notably worse than the likely alternatives. And although his party organized the genocide, they did so only after his death. In any case, the genocide was under way before most foreigners clearly understood what was happening. Even immediate threats to prosecute all parties to the massacre probably would have had little deterrent effect.

In June 1994, several months after the mass murders began, France obtained authorization from the United Nations to intervene militarily for a period of two months. French troops created a protected zone for all refugees, Hutu and Tutsi. The French declared that their goal was humanitarian and that they did not intend to fight in the ongoing civil war. At first, many observers criticized the intervention on grounds that the French had ulterior motives. Some claimed that France was merely flexing its muscles, a view partially supported by Prime Minister Edouard Balladur's declaration regarding the intervention:

> France sees itself as a world power. This is its ambition and its honor and I wish for it to preserve this ambition. And its main field of action is Africa, where it has an important role to play because of longstanding tradition— especially in French-speaking Africa.[19]

Other critics suspected that France was trying to prevent a victory by the Tutsi-led RPF and was too closely tied to the murderous Hutu regime to intervene fairly. Still others suggested that French action arose primarily out of guilt stemming from France's prior support of the Hutu murderers.[20]

By the time French troops left the country in late August, however, most observers praised the intervention.[21] In the summer of 1994, it quickly became clear that France's establishment of a safe zone had been responsible for the survival of many Tutsis. In addition, large numbers of Hutus poured into the French-controlled areas, fearing reprisals from the RPF. Many of these refugees, including some perpetrators of prior atrocities, also were saved. But the intervention was too little and too late to rescue hundreds of thousands of victims. Nonetheless, in this imperfect world, France's establishment of a safe zone was a better response than most; it saved Rwandan lives and cost little in terms of French casualties.

Much earlier, the West, especially the French, might have wielded foreign aid as a tool to discourage genocide. Hutu extremist leaders perhaps would have thought twice about launching the massacre if they believed that they would forever be regarded as outcasts. But the West's cool response to the tragedies in Burundi had told a different story. In that instance, condemnations were few, and mass killings were treated as "business as usual." Moreover, policymakers in the West faced a difficult dilemma: cuts in foreign aid generally have the greatest impact on innocent parties who need it most. Still, the Western nations might have made it immediately clear that any perpetrators of genocide in Rwanda would retain lifelong pariah status.

The massacres in Rwanda took place so rapidly that it is likely that any military effort would have been too late for many victims. On the other hand, a very rapid American military action and successful occupation of Rwanda would probably have saved the majority of those killed, even if it did not prevent the massacre altogether. Judging by the state of the Rwandan armed forces, American casualties probably would have been light. Another proposed intervention would have been less costly. Some suggest that the United States might have been able to jam the Rwandan radio broadcasts that played so important a role in motivating and directing the killers during the genocide. As many recent analysts note, however, this action would have been "no panacea." And knocking out the broadcasting stations may well have required air attacks or commando raids. American military leaders understood, at the time, that stopping the genocide required a military approach, and neither they nor anyone else with influence in Washington wanted any part in such a solution.[22]

Central Africa lies beyond America's sphere of vital interest. Any case for intervention had to rest purely on humanitarian grounds. And, after the Somalia fiasco, few American policymakers had much confidence in their ability to influence the African quality of life at a cost tolerable to American taxpayers. The humanitarian intervention in Somalia hammered home how easily American good intentions could become mired in the complexities of local politics and how frequently they turned out to be of no avail. After the September 11, 2001, attack on New York and Washington, the United States will likely grow even less enthusiastic about international ventures that are purely humanitarian.

Had the United States intervened in Rwanda, its ability to restrain violence might have lasted only as long as American soldiers occupied the country. Troop withdrawal might well have been followed by the status quo ante, or by some unpredictable but equally undesirable situation. Few Americans or Europeans had a desire to see Western troops administering a long-term occupational government in central Africa. Even fewer non-Western countries would have welcomed such a move. Yet that may well have been what it would have taken to stabilize the country and break the cycle of genocide.

A related problem with early, large-scale military intervention is that opposing one leader inevitably means supporting another. And often none of the contenders for power merits the backing of a democratic nation. Americans, after Vietnam, have grown sensitive to what might be called the "Ngo Dinh Diem" problem, the troubles inherent in committing American troops to support the lesser of two evils, who may, himself, be quite evil.

In Rwanda, however, the leaders of the Rwandan Patriotic Front, the rebel organization that deposed the murderous Hutu government, now deserve their chance to govern the country. True, some revenge killings have taken place and the RPF has some blood on its hands. But the central RPF government has, for the most part, attempted to restrain its soldiers under extremely difficult conditions. The government to date seems committed to dealing with perpetrators of the 1994 genocide within the confines of legal proceedings. Tutsis dominate the RPF, but the organizational leadership includes many Hutus. It is hard to be optimistic about Rwanda, especially since Tutsi leaders are not apt to push for elections in a country with a Hutu majority. But the RPF has shown commitment to working with the Hutus, perhaps because it has no feasible alternative, especially after the decimation of the Tutsi population.

Complexities similar to those in Rwanda surround all questions of Western intervention to combat mass hatred, as the situation in Bosnia illustrates. Historians and political scientists will debate for decades what the West should have done to prevent the outbreak and perpetuation of disaster in the former Yugoslavia. By withholding recognition of Croatia, Slovenia, and/or Bosnia, the West might have encouraged a negotiated solution to the clash of nationalisms in the Balkans. Or by dropping a few well-placed bombs on Serbian strongholds, the West might have discouraged the Serbs from pursuing their plans for aggression. But responses such as these may have snowballed into Western involvement in a drawn-out Balkan war, one with the potential to turn into a military quagmire on the scale of Vietnam because of the difficult topography of the region. Even in a relatively short conflict, the West would still face the problem of what to do after victory. As the 1991 Persian Gulf war demonstrated with great clarity, success on the battlefield does not necessarily lead to a desirable postwar settlement. In 1999 seventy-eight days of NATO bombing resolved the immediate dilemma in Kosovo, but the political future of the region remains a giant question mark and a seemingly permanent headache for the international community. Moreover, there was no guarantee that fewer people would have died in a West-supported war.

Once the fighting in Bosnia began, the United States pursued three goals that seemed eminently reasonable. America wanted to (1) end the war quickly, (2) keep out of the conflict, and (3) support the Bosnian Muslims. Unfortunately, as Johns Hopkins University political scientist Michael Mandelbaum has pointed out, "the three are incompatible. Achieving any one of them requires abandoning another. But the Administration has been unwilling or unable to abandon any of them." As a result, the United States pursued what became a "self-canceling policy" in the Balkans.[23]

The West may occasionally possess the means to intervene to keep a genocidal regime from carrying out its plans. More often, the moral and practical issues surrounding intervention are too complex to be resolved without much debate and deliberation. Yet it is precisely the time required for such deliberation that often diminishes the chances that an intervention might prevent or limit the scale of a genocidal massacre. In this situation, leaders sometimes must decide to intervene at the first sign of an impending massacre, or risk being too late. These leaders are in an unenviable position, for the costs of action as well as inaction are apt to be high. Failure to intervene may result in countless dead civilians, but intervention may lock Western nations into a divisive quagmire with unpredictable casualties. Not surprisingly, when humanitarian issues are the only ones involved, most leaders opt for inaction. And while Western publics frequently protest the consequences after the fact, it is by no means apparent that they would be willing to endure the costs of a drawn-out intervention.

Indeed, no nation can, or should, embark thoughtlessly on a program of policing the earth, for such programs often create as many problems as they solve.[24] When a quixotic desire to fight evil is not weighed against the realistic costs of involvement, the result may be endless and futile involvement in bloody conflicts around the world. Broadcasting a military or economic *threat* may work. But Bosnia provides the classic example of saber-rattling bluffs that did not succeed. Failed threats force decisions concerning the use of the armed forces. On infrequent occasions, military interventions by the United States or a coalition of Western nations may be practical, and the moral costs of inaction may outweigh the economic, political, diplomatic, and human costs of action. An example of such an occasion was the period immediately preceding the Bosnian Serbs' overrunning of the United Nations "safe" haven in Srebrenica in 1995. Heavy bombing of Serb positions might have prevented this onslaught, as well as

the subsequent massacre of thousands of Muslim prisoners. Such bomb-
ing did take place shortly afterward, and may have prodded the Bosnian
Serbs toward negotiations—but only after many had died unnecessarily.
The Kosovo intervention was also justifiable.

There is a response to mass murder that can be more readily implemented. The West should make it known that the perpetrators of destructiveness will be regarded forever as villains and pariahs. For the rest of
their lives, they will be denied admission to the world of the civilized. The
sooner such a message is delivered to the heads of murderous regimes, the
better. Since the 1991 war in the Gulf, the United States has worked hard
to isolate Saddam Hussein. But threats of isolation will deter genocide
only if nations impose the policy even when doing so is politically costly.

At times, civilized countries have to deal with the devil, as in the case of
the Allies' cooperation with Stalin during World War II. Nations should
be willing to go to great lengths not to deal with unsavory killers. Doing
business with murderers may be justified as the lesser of two evils, but
only if one figures into the equation the long-term impact of legitimizing
evil conduct.

PROMOTING A WORLD WITH LESS MASS HATRED

None of the strategies for dealing with a currently existing genocidal situation can inspire much hope. But perhaps steps may be taken to lower the
probability that such situations will develop in the first place. Nobody has
presented a clear, comprehensive, and convincing strategy for encouraging and maintaining a nongenocidal society. But a variety of tactics merit
consideration.

As noted, many atrocities are crimes of submission, where the perpetrator lacks the psychological wherewithal to resist. Some students of mass
hate have reasoned, therefore, that one might reduce the following of
hatemongers by "breaking the habit of unquestioning obedience."[25] In
theory, a society would resist mass hatred more effectively if many people
possessed the courage of their convictions, the strength to assert their independence, and the ability to distinguish between just and unjust directives. Better still, people who actively protested and resisted evil orders
would become a powerful force that could thwart the schemes of a destructive regime. In situations where the tendency toward blind obedience

drives compliance with a hateful regime, the promotion of personal responsibility and independent judgment might be a significant step toward preventing mass atrocities.

In practice, however, a program promoting such virtues would have severe limitations. First, when one considers the energy that psychologists devote to fostering independence and new values in a single person, it seems doubtful that anyone could carry out such a complex restructuring of personality on a mass scale. More likely, any educational or social programs devoted to this end would miss the mark. Instead of developing individuals with a rich philosophical capacity to distinguish between rules that merit obedience and rules that do not, the programs might instill a generalized disrespect for social conventions and a desire to disobey authority indiscriminately.

In the military especially, the ethic of obedience underlies effective organization; this need for obedience applies to democratic armies fighting just wars, not merely to thugs doing the work of the devil. Additionally, attempts to reduce unquestioning obedience presuppose that people will evaluate the merits of rules and directives by reference to a well-formed conscience. But people can be directed toward all sorts of warped thinking by their consciences.

When fanatics commit crimes of initiative, misguided consciences are more responsible than anything else for promoting mass hatred. Even if successful in lessening crimes of submission, efforts to promote independent judgment would not reduce participation in atrocities by those who commit crimes of initiative. Indeed, in just wars fought by democratic armies, a reduction in obedience might result in an *increase* in war crimes. Military authorities typically restrain those soldiers who would not, by themselves, control their greed, hate, or aggression. But the biggest problem with a strategy based on teaching independence of thought is that the places most at risk for mass hatred would be least likely to participate. In those parts of the world that are least modern, people tend to be less oriented toward individualism, more collective-minded, and, hence, highly resistant to this type of training. Even more important, countries at the greatest risk for mass hatred are usually run by dictators with little interest in promoting the values of selective obedience.

One might consider other varieties of psychological retraining. Some have suggested programs to build greater caring and superior ethics. A hint of exasperation with everyday humanity may lie beneath the utopian character of such schemes to remake human nature. But these approaches, too, are unlikely to have much success in halting mass hatred. Like antiobedience training, the well-intentioned plans for recasting personalities might be accepted most in the corridors where they are needed least. And they may well result in an enhanced *language* of caring without having any impact on the real feelings of those most apt to commit atrocities. Two noted scholars of genocide, Robert Jay Lifton and Eric Markusen, rest their antigenocidal policy on hopes for the development of a "species mentality."[26] They call for "full consciousness of ourselves as members of the human species."[27] And they explain:

> Species awareness inevitably extends to the habitat of all species, to the earth and its ecosystem. Our awareness of our relationship to the sun, to the oceans, to the earth's resources of food, energy, and materials of every kind, to all animals and plants—becomes intensified as both we and that ecosystem are simultaneously threatened.[28]

Sensible people may hope to live in such a world, but it seems wishful thinking to hinge efforts to combat mass murder on an endeavor with such a low probability of success.

Another respected authority on mass hatred, Professor Ervin Staub of the University of Massachusetts, concludes his study of genocide by calling for the creation of "caring, connection, and nonaggression."[29] More realistically, an antigenocide policy might start with a very different assumption: acknowledging the implausibility of eliminating ethnocentrism and focusing on controlling its most egregious manifestations. No one can deny that building a caring society is a laudable goal, but it seems a remote strategy for reducing the casualties of mass murder in the foreseeable future.

Some have suggested that economic policy provides a potent weapon in the war against terrorism and mass hatred. This strategy rests on English writer Samuel Johnson's eighteenth-century dictum: "Poverty is a great enemy to human happiness; it certainly destroys liberty, and it makes some virtues impracticable and others extremely difficult." Advocates of the economic approach suggest that the character traits needed to resist hatred require a foundation of prosperity, or at least a minimal ability to meet one's basic needs. The economic approach maintains that efforts to control mass hatred will succeed in the long run only if they attack the problem at its "root cause." Terrible poverty prevails in many societies where mass hate has erupted, and in many more where it threatens to strike in the future. As noted above, hatred frequently grows out of anger, which has its source in frustration. Frustration, in turn, develops most easily under conditions of deprivation. The economic approach presupposes that increasingly prosperous people will less often cling to doctrines of hate.

This approach, too, has serious limitations. The West has funneled huge sums of money into the economies of under-developed nations in the decades since their independence. By all accounts, however, these efforts have yielded disappointing results. Although the American public has lost much of its never-too-great enthusiasm for foreign aid, one could in theory envision a massive injection of Western capital into the most economically deprived parts of the world. Even if this happened, however, the investment might never reach the impoverished masses, because countries most at risk for mass hatred usually have dictatorial forms of government. And many dictators, by habit, grab for as much as they can. In addition, citizens of Western nations might resist, on moral grounds alone, the donation of massive sums of money to those who may soon launch genocidal or terrorist campaigns.

If one makes the unlikely assumption that aid will reach those who need it most, yet another problem remains. Improvements in living standards may raise expectations to a point beyond the practical reach of economic development. One person may see another person's new tractor, and grow even more frustrated. Or new resources may bring access to the mass media with its depictions of the (relatively) tremendous wealth of Western families. Such contrasts may leave large numbers of people feeling more frustrated even though actual economic conditions have improved.

A more just distribution of resources does not result automatically in greater subjective feelings of justice. In addition, many perpetrators of mass hatred *seek* an unfair distribution of wealth, in their favor. As noted, some crimes of initiative are motivated by a desire for material gain at the expense of victims. Other crimes of initiative, such as terrorism, frequently grow out of misguided ideologies that teach people to attribute

their misfortunes to others. For these perpetrators, nothing is apt to reduce their feelings of mistreatment except for the utter subjugation or
death of the targets of their hatred. Finally, perceptions of injustice play
no role in motivating those who commit crimes of submission, so re-
dressing collective grievances will not diminish their participation in
atrocities.

In recent years, educators have devoted much energy to designing educational programs to increase knowledge of mass hatred and, hence, resistance to it. Such educational programs can be intellectually significant,
but their usefulness in building resistance to genocide is limited. As we
have seen, ignorance is seldom the force that propels perpetrators to commit atrocities. More often, such crimes originate in greed, ambition,
anger, hatred, fear, lust for revenge, and weakness in the face of social
pressures. Moral decency and character can strengthen resistance to these
forces, but there is little reason to believe that such attributes can be imparted through genocide education in a matter of weeks or months. An
intellectual understanding of genocide constitutes a very weak defense
against the pressures, emotions, and beliefs that typically lead to mass
murder.

Moreover, curricula that focus on genocide are apt to reach the wrong
audience. One of the most influential curricula, a Holocaust education
program called "Facing History and Ourselves," reaches an estimated five
hundred thousand American students each year; though this audience is
large, it represents a small percentage of American students. And those
adolescents most afflicted by hatred probably insulate themselves best
from the program's message by ignoring, discounting, or ridiculing the
material. Students least likely to join in movements of mass hate no doubt
judge the experience a moving and important one.

Television miniseries like *Holocaust* (originally broadcast in April 1978)
and *Roots* (originally broadcast in January 1977) have reached hundreds
of millions of viewers, but with limited effect. Research suggests that these
programs can be educational for many who watch, but they apparently
preach to the converted. In *Roots* and *Holocaust*, the television depictions
of hatred and bigotry succeeded magnificently in evoking powerful emotions and sympathy, but largely among people who already agreed with
the programs' orientations. These television miniseries changed the attitudes of very few bigots.[30]

In any event, there is no reason to believe that haters who learn more about past atrocities will always reject their own hateful beliefs. Some of the greatest students of past atrocities turn out to be supporters of present hatred. Around the world, neo-Nazis study the Hitler era with a sense of pride and nostalgia. Among Serbs, heightened consciousness of the World War II era seems to result in greater anger toward contemporary Croats and Muslims. Though instructors attempt to impart a socially responsible interpretation of past events, many bigoted students reject the spin. Of course, these limitations do not mean that one should avoid teaching about past eras of destructiveness. Some budding haters will be shamed into abandoning or rethinking their views. But no one should hold in-flated hopes regarding the ability of genocide education to inoculate societies against genocide. This is particularly true since those countries most at risk are least likely to sponsor or permit such educational efforts.

Yet another problem plagues genocide educators: what to teach. Programs take many forms and thus cannot be adequately reviewed here. But a recent controversy surrounding the "Facing History and Ourselves" curriculum illustrates some of the problems involved in creating junior high school and high school units based on case studies of mass hatred.[31] The two-decades-old curriculum for eighth and ninth graders reviews the history of Hitler's rise to power, focusing on Nazi anti-Semitism and its consequences. Yet, as Holocaust historian Deborah Lipstadt notes, the curriculum does not stop here:

> It attempts to bring the Holocaust into the orbit of the students' experiences by providing a section at the end of each chapter called "Connections," which includes subjects such as racism and violence in America—though not contemporary anti-Semitism. It presents the Holocaust as an occasion for teaching lessons in moral reasoning and good (American) citizenship; as an object lesson, a generic inoculation against prejudice.[32]

The curriculum even suggests that the Holocaust and a potential nuclear "holocaust" share certain "basic principles." Lipstadt further objects that "No teacher using this material can help but draw the historically fallacious parallel between Weimar Germany and contemporary America."[33]

Undoubtedly, whenever teachers try to draw morals from the Holocaust or other instances of mass atrocities, they rely on their personal politics and values. Ideally, a firm student grounding in general history, psychology, and the particulars of various instances of genocide would come first in studying mass murder. Then, students could derive "lessons" and locate appropriate parallels. In reality, only a very small fraction of students would achieve this level of understanding, particularly in the eighth or ninth grade. As a result, Holocaust education curricula often choose to leapfrog over, or abbreviate, much of the prerequisite background, skipping quickly to the "lessons."

The problem lies not so much with extracting lessons, but with extracting the right lessons. Influenced by Stanley Milgram and Hannah Arendt, Holocaust curricula often teach that "blind obedience" is what the Holocaust is all about; the remedy is questioning authority. Additionally, they suggest to students to "follow your conscience," without noting that Hitler and many Nazi fanatics did precisely that. One might more sensibly advise students to "examine" their consciences, but even that approach has the severe drawback that different examiners will arrive at different judgments.[34]

Some critics have argued that the search for contemporary relevance usually results in a failure to emphasize the roots of Nazi mass murder in two thousand years of anti-Semitism; these critics suggest that anti-Semitism in Germany had its own peculiar dynamics and cannot be portrayed as essentially similar to other sorts of prejudice, say, in contemporary America.

Still others object that a comparative study of genocidal massacres deprives the Holocaust of its uniqueness. They correctly assert that certain features of the Holocaust—its scope, ideological foundation, roots in historical anti-Semitism, and international character—should guarantee it a position of centrality in the study of genocide. But these critics miss an important point. Mass hatred has unique characteristics in every situation, but it also has some common elements that cut across contexts. "Facing History and Ourselves" goes too far in its quest for relevance, noting commonalities among the Nazi Holocaust, the dropping of the atomic bomb that ended World War II, the My Lai massacre in Vietnam, and white racism in the United States. Many critics have objected particularly to the curriculum's overly tolerant approach to those who flock to Louis Farrakhan, the black, anti-Semitic leader of the Nation of Islam. In these and other ways, the curriculum reveals its political orientation, well to the left of center and strongly multiculturalist.[35] Perhaps it would have been wiser and more effective to adopt a centrist political perspective in a curriculum for fourteen-year-olds.

With so much disagreement about appropriate moral lessons, it might seem best to stick as close as possible to those past events about which mainstream historians agree. However, it seems imprudent to teach junior high and high school students about the horrible consequences of genocide without attempting to draw some conclusions with contemporary relevance. If lessons are drawn, they should, at a minimum, emphasize (1) the wide variety of psychological forces, greed, fear, ambition, hatred, misjudgment, and others, that have propelled individuals toward involvement in genocide; (2) the ease with which many people abandoned morality in the face of psychological, social, and political pressure; (3) the need for strong cultural, legal, and constitutional institutions to restrain the growth of mass hatred; (4) the differences, as well as similarities, among various instances of mass murder; (5) the dangers arising from seductive, charismatic leaders; (6) the murderous implications of dehumanizing ideologies; and (7) the fundamental strengths of Western democratic institutions in contrast to nondemocratic ones.

Our conclusion is clear. Education about past instances of mass hate provides no magical inoculation against such hate in the future. "If men could learn from history," averred poet Samuel Coleridge in 1831, "What lessons it might teach us! But passion and party blind our eyes, and the light which experience gives is a lantern on the stern, which shines only on the waves behind us!"

*   *   *

The two best strategies for combating mass hatred are the relentless pursuit and punishment of the perpetrators of atrocities and the promotion of stable democracies wherever possible. The trial of perpetrators can be particularly important. At Nuremberg and elsewhere after World War II, war criminals answered to international and national legal authorities for deeds committed under the auspices of the Third Reich. Many criminals were executed and many more publicly carried the disgrace of their deeds with them for the rest of their lives. Present-day prosecutions of Nazis do not always

command the support of a weary public. Well-intentioned people sometimes ask whether it makes sense to toss an eighty-year-old man in jail,
when he has been such a fine neighbor all these years. They wonder
whether the time has come to forgive and forget.

But that time can never come. Whatever their motivation, those contem-
plating participation in crimes of mass hatred should know that the civilized
world will never allow them peace. Though, as we've seen, some individuals
may have become war criminals in response to situational pressures, public
prosecutions will broadcast the message that "just following orders" excuses
no one. Public trials will inform those who indulge their aggressive or sexual
impulses that they will pay a price for their misdeeds. In the future, then,
some individuals facing situational inducements to evil may pause to consider the possible cost of their acts, not to the victims, but to themselves.

Perhaps most important, prosecutions help meet the victims' need for
justice. In addition, when a group has been the target of mass murders in
the past, and when the murderers have escaped punishment and world
condemnation, opportunistic leaders have built on the victimized peoples' unresolved grief and desire for revenge. Such a scenario recently
played out with terrible effect among both Hutus and Serbs.

It is the obligation of the successors to murderous regimes to dissociate
themselves, in the clearest of terms, from the perpetrators of past atrocities. The German government has done this, and the contemporary
Japanese are doing so, but many other successor governments have not.
Until his death, President Tudjman of Croatia continued to make comments about World War II that can be interpreted as being sympathetic to
the Croatian fascist Ustashas. Turkey, eight decades after the massacre of
the Armenians, refuses to acknowledge responsibility for that crime. And,
in 1995, the president of Argentina, Saúl Menem, urged the torturers and
murderers of the military regime of the 1970s not to "rub salt in old
wounds" by confessing and recounting past deeds.[36]

Putting perpetrators of genocide on trial is always desirable, but not always easy to accomplish. Regarding the Serbs, for example, the West devoted great energy to cutting a deal with the vilest war criminals. By 1995,
Slobodan Milosevic, a man earlier identified by the United States and
many international organizations as a good candidate for prosecution,
had recast himself as a peacemaker. Although few Westerners bought the
new image, he could not be placed on trial until he lost a war in Kosovo

and, some time later, fell from power in Belgrade. One by one, leaders of the genocide are being brought to justice, which is as it should be. But the process may take many years.[37]

Prosecutors must decide how many people to indict. If only the leaders are indicted, then a tribunal may leave the dangerous impression that underlings bear no responsibility for their deeds. But, concerning Rwanda, for example, the list of indictments could include tens of thousands of names. And large-scale trials seem to stand in the way of national reconciliation in both Rwanda and Bosnia.

Some concession to reality must be made, perhaps by focusing on leaders, those responsible for the worst crimes, and those for whom documentation is most readily available. But a lasting peace cannot rest on illusion. In April 1995, a United Nations official in Rwanda noted, "There is a great frustration because of the lack of justice. People are saying it is one year since the massacres and everyone knows who the killers are—they are running free in the camps. Yet the world community gives them free food. They are saying, where is the justice?"[38]

The best current policy with respect to the perpetrators of genocide is to support ongoing international tribunals, but this does not require opposition to trials held by national governments. In the eyes of many victims and their families, one limitation of the United Nations tribunals is that they cannot impose the death penalty. Nazis were tried in many different types of courts. Even if some trials of war criminals from Bosnia and Rwanda are conducted in absentia, the word might go forth that perpetrators of genocide will be held before the world as reprehensible criminals, never again welcome among company that values the rules of civilized society.

The new century has taught us much about terrorism, starting with the realization that it can produce casualties approaching or even exceeding those associated with genocidal slaughter. In contrast to most genocides, well-organized international terrorist assaults like the one that struck New York and Washington in September 2001 can be destabilizing on a global scale. They can affect the lives of billions in ways that are difficult to calculate. As in the case of genocide, terrorism typically arises out of an ideology of hatred. A difference is that in terrorism atrocities are perpetrated by a relatively small number of people whose modus operandi may render them beyond the reach of the world's criminal justice machinery, even when states wish to deploy their law enforcement apparatus. In addition, neither traditional statecraft nor light military countermeasures may prove equal to the task of breaking up or weakening a well-established terrorist network.

Clearly, the old approaches to controlling terror have failed. In light of the vulnerabilities identified and exploited by bin Laden and the al-Qaeda operatives, the world needs to develop a new strategy for fighting sophisticated and state-sponsored terrorism, especially when it is bolstered by a web of misguided popular support. As President George W. Bush has announced, this battle will take place on many fronts, some of which have yet to be identified. Undoubtedly, it will involve more than America's traditional tactics, which is to say, reliance on lengthy but relentless legal investigations and courtroom prosecutions. In some cases, where the risk of inaction is great, preemptive military strikes against state sponsors will be critical. Leaders of such states must receive the message that their days are numbered if they—for whatever reason and on whatever grounds—permit those who would cause mass atrocities to operate from within their borders. When weighing the desirability of military approaches, the heads of responsible states must consider not only what crimes have been committed, but also which ones are likely to occur if no action is taken. As we approach the era of nuclear, biological, and chemical terror, it may be unwise to wait for a terrorist foe to launch a first strike. As always, overreaction remains a danger. We have learned, however, that inaction may pose as great a danger or a greater one under certain circumstances. And, as in the case where America was attacked, as columnist Michael Kelley has written, pacifism can be inescapably and profoundly immoral, ". . . on the side of the murderers, and . . . on the side of letting them murder again."[39]

*   *   *

In the long run, nothing will block the emergence of terrorism or genocide as effectively as the establishment of stable democratic governments resting on respect for constitutional procedures, a free media, and human rights. A democracy acquires stability not merely through its formal institutions but also from the psychological and emotional support of its citizens. Democracies will turn to mass hate on the scale seen in nondemocracies only if the governmental system falls to pieces. The best way to insure that this does not happen is through an educational program that imparts respect for the democratic system, critical thinking, and tolerance for diverse political, religious, ethnic, and racial groups.

The Western nations have learned that they cannot often export their democratic systems. Japan and Germany are two great exceptions, and both cases followed total war and long-term occupation. More often, Western powers must promote democracy from afar. But, as social psychologist Kurt Lewin noted in 1943:

> It is a fallacy to assume that people, if left alone, follow a democratic pattern in their group life. . . . In regard to changing from one cultural pattern to another experiments indicate that autocracy can be "imposed upon a person." . . . Democracy cannot be imposed upon a person; it has to be learned by a process of voluntary and responsible participation.[40]

Referring to the prospect of developing a democratic culture in Germany, Lewin rejected the view that satisfaction of the many needs of the German people would suffice to make them democratic. He noted: "Such suggestions are based on the naive idea that 'human nature' is identical with 'democratic culture'; that one needs but to destroy the causes of maladjustment to create a democratic world."[41] Lewin's psychologically sophisticated plan to build democracy in Germany paralleled the actual procedures that followed.

In the contemporary world, the export of democracy is generally more complicated. Most recent efforts to promote democracy have been unenthusiastic and ineffectual. When progress toward democracy becomes a condition of foreign aid, countries typically adopt at most some of the forms of democracy, but little of the underlying culture of tolerance. Elections which take place outside the context of democratic values usually contribute little to stabilizing a nation. Sometimes, they even precipitate the outbreak of violence, when as in Bosnia the likely loser sabotages the electoral system. But the West must continue to develop new strategies to spread the democratic message to those nations that persist in shutting it out. Few goals should be higher on the agenda of Western nations.

*   *   *

No study of mass hatred can conclude optimistically. Genocidal massacres and terrorist attacks will surely occur in the future as they have in the past. The West is not generally the source of the mass hatred that leads to terrorism or massacres. Western nations usually are not the solution either. When genocidal situations arise, outside military interventions may offer the only hope, but such interventions run the risk of adding to the bloodshed in unpredictable ways. They also may carry a high price in the lives of Western soldiers. Even so, the military option may be better than standing idly by, while tens of thousands, hundreds of thousands, or millions, die.

The establishment of superior legal, political, and cultural institutions provides the best protection for any nation against degeneration into mass hate and murderousness. Without such institutions firmly in place, many people give way to the purveyors of hate, whether opportunists or fanatics. Once democratic laws, procedures, and cultural values have been established, they should be recognized and respected for the pillars they are.

NOTES

PREFACE

1. George W. Bush, "September 20: Bush's Speech to Congress," MSNBC [On-line], 20 September 2001, accessed 21 September 2001, available from www.msnbc.com/news/631906.asp.

2. Neil J. Kressel, *Mass Hate: The Global Rise of Genocide and Terror* (New York: Plenum, 1996), 49.

3. Ibid.

4. Ibid.

5. Bush, "September 20: Bush's Speech to Congress."

6. Quoted in James Risen, "U.S. Pursued Secret Efforts to Catch or Kill bin Laden," *New York Times*, 30 September 2001, A1, B3.

7. For intelligent treatments of this issue, see Paul Hollander, *Anti-Americanism: Critiques at Home and Abroad, 1965–1990* (New York: Oxford University Press, 1992); Thomas Perry Thornton, ed. "Anti-Americanism: Origins and Context," special issue, *Annals of the American Academy of Political and Social Science* (May 1988). See also the spirited—though dated—book, Arnold Beichman, *Nine Lies About America* (London: Alcove Press, 1972).

8. Reuel Marc Gerecht, "The Face of Holy War," *New York Post*, 17 September 2001, 44, reprinted from *Weekly Standard*, 24 September 2001.

9. Simon Reeve, *The New Jackals: Ramzi Yousef, Osama bin Laden and the Future of Terrorism* (Boston: Northeastern University Press, 1999), 227.

10. "Osama Bin Laden: FAQ," MSNBC online, accessed 21 September 2001, available from www.msnbc.com/news/627355.asp.

11. "Statement Attributed to Osama bin Laden," MSNBC online, accessed 25 September 2001, available from www.msnbc.com/news/633244.asp.

12. "Suspected Terrorist's Will Details Final Wishes," CNN online, 2 October 2001, accessed 3 October 2001, available from www.cnn.com.

13. Boris Johnson, "What Islamic Terrorists Are Really Afraid of Is Women," *Daily Telegraph* [London], 27 September 2001, 29, accessed 3 October 2001, available from LEXIS-NEXIS Academic Universe, www.lexis-nexis.com/universe.

14. Caleb Carr, "Americans Don't Understand That Their Heritage Is Itself a Threat," *New York Times Magazine*, 23 September 2001, 92.

15. Christopher Dickey, "Training for Terror," *Newsweek* 24 September 2001, accessed 21 September 2001, available from www.msncb.com/news/629583.asp.

16. Psychologists have learned much about brainwashing in other contexts, but the concept refers primarily to people who are coercively persuaded to act against their will; this does not appear to describe what typically occurred in bin Laden's training camps. See, for example, Edgar H. Schein, Inge Schneier, and Curtis H. Baker, *Coercive Persuasion: A Socio-Psychological Analysis of the "Brainwashing" of American Civilian Prisoners by the Chinese Communists* (New York: MIT Press, 1961).

17. Ibid.

18. Jodi Wilgoren, "The Hijackers: A Terrorist Profile Emerges That Confounds the Experts," *New York Times*, 15 September 2001, A2.

19. "Excerpts from Letter Found in Car of a Suspect," *New York Times*, 28 September 2001, B4.

20. Thomas L. Friedman, "Terrorism Game Theory," *New York Times*, 25 September 2001, A29.

21. Neil MacFarquhar, "U.S. Has a Long Way to Go to Bring Around Egyptians," *New York Times*, 26 September 2001, B5.

22. Neil MacFarquhar, "Saudi Dilemma: A Native Son, A Heinous Act," *New York Times*, 5 October 2001, A1.

23. Ibid., B3.

24. Ian Fisher, "An Exhibit on Campus Celebrates Grisly Deed," *New York Times*, 26 September 2001, A10.

25. Emerson is quoted in Reeve, *The New Jackals*, 232.

26. See, for example, Patricia Cohen, "Response to Attack Splits Arabs in the West," *New York Times*, 29 September 2001, A9.

27. Warren Hoge, "A Sense of Unfairness Erodes Support in Gulf States," *New York Times*, 2 October 2001, A8.

28. George W. Bush, "Remarks by President Bush and His Majesty King Abdullah of Jordan in a Photo Opportunity," 28 September 2001, accessed 4 October 2001, available from www.whitehouse.gov/news/releases/2001/09/20010928–4.html.

29. Peter Steinfels, "Beliefs: Amid Islam's Complexity, Scholars Are Challenged to Influence Change Without Compromising," *New York Times*, 29 September 2001, D3.

30. Lamin Sanneh, "Faith and the Secular," *New York Times*, 23 September 2001, Section 4, 17.

31. See, for example, Paul Johnson, "'Relentlessly and Thoroughly:' The Only Way to Respond," *National Review*, 15 October 2001, accessed 4 October 2001, available from www.nationalreview.com. Two excellent scholarly volumes are also relevant. Johannes J. G. Jansen, *The Neglected Duty: The Creed of Sadat's Assassins and Islamic Resurgence in the Middle East* (New York: Macmillan, 1986), and Bernard Lewis, *The Political Language of Islam* (Chicago: University of Chicago Press, 1988).

32. George W. Bush, "President Meets with Muslim Leaders : Remarks by the President in Meeting with Muslim Community Leaders," 26 September 2001, available from www.whitehouse.gov.

33. Ibid.

34. Quoted in "Bush's Big Blunder," *Smartertimes* online, 19 September 2001, accessed 24 September 2001, available from www.smartertimes.com. This information is based on research conducted by Daniel Pipes, a former Reagan administration Middle East aide who runs the Middle East Forum in Philadelphia.

35. William Safire, "For a Muslim Legion," *New York Times*, 1 October 2001, A23.

36. Quoted in Tim Pulman, "British Overture May Have Hardened Iran's Stance," *Jewish Community News* (New Jersey), 5 October 2001, 12.

37. Larry B. Stammer, Teresa Watanabe, "Muslims in Southland Brace for Retaliation," *Los Angeles Times*, 12 September 2001, A38.

38. Tom Tugend, "U.S. Jewish–Muslim Relations Grow Dim," *Jerusalem Post*, 30 September 2001, section "Jewish World," 7, available from LEXIS-NEXIS Academic universe, www.lexis-nexis.com/universe.

39. Thomas L. Friedman, "Yes, But What?" *New York Times*, 5 October 2001, A27.

40. Serge Schmemann, "Israel As Flashpoint, Not Cause," *New York Times*, 23 September 2001, Section 4, 8.

41. Alan M. Dershowitz, "The Muslim Clerics" [letter], *New York Times*, 2 October 2001, A24.

42. Ibid.

Chapter 1

1. Abraham H. Maslow, *Toward a Psychology of Being*, 2d ed. (New York: Van Nostrand, 1968), 6.

2. Paul Lewis, "Rape Was Weapon of Serbs, UN Says," *New York Times*, 20 October 1993, A1, late ed.; Charles Lane, "Washington Diarist: War Stories," *New Re-

public, 3 January 1994, 43; Aryeh Neier, "Watching Rights," *Nation,* 1 March 1993, 259. Steven L. Burg and Paul S. Shoup review the current state of knowledge about the number of rapes committed, concluding that—while the precise number will never be known—12,000 is a conservative estimate. See Steven L. Burg and Paul S. Shoup, *The War in Bosnia-Herzegovina: Ethnic Conflict and International Intervention* (Armonk, NY: M.E. Sharpe, 1999), 170.

3. Anna Quindlen, "Gynocide," *New York Times,* 10 March 1993, A19, late ed. See also Beverly Allen, *Rape Warfare: The Hidden Genocide in Bosnia-Herzegovina and Croatia* (Minneapolis: University of Minnesota Press, 1996), and Alexandra Stiglmayer, ed., *Mass Rape: The War Against Women in Bosnia-Herzegovina,* trans. Marion Faber (Lincoln: University of Nebraska Press, 1994).

4. Tom Post et al., "A Pattern of Rape," *Newsweek,* 4 January 1993, 34.

5. Ibid., 35–36.

6. Roy Gutman, *A Witness to Genocide* (New York: Macmillan, 1993), 166.

7. Susan Brownmiller, "Making Female Bodies the Battlefield," *Newsweek,* 4 January 1993, 37.

8. Post et al., p. 34. Herak's story is also reported in several other sources: John F. Burns, "Bosnia War Crime Trial Hears Serb's Confession," *New York Times,* 14 March 1993, sec. 1, 10, late ed.; John F. Burns, "2 Serbs to Be Shot for Killings and Rapes," *New York Times,* 31 March 1993, A6, late ed.; Peter Maass, "Two Serbs Face Murder, Rape Charges in Bosnia's First War Crimes Trial," *Washington Post,* 12 March 1993, A17, final ed.; Peter Maass, "Bosnia War Crimes Case Opens: Serbs Accused of Massacres, Rapes Face Sarajevo Court," *Washington Post,* 13 March 1993, A14, final ed.; David Crary, "The Anatomy of a War Crime," *Boston Globe,* 28 November 1992, 2. Herak was convicted in a Bosnian court and sentenced to death. His sentence was later commuted to forty years in prison when Bosnia abolished the death penalty. Three years after his trial, he recanted his stunning confession, claiming that it had been extracted under torture. In the changed climate that followed the end of the war, however, Herak may well have concocted his recantation in an effort to procure his release. What is more disturbing, two of the victims he allegedly killed later turned up alive, perhaps corroborating some portion of his new story or perhaps owing to the confusions of a wartime trial. In any event, a Bosnian court in May 1999 further reduced his sentence to twenty years. It remains hard to accept Herak's assertion that he was a simple front-line soldier who never killed anyone. His alleged accomplice in rape and murder, Sretko Damjanovic, who also confessed and recanted, rejects Herak's declarations of innocence, saying "Let Herak talk if he wants, but it's all lies. . . . Now he says he didn't do anything. Well, that is a guy that I know pretty well. He's not really clean, if you know what I mean. He never was. He's an ani-

mal. They never should have given him a gun" (quoted in Kit R. Roane, "Symbol of Inhumanity in Bosnia Now Says 'Not Me,'" *New York Times*, 31 January 1996, A6, accessed 17 August 2001, available from LEXIS-NEXIS Academic universe, www.lexis-nexis.com/universe). See also Jonathan Randal, "Serb Convicted of Murders Demanding Retrial After 2 'Victims' Found Alive," *Washington Post*, 15 March 1997, A17, accessed 17 August 2001, available from LEXIS-NEXIS Academic universe, www.lexis-nexis.com/universe; Burg and Shoup, *The War in Bosnia-Herzegovina*, 160.

9. Post et al., 34.

10. Burns, "Bosnia War Crime Trial Hears Serb's Confession," 10.

11. Alison Mitchell, "Specter of Terror: The Links," *New York Times*, 25 June 1993, A1, late ed.

12. David Johnston, "The Cleric's Indictment; Reno Sees Growing Evidence and Makes Call," *New York Times*, 26 August 1993, B4, late ed.; Jill Smolowe, "A Voice of Holy War," *Time*, 15 March 1993, 31; "Specter of Terror: The Suspects," *New York Times*, 25 June 1993, B3, late ed.; Richard Behar, "The Secret Life of Mahmud the Red," *Time*, 4 October 1993, 54–61; Francis X. Clines, "U.S.-Born Suspect in Bombing Plots: Zealous Causes and Civic Roles," *New York Times*, 28 June 1993, B2, late ed.; Francis X. Clines, "Bomb-Plot Suspects' Lives Emerge in Sharper Detail," *New York Times*, 4 July 1993, sec. 1, 27, late ed.; Joseph P. Fried, "Sheik and 9 Followers Guilty of a Conspiracy of Terrorism," *New York Times*, 2 October 1995, A1, late ed.

13. Joseph B. Treaster, "Secret Tapes Are Disclosed in Bomb Plot," *New York Times*, 3 August 1993, B1, late ed.

14. Clines, "U.S.-Born Suspect in Bombing Plots," B2.

15. Michael Shermer and Alex Grobman, *Denying History: Who Says the Holocaust Never Happened and Why Do They Say It?* (Berkeley: University of California Press, 2000); Deborah E. Lipstadt, *Denying the Holocaust: The Growing Assault on Truth and Memory* (New York: Free Press, 1993); Pierre Vidal-Naquet, *Assassins of Memory: Essays on the Denial of the Holocaust*, trans. Jeffrey Mehlman (New York: Columbia University Press, 1993). See also Brian Siano, "False History, Gas Chambers, Blue Smoke and Cracked Mirrors," *Humanist*, July–August 1993, 31.

16. Gerald Fleming, "Engineers of Death," *New York Times*, 18 July 1993, sec. 4, 19, late ed. This article includes translated transcripts of interviews with the engineers conducted by the intelligence branch of the Soviet army in the late 1940s. The engineers' statements are taken from these transcripts.

17. Hannah Arendt, *Eichmann in Jerusalem: A Report on the Banality of Evil,* rev. ed. (New York: Penguin Books, 1977).

18. Ibid., 25.

19. Stanley Milgram, *Obedience to Authority: An Experimental View* (New York: Harper-Colophon, 1974); Craig Haney, Curtis Banks, and Philip Zimbardo, "A Study of Prisoners and Guards in a Simulated Prison," in *Readings about the Social Animal*, 7th ed., Elliot Aronson, ed. (New York: W.W. Freeman, 1995).

20. Robert Jay Lifton, *The Nazi Doctors: Medical Killing and the Psychology of Genocide* (New York: Basic Books, 1988), 418–65.

21. See Daniel Jonah Goldhagen, *Hitler's Willing Executioners: Ordinary Germans and the Holocaust* (New York: Vintage Books, 1997).

CHAPTER 2

1. Susanne Hoeber Rudolph and Lloyd I. Rudolph, "Modern Hate: How Ancient Animosities Get Invented," *New Republic*, 22 March 1993, 24.

2. U.S. Dept. of State, *Seventh Report on War Crimes in the Former Yugoslavia: Supplemental United States Submission of Information to the United Nations Security Council*, U.S. Dept. of State Dispatch, vol. 4 (Washington, DC: Government Printing Office, 1993), 257, online, Nexis.

3. Roy Gutman, *A Witness to Genocide* (New York: Macmillan, 1993), 144–49. In February 1995 Meakic was charged with atrocities by the International Criminal Tribunal for Former Yugoslavia and a warrant was issued for his arrest. At the time of this writing, he remains at large.

4. Chuck Sudetic, "In Bosnia Again, a Grim 'Ethnic Cleansing,'" *New York Times*, 17 February 1994, A1, late ed.

5. Slavenka Drakulic, *The Balkan Express: Fragments from the Other Side of War* (New York: WW Norton, 1993), 3. For further discussion of the analogy between Bosnia and Nazi Germany, see Mary Coleman, "Human Sacrifice in Bosnia," *Journal of Psychohistory* 21 (Fall 1993): 157–69.

6. Erich Goldhagen, "Nazi Sexual Demonology," *Midstream*, May 1981, 7–15.

7. A. M. Rosenthal, "Bombs for Bosnia," *New York Times*, 21 July 1995, A5, late ed. For various perspectives on the question of whether the Holocaust should be regarded as unique, see Alan S. Rosenbaum, ed., *Is the Holocaust Unique? Perspectives on Comparative Genocide* (Boulder, CO: Westview Press, 1996).

8. Steven L. Burg and Paul S. Shoup, *The War in Bosnia-Herzegovina: Ethnic Conflict and International Intervention* (Armonk, NY: M.E. Sharpe, 1999), 169, offers a balanced discussion of casualty figures. See also Carole Rogel, *The Breakup of Yugoslavia and the War in Bosnia* (Westport, CT: Greenwood Press, 1998), 73, and John R. Lampe, *Yugoslavia As History: Twice There Was a Country*, 2d ed. (New York: Cambridge University Press, 2000), 373. George Kenney, "The

Bosnia Calculation," *New York Times*, 23 April 1995, sec. 6, 42–43, was highly influential when written but it is now somewhat dated.

9. Gutman, xix.

10. Drakulic, 91. Western influence was not always inconsistent with the wartime ethos in Bosnia. In September 1992 Sonja Karadzic, daughter of Bosnian Serb leader Radovan Karadzic and a budding rock singer, told a Belgrade magazine: "If the Americans come to Bosnia, they'll see that our soldiers look at the world like theirs do. . . . The Serbian chetnik fighters have grown up with a Coke in their hand and watching the same TV spots as someone their own age in Alabama, and we're into the latest styles just the way guys or girls from Florida are. Together we got our battle ethics from the movies about Mad Max and Terminator, Rambo and Young Guns. And what happened when the war began—we started identifying with the media images and heroes. . . . Nobody is dirty or sloppy or smelly or unshaven—we're still into good cigarettes and Coca-Cola, nice perfume and makeup, and we're up on the latest movies and music. And we still like a good laugh—not the Moslem nonsense down in town" (Sonja Karadzic, "America's Influence on the Bosnian Serbs," trans. by Ann Clymer Bigelow, in Rogel, 132, excerpted and reprinted from an interview that appeared in the Belgrade biweekly *Duga*, September 1992).

11. As quoted in William Pfaff, "Invitation to War," *Foreign Affairs* 72 (Summer 1993): 104.

12. Paul Lewis, "Rape Was Weapon of Serbs, U.N. Says," *New York Times*, 20 October 1993, A1, late ed. For a list of current indictments and reports on the progress of individual trials at the International Criminal Tribunal for Former Yugoslavia at the Hague, see ICTY at a Glance [Online], accessed 8 August 2001, available from www.un.org/icty/glance.htm.

13. Roger Cohen, "C.I.A. Report on Bosnia Blames Serbs for 90% of the War Crimes," *New York Times*, 9 March 1995, A1, late ed. The Croatian army's summer 1995 offensive in the Krajina region of Croatia effectively emptied the area of Serbs with the tacit approval of the West, but—taking place, as it did, in the latter days of the Bosnian war and producing relatively few casualties—it cannot be equated with Serbian ethnic cleansing in Bosnia. See Burg and Shoup, 326.

14. Gutman, 169.

15. Gutman, 168–73.

16. Eric Schmitt, "Spy Photos Indicate Mass Grave at Serb-Held Town, U.S. Says," *New York Times*, 10 August 1995, A1, late ed. Stephen Engelberg and Tim Weiner, "Srebrenica: The Days of Slaughter," *New York Times*, 29 October 1995, A1, late ed. For detailed descriptions of the horrific events at Srebrenica and the politics behind them, see Jan Willem Honig and Norbert Both, *Srebrenica: Record*

of a War Crime (New York: Penguin USA, 1997) and David Rohde, *Endgame: The Betrayal and Fall of Srebrenica* (New York: Farrar, Straus & Giroux, 1997). Political psychologists Maja Djikic and Jordan Peterson argue that a "spirit of moral equivalence was accepted by staff at all levels of the UN hierarchy (including peacekeepers on the field)" and that this spirit played an important part in the genesis of the Srebrenica disaster where civilians, presumably under the protection of the United Nations, were massacred. See Maja Djikic and Jordan B. Peterson, "Self-Deception in the United Nations: A Contributing Factor to Genocide," paper presented at the 24th Annual Scientific Meeting of the International Society of Political Psychology, 18 July 2001, Cuernavaca, Mexico (available from the authors at the University of Toronto, Canada).

17. Jeri Laber, "The Brutalized Become the Brutal," *New York Times,* 11 October 1993, A17, late ed.

18. United States, Dept. of State, *Seventh Report on War Crimes in the Former Yugoslavia.* This report and Gutman's *A Witness to Genocide* describe most of the atrocities discussed below.

19. Rebecca West, *Black Lamb and Grey Falcon: A Journey Through Yugoslavia* (1942; reprint New York: Penguin, 1982) as quoted in Cvijeto Job, "Yugoslavia's Ethnic Furies," *Foreign Policy* 92 (Fall 1993): 53.

20. Pfaff, 97. For another critique of the "ancient animosities" explanation, see Robert J. Donia and John V. A. Fine, Jr., *Bosnia and Hercegovina: A Tradition Betrayed* (New York: Columbia University Press, 1994), 220, dubbing the conflict in Bosnia "an historical aberration, albeit with a single important historical precedent: the interethnic slaughter of the World War II era." Similarly, Susan L. Woodward, *Balkan Tragedy* (Washington, DC: Brookings, 1995), argues against the historical inevitability of the violence in Bosnia.

21. Roger Cohen, "In a Town 'Cleansed' of Muslims, Serb Church Will Crown the Deed," *New York Times,* 7 March 1994, A1, late ed.

22. Fred Singleton, *A Short History of the Yugoslav Peoples* (New York: Cambridge, 1985), 285.

23. Jeri Laber, "Bosnia: Questions About Rape," *New York Review of Books,* 25 March 1993, 3–6.

24. Fouad Ajami, "In Europe's Shadows," *New Republic,* 21 November 1994, 35. Alija A. Izetbegovic, *Islam between East and West,* 3d ed. (Plainfield, IN: American Trust Publications, 1993). Two excellent studies have increased our understanding of Islam in Bosnia. See Tone Bringa, *Being Muslim the Bosnian Way: Identity and Community in a Central Bosnian Village* (Princeton, NJ: Princeton University Press, 1995), and Francine Friedman, *The Bosnian Muslims: Denial of a Nation* (Boulder, CO: Westview Press, 1996). The first is an anthropological study of reli-

gion and identity in a village that was destroyed during the recent war; the second traces the history of Bosnian Muslims over many centuries.

25. Ivo Banac, "Croatianism: Franjo Tudjman's Brutal Opportunism," *New Republic,* 25 October 1993, 20.

26. Tito is quoted in Ante Cuvalo, *The Croatian National Movement: 1966–1972* (New York: Columbia University Press, 1990), 3.

27. For a well-written history of Kosovo, including a brief account of the 1998–1999 conflict, see Noel Malcolm, *Kosovo: A Short History,* updated ed. (New York: HarperPerennial, 1999).

28. Christopher Bennett, *Yugoslavia's Bloody Collapse* (New York: New York University Press, 1995), 206.

29. Misha Glenny, *The Fall of Yugoslavia: The Third Balkan War,* rev. ed. (New York: Penguin, 1993), 31. See also Aleksa Djilas, "A Profile of Slobodan Milosevic," *Foreign Affairs* 72 (Summer 1993): 81–96. For a discussion of Milosevic's opportunism during the 1995 peace negotiations, see Roger Cohen, "Peace in the Balkans Now Relies on Man Who Fanned Its Wars," *New York Times,* 31 October 1995, late ed., A1. Lenard J. Cohen, *Serpent in the Bosom: The Rise and Fall of Slobodan Milosevic* (Boulder, CO: Westview Press, 2000), traces the dictator's career until his fall from power in October 2000.

30. Bennett, 208. David Rieff, *Slaughterhouse: Bosnia and the Failure of the West* (New York: Simon & Schuster, 1995), similarly emphasizes the power of propaganda in manufacturing violent nationalistic sentiments. Additionally, Slovenian scholar Svetlana Slapsak has analyzed the content of Belgrade's daily *Politika* and concluded that, even prior to the outbreak of fighting, the newspaper employed all manner of exaggeration and propaganda. See Svetlana Slapsak, "Some Mechanisms of Making Stereotypes: The Belgrade Daily *Politika* and its Rubric 'Echoes and Reactions,' January–July 1990" (Unpublished manuscript, Ljubljana, Slovenia, 1994).

31. Bette Denich, "Dismembering Yugoslavia: Nationalist Ideologies and the Symbolic Revival of Genocide," *American Ethnologist* 21 (1994): 370.

32. A flood of books and articles—many of them quite good—have brought light to various aspects of the breakup of Yugoslavia. In addition to those cited earlier, see Laura Silber and Allan Little, *Yugoslavia: Death of a Nation* (New York: TV Books/Penguin, 1996); Tim Judah, *The Serbs: History, Myth and the Destruction of Yugoslavia* (New Haven, CT: Yale University Press, 1997); Richard West, *Tito and the Rise and Fall of Yugoslavia* (New York: Carroll and Graf, 1996); Marcus Tanner, *Croatia: A Nation Forged in War* (New Haven, CT: Yale University Press, 1998); Branimir Anzulovic, *Heavenly Serbia: From Myth to Genocide* (New York: New York University Press, 1999); Alex Dragnich, *Serbs*

and Croats: The Struggle in Yugoslavia (New York: Harcourt Brace Jovanovich, 1992); Jasminka Udovicki and James Ridgeway, eds., *Burn This House: The Making and Unmaking of Yugoslavia* (Durham, NC: Duke University Press, 1997); Lenard J. Cohen, *Broken Bonds: Yugoslavia's Disintegration and Balkan Politics in Transition,* 2d ed. (Boulder, CO: Westview Press, 1995); John B. Allcock, *Explaining Yugoslavia* (New York: Columbia University Press, 2000); Warren Zimmerman, *Origins of a Catastrophe: Yugoslavia and Its Destroyers—America's Last Ambassador Tells What Happened and Why* (New York: Times Books, 1996).

33. In the first years of independence, Macedonians faced a threat from Greece. The Greek government objected to the use of the name "Macedonia," which it judged to be part of Greek national heritage. But by autumn of 1995, Greeks and Macedonians had, as a result of negotiations, resumed trade, and the problem seemed to recede in importance. Then, in 2001, long-simmering tensions between the Macedonian Slavic majority and the ethnic Albanian minority erupted into small-scale fighting. At its core, the conflict concerned widespread perceptions among Albanians that they were treated by law and common practice as second-class citizens. To what extent Macedonia would become yet another site for Balkan bloodshed remained uncertain as of this writing. See Anne Husarka, "A Last Chance in Macedonia," *New York Times,* 27 June 2001, A23; Ian Fisher, "Macedonian Leader, Warning of Civil War, Urges Calm," *New York Times,* 27 June 2001, A6; Carlotta Gall, "Albanians in Macedonia Are Suspicious of the Police," *New York Times,* 27 June 2001, A6; Ian Fisher, "Albanians' Many Children Unnerve Macedonia's Slavs," *New York Times,* 11 August 2001, A3; Unrepresented Nations and Peoples Organization, "Statement on the Political Situation in the Former Yugoslav Republic of Macedonia," United Nations and Peoples Organization [Online], 29 May 2001, accessed 14 August 2001, available from www.unpo.org/press/010529albans.htm.

34. Glenny, 174.

35. Drakulic, 51.

36. Ibid., 52.

37. Ibid.

38. One by one, war criminals from the wars in Bosnia and Kosovo have been indicted, arrested, and—in some cases—convicted. See, for example, Joshua Hammer and Zoran Cirjakovic, "'The Empress' Deposed," *Newsweek,* 22 January 2001, 36; Michael Meyer, "His Willing Executioners," *Newsweek,* 9 April 2001, 18; Carlotta Gall, "Yugoslavs Act on Hague Trial for Milosevic," *New York Times,* 24 June 2001, A1; Marlise Simons, "Milosevic to Face Charges Covering 3 Wars in Balkans," *New York Times,* 31 August 2001, A1; Marlise Simons, "Tribunal in

Hague Finds Bosnian Serb Guilty of Genocide," *New York Times*, 3 August 2001; "Bosnian Serb Officer Arrested on War Crimes Charges," *New York Times*, 11 August 2001, A3.

39. John Kifner, "An Outlaw in the Balkans Is Basking in the Spotlight," *New York Times*, 23 November 1993, A1, late ed.

40. Ibid.

41. Judah, 187; Rogel, 109.

42. Gutman, 157–63.

43. Glenny, 185–87.

44. Donia and Fine, 245.

45. Gutman, 60.

46. John E. Mack, "The Psychodynamics of Victimization Among National Groups in Conflict," in *The Psychodynamics of International Relationships*, vol. 1, V. Volkan, D. Julius, and J. Montville, eds. (Lexington, MA: Heath, 1990), 125, as quoted in Denich, 382.

47. Mark R. Levy and Michael S. Kramer, *The Ethnic Factor* (New York: Simon & Schuster, 1973), 95–121.

48. Vamik Volkan, *The Need to Have Enemies and Allies: From Clinical Practice to International Relationships* (Northvale, NJ: Aronson, 1988), 172, as quoted in Denich, 378.

49. Glenny, 26–29.

50. Gutman, ix.

51. Ibid., x.

52. Drakulic, 39.

53. Stephen Kinzer, "In Stronghold, Serbs Cite Dread of Muslim Rule," *New York Times*, 1 July 1995, 3, late ed.

54. Susan Brownmiller, "Making Female Bodies the Battlefield," *Newsweek*, 4 January 1993, 37.

55. Susan Brownmiller, *Against Our Will: Men, Women and Rape* (New York: Fawcett Columbine, 1975), 32.

56. Brownmiller, *Against Our Will*, 35. Rwanda in 1994 constitutes an exception to Brownmiller's contention that the winning side in a war typically does more raping than the losing side. As Chapter 4 documents, the Hutu government and militia forces committed far more violations of human rights, including rapes, than did the RPF rebels who won the war. See Donatella Lorch, "Wave of Rape Adds Horror to Rwanda's Trail of Brutality," *New York Times*, 15 May 1995, A1, late ed.

57. Brownmiller, *Against Our Will*, 32.

58. Ibid., 14–15, 31–113. See also Lee Ellis, *Theories of Rape: Inquiries into the Causes of Sexual Aggression* (New York: Hemisphere, 1989), for a balanced overview of several perspectives, including the feminist theory.

59. James Sterngold, "Japan Admits Army Forced Women Into War Brothels," *New York Times,* 5 August 1993, A2, late ed.; Nicholas D. Kristof, "Japan to Pay Women Forced Into Brothels," *New York Times,* 15 June 1995, A10, late ed.

60. Brownmiller, "Making Female Bodies the Battlefield," 37.

61. Gutman, 68–73. Though, understandably, most victims have been reluctant to speak of their ordeals, one can gain insights into what happened and why from various sources, including refugee testimony and records of war crime trials. See, for example, Michael P. Scharf, *Balkan Justice: The Story Behind the First International War Crimes Trial Since Nuremberg* (Durham, NC: Carolina Academic Press, 1997); Radmila Manojlovic Zarkovic and Fran Peavey, eds., I *Remember Sjecam Se: Writings by Bosnian Women Refugees* (San Francisco: Aunt Lute Books, 1996); Julie Mertus, Jasmina Tesanovic, Habiba Metikos, and Rada Boric, *The Suitcase: Refugee Voices from Bosnia and Croatia* (Berkeley: University of California Press, 1997); Alexandra Stiglmayer, ed., *Mass Rape: The War Against Women in Bosnia-Herzegovina,* trans. by Marion Faber (Lincoln: University of Nebraska Press, 1994); Beverly Allen, *Rape Warfare: The Hidden Genocide in Bosnia-Herzegovina and Croatia* (Minneapolis: University of Minnesota Press, 1996).

62. Gutman, 68.

63. Richard B. Felson, "Motives for Sexual Coercion," in *Aggression and Violence,* eds. Richard B. Felson and James T. Tedeschi (Washington, DC: American Psychological Association, 1993), 238–42.

64. Glenny, 209.

65. V. L. Quinsey, T. C. Chaplin, and D. Upfold, "Sexual Arousal to Nonsexual Violence and Sadomasochistic Themes Among Rapists and Non-Sex Offenders," *Journal of Consulting and Clinical Psychology* 52 (1984): 651–57.

66. D. Zillman, *Connections Between Sex and Aggression* (Hillsdale, NJ: Erlbaum, 1984).

67. N. M. Malamuth, R. J. Sockloskie, M. P. Koss, and J. S. Tanaka, "Characteristics of Aggressors Against Women," *Journal of Consulting and Clinical Psychology* 59 (1991): 670–81.

68. E. J. Kanin, "Date Rapists," *Archives of Sexual Behavior* 14 (1985): 219–31.

69. Felson, 240.

70. Neil M. Malamuth, "Predictors of Naturalistic Sexual Aggression," *Journal of Personality and Social Psychology* 50 (1986): 953–62.

71. See Ellis, *Theories of Rape,* for a review of the relevant evidence.

CHAPTER 3

1. Sheikh Omar Abdel Rahman is quoted in Steven Emerson, "Political Islam Promotes Terrorism," in *Islam: Opposing Viewpoints*, Paul A. Winters, ed. (San Diego, CA: Greenhaven Press, 1995), 160.

2. Daniel Pipes, "Same Difference," *National Review*, 7 November 1994, reprinted in "Political Islam is a Threat to the West," in *Islam: Opposing Viewpoints*, Paul A. Winters, ed. (San Diego, CA: Greenhaven Press, 1995), 191. See also Daniel Pipes, *In the Path of God: Islam and Political Power* (New York: Basic Books, 1983).

3. "Bombing Victim's Husband Speaks Out," *New York Times*, 25 May 1994, B4, late ed.

4. In 1999, as a consequence of a legal technicality, and at a cost to taxpayers of about $1 million, the first four defendants convicted in the World Trade Center bombing were resentenced; their terms, this time, ran 108 to 117 years apiece, still amounting, of course, to life in prison. See Richard Bernstein, "Trade Center Bombers Get Prison Terms of 240 Years," *New York Times*, 25 May 1994, A1, late ed.; Larry Neumeister, "Admitted Terrorist Gets Life," *Chicago Sun-Times*, 9 January 1998, A24, accessed 21 August 2001, available from LEXIS-NEXIS Academic universe, www.lexis-nexis.com/universe; Greg B. Smith, "WTC Bombers Are Resentenced," *New York Daily News*, 14 October 1999, 12, accessed 21 August 2001, available from LEXIS-NEXIS Academic universe, www.lexis-nexis.com/universe.

5. Steven Emerson, "The Other Fundamentalists," *New Republic*, 12 June 1995, 22. See also Adam Brodsky, "Jihad on American Soil? You'd Better Believe It," *Daily News* [New York], 1 February 1993, 27.

6. Several recent books address the chilling scenario of nuclear and biological terrorism. See, for example, Jessica Stern, *Ultimate Terrorists*, paperback ed. (Cambridge, MA: Harvard University Press, 2000); Walter Laqueur, *The New Terrorism: Fanaticism and the Arms of Mass Destruction* (New York: Oxford University Press, 1999); Harvey Kushner, ed., *The Future of Terrorism: Violence in the New Millennium* (Thousand Oaks, CA: Sage Publications, 1998).

7. Sheikh Metwali el-Shaarawi, a popular Islamic cleric in Cairo, issued a fatwa that, in view of the Serbs' campaigns of "ethnic cleansing," it was permissible for Bosnian Muslims to force the wives and daughters of their Serb prisoners to engage in sex. Youssef M. Ibrahim, "Muslim Edicts Take on New Force," *New York Times*, 12 February 1995, sec. 1, 14, late ed.

8. Flora Lewis, "The War on Arab Intellectuals," *New York Times*, 7 September 1993, A19, late ed.; Youssef M. Ibrahim, "Muslim Edicts Take on New Force," 14;

Youssef M. Ibrahim, "Algeria Militants Vow to Kill Women Linked to Government," *New York Times,* 4 May 1995, A3, late ed.; Youssef M. Ibrahim, "With 46th Algerian Journalist Slain, It's a Furtive Vocation," *New York Times,* 31 May 1995, A11, late ed.

9. "Cairo Militants Win Annulment," *New York Times,* 15 June 1995, A3, late ed. Khaled Dawoud, "Egyptian Feminist Allowed to Stay Married," *The Guardian,* 31 July 2001, 13, accessed 20 August 2001, available from LEXIS-NEXIS Academic universe, www.lexis-nexis.com/universe.

10. Emerson, "The Other Fundamentalists," 22. Simon Reeve, *The New Jackals: Ramzi Yousef, Osama bin Laden and the Future of Terrorism* (Boston: Northeastern University Press, 1999), 156. See also Michael Grunwald, "U.S. Tries to Link N.Y., Africa Bombs: Prosecutors Say Bin Laden Aide Got Guns for Trade Center Plotter," *Washington Post,* 24 September 1998, A29, accessed 21 August 2001, available from LEXIS-NEXIS Academic universe, www.lexis-nexis.com/universe, Internet.

11. Eric Pooley, "The Arab Connection: Breaking the World Trade Center Bombing Case," *New York,* 15 March 1993, 30.

12. Terrorism expert Simon Reeve paints a fascinating portrait of Ramzi Yousef. A senior Pakistani intelligence officer told Reeve: "Everywhere Yousef went he was able to convert religious young men to his terrorist cause. His power was based partly on fear and partly on persuasion—he convinced some of these youngsters that what they were doing was in the name of Allah. He knew exactly what to say and what to do to win them over. Ramzi Yousef is an evil genius" (quoted in Reeve, 132).

13. Richard Behar, "The Secret Life of Mahmud the Red," *Time,* 4 October 1993, 57. Many of the details of Abouhalima's life are taken from this article. Hannah Arendt's views are discussed in Chapters 5 and 6.

14. Tim Weiner, "Blowback from the Afghan Battlefield," *New York Times,* 13 March 1994, sec. 6, 53, late ed.

15. Hekmatyar was defeated by the even more extremist Taliban. However, he is still alive and retains some support in the region.

16. The information presented here comes principally from press reports and court proceedings. For some of the terrorists, information is unavailable and for others it is difficult to confirm.

17. Francis X. Clines, "U.S.-Born Suspect in Bombing Plots: Zealous Causes and Civic Roles," *New York Times,* 28 June 1993, B2, late ed.

18. Ibid.

19. James C. McKinley, Jr., "Parents of Bomb Suspect Weep and Insist He Is No Terrorist," *New York Times,* 17 August 1995, B4, late ed. Though Ramzi Yousef

claims to be a Muslim whose terrorist acts derive from religious motives, Simon Reeve argues against calling him an Islamic fundamentalist, citing numerous instances when Yousef readily abandoned the precepts of his purported faith. Whether one accepts this logic or not, Reeve is no doubt correct in calling Yousef "the archetypal angry young man" who rants and rails against the world's inequities, real and imagined. The psychological origins of his anger remain obscure, but its main target has been the United States, largely because of its sympathetic orientation toward the state of Israel. Yousef describes himself as "Pakistani by birth, Palestinian by choice" (quoted in Reeve, 127).

20. Yvonne Yazbeck Haddad, ed., *The Muslims of America* (New York: Oxford University Press, 1991).

21. "The Immigrants: Fundamentalist Islamic Terrorists in the US," editorial, *New Republic*, 19 April 1993, 7.

22. Richard Bernstein, "Hate-Literature Documents Weighed in Bombing Trial," *New York Times*, 27 January 1994, B4, late ed.

23. Ibid.

24. Ibid.

25. Ibid.

26. Ibid.

27. Richard Bernstein, "Bomb Trial Focuses on Origin of Video," *New York Times*, 2 February 1994, B3, late ed.

28. Ibid.

29. Bernstein, "Trade Center Bombers Get Prison Terms of 240 Years," B4.

30. Ibid.

31. Mary B. W. Tabor, "Transcript of Tapes Reveals Sheik Talked of Merits of Bomb Targets," *New York Times*, 4 August 1993, A1, late ed.

32. "Sheik Urged Attack on U.S. Army, Transcripts of Tapes Show," *New York Times*, 7 March 1994, B4, late ed.

33. Tabor, A1.

34. Ibid., B4.

35. Joseph P. Fried, "Ex-Aide Says Sheik Wanted Mubarak Dead," *New York Times*, 5 May 1995, A1, late ed. Abdo Haggag testified as part of a plea bargain in which charges were dropped for his involvement in the Mubarak plot. As part of the deal, he pled guilty in an unrelated arson case.

36. Jill Smolowe, "A Voice of Holy War," *Time*, 15 March 1993, 31; Richard Bernstein, "Sheik Asserts Innocence in Terror Conspiracy Case," *New York Times*, 16 October 1993, 27, late ed.

37. John L. Esposito, *The Islamic Threat: Myth or Reality* (New York: Oxford University Press, 1992), 47–76, presents this classification. Numerous recent

works have addressed the rise of Islamic extremism from a variety of perspectives. See Milton Viorst, *In the Shadow of the Prophet: The Struggle for the Soul of Islam* (New York: Anchor, 1998); Mark Huband, *Warriors of the Prophet: The Struggle for Islam* (Boulder, CO: Westview Press, 1998); Morgan Norval, *Triumph of Disorder: Islamic Fundamentalism, the New Face of War* (Bend, OR: Sligo Press, 1999); Edgar O'Ballance, *Islamic Fundamentalist Terrorism, 1979–95: The Iranian Connection* (New York: New York University Press, 1996); John K. Cooley, *Unholy Wars: Afghanistan, America and International Terrorism,* new ed. (London: Pluto Press, 2000); Anthony J. Dennis, *The Rise of the Islamic Empire and the Threat to the West* (Bristol, IN: Wyndham Hall Press, 1996). Several of these works should be read with caution. Consult Daniel Pipes, "Review of Milton Viorst, *In the Shadow of the Prophet: The Struggle for the Soul of Islam,*" *Middle East Quarterly* (September 1998), and "Review of Mark Huband, *Warriors of the Prophet: The Struggle for Islam,*" *Middle East Quarterly* (June 1999), both accessed 20 August 2001, available from www.danielpipes.org. See also two excellent—but older and more general—works: Raphael Patai, *The Arab Mind,* rev. ed. (New York: Charles Scribner's Sons, 1983), and David Pryce-Jones, *The Closed Circle: An Interpretation of the Arabs* (New York: HarperPerennial, 1991).

38. Esposito, 7–8.

39. Bernard Lewis, *The Political Language of Islam* (Chicago: University of Chicago Press, 1988), 117–18, n. 3.

40. Ibid.

41. Ibid.

42. Hrair Dekmejian, *Islam in Revolution: Fundamentalism in the Arab World* (Syracuse, NY: Syracuse University Press, 1985), 4–5.

43. Ibid.

44. Ibid., 179–91.

45. Esposito, 122.

46. Ibid., 32.

47. Bernard Lewis, 73.

48. Patrick J. Bannerman, *Islam in Perspective* (London: Routledge, 1988), 86, as quoted in Esposito, 33.

49. Fathi Yakin, *Mushkilat al-Da'wa wad-Da'iyya* [*Problems of the Call and the Caller*] (Beirut: Mu'assasat al-Risala, 1981), 220–21, as quoted in Ziad Abu-Amr, *Islamic Fundamentalism in the West Bank and Gaza: Muslim Brotherhood and Islamic Jihad* (Bloomington: Indiana University Press, 1994), 120.

50. Johannes J. G. Jansen, *The Neglected Duty: The Creed of Sadat's Assassins and Islamic Resurgence in the Middle East* (New York: Macmillan, 1986). Jansen's work includes as an appendix an English translation of Faraj's 1981 manifesto.

Jansen writes that: "Western writers who give accounts of Islam to a Western public often do not stress those elements in Islam that would be offensive or nonsense in the eyes of their Western readers. They rather see it as their duty to present Islam in as acceptable a light as possible to the West. They state the case of Islam with as much coherence as possible and construct the most feasible explanation for various Islamic aspirations. In general, they take on the role of a counsel for the defense" (xxi).

51. *Faridah,* sec. 16 as quoted in Jansen, 7. Contrast this with King Hussein's perspective, expressed at the time of the signing of an accord with Israel in July 1994. He quoted the Koran: "Then if they should be inclined to make peace, do thou incline toward it also, and put thy trust in Allah. Surely, it is He who is all-hearing, all-knowing." Elaine Sciolino, "Quoting Bible and Koran, Two Old Foes Pledge Peace," *New York Times,* 27 July 1994, A8, late ed.

52. *Faridah,* sec. 50, as quoted in Jansen, 183–84.

53. *Faridah,* sec. 54, as quoted in Jansen, 185.

54. *Faridah,* sec. 55, as quoted in Jansen, 186.

55. *Faridah,* sec. 3, as quoted in Jansen, 160–61.

56. *Faridah,* sec. 84, as quoted in Jansen, 199.

57. *Faridah,* sec. 109, as quoted in Jansen, 211.

58. *Faridah,* sec. 121, as quoted in Jansen, 217.

59. *Faridah,* sec. 100, as quoted in Jansen, 205.

60. James C. McKinley Jr., "Sheik's Speech Encouraging Guerrillas is Entered at Trial," *New York Times,* 1 March 1995, B2, late ed.

61. David Lamb, *The Arabs: Journeys Beyond the Mirage* (New York: Vintage-Random, 1988), 108.

62. Bernard Lewis, 4.

63. Fatima Mernissi, *Islam and Democracy: Fear of the Modern World,* trans. Mary Jo Lakeland (New York: Addison-Wesley, 1992), 145–47.

64. James A. Bill, "Resurgent Islam in the Persian Gulf," *Foreign Affairs* 63 (Fall 1984): 126.

65. Bernard Lewis, "Islam and Liberal Democracy," *The Atlantic Monthly,* February 1993, excerpted as "Islam Has Weak Democratic Traditions," in *Islam: Opposing Viewpoints,* Paul A. Winters, ed. (San Diego, CA: Greenhaven Press, 1995), 103.

66. Mernissi, 32–41.

67. Ibid., 43.

68. Ibid., 47.

69. See also Peter Waldman, "Leap of Faith: Some Muslim Thinkers Want to Reinterpret Islam for Modern Times," *Wall Street Journal,* 15 March 1995, 1.

70. Chapter 7 considers the psychology of injustice and its impact on aggressive behavior.

71. C. A. Russell and B. H. Miller, "Profile of a Terrorist," *Terrorism: An International Journal* 1 (1977): 17–24.

72. United States Federal Bureau of Investigation, *Terrorism in the United States: 1987* (Washington, DC: Government Printing Office, 1988).

73. Walter Laqueur, *The Age of Terrorism* (Boston: Little, Brown, 1987), 149–50.

74. Leonard Weinberg and Paul Davis, *Introduction to Political Terrorism* (New York: McGraw-Hill, 1989), 98–99. See also Walter Reich, ed., *Origins of Terrorism: Psychologies, Ideologies, Theologies, States of Mind* (Washington, DC: Woodrow Wilson Center Press, 1998); Laura K. Engendorf, *Terrorism: Opposing Viewpoints* (San Diego, CA: Greenhaven Press, 2000).

75. Phillip W. Johnson and Theodore B. Feldmann, "Personality Types and Terrorism: Self-Psychology Perspectives," *Forensic Reports* 5 (1992): 300–301.

76. Laqueur, 142–73.

77. Dekmejian, 32–36.

78. Ibid., 33.

79. Ibid., 35.

80. Lamb, 89.

CHAPTER 4

1. Roger Rosenblatt, "A Killer in the Eye," *New York Times*, 5 June 1994, sec. 6, 40, late ed.

2. Donatella Lorch, "Children's Drawings Tell Horror of Rwanda in Colors of Crayons," *New York Times*, 16 September 1994, A1, late ed.

3. United Nations, *Final Report of the Commission of Experts Submitted Pursuant to Security Council Resolution 935* (Geneva, Switzerland: United Nations, 1994), 9. The victims' hope, based on past respect for the sanctuary of the church, was particularly ill-founded. Although some clergy did attempt to shield the victims, witnesses have accused more than a score of priests and nuns of complicity in genocide. Raymond Bonner, "Clergy in Rwanda Is Accused of Abetting Atrocities," *New York Times*, 7 July 1995, A3, late ed. Hugh McCullum, *The Angels Have Left Us: The Rwanda Tragedy and the Churches* (Geneva: World Council of Churches Publications, 1995), elaborates on the role of religious leaders and institutions in the Rwanda genocide. For a competent discussion of the death toll, see Alison Des Forges, *"Leave None to Tell the Story": Genocide in Rwanda* (New York: Human Rights Watch, 1999), 15.

4. Donatella Lorch, "Heart of Rwanda's Darkness: Slaughter at a Rural Church," *New York Times*, 3 June 1994, A1, late ed.

5. United Nations, *Final Report of the Commission of Experts*, 12–14.

6. Wolfgang Schweitzer, "Un Millier de morts en avril à l'hôpital psychiatrique de Kigali," *Agence France Presse*, 10 October 1994, online, Nexis.

7. Serge Arnold, "37 Journalistes tués dans les massacres au Rwanda," *Agence France Presse*, 23 September 1994, online, Nexis.

8. Donatella Lorch, "Thousands of Rwanda Dead Wash Down to Lake Victoria," *New York Times*, 21 May 1994, 1, late ed.

9. Howard W. French, "An Ignorance of Africa as Vast as the Continent," *New York Times*, 20 November 1994, sec. 4, 3, late ed.

10. Jean Hélène, "En Dépit de nombreux témoignages le chef des milices Rwandaises réfute les accusations de génocide," *Le Monde*, 17 May 1994, online, Nexis.

11. Ibid.

12. Raymond Bonner, "Rwanda Now Faces Painful Ordeal of Rebirth," *New York Times*, 29 December 1994, A1, late ed.

13. United Nations, *Final Report of the Commission of Experts*, 9. In the years since the 1994 genocide, scholars and journalists have established beyond doubt that the mass killings of Tutsis and Hutu moderates occurred not as spontaneous aggressive outbursts, but rather in fulfillment of carefully devised schemes formulated by political, military, and intellectual leaders. See, especially, Des Forges, 4; Philip Gourevitch, *We Wish to Inform You That Tomorrow We Will Be Killed with Our Families: Stories from Rwanda* (New York: Farrar, Straus & Giroux, 1998), 95; Fergal Keane, *Season of Blood: A Rwandan Journey* (London: Penguin, 1995), 8; Joan Kakwenzire and Dixon Kamukama, "The Development and Consolidation of Extremist Forces in Rwanda, 1990–1994," in Howard Adelman and Astri Suhrke, eds., *The Path of a Genocide: The Rwanda Crisis from Uganda to Zaire* (New Brunswick, NJ: Transaction Publishers, 1999), 61; François Byarahamuwanzi, untitled remarks in John A. Berry and Carol Pott Berry, eds., *Genocide in Rwanda: A Collective Memory* (Washington, DC: Howard University Press, 1999), 52; Mahmood Mamdani, *When Victims Become Killers: Colonialism, Nativism, and the Genocide in Rwanda* (Princeton, NJ: Princeton University Press, 2001).

14. Raymond Bonner, "Unsolved Rwanda Mystery: The President's Plane Crash," *New York Times*, 12 November 1994, 1, late ed. See Des Forges, *"Leave None,"* 181, for an interesting but, in the end, unfruitful attempt to get to the bottom of the mystery surrounding the downing of Habyarimana's plane. Her conclusion bears repeating: "Responsibility for killing Habyarimana is a serious is-

sue, but it is a different issue from responsibility for the genocide. We know little about who assassinated Habyarimana. We know more about who used the assassination as the pretext to begin a slaughter that had been planned for months. Hutu Power leaders expected that killing Tutsi would draw the RPF back into combat and give them a new chance for victory or at least for negotiations that might allow them to win back some of the concessions made at Arusha" (p. 185).

15. René Lemarchand, "The Apocalypse in Rwanda," *Cultural Survival Quarterly,* Summer/Fall 1994, 29–33.

16. Raymond Bonner, "Nyakizu Journal: And the Church Refuge Became a Killing Field," *New York Times,* 17 November 1994, A4, late ed.

17. This subhead comes from Jacques J. Maquet, *The Premise of Inequality in Rwanda* (New York: Oxford University Press, 1961).

18. George Thomas Kurian, "Rwanda," *Encyclopedia of the Third World,* 4th ed. (New York: Facts on File, 1992), 1609–23; Richard F. Nyrop et al., *Rwanda: A Country Study* (Washington, DC: Government Printing Office, 1982), 5–89.

19. Sometimes the groups are identified with prefixes from Kinyarwanda, the national language, as in Bahutu, Batutsi, Batwa, Watutsi.

20. Alex Shoumatoff, "Rwanda's Aristocratic Guerrillas," *New York Times,* 13 December 1992, sec. 6, 42, late ed.

21. Ibid.

22. As quoted in Frank Smyth, "The Horror—Rwanda: A History Lesson," *New Republic,* 20 June 1994, 19.

23. Maquet, 129–35, 158–70.

24. Ali Yusuf Mugenzi, "Brewing Hatred," *Focus on Africa,* October–December 1994, 10–12.

25. Leo Kuper, *Genocide: Its Political Use in the Twentieth Century* (New Haven, CT: Yale University Press, 1981), 47–48.

26. Jacques J. Maquet, *The Premise of Inequality in Rwanda* (New York: Oxford University Press, 1961). Three other sources on the history of this period are: René Lemarchand, "Rwanda," in *African Kingships in Perspective: Political Change and Modernization in Monarchical Settings,* René Lemarchand, ed. (London: Frank Cass, 1977), 67–92; Lucy Mair, *African Kingdoms* (New York: Oxford University Press, 1977); Catharine Newbury, *The Cohesion of Oppression: Clientship and Ethnicity in Rwanda* (New York: Columbia University Press, 1988). See also Learthen Dorsey, *Historical Dictionary of Rwanda* (Metuchen, NJ: Scarecrow Press, 1994).

27. Maquet, 160.

28. Ibid., 66–77.

29. Ibid., 129–36.

30. Ibid., 143.

31. William Roger Louis, *Ruanda-Urundi 1884–1919* (Oxford: Clarendon, 1963). In the preindependence period, Rwanda was usually spelled "Ruanda" and Burundi was spelled "Urundi."

32. Nyrop et al., 14.

33. Lemarchand, "The Apocalypse in Rwanda," 30–31.

34. Nyrop et al., 14–15.

35. Kuper, 61.

36. Kuper, 62; Lemarchand, "Rwanda," in *African Kingships in Perspective,* 67–92.

37. As quoted in Smyth, 19.

38. René Lemarchand, "Burundi," in *African Kingships in Perspective: Political Change and Modernization in Monarchical Settings,* René Lemarchand, ed. (London: Frank Cass, 1977), 93–126. See also René Lemarchand, *Burundi: Ethnocide As Discourse and Practice* (New York: Cambridge University Press, 1994; paperback ed., 1996).

39. Irving Louis Horowitz, *Genocide: State Power and Mass Murder,* 2d ed. (New Brunswick, NJ: Transaction, 1977), 38–39.

40. Stanley Meisler, "Holocaust in Burundi, 1972," in *Case Studies on Human Rights and Fundamental Freedoms: A World Survey,* vol. 5, Willem A. Veenhoven, ed. (The Hague: Martinus Nijhoff, 1976), 227–32, reprinted in *The History and Sociology of Genocide,* Frank Chalk and Kurt Jonassohn, eds. (New Haven, CT: Yale University Press, 1990), 384–93; Kuper, 63.

41. Jerry Gray, "2 Nations Joined by Common History of Genocide," *New York Times,* 9 April 1994, 6, late ed. René Lemarchand sets the number of Hutu victims a bit lower, at 15,000. See Lemarchand, *Burundi,* 126.

42. Some independent sources have set the death toll as high as one hundred thousand, or even one hundred fifty thousand. These numbers are difficult to verify. See Donatella Lorch, "Now, Rwanda's Neighbor Hovers Near the Brink," *New York Times,* 3 February 1995, A3, late ed.

43. Gray, 6.

44. See, for example, Donatella Lorch, "Burundi's Ethnic Divide Widens, Feeding Fear of Greater Violence," *New York Times,* 2 April 1995, sec. 1, 1, late ed.; "South African Mediators Leave Burundi with Little Progress," *New York Times,* 4 August 1995, A4; "Doubtful Peace," *Economist* (21 July 2001), accessed 2 September 2001, available from LEXIS-NEXIS Academic universe, www.lexis-nexis.com/universe.

45. Meisler, "Holocaust in Burundi, 1972," reprinted in *The History and Sociology of Genocide,* 389–93.

46. Lemarchand, "The Apocalypse in Rwanda," 29–33.

47. Mugenzi, 11.

48. Ibid.

49. Donatella Lorch, "Rwanda Rebels: Army of Exiles Fights for a Home," *New York Times,* 9 June 1994, A10, late ed.; Jane Perlez, "Violence Roils Rwanda's Embryo Democracy," *New York Times,* 1 June 1992, A11, late ed.; Raymond Bonner, "How Minority Tutsi Won the War," *New York Times,* 6 September 1994, A6, late ed.

50. Shoumatoff, 42.

51. Raymond Bonner, "Rwanda's Leaders Vow to Build a Multiparty State for Both Hutu and Tutsi," *New York Times,* 7 September 1994, A10, late ed.

52. Shoumatoff, 42.

53. Independent sources have identified instances of RPF human rights violations during the fighting, and as revenge afterward, but there seems to be little evidence of a systematic, centrally directed policy by the RPF to commit such atrocities. The RPF leaders have made efforts to prevent the atrocities and appear committed to legal proceedings against those Hutu who participated in the genocide.

54. Jane Perlez, "Under the Bougainvillea, A Litany of Past Wrongs," *New York Times,* 15 August 1994, A6, late ed.

55. Ibid.

56. United Nations, *Final Report of the Commission of Experts,* 10; Andrew Jay Cohen, "On the Trail of Genocide," *New York Times,* 7 September 1994, A23, late ed.

57. Cohen, A23. Berry and Berry, *Genocide in Rwanda,* 113, reprint the complete text of the Hutu Ten Commandments. Two examples provide a glimpse into the soul of Hutu power: "Every Muhutu should know that a Mututsi woman, wherever she is, works for the interest of her Tutsi ethnic group. As a result, we shall consider a traitor any Muhutu who marries a Tutsi woman, befriends a Tutsi woman, employs a Tutsi woman as a secretary or a concubine"; and "All strategic positions, political, administrative, economic, military, and security should be entrusted only to Bahutu."

58. *Kangura,* issue No. 47, 5 as quoted in Mugenzi, 12.

59. Mugenzi, 11.

60. Bill Berkeley, "Sounds of Violence: Rwanda's Killer Radio," *New Republic,* 22 August 1994, 18. See also Frank Chalk, "Hate Radio in Rwanda," in Adelman and Suhrke, *Path of a Genocide,* 93.

61. Chris McGreal, article, *The Guardian* [London], 3 December 1994, reprinted in "Building Cases in Rwanda and Bosnia: Will War Criminals Be Tried?" *World Press Review,* February 1995, 19.

62. United Nations, *Final Report of the Commission of Experts,* 10.

63. Berkeley, 18.

64. Ibid.

65. Ibid.

66. Sidney Kraus and Dennis Davis, *The Effects of Mass Communication on Political Behavior* (University Park: Pennsylvania State University Press, 1976), 117–24.

67. Jerry Gray, "Rumor Mills Spin Mistrust in 2 Countries," *New York Times*, 17 August 1994, A12, late ed.

68. Mugenzi, 11.

69. Peter Smerdon, "Rwandan Prisoners Say They Were Forced to Kill Tutsi," *New York Times*, 6 June 1994, A8, late ed.

70. Ibid.

71. Ibid.

72. Rosenblatt, 40. See also reports of the militia members' cruel behavior in Thomas Kamilindi, untitled remarks in Berry and Berry, *Genocide in Rwanda*, 14.

73. Berkeley, 18.

74. Ibid.

75. Lemarchand, "The Apocalypse in Rwanda," 32.

76. Frank Rusagara, untitled remarks in Berry and Berry, *Genocide in Rwanda*, 60.

77. McGreal, 18.

78. Lemarchand, "The Apocalypse in Rwanda," 31.

79. Gustave Le Bon, *The Crowd* (London: T. Fisher Unwin, 1896, trans. *Psychologie des foules* [Paris]), 26.

80. Social psychologist Ervin Staub has attempted to understand the origins of genocide in Rwanda by applying his well-regarded theoretical model. See Ervin Staub, "The Origins and Prevention of Genocide, Mass Killing, and Other Collective Violence," *Peace and Conflict: Journal of Peace Psychology* 5 (1999): 303–36; Ervin Staub, "The Roots of Evil: Social Conditions, Culture, Personality, and Basic Human Needs," *Personality and Social Psychology Review* 3 (1999): 179–92. Staub has also gone to Rwanda to work with survivors of the genocide.

81. Bonner, "Nyakizu Journal: And the Church Refuge Became a Killing Field," A4.

Chapter 5

1. Gilbert Allardyce, ed., *The Place of Fascism in European History* (Englewood Cliffs, NJ: Prentice-Hall, 1971), 2.

2. Peter Viereck, *Metapolitics: The Roots of the Nazi Mind*, rev. ed. (1941; New York: Capricorn, 1965), 318.

3. Edouard Calic, *Reinhard Heydrich: The Chilling Story of the Man Who Masterminded the Nazi Death Camps,* trans. Lowell Bair (New York: William Morrow, 1985). Calic provides a fair discussion of his disagreements with Charles Wighton, Shlomo Aronson, and other earlier biographers; Calic, 52–54. There were apparently unfounded rumors that Heydrich's father Bruno, a composer and Wagner enthusiast, was Jewish. They caused Bruno Heydrich much anxiety and led him to preach strict anti-Semitism, both out of conviction and as a preemptive strike against the anti-Semitism of neighbors and professional colleagues.

4. Wilhelm Keitel, *The Memoirs of Field-Marshal Keitel,* ed. Walter Gorlitz, trans. David Irving (New York: Stein & Day, 1966), 238.

5. Telford Taylor, *The Anatomy of the Nuremberg Trials: A Personal Memoir* (New York: Alfred A. Knopf, 1992).

6. Albert Speer, *Inside the Third Reich,* trans. Richard and Clara Winston (New York: Avon, 1970), 47–48.

7. Ibid., 49.

8. Ibid., 48. For critical perspectives on Speer's book, see Erich Goldhagen, "Albert Speer, Himmler, and the Secrecy of the Final Solution," *Midstream,* October 1971, 43–50; Matthias Schmidt, *Albert Speer: The End of a Myth,* trans. Joachim Neugroschel (New York: St. Martin's Press, 1984); Gitta Sereny, *Albert Speer: His Battle with Truth* (New York: Albert A. Knopf, 1995). Schmidt writes that Speer "was anything but a man 'trapped in narrow technology' . . . His rapid climb to the top of the Nazi hierarchy, his abrupt moral about-face at the end of the war, and his self-portrayal as an apolitical National Socialist all point to the same thing. Speer had only one goal in mind: to make history. The positions he held during the 'thousand' years of the Third Reich were purely means to an end" (5).

9. Rudolf Hoess, *Commandant at Auschwitz: The Autobiography of Rudolf Hoess* (London: George Weidenfeld & Nicolson, 1959), excerpted in "Excerpts from *The Autobiography of Rudolf Hoess,*" in *Survivors, Victims, and Perpetrators: Essays on the Nazi Holocaust,* ed. Joel E. Dimsdale (New York: Hemisphere, 1980), 289–304.

10. Taylor, 363. For an analysis of interviews conducted by Dr. Gustave Gilbert, the prison psychologist at Nuremberg, and Dr. Douglas Kelley, the prison psychiatrist, see Eric A. Zillmer, Molly Harrower, Barry A. Ritzler, and Robert P. Archer, *The Quest for the Nazi Personality: A Psychological Investigation of Nazi War Criminals* (Hillsdale, NJ: Erlbaum, 1995). This book also contains a fascinating history of the feud between Gilbert and Kelley and its impact on the utilization of data stemming from the Nuremberg interviews.

11. Gitta Sereny, *Into That Darkness: From Mercy Killing to Mass Murder* (New York: McGraw-Hill, 1974).

12. Leonard Mosley, *The Reich Marshal: A Biography of Hermann Goering* (Garden City, NY: Doubleday, 1974), 329.

13. Ibid., 337.

14. Ibid., 333.

15. Raul Hilberg, *Perpetrators Victims Bystanders: The Jewish Catastrophe 1933–1945* (New York: HarperPerennial, 1992), 1.

16. Other biographies of Goering include: Roger Manvell and Heinrich Fraenkel, *Hermann Göring* (London: Heineman, 1962); David Irving, *Göring: A Biography* (New York: William Morrow, 1989); Asher Lee, *Goering: Air Leader* (New York: Hippocrene, 1972).

17. Walter Gorlitz, introduction, *The Memoirs of Field-Marshal Keitel*, by Wilhelm Keitel, 29.

18. Michael R. Marrus, *The Holocaust in History* (New York: New American Library, 1987), 32.

19. Hilberg, *Perpetrators Victims Bystanders*, 20.

20. Marrus, 46.

21. Viereck, 317.

22. Robert G. L. Waite, preface, *The Psychopathic God: Adolf Hitler* (New York: Basic Books, 1977), xi.

23. Fred I. Greenstein, *Personality and Politics: Problems of Evidence, Inference, and Conceptualization*, new ed. (Princeton, NJ: Princeton University Press, 1987). Greenstein discusses the conditions under which a leader's personality is apt to influence the course of policy. See also Neil J. Kressel, ed., *Political Psychology: Classic and Contemporary Readings* (New York: Paragon House, 1993).

24. Marrus, 37. For discussions of Hitler's role in ordering the Final Solution, see Marrus, 31–54; Christopher R. Browning, *The Path to Genocide: Essays on Launching the Final Solution* (New York: Cambridge University Press, 1992), 86–121.

25. Marrus, 31–54.

26. Rudolph Binion, *Hitler among the Germans* (New York: Elsevier, 1976), 27, contains this and many other telling anti-Semitic quotations from Hitler's early years as a political activist.

27. Lucy S. Dawidowicz, *The War Against the Jews 1933–1945* (New York: Bantam, 1976), 27.

28. Adolf Hitler, *Mein Kampf*, trans. Ralph Manheim (Boston: Houghton Mifflin, 1943), 51–65.

29. Historians and biographers have long debated the question of when Hitler became an anti-Semite; many question his own account in *Mein Kampf*, preferring an earlier or later date. Moreover, Hitler apparently rewrote the details of his

years in Vienna to suit his political purposes, quite consciously attempting to forge a useful personal myth. For a refutation of the *Mein Kampf* account, see Karl Dietrich Bracher, *The German Dictatorship: The Origins, Structure, and Effects of National Socialism,* trans. Jean Steinberg (New York: Praeger, 1970). For Hitler's attempt to manage his own image, see Ian Kershaw, *The "Hitler Myth": Image and Reality in the Third Reich* (New York: Oxford University Press, 1987). There are many good books about Hitler; see especially John Toland, *Adolf Hitler* (Garden City, NY: Anchor-Doubleday, 1976); Ian Kershaw, *Hitler: 1889–1936 Hubris,* paperback ed. (New York: WW Norton, 2000); Ian Kershaw, *Hitler: 1936–1945 Nemesis,* paperback ed. (New York: WW Norton, 2000). For a discussion of attempts to unravel the mysteries of Hitler that pays particular attention to what such endeavors reveal about the explainers, see Ron Rosenbaum, *Explaining Hitler: The Search for the Origins of His Evil,* paperback ed. (New York: HarperCollins, 1999).

30. Waite, 39.

31. See Erich Fromm, *The Anatomy of Human Destructiveness* (New York: Fawcett-Crest, 1973). The renowned neo-Freudian analyst offers a well-argued dissent from the mainstream psychoanalytic perspective on Hitler's family life. He notes that the Oedipus complex is supposed to be universal, and though Hitler's was powerful and unresolved, it is hard to see how it could have accounted for his destructive character. Moreover, Fromm rejects the image of Hitler's father, Alois, as brutal and sees Hitler's parents as essentially normal. He sees the roots of the problem in Hitler's unloving relationship with his mother. This relationship ultimately led to Hitler's imprisonment in a cold, narcissistic shell, his inability to deal with reality, and his deeply "necrophilous" lust for destruction. Fromm's very long book is worth reading for its brilliant critique of other approaches, but Carr, among others, has shown its poor grounding in historical knowledge about Hitler's early life. See William Carr, *Hitler: A Study in Personality and Politics* (New York: St. Martin's Press, 1979), 152–53.

32. Binion, 21–22; Gertrud M. Kurth, "The Jew and Adolf Hitler," *Psychoanalytic Quarterly* 16 (1947): 11–32.

33. Shlomo Aronson, "Reinhard Heydrich," in *The Encyclopedia of the Holocaust,* Israel Gutman, ed. (New York: Macmillan, 1990), 655–57. See also Calic, *Reinhard Heydrich: The Chilling Story of the Man Who Masterminded the Nazi Death Camps.*

34. Walter Langer, *The Mind of Adolf Hitler: The Secret Wartime Report* (New York: Basic Books, 1972); Waite, *The Psychopathic God: Adolf Hitler;* Norbert Bromberg and Verna Volz Small, *Hitler's Psychopathology* (New York: International Universities Press, 1983). The best summaries of the psychoanalytic per-

spectives on Hitler are Fritz Redlich, *Hitler: Diagnosis of a Destructive Prophet* (New York: Oxford University Press, 1998); George Victor, *Hitler: The Pathology of Evil* (Dulles, VA: Brasseys, 1999); Waite, *The Psychopathic God: Adolf Hitler;* Carr, *Hitler: A Study in Personality and Politics;* George M. Kren and Leon Rappoport, *The Holocaust and the Crisis of Human Behavior,* rev. ed. (New York: Holmes and Meier, 1994).

35. David E. Stannard, *Shrinking History* (New York: Oxford University Press, 1980). Stannard delivers a passionate attack on psychohistory. Though he tends to throw out the baby with the bath water, his book should be consulted by those interested in the serious limitations of this mode of explanation. For discussion of the role of psychology in the historiography of anti-Semitism and the Holocaust, see Neil J. Kressel, "Studying Anti-Semitism: Is It Worthwhile?" *Reconstructionist,* March 1979, 20–25; Neil J. Kressel, "Hating the Jews: A New View from Social Psychology," *Judaism* 30 (Summer 1981): 269–75; Klaus P. Fischer, "Shrinkwrapped Führer," *Los Angeles Times,* 21 February 1999, 7 (book review), accessed 5 September 2001, available from LEXIS-NEXIS Academic universe, www.lexis-nexis.com/universe.

36. D. M. Kelley, *22 Cells in Nuremberg: A Psychiatrist Examines the Nazi Criminals* (New York: Greenberg, 1947); Carr, *Hitler: A Study in Personality and Politics.*

37. Bromberg and Small, 8.

38. Redlich, *Hitler;* see also Erica Goode, "Insane or Just Evil: A Psychiatrist Takes a New Look at Hitler," *New York Times,* 17 November 1998, F3, accessed 5 September 2001, available from LEXIS-NEXIS Academic universe, www.lexis-nexis.com/universe.

39. Binion, xv.

40. Peter H. Merkl, *The Making of a Stormtrooper* (Princeton, NJ: Princeton University Press, 1980), 11. Bruening had no credible solutions to offer, and his remarks were, of course, self-serving.

41. See Bracher, *The German Dictatorship;* Toland, *Adolf Hitler;* Alan Bullock, *Hitler: A Study in Tyranny,* abr. ed. (New York: HarperPerennial, 1971); A. J. Nicholls, *Weimar and the Rise of Hitler* (New York: St. Martin's Press, 1968).

42. Michael Kater has collected statistical evidence that demonstrates some serious limitations of the "economic" explanation. In some instances, it seems those least affected by the depression proved most likely to support Hitler. Michael H. Kater, *The Nazi Party: A Social Profile of Members and Leaders, 1919–1945* (Cambridge, MA: Harvard University Press, 1983), 157.

43. R. Palme Dutt, *Fascism and Social Revolution* (London: Lawrence and Wishart, 1934).

44. Erich Fromm, *Escape from Freedom* (New York: Holt, Rinehart & Winston, 1941), as quoted in Allardyce, 38.

45. Peter F. Drucker, *The End of Economic Man* (London: Curtis Brown, 1939). Excerpts from Drucker, Dutt, Fromm, and other important works on European fascism are reprinted in Allardyce, ed., *The Place of Fascism in European History.*

46. Ervin Staub, *The Roots of Evil: The Origins of Genocide and Other Group Violence* (New York: Cambridge University Press, 1989), 100–115; Kren and Rappoport, 29–49.

47. Edmond Vermeil, *Germany in the Twentieth Century* (New York: Praeger, 1956). Peter H. Merkl elaborates on the weaknesses of approaches based on "age-old German tendencies or trends in German intellectual thought." Merkl, *The Making of a Stormtrooper*, 13.

48. Raul Hilberg, *The Destruction of the European Jews* (New York: Franklin Watts, 1973), 9. See also Paul E. Grosser & Edwin G. Halperin, *Anti-Semitism: The Causes and Effects of a Prejudice* (Secaucus, NJ: Citadel Press, 1979), 164.

49. In his controversial but meticulously researched book, Daniel Jonah Goldhagen usefully focuses attention on the development of "eliminationist anti-semitism" in modern Germany. In my view, he errs by overemphasizing this undeniable source of genocidal behavior when it could, more reasonably, be viewed as one component of a multivariate causal model. See Daniel Jonah Goldhagen, *Hitler's Willing Executioners: Ordinary Germans and the Holocaust*, paperback ed. (New York: Vintage, 1997). For a summary of these long-term forces, see Kren and Rappoport, *The Holocaust and the Crisis of Human Behavior*; Staub, *The Roots of Evil*. For an argument that the roots of Nazism lie in German romanticism, see Viereck, *Metapolitics: The Roots of the Nazi Mind*. For the roots of anti-Semitism in the intellectual history of Europe prior to the Holocaust, see Jacob Katz, *From Prejudice to Destruction: Anti-Semitism, 1700–1933* (Cambridge, MA: Harvard University Press, 1980).

50. Kater, 237–38.

51. Hjalmar H. G. Schacht, *Account Settled*, trans. Edward Fitzgerald (London: Weidenfeld & Nicolson, 1949), 206.

52. Ian Kershaw, "Ideology, Propaganda, and the Rise of the Nazi Party," in *The Nazi Machtergreifung*, Peter D. Stachura, ed. (Boston: George Allen & Unwin, 1983), 162–81.

53. Carr, 8–9.

54. See Kershaw, *The "Hitler Myth."*

55. Ibid., 21–31. This summary is a bit of a simplification, insofar as the myth functioned differently for those inside the movement and those outside. Additionally, the content and function of the myth changed with events.

56. Ibid., 1–10.

57. Paul Johnson, *A History of the Jews* (New York: Harper & Row, 1987), recounts how anti-Semitism changed through the ages. The ubiquitous anti-Semitism of Christian leaders dating back to the first century had made Europe fertile for this doctrine. So had Martin Luther, whose desire to burn the Jews did not detract in the least from his success in leading the Protestant Reformation in Germany. In this sense, many European intellectuals and artists, not merely Richard Wagner, Compte de Gobineau, Houston Stewart-Chamberlain, and Karl Marx (despite his Jewish roots), can be counted among Hitler's advance men. Most important of all, the late nineteenth-century anti-Semitic movements in France, Germany, and Austria articulated for the first time a strictly racial basis for hating the Jews; until then, Christians ostensibly hated the Jews for their alleged religious transgressions, and Jews could therefore enter society by converting. But by the twentieth century, a converted Jew remained a Jew. Katz, *From Prejudice to Destruction*, describes the development of anti-Semitism in modern intellectual history. The history of the Spanish inquisition reveals that it is a bit of a simplification to say that Christian anti-Semitism always ended at the point of conversion. Additionally, Jew-hatred did not begin with Christianity, but in fact existed in a different form during the period before Christ. Finally, one might suggest that we discard the term anti-Semitism, which in fact was coined by Wilhelm Marr, a Jew-baiting journalist of nineteenth-century Germany. It is imprecise, in regarding Jews as coterminous with Semites, and reflects the racist thinking of its originator. Still, the term is widely understood and, as long as one understands its limitations, no harm is done by continuing to use it.

58. Marrus, 11. See also Peter H. Merkl, *Political Violence Under the Swastika: 581 Early Nazis* (Princeton, NJ: Princeton University Press, 1975); Henry V. Dicks, *Licensed Mass Murder: A Socio-psychological Study of Some SS Killers* (New York: Basic Books, 1972). Many studies of Nazi supporters, even those in the SS and the SA, but especially among mere voters, show anti-Semitism to be, at most, a secondary part of the attraction.

59. Ernst Nolte, *Three Faces of Fascism*, trans. Leila Vennewitz (New York: Holt, Rinehart & Winston, 1965), excerpted in Ernst Nolte, "Infantilism, Monomania, Mediumism," in *The Nazi Revolution: Hitler's Dictatorship and the German Nation*, eds. John L. Snell and Allan Mitchell, 2d ed. (Lexington, MA: D.C. Heath, 1973), 76.

60. Ibid., 75.

61. Ibid., 76.

62. Helm Stierlin, *Adolf Hitler: A Family Perspective* (New York: Psychohistory Press, 1976). See also analysis in Carr, *Hitler: A Study in Personality and Politics.*

63. Binion, xii.

64. Ibid., 127.

65. Peter Loewenberg, "The Psychohistorical Origins of the Nazi Youth Cohort," *American Historical Review 76* (December 1971), excerpted in Peter Loewenberg, "The Appeal to Youth," in *The Nazi Revolution: Hitler's Dictatorship and the German Nation,* eds. John L. Snell and Allan Mitchell, 93–116. Wangh, in 1964, argued along similar lines that young followers of Hitler reacted as they did to the Great Depression because their childhoods had been "subjected to particularly noxious influences," including their fathers' prolonged absence and return in defeat, their fathers' failure to shield the family from the postwar economic crises, and their mothers' heightened anxiety. M. Wangh, "National Socialism and the Genocide of the Jews," *International Journal of Psycho-Analysis* 45 (1964): 386.

66. See Theodore Abel, *Why Hitler Came into Power: An Answer Based on the Original Life Stories of Six Hundred of His Followers* (New York: Prentice-Hall, 1938); Theodore Abel, *The Nazi Movement* (New York: Atherton, 1965); Merkl, *Political Violence Under the Swastika;* Merkl, *The Making of a Stormtrooper.* All these books include analyses of the Nazi essays; the text draws principally on Merkl's reanalysis of the Abel data.

67. Merkl, *The Making of a Stormtrooper,* 307–8.

68. David Schoenbaum, *Hitler's Social Revolution: Class and Status in Nazi Germany 1933–1939* (Garden City, NY: Anchor, 1967), 283.

69. Kershaw, *The "Hitler Myth,"* 105–20, develops this argument in more detail. For a discussion of the role of Pope Pius XII and the Catholic church, see John Cornwell, *Hitler's Pope: The Secret History of Pius XII,* paperback ed. (New York: Penguin, 2000).

70. Neil J. Kressel, "Hitler's Public Support," *Heuristics: The Journal of Innovative Sociology* 10, 2 (Fall 1980): 34–47, deals with this question in some detail. See also Neil J. Kressel, "Hating the Jews: A New View from Social Psychology." For a different perspective on the development of support for Hitler in post-1933 Germany, see Robert Gellately, *Backing Hitler: Consent and Coercion in Nazi Germany* (New York: Oxford University Press, 2001); this book emphasizes the purposeful publicizing of Nazi terror against selected groups of "undesirables" and the public's support for such measures.

71. For background on this research, see Elliot Aronson, Timothy D. Wilson, and Robin M. Akert, *Social Psychology: The Heart and the Mind* (New York: HarperCollins, 1994), 284–323. For applications to the understanding of mass hatred, see Staub, *The Roots of Evil.*

72. Daryl J. Bem, *Beliefs, Attitudes, and Human Affairs* (Belmont, CA: Brooks/Cole, 1970), 50. Bem developed self-perception theory, drawing on Skin-

nerian principles. Cognitive dissonance theory was originally developed by Leon Festinger in 1957 and has been one of the most heavily researched topics in contemporary social psychology. See Leon Festinger, *A Theory of Cognitive Dissonance* (Evanston, IL: Row-Peterson, 1957).

73. Kurt Lewin, "Cultural Reconstruction," *Journal of Abnormal and Social Psychology* 38 (1943): 166–73, reprinted in Kurt Lewin, *Resolving Social Conflicts: Selected Papers on Group Dynamics*, Gertrud Weiss Lewin, ed. (New York: Harper & Row, 1948), 38.

74. Staub, 116–27.

75. Ibid., 119.

76. Dicks, 255. Dicks builds his analysis on the work of W. von Baeyer-Katte.

77. Browning, *The Path to Genocide*, 125–44. Browning's books are the best source of case studies of Nazi perpetrators. See also Christopher R. Browning, *Ordinary Men: Reserve Police Battalion 101 and the Final Solution in Poland* (New York: HarperPerennial, 1993).

78. Dicks, 60–61. As the war progressed, it became more difficult to opt out of the SS, especially for those privy to the "guilty secrets" about the genocidal policies. From this point forward, very few left the SS except for reason of ill-health; there were also some suicides.

79. Gerald L. Borofsky and Don J. Brand, "Personality Organization and Psychological Functioning of the Nuremberg War Criminals: The Rorschach Data," in *Survivors, Victims, and Perpetrators: Essays on the Nazi Holocaust*, Joel E. Dimsdale, ed. (New York: Hemisphere, 1980), 359–403. This chapter summarizes and interprets other studies on the Nuremberg Rorschachs. A lengthier and more comprehensive treatment can be found in Zillmer, Harrower, Ritzler, and Archer. But see also Neil J. Kressel, "Review: *The Quest for the Nazi Personality: A Psychological Investigation of Nazi War Criminals*," *Aggressive Behavior* 23 (1997): 301–3, for a discussion of the book's limitations.

80. The IQ scores appear in Mosley, 330.

81. Ronald Jay Cohen, Mark E. Swerdlik, and Douglas K. Smith, *Psychological Testing and Assessment: An Introduction to Tests and Measurement*, 2d ed. (Mountain View, CA: Mayfield, 1992), 445–53.

82. M. Harrower, "Were Hitler's Henchmen Mad?" *Psychology Today* 76 (July 1976): 80.

83. Borofsky and Brand, 398. The three studies were F. R. Miale and M. Selzer, *The Nuremberg Mind* (New York: Quadrangle, 1975); B. A. Ritzler, "The Nuremberg Mind Revisited: A Quantitative Approach to Nazi Rorschachs," *Journal of Personality Assessment* 42 (1978): 344–53; M. Harrower, "Rorschach Records of the Nazi War Criminals: An Experimental Study After Thirty Years," *Journal of*

Personality Assessment 40 (1976): 341–51. See also, Harrower, "Were Hitler's Henchmen Mad?" 79–80. Miale and Selzer claim to have detected some evidence of psychopathology, but Borofsky and Brand convincingly demonstrate the severe flaws in their methodology. Borofsky and Brand, 384–87.

84. Dicks, 230.

85. Browning, *The Path to Genocide*, 125–83; Browning, *Ordinary Men*.

86. Hannah Vogt, *The Burden of Guilt: A Short History of Germany, 1914–1945*, trans. Herbert Strauss (New York: Oxford University Press, 1964), 173.

87. Bernd Naumann, *Auschwitz: A Report on the Proceedings Against Robert Karl Ludwig Mulka and Others Before the Court at Frankfurt* (London: Pall Mall Press, 1966), 91, as quoted in Kren and Rappoport, 76, 186 n. 33. Erich Fromm cites former prisoners' estimates of sadistic behavior among guards as ranging from 10 to 90 percent, with lower estimates coming more often from political prisoners; perhaps the disparity originates in differing criteria for sadism. Fromm, *The Anatomy of Human Destructiveness*, 84.

88. Viktor E. Frankl, *Man's Search for Meaning: An Introduction to Logotherapy*, 3d ed. (New York: Simon & Schuster, 1984), 92–94.

89. Kren and Rappoport, 70; Heinz Höhne, *The Order of the Death's Head: The Story of Hitler's SS* (New York: Ballantine, 1971).

90. See Browning, *Ordinary Men*.

91. Sigmund Freud, *Civilization and Its Discontents*, trans. James Strachey (New York: WW Norton, 1962).

92. Fromm, *The Anatomy of Human Destructiveness*, 98.

93. John M. Steiner, "The SS Yesterday and Today: A Sociopsychological View," in *Survivors, Victims, and Perpetrators: Essays on the Nazi Holocaust*, Joel E. Dimsdale, ed. (New York: Hemisphere, 1980), 405–56. See also Kren and Rappoport, *The Holocaust and the Crisis of Human Behavior*; Dicks, *Licensed Mass Murder*.

94. Steiner, 407.

95. Hannah Arendt, *Eichmann in Jerusalem: A Report on the Banality of Evil*, rev. ed. (New York: Penguin Books, 1977), 150.

96. Jacob Robinson, *And the Crooked Shall Be Made Straight: The Eichmann Trial, The Jewish Catastrophe, and Hannah Arendt's Narrative* (New York: Macmillan, 1965), 1–59.

97. Arendt, 278.

98. Robert Jay Lifton, *The Nazi Doctors: Medical Killing and the Psychology of Genocide* (New York: Basic Books, 1986), 417–500.

99. Ibid., 430–65.

100. Kren and Rappoport, 20.

101. Dicks, 61.

102. Several theories of Nazi murderousness have appeal, in part, because they serve a psychological function for the people who believe them. To view Nazis as severely disturbed madmen preserves the image of a benevolent humanity in which *most* people, even most Germans, lack the potential for genocidal activity; this notion, born partly of astonishment at the heinousness of Nazi crimes, can be comforting and restores some order to the world. To see Nazi killers as evil-to-the-core, sadistic, and incapable of warmth in any aspect of their lives serves similar functions. People who see the Nazi killers as petrified slaves ignore the historical record in order to express their overly strong need to empathize; they also simplify the world and reduce their conflict in dealing with Germans and Germany after Hitler. The most troubling explanations of Nazi murderousness focus on careerism and duty, because these goals feel familiar to most people in the West. These latter explanations, and the attribution of Nazi murderousness to obedience, shift the onus of guilt from the Nazis to virtually everyone in the world; by so doing, these explanations provide additional justification for those who wish to overhaul "the system." Theories can be true, even if they serve extraneous psychological purposes, but it is useful to keep such purposes in mind.

CHAPTER 6

1. John P. Sabini and Maury Silver, "Destroying the Innocent with a Clear Conscience: A Sociopsychology of the Holocaust," in *Survivors, Victims, and Perpetrators: Essays on the Nazi Holocaust,* Joel E. Dimsdale, ed. (New York: Hemisphere, 1980), 357.

2. Stanley Milgram, interview, "I Was Only Following Orders," *60 Minutes,* CBS, 31 March 1979, 7–8 of transcript, as quoted in Thomas Blass, "The Social Psychology of Stanley Milgram," in *Advances in Experimental Social Psychology,* vol. 25, Mark P. Zanna, ed. (New York: Academic Press, 1992), 305.

3. See Stanley Milgram, *Obedience to Authority: An Experimental View* (New York: Harper-Colophon, 1974). Milgram's book summarizes and interprets the experiments which originally appeared as a series of articles in social psychology journals. Thomas Blass traces the impact of Milgram's obedience studies in Blass, "The Social Psychology of Stanley Milgram," 277–329. See also Thomas Blass, ed., *Obedience to Authority: Current Perspectives on the Milgram Paradigm* (Mahwah, NJ: Erlbaum, 2000).

4. Roger Brown, *Social Psychology: The Second Edition* (New York: Free Press, 1986), 2. Brown's book contains an excellent introduction to the implications of Milgram's research, and originates the concept of the "Eichmann fallacy"—the belief that evil acts presuppose an evil person as actor (5).

5. The South African trial that allowed the "obedience to authority" defense is discussed in A. M. Colman, "Crowd Psychology in South African Murder Trials," *American Psychologist* 46 (1991), 1071–79.

6. C. P. Snow, "Either-Or," *Progressive,* February 1961, 24, as quoted in Milgram, *Obedience to Authority,* 2.

7. Milgram, *Obedience to Authority,* 2.

8. See, for example, Herbert C. Kelman and V. Lee Hamilton, *Crimes of Obedience: Toward a Social Psychology of Authority and Responsibility* (New Haven, CT: Yale University Press, 1989); Irwin A. Horowitz and Kenneth S. Bordens, *Social Psychology* (Mountain View, CA: Mayfield, 1995), 357–95.

9. John B. Watson, *Behaviorism,* 2d ed. (New York: WW Norton, 1930), 104.

10. Lee Ross and Richard E. Nisbett, *The Person and the Situation: Perspectives of Social Psychology* (New York: McGraw-Hill, 1991), 3, 125–33.

11. A major controversy surrounds Hannah Arendt's *Eichmann in Jerusalem: A Report on the Banality of Evil,* rev. ed. (New York: Penguin Books, 1977). See, for example, Jacob Robinson, *And the Crooked Shall Be Made Straight: The Eichmann Trial, the Jewish Catastrophe, and Hannah Arendt's Narrative* (New York: Macmillan, 1965); Norman Podhoretz, "Hannah Arendt on Eichmann: A Study in the Perversity of Brilliance," *Commentary,* September 1963, 201–8; Lucy S. Dawidowicz, *The Holocaust and the Historians* (Cambridge, MA: Harvard University Press, 1981).

12. Kelman and Hamilton, 1–22, 167–94, 211–35.

13. Solomon Asch's conformity studies appeared in the 1950s. For a summary of the classic studies, see Charles A. Kiesler and Sara B. Kiesler, *Conformity* (Reading, MA: Addison-Wesley, 1969). A good review of recent work appears in Elliot Aronson, Timothy D. Wilson, and Robin M. Akert, *Social Psychology: The Heart and the Mind* (New York: HarperCollins, 1994), 257–75. For a situationist interpretation of many laboratory studies in social psychology, including those by Asch, see Ross and Nisbett, 27–58. The next chapter considers some relevant personal traits that bear on conformity and obedience.

14. B. Latané and J. M. Darley, *The Unresponsive Bystander: Why Doesn't He Help?* (New York: Appleton-Century-Crofts, 1970), summarizes the authors' early studies on bystander intervention, including the first two studies discussed here. J. M. Darley and C. D. Batson, "From Jerusalem to Jericho: A Study of Situational and Dispositional Variables in Helping Behavior," *Journal of Personality and Social Psychology* 27 (1973), 100–108, presents the third study. For a summary of social psychological research on altruism, see Horowitz and Bordens, 537–88.

15. Stanley Milgram, "Nationality and Conformity," *Scientific American* (December 1961): 45–51. Milgram also found that Norwegians tended to be some-

what more obedient than the French. For a review of current evidence on the cross-cultural generalizability of the Asch study and other conformity experiments, see Peter B. Smith and Michael Harris Bond, *Social Psychology Across Cultures: Analysis and Perspectives* (Boston: Allyn & Bacon, 1994).

16. Stanley Milgram, interview, in *The Making of Social Psychology,* Richard Evans, ed., (New York: Gardner, 1980), excerpted in Stanley Milgram, *The Individual in a Social World: Essays and Experiments,* 2d ed., John Sabini and Maury Silver, eds. (New York: McGraw-Hill, 1992), 127–28.

17. Milgram, *Obedience to Authority,* 18. All references to Milgram's experimental procedure are taken from this book, although his write-ups in scientific journals contain some details not reproduced in his book.

18. Ibid., 19.

19. Ibid., 20–21.

20. Ibid., 23.

21. Ibid., 21.

22. Stanley Milgram, "Some Conditions of Obedience and Disobedience to Authority," *Human Relations* 18, 1 (1965), reprinted in Milgram, *The Individual in a Social World,* 155.

23. Milgram, *Obedience to Authority,* 6–7.

24. Milgram, "Some Conditions of Obedience and Disobedience to Authority," 157.

25. Milgram, *Obedience to Authority,* 149.

26. Stanley Milgram, interview by Carol Tavris, "The Frozen World of the Familiar Stranger," *Psychology Today* 8 (June 1974): 71, excerpted in Milgram, *The Individual in a Social World,* xxiv.

27. Ibid.

28. Stanley Milgram, "Interpreting Obedience: Error and Evidence (A Reply to Orne and Holland)," in *The Social Psychology of Psychological Research,* Arthur G. Miller, ed. (New York: Free Press, 1972), 153, n. 5.

29. Another line of criticism focuses on the ethics of the study. Milgram took unsuspecting people off the street and showed them some of their unsuspected capacities. No doubt, the British playwright Abse went way too far in condemning Milgram and stating that many people "may feel that in order to demonstrate that subjects may behave like so many Eichmanns the experimenter had to act the part, to some extent, of a Himmler." D. Abse, *The Dogs of Pavlov* (London: Valentine, Mitchell, 1973), 29, as quoted in Blass, "The Social Psychology of Stanley Milgram," 287. In fact, Milgram took many precautions to ensure the well-being of the subjects and his follow-up research showed few negative consequences. Milgram, plausibly, felt that his study aroused so much ethical controversy because

people felt threatened by its findings. In any case, the study spawned new ethical guidelines for research. While studies similar to Milgram's are not expressly prohibited, few researchers have proved willing to face a barrage of criticism and the study has not been replicated in the United States in recent years.

30. Martin T. Orne and Charles H. Holland, "On the Ecological Validity of Laboratory Deceptions," *International Journal of Psychiatry* 6 (1968): 282–93, reprinted in *The Social Psychology of Psychological Research*, Arthur G. Miller, ed., 129. Milgram's response also appears in this volume.

31. Ibid., 130–31.

32. Milgram, "Interpreting Obedience: Error and Evidence (A Reply to Orne and Holland)," in *The Social Psychology of Psychological Research*, 140.

33. Orne's criticism of the unreality of experimental situations has held up much better in regard to other studies. Milgram's well-designed research managed to avoid many of the problems with experimentation in social psychology that were later identified. See, for example, Neil J. Kressel, "Systemic Barriers to Progress in Academic Social Psychology," *Journal of Social Psychology* 130 (February 1990): 5–27.

34. D. Mixon, *Obedience and Civilization: Authorized Crime and the Normality of Evil* (London: Pluto Press, 1989); J. D. Greenwood, "Role-playing as an Experimental Strategy in Social Psychology," *European Journal of Social Psychology* 13 (1983): 235–54.

35. Erich Fromm, *The Anatomy of Human Destructiveness* (New York: Fawcett Crest, 1973), 74. He was, apparently, unaware of the variation that took place away from Yale. As usual, Fromm offers a unique viewpoint, seeing the presence of conscience in the people who delivered the shocks as the most interesting finding of the study.

36. S. C. Patten, "Milgram's Shocking Experiments," *Philosophy* 52 (1977): 425–40.

37. Ross and Nisbett, 57.

38. Ibid., 57–58.

39. Gordon W. Allport, *The Nature of Prejudice*, abr. ed. (Garden City, NY: Doubleday-Anchor, 1958).

40. Milgram, *Obedience to Authority*, 175–76.

41. See Robert Jay Lifton, *The Nazi Doctors: Medical Killing and the Psychology of Genocide* (New York: Basic Books, 1986), 415–500; Henry V. Dicks, *Licensed Mass Murder: A Socio-Psychological Study of Some SS Killers* (New York: Basic Books, 1972).

42. Raul Hilberg, *Perpetrators Victims Bystanders: The Jewish Catastrophe 1933–1945* (New York: HarperPerennial, 1992), 51–64. Daniel Goldhagen argues

that many German killers of Jews felt little guilt, even those people who might have been driven by their consciences on other matters. They participated in genocide without guilt precisely because they shared Hitler's anti-Semitic vision. See Daniel Jonah Goldhagen, *Hitler's Willing Executioners: Ordinary Germans and the Holocaust,* paperback ed. (New York: Vintage, 1997).

43. Several writers have addressed the fit between the Milgram paradigm and Nazism. See Ann L. Saltzman, "The Role of Obedience Experiments in Holocaust Studies: The Case for Renewed Visibility," in Blass, *Obedience to Authority,* 125–43; Thomas Blass, "Psychological Perspectives on the Perpetrators of the Holocaust: The Role of Situational Pressures, Personal Dispositions, and Their Interactions," *Holocaust and Genocide Studies* 7 (1993): 30–50; Sabini and Silver, "Destroying the Innocent with a Clear Conscience," in *Survivors, Victims, and Perpetrators,* Joel E. Dimsdale, ed., 329–58; Fromm, 68–90. See also Milgram, *Obedience to Authority,* 174–78.

44. See especially Kelman and Hamilton, *Crimes of Obedience.*

45. Milgram, *Obedience to Authority,* 182.

46. Milgram, interview by Carol Tavris, excerpted in *The Individual in a Social World,* xxxiii.

47. Kelman and Hamilton, 15–16. Kelman's perspective also appears in an earlier article, H. C. Kelman, "Violence Without Moral Restraint: Reflections on the Dehumanization of Victims and Victimizers," *Journal of Social Issues* 29 (1973): 25–61.

48. Kelman and Hamilton, 16–20.

49. John Sabini, *Social Psychology,* 2d ed. (New York: WW Norton, 1995), 58. See also Ervin Staub's discussion of cultural devaluation and ideologies of antagonism: Ervin Staub, "The Roots of Evil: Conditions, Culture, Personality, and Basic Human Needs," *Personality and Social Psychology Review* 3 (1999): 183.

50. For more detail on this mechanism, see the discussion of cognitive dissonance and self-perception in Chapter 5.

51. Craig Haney, Curtis Banks, and Philip Zimbardo, "A Study of Prisoners and Guards in a Simulated Prison," in *Readings About the Social Animal,* 7th ed., Elliot Aronson, ed. (New York: W. H. Freeman, 1995), 52–67. See also Philip G. Zimbardo, "Pathology of Imprisonment," *Society* 9 (April 1972): 4–8. An excellent analysis of the prison study appears in Sabini, *Social Psychology,* 55–60. See also the interesting retrospective essay by three of the researchers who conducted the study: Philip G. Zimbardo, Christina Maslach, and Craig Haney, "Reflections on the Stanford Prison Experiment: Genesis, Transformations, Consequences," in Blass, *Obedience to Authority,* 193–237.

52. Haney, Banks, and Zimbardo, "A Study of Prisoners," in *Readings About the Social Animal*, Elliot Aronson, ed., 54.

53. Ibid., 63–64.

54. Zimbardo, "Pathology of Imprisonment," 4.

55. In another study by Zimbardo, female undergraduates who wore hoods and concealing costumes delivered more electric shocks to a (confederate) victim than did women who did not wear such costumes and were easy to identify. See P. G. Zimbardo, "The Human Choice: Individuation, Reason, and Order Versus Deindividuation, Impulse, and Chaos," in *Nebraska Symposium on Motivation: 1969*, vol. 17, eds. W. J. Arnold and D. Levine (Lincoln: University of Nebraska Press, 1970), 237–307.

56. Janice T. Gibson and Mika Haritos-Fatouros, "The Education of a Torturer," *Psychology Today* (November 1986): 50–58, reprinted in Steve L. Ellyson and Amy G. Halberstadt, *Explorations in Social Psychology* (New York: McGraw-Hill, 1995), 108–15.

57. Ibid., 111.

58. Dicks, 253–63. See also the discussion in Chapter 5.

CHAPTER 7

1. Gordon W. Allport, *The Nature of Prejudice*, abr. ed. (Garden City, NY: Doubleday-Anchor, 1958), 343.

2. Stanley Milgram, *Obedience to Authority: An Experimental View* (New York: Harper-Colophon, 1975), 51.

3. Ibid., 205.

4. Additionally, for practical reasons, experts on the prejudiced personality have not conducted many studies with actual mass murderers or terrorists, relying instead on milder manifestations of bigotry and hatred from which conclusions are extrapolated. There are many reasons for this, including difficulties of access, language problems, and "scientific" disciplinary norms favoring heavily statistical approaches which are not feasible with this population. For an examination of these issues, see Neil J. Kressel, "Systemic Barriers to Progress in Academic Social Psychology," *Journal of Social Psychology* 130 (February 1990): 5–27.

5. Nevitt Sanford, "Authoritarianism and Social Destructiveness," in *Sanctions for Evil: Sources of Social Destructiveness*, eds. Nevitt Sanford and Craig Comstock (San Francisco: Jossey-Bass, 1971), 139.

6. T. W. Adorno, Else Frenkel-Brunswik, Daniel J. Levinson, and Nevitt Sanford, *The Authoritarian Personality* (New York: Harper & Row, 1950).

7. Nevitt Sanford, "Authoritarian Personality in Contemporary Perspective," in *Handbook of Political Psychology*, Jeanne N. Knutson, ed. (San Francisco: Jossey-

Bass, 1973), 139–40. The best review of the contributions of Horkheimer and the Institute of Social Research to the analysis of fascism is Martin Jay, *The Dialectical Imagination: A History of the Frankfurt School and the Institute of Social Research 1923–1950* (Boston: Little, Brown, 1973).

8. See discussion in Adorno et al., *The Authoritarian Personality;* and Roger Brown, *Social Psychology* (New York: Free Press, 1965), 477–79.

9. Good summaries of authoritarian personality research are found in: Brown, *Social Psychology,* 477–546; Sanford, "Authoritarian Personality in Contemporary Perspective"; Alan C. Elms, *Personality in Politics* (New York: Harcourt Brace Jovanovich, 1976), 30–41; William S. Sahakian, *History and Systems of Social Psychology,* 2d ed. (New York: Hemisphere, 1982), 247–61; F. Samelson, "Authoritarianism from Berlin to Berkeley," *Journal of Social Issues* 42 (1986): 191–208; Fred I. Greenstein, *Personality and Politics: Problems of Evidence, Inference, and Conceptualization,* new ed. (Princeton, NJ: Princeton University Press, 1987), 96–119; William F. Stone and Paul E. Schaffner, *The Psychology of Politics,* 2d ed. (New York: Springer-Verlag, 1988), 143–55; Jos Meloen, "The Fortieth Anniversary of 'The Authoritarian Personality'," *Politics and the Individual* 1 (1991): 119–27; Robert S. Erikson, Norman R. Luttbeg, and Kent L. Tedin, *American Public Opinion: Its Origins, Content, and Impact,* 4th ed. (New York: Macmillan, 1991), 128–33. John Levi Martin, "The Authoritarian Personality, 50 Years Later: What Lessons Are There for Political Psychology?" *Political Psychology* 22 (2001): 1–26.

10. Theodor W. Adorno, "Freudian Theory and the Pattern of Fascist Propaganda," in *Psychoanalysis and the Social Sciences,* vol. 7, Geza Roheim, ed. (New York: International Universities Press, 1951), 291n, as quoted in Greenstein, 103.

11. All statements measuring authoritarian opinions are taken from the scale used in *The Authoritarian Personality.*

12. Adorno et al., *The Authoritarian Personality,* 482.

13. Else Frenkel-Brunswik, "Further Explorations by a Contributor," in *Studies in the Scope and Method of "The Authoritarian Personality",* eds. Richard Christie and Marie Jahoda (New York: Free Press, 1954), 236–37.

14. Adorno et al., *The Authoritarian Personality,* 976.

15. Sanford, "Authoritarian Personality in Contemporary Perspective," 152–63; Stone and Schaffner, 149–55; Erikson, Luttbeg, and Tedin, 128–32; Jean A. Cunningham, Stephen J. Dollinger, Madelyn Satz, and Nancy S. Rotter, "Personality Correlates of Prejudice Against AIDS Victims," *Bulletin of the Psychonomic Society* 29 (March 1991): 165–67. One recent article has questioned whether anti-Semitism remains a key component of the syndrome. See David Raden, "Is Anti-Semitism Currently Part of an Authoritarian Attitude Syndrome?" *Political Psychology* 20 (1999): 323–43.

16. Sahakian, 259.

17. Stone and Schaffner, 150.

18. Theodor Adorno, "Scientific Experiences of a European Scholar in America," in *The Intellectual Migration,* eds. Donald Fleming and Bernard Bailyn (Cambridge, MA: Harvard University Press, 1969), 363.

19. Bob Altemeyer, *The Authoritarian Specter* (Cambridge, MA: Harvard University Press, 1996); Bob Altemeyer, *Right-Wing Authoritarianism* (Winnipeg: University of Manitoba Press, 1981); Bob Altemeyer, *Enemies of Freedom: Understanding Right-Wing Authoritarianism* (San Francisco: Jossey-Bass, 1988); John J. Ray and F. H. Lovejoy, "The Behavioral Validity of Some Recent Measures of Authoritarianism," *Journal of Social Psychology* 120 (1983): 91–99; J. D. Meloen, L. Hagendoorn, Q. Raaijmakers, and L. Visser, "Authoritarianism and the Revival of Political Racism," *Political Psychology* 9 (1988): 413–29.

20. Milton Rokeach, *The Open and Closed Mind: Investigations into the Nature of Belief Systems and Personality Systems* (New York: Basic Books, 1960).

21. John L. Sullivan, James Piereson, and George E. Marcus, *Political Tolerance and American Democracy* (Chicago: University of Chicago Press, 1982), 155.

22. Rokeach, 80–87.

23. John J. Ray, "Do Authoritarians Hold Authoritarian Attitudes?" *Human Relations* 29 (1976): 307–25; John J. Ray, "Explaining Australian Attitudes Towards Aborigines," *Ethnic and Racial Studies* 4 (July 1981): 348–52. Other recent measures of authoritarianism are described in: T. G. Goertzel, "Authoritarianism of Personality and Political Attitudes," *Journal of Social Psychology* 127 (1987): 7–18; P. C. L. Heaven, "Construction and Validation of a Measure of Authoritarian Personality," *Journal of Personality Assessment* 49 (1985): 545–51.

24. Altemeyer, *Enemies of Freedom,* 3.

25. Ibid., 2–3.

26. Ibid., 8–15.

27. Marianne Szegedy-Maszak, review, "Enemies of Freedom: Understanding Right-Wing Authoritarianism," by Bob Altemeyer, *Psychology Today* 23 (March 1989): 66.

28. Altemeyer, *Enemies of Freedom,* 22–23.

29. John J. Ray, "Defective Validity in the Altemeyer Authoritarianism Scale," *Journal of Social Psychology* 125 (1985): 271–72. Altemeyer also employs a biased measure of prejudice. In his 20-item scale designed to measure prejudice among Canadians, a prejudiced response is *disagreeing* with statements such as: "Canada should open its doors to more immigration from the West Indies"; "Much of the white race's accomplishments have occurred because it has continually exploited the other races"; and "The main reason certain groups like our native Indians end

up in slums is because of prejudice on the part of white people." Altemeyer, *Enemies of Freedom*, 110. Each of these propositions is arguable, and disagreement hardly equals prejudice.

30. The attempt to do so in Altemeyer, *Enemies of Freedom*, 273, is unconvincing. The debate over the validity of the Altemeyer scale continues. See, for example, Christina Fiebich and Ian Williamson, "Cutting Out the Fat: Modifying the Authoritarian Personality Scale to Avoid Tautologies," paper presented at the 24th Annual Scientific Meeting of the International Society of Political Psychology, Cuernavaca, Morelos, Mexico, 15 July 2001. Available from the authors at the University of Minnesota.

31. Felicia Pratto, Jim Sidanius, Lisa M. Stallworth, and Bertram F. Malle, "Social Dominance Orientation: A Personality Variable Predicting Social and Political Attitudes," *Journal of Personality and Social Psychology* 67 (1994): 741–63; Jim Sidanius and Felicia Pratto, "The Dynamics of Social Dominance and the Inevitability of Oppression," in *Prejudice, Politics, and Race in America Today*, eds. Paul Sniderman and Philip E. Tetlock (Stanford, CA: Stanford University Press, 1993), 173–211; Bernard E. Whitley, Jr., "Right-wing Authoritarianism, Social Dominance Orientation, and Prejudice," *Journal of Personality and Social Psychology* 77 (1999): 126–34.

32. Pratto et al., "Social Dominance Orientation," 741.

33. Ibid.

34. Ibid., 741–43.

35. Ibid., 742.

36. Ibid., 760–63.

37. Sanford, "Authoritarian Personality in Contemporary Perspective," 163.

38. Ibid., 164.

39. Sam G. McFarland, Vladimir S. Ageyev, and Marina A. Abalakina-Paap, "Authoritarianism in the Former Soviet Union," *Journal of Personality and Social Psychology* 63 (December 1992): 1004–10. See also Sam G. McFarland, Vladimir S. Ageyev, and Nadya Djintcharadze, "Russian Authoritarianism: Two Years After Communism," *Personality and Social Psychology Bulletin* 22 (1996): 210–17.

40. Ervin Staub, *The Roots of Evil: The Origins of Genocide and Other Group Violence* (New York: Cambridge University Press, 1992), has suggested that Cambodian society prior to the genocide of the late 1970s had an authoritarian-hierarchical character (197). Also, Ottoman society prior to the World War I massacre of the Armenians also had a strong pro-obedience orientation rooted in Islamic law and the empire's feudal traditions (176).

41. Ivan Siber, "Review of Research on the 'Authoritarian Personality' in Yugoslav Society," *Politics and the Individual* 1 (1991): 21–28, is the source of this

discussion of studies that appeared in Serbo-Croatian. See also Bojan Todosijevic and Zsolt Enyedi, "Nationalism and Socialist Ideology: The Case of Yugoslavia," paper presented at the 24th Annual Scientific Meeting of the International Society of Political Psychology, Cuernavaca, Morelos, Mexico, 15 July 2001. Available from the authors at Central European University, Budapest, Hungary.

42. As quoted in Siber, 22.

43. Siber, 28.

44. Henry V. Dicks, *Licensed Mass Murder: A Socio-psychological Study of Some SS Killers* (New York: Basic Books, 1972), 70–71.

45. Ibid., 253.

46. John M. Steiner, "The SS Yesterday and Today: A Sociopsychological View," in *Survivors, Victims, and Perpetrators: Essays on the Nazi Holocaust*, Joel E. Dimsdale, ed. (New York: Hemisphere, 1980), 433–34. Peter H. Merkl, *Political Violence Under the Swastika: 581 Early Nazis* (Princeton, NJ: Princeton University Press, 1975), 489–97, tried to assess authoritarianism as an explanation of early Nazi sympathizers and supporters. He didn't get very far because of a lack of relevant information, but his findings were basically unsupportive.

47. Hrair Dekmejian, *Islam in Revolution: Fundamentalism in the Arab World* (Syracuse, NY: Syracuse University Press, 1985), 32–36. See discussion in Chapter 3. According to a study by Sheena Sethi and Martin E. P. Seligman, "Optimism and Fundamentalism," *Psychological Science* 4 (July 1993): 256–59, fundamentalism in various religions, including Islam, is associated with greater optimism. However, this study does not compare the Islamic fundamentalists to "moderate" or "liberal" Islamic groups, and it is based on a response rate of 30 percent (i.e., 70 percent did not return the questionnaires) and a total sample size of 78. Optimism does not seem logically or psychologically consistent with the cynicism of authoritarians. But this study, with its weak methodology and lack of distinction among Muslim groups, doesn't provide much evidence for a tendency toward optimism.

48. William Graham Sumner, *Folkways* (Boston: Ginn, 1906), 12, as quoted in Roger Brown, *Social Psychology: The Second Edition* (New York: Free Press, 1986), 533.

49. Brown, *Social Psychology: The Second Edition*, 534.

50. Susan T. Fiske and Shelley E. Taylor, *Social Cognition*, 2d ed. (New York: McGraw-Hill, 1991), 133. These authors summarize research on how normal thought processes can bolster stereotypical, ethnocentric, and prejudiced beliefs. See also David A. Wilder, "Social Categorization: Implications for Creation and Reduction of Intergroup Bias," in *Advances in Experimental Social Psychology*, vol. 19, Leonard Berkowitz, ed. (New York: Academic Press, 1986), 291–355.

51. Mark Schaller, Carrie Boyd, Jonathan Yohannes, and Meredith O'Brien, "The Prejudiced Personality Revisited: Personal Need for Structure and Formation of Erroneous Group Stereotypes," *Journal of Personality and Social Psychology* 68 (1995): 544–55.

52. Elliot Aronson, Timothy D. Wilson, and Robin M. Akert, *Social Psychology: The Heart and the Mind* (New York: HarperCollins, 1994), 514.

53. Schaller et al., 545.

54. R. T. LaPiere, "Attitudes vs. Actions," *Social Forces* 13 (1934): 230–37.

55. John Harding, Harold Proshansky, Bernard Kutner, and Isidor Chein, "Prejudice and Ethnic Relations," in *The Handbook of Social Psychology*, 2d ed., vol. 5, Gardner Lindzey and Elliot Aronson, eds. (Reading, MA: Addison-Wesley, 1969), 43. For a more general perspective on the relationship between attitudes, behavior, and personality, see Icek Ajzen, *Attitudes, Personality, and Behavior* (Chicago, IL: Dorsey, 1988).

56. Quoted in Philip Gourevitch, *We Wish to Inform You That Tomorrow We Will Be Killed with Our Families: Stories from Rwanda* (New York: Farrar, Straus & Giroux, 1998), 23.

57. Herbert C. Kelman and V. Lee Hamilton, *Crimes of Obedience: Toward a Social Psychology of Authority and Responsibility* (New Haven, CT: Yale University Press, 1989), 172–73.

58. V. Lee Hamilton, Joseph Sanders, and Scott J. McKearney, "Orientations Toward Authority in an Authoritarian State: Moscow in 1990," *Personality and Social Psychology Bulletin* 21 (April 1995): 356–65.

59. Milgram, 205.

60. Thomas Blass, "Understanding Behavior in the Milgram Obedience Experiment: The Role of Personality, Situations, and Their Interactions," *Journal of Personality and Social Psychology* 60 (1991): 398–413. This article also presents mixed evidence linking obedience to how religious one is and how trusting.

61. Stanford University political scientist Paul M. Sniderman, in *Personality and Democratic Politics* (Berkeley: University of California Press, 1975), carefully probes the complex relationship between low self-esteem, conformity, and political extremism. He notes that while people with low self-esteem, generally, are less tolerant, less supportive of democratic procedures, and more cynical about democracy, they also tend to be weak opponents of democratic institutions. This is because low self-esteem makes them less likely to pay attention to politics and less likely to respond to political messages of any sort. Sniderman states that "the very psychological needs that tend to motivate those with low self-esteem toward extremist politics tend to make it difficult for extremist movements to mobilize them" (308). In democratic countries, high self-esteem usually leads to greater

support for democratic values, but the opposite may be the case in authoritarian countries. High self-esteem enhances the ability and motivation to absorb information and values from one's society; it also leads to greater participation in political life. Thus, in non-democratic countries, high self-esteem may actually increase support for authoritarian institutions (322). According to psychologist Roy F. Baumeister, empirical evidence supports the counterintuitive proposition that bullies, domestic abusers, and other perpetrators of violence frequently have high self-esteem. He further argues that many evil leaders throughout history have possessed inflated self-images. When these images become tarnished or damaged, the result may be a powerful drive for revenge. Meek and humble men do not generally initiate great crimes against humanity. See Roy F. Baumeister, *Evil: Inside Human Violence and Cruelty* (New York: Freeman, 1997).

62. Staub, 188–209. For a horrifying but insightful account of atrocities committed in a Khmer Rouge prison, see David Chandler, *Voices from S-21: Terror and History in Pol Pot's Secret Prison* (Berkeley: University of California Press, 1999).

63. Gertrude J. Selznick and Stephen Steinberg, *The Tenacity of Prejudice: Anti-Semitism in Contemporary America* (New York: Harper & Row, 1969). See also discussions of this work in Sanford, "Authoritarian Personality in Contemporary Perspective," 159–63; Harold E. Quinley and Charles Y. Glock, *Anti-Semitism in America* (New York: Free Press, 1979); Neil J. Kressel, "Hating the Jews: A New View From Social Psychology," *Judaism* 30 (Summer 1981): 269–75.

64. Erikson, Luttbeg, and Tedin, 106–16.

65. Ibid., 114.

66. J. Dollard, L. W. Doob, N. E. Miller, O. H. Mowrer, and R. R. Sears, *Frustration and Aggression* (New Haven, CT: Yale University Press, 1939).

67. The best summaries of current perspectives on aggression are: Leonard Berkowitz, "Frustration-Aggression Hypothesis: Examination and Reformation," *Psychological Bulletin* 106 (1989): 59–73; Leonard Berkowitz, *Aggression* (New York: McGraw-Hill, 1993); R. A. Baron and D. R. Richardson, *Human Aggression*, 2d ed. (New York: Plenum, 1992).

68. Wilder, "Social Categorization."

CHAPTER 8

1. Roger Brown, *Social Psychology*, 2d ed. (New York: Free Press, 1986), 533.

2. D. T. Miller and M. Ross, "Self-Serving Biases in the Attribution of Causality," *Psychological Bulletin* 82 (1975): 213–25.

3. See, especially, David Pryce-Jones, *The Closed Circle: An Interpretation of the Arabs* (New York: HarperPerennial, 1991), 21–57.

4. R. J. Rummel, "Democide in Totalitarian States: Mortacracies and Mega-murderers," in *The Widening Circle of Genocide,* Israel W. Charny, ed., vol. 3 of the Genocide: A Critical Bibliographic Review Series (New Brunswick, NJ: Transaction, 1994), 7–9.

5. Ibid., 7.

6. Ibid., 11.

7. Michael Janofsky, "Skinhead Violence Is Worldwide and Growing, a Report Finds," *New York Times,* 28 June 1995, A11, late ed. See also Robert L. Snow, *The Militia Threat: Terrorists Among Us* (New York: Plenum Trade, 1999); Kenneth S. Stern, *A Force upon the Plain: The American Militia Movement and the Politics of Hate* (New York: Simon and Schuster, 1996); Philip Lamy, *Millennium Rage: Survivalists, White Supremacists, and the Doomsday Prophecy* (New York: Plenum Press, 1996); Jack Levin and Jack McDevitt, *Hate Crimes: The Rising Tide of Bigotry and Bloodshed* (New York: Plenum Press, 1993).

8. Timothy Egan, "Inside the World of the Paranoid," *New York Times,* 30 April 1995, sec. 4, 1, late ed.

9. Janofsky, A11.

10. Herbert McClosky and Alida Brill, *Dimensions of Tolerance* (New York: Russell Sage, 1983).

11. John L. Sullivan, James Piereson, and George E. Marcus, *Political Tolerance and American Democracy* (Chicago: University of Chicago Press, 1982), discuss the theory of pluralistic intolerance. See also, Robert S. Erikson, Norman R. Luttbeg, and Kent L. Tedin, *American Public Opinion: Its Origins, Content, and Impact,* 4th ed. (New York: Macmillan, 1991), 115.

12. Israel W. Charny, "The Psychology of Denial of Known Genocides," in *Genocide: A Critical Bibliographic Review,* vol. 2, Israel W. Charny, ed. (New York: Facts on File, 1991), 15. A focus on blaming Western institutions and a failure to distinguish adequately among levels of evil has marred much recent writing on the origins of interpersonal and collective violence. See, for example, Jennifer Turpin and Lester R. Kurtz, eds., *The Web of Violence: From Interpersonal to Global* (Chicago: University of Illinois Press, 1997). See also my review of the Turpin and Kurtz anthology: Neil J. Kressel, "A Tangled Web," *Peace and Conflict: Journal of Peace Psychology* 4 (1998): 311–14.

13. Ibid.

14. Ibid.

15. Alan C. Elms, *Personality in Politics* (New York: Harcourt Brace Jovanovich, 1976), 50.

16. Larry Martz, "From the Editor," *World Press Review* (September 1994): 4.

17. Samantha Power, "Bystanders to Genocide," *Atlantic,* September 2001, 84; Holly Burkhalter, "A Preventable Horror?" *Africa Report* (November–December 1994): 17–21.

18. Frank Smyth, "French Guns, Rwandan Blood," *New York Times,* 14 April 1994, A21, late ed.

19. Marlise Simons, "France's Rwanda Connection," *New York Times,* 3 July 1994, sec. 1, 6, late ed.

20. Ibid.

21. Raymond Bonner, "As French Leave Rwanda, Critics Reverse Position," *New York Times,* 23 August 1994, A6, late ed.

22. Power, 101. See also Frank Chalk, "Hate Radio in Rwanda," in Howard Adelman and Astri Suhrke, eds., *The Path of a Genocide: The Rwanda Crisis from Uganda to Zaire* (New Brunswick, NJ: Transaction Publishers, 1999), 104.

23. Michael Mandelbaum, "America's Self-Canceling Bosnia Policy," *New York Times,* 18 June 1995, sec. 4, 15, late ed.

24. See Robert S. McNamara and James G. Blight, *Wilson's Ghost: Reducing the Risk of Conflict, Killing, and Catastrophe in the 21st Century* (New York: Public Affairs, 2001), for an argument that, even when intervention is required to prevent communal killing, the United States should resist any tendency to go it alone.

25. Herbert C. Kelman and V. Lee Hamilton, *Crimes of Obedience: Toward a Social Psychology of Authority and Responsibility* (New Haven, CT: Yale University Press, 1989), 307–38.

26. Robert Jay Lifton and Eric Markusen, *The Genocidal Mentality: Nazi Holocaust and Nuclear Threat* (New York: Basic Books, 1990), 255–79.

27. Ibid., 258.

28. Ibid., 275.

29. Ervin Staub, *The Roots of Evil: The Origins of Genocide and Other Group Violence* (New York: Cambridge University Press, 1992), 274. Staub has attempted to put some of his ideas into practice with survivors of the genocide in Rwanda. See Ervin Staub, "Genocide and Mass Killings: Origins, Prevention, Healing and Reconciliation," *Political Psychology* 21 (2000): 367–82.

30. Neil J. Kressel, "Televised History and Race Relations: The Impact of *Roots* and *Holocaust,*" *Clearinghouse for Civil Rights Research* 8 (Summer–Fall 1980): 7–13.

31. In January 1995, the debate concerning "Facing History and Ourselves" figured in a minor political scandal. Just days after announcing Professor Christina Jeffrey's appointment as historian of the U.S. House of Representatives, Speaker Newt Gingrich dismissed her from the post. The decision to sack the political scientist followed a flood of objections by liberal writers and politicians. Jeffrey, in

1986, had evaluated a grant proposal from the Facing History and Ourselves Foundation that focused on training teachers for a values clarification program. She had, ostensibly, criticized the curriculum for not presenting the Nazi point of view. Several liberal politicians branded her an anti-Semite, a "wacko," and a Nazi sympathizer. Gingrich, who had hand-picked his old colleague Jeffrey for the job, acted quickly to minimize what he suspected would be a damaging political controversy over a minor appointment. Jeffrey's words in her own defense appeared in the *Wall Street Journal*, but did not get the attention they deserve. She argues, convincingly, that her remark was taken out of context and twisted for political reasons. According to Jeffrey, her actual views on Holocaust education reflect a conservative political orientation, but fall within the bounds of the mainstream. Moreover, she was the only one of fifteen reviewers who gave the grant proposal a passing score. Adam Brodsky, managing editor of *The Forward*, a prominent Jewish newspaper, argues that Jeffrey received a "bum rap." He writes: "It is not lessons in morality that critics [like Jeffrey] oppose; it is using the Holocaust to indoctrinate students with a left-leaning agenda. That is a lot more likely what this fight was about, and if so, then the Jewish community was suckered into allowing the term anti-Semite to be exploited by politics and to be used to slur someone who opposed exploitation of one of the most sacred memories in Jewish history." Adam Brodsky, "Jeffrey's Bum Rap," *Forward* [New York], 7 April 1995, 7. See also Christina Jeffrey, "Playing Politics with History," *Wall Street Journal*, 28 March 1995, A26.

32. Deborah E. Lipstadt, "Not Facing History," *New Republic*, 6 March 1995, 27. According to the project's 2001 home page, "Facing History and Ourselves" offers teachers and others in the community occasions to study the past, explore new ideas and approaches, and develop practical models for civic engagement that link history to the challenges of an increasingly interconnected world and the choices that young people make daily. "Facing History" students learn that apathy and indifference stifle hope. They discover how violence destroys families and nations. They seek opportunities to confront the isolation that fuels the misunderstandings, myths, and misinformation they have about the 'other.'" Facing History and Ourselves [Online], accessed 8 September 2001, www.facing.org.

33. Ibid.

34. For an argument that Holocaust studies curricula should place even greater emphasis on Milgram's work, see Ann L. Saltzman, "The Role of Obedience Experiments in Holocaust Studies: The Case for Renewed Visibility," in Thomas Blass, ed., *Obedience to Authority: Current Perspectives on the Milgram Paradigm* (Mahwah, NJ: Erlbaum, 2000), p. 126.

35. Neil J. Kressel and Adam Brodsky, "Multiculturalism and Sensitivity on Campus," *Midstream* (December 1992): 26–29, discuss the insensitivity of the multicultural movement to traditional Jewish concerns.

36. Calvin Sims, "Argentine President Discourages New Revelations on 'Dirty War,'" *New York Times*, 30 March 1995, A10, late ed. See also "For the First Time, Argentine Army Admits 'Dirty War' Killings," *New York Times*, 26 April 1995, A13, late ed.

37. Numerous books and articles have addressed the challenges faced by tribunals handling the trials of accused war criminals from wars in Bosnia, Kosovo, and Rwanda. See, for example, Howard Ball, *Prosecuting War Crimes and Genocide: The Twentieth Century Experience* (Lawrence: University Press of Kansas, 1999); William A. Schabas, *Genocide in International Law: The Crime of Crimes* (New York: Cambridge University Press, 2000); Aryeh Neier, *War Crimes: Brutality, Genocide, Terror, and the Struggle for Justice* (New York: Times Books/Random House, 1998).

38. Donatella Lorch, "As Rwanda Trials Open, A Nation Struggles," *New York Times*, 7 April 1995, A1, late ed.

39. Michael Kelley, "The Pacifist Threat," MSNBC online, 26 September 2001, accessed 26 September 2001, www.msnbc.com/news/634264.asp [Internet].

40. Kurt Lewin, *Resolving Social Conflict: Selected Papers on Group Dynamics*, Gertrud Weiss Lewin, ed. (New York: Harper & Row, 1948), 38–39.

41. Ibid., 48.

INDEX